Microsoft® Windows® Scripting with WMI: Self-Paced Learning Guide

Ed Wilson

PUBLISHED BY
Microsoft Press
A Division of Microsoft Corporation
One Microsoft Way
Redmond, Washington 98052-6399

Library of Congress Control Number 2005933639

Printed and bound in the United States of America.

1 2 3 4 5 6 7 8 9   QWT   8 7 6 5

Distributed in Canada by H.B. Fenn and Company Ltd.

A CIP catalogue record for this book is available from the British Library.

Microsoft Press books are available through booksellers and distributors worldwide. For further information about international editions, contact your local Microsoft Corporation office or contact Microsoft Press International directly at fax (425) 936-7329. Visit our Web site at www.microsoft.com/mspress. Send comments to *mspinput@microsoft.com*.

Microsoft, Active Directory, Excel, JScript, Microsoft Press, MSDN, Outlook, Visual Basic, Win32, Windows, Windows NT, and Windows Server are either registered trademarks or trademarks of Microsoft Corporation in the United States and/or other countries.

The example companies, organizations, products, domain names, e-mail addresses, logos, people, places, and events depicted herein are fictitious. No association with any real company, organization, product, domain name, e-mail address, logo, person, place, or event is intended or should be inferred.

This book expresses the author's views and opinions. The information contained in this book is provided without any express, statutory, or implied warranties. Neither the authors, Microsoft Corporation, nor its resellers, or distributors will be held liable for any damages caused or alleged to be caused either directly or indirectly by this book.

Acquisitions Editor: Martin DelRe
Project Editors: Melissa von Tschudi-Sutton and Barbara Moreland
Technical Editor: Bob Hogan
Copy Editor: Christina Palaia
Indexer: Julie Bess

Body Part No. X11-50076

This book is dedicated to my best friend and wife, Teresa.

Contents at a Glance

Part VI Appendixes

Table of Contents

Part I   ## Getting Started with WMI

Part VI   Appendixes

Acknowledgments

Many people assisted in bringing this book to fruition. First and foremost, I must thank my agent, Claudette Moore of the Moore Literary Agency, who ensured the proper publisher was found for this book. Martin DelRe at Microsoft Press has been awesome to work with and is an enthusiastic supporter of scripting in general and of Windows Management Instrumentation (WMI) in particular. Melissa von Tschudi-Sutton, Barbara Moreland, and Maureen Zimmerman, also at Microsoft Press, have kept my nose to the grindstone and forestalled my natural tendency to procrastinate. Bob Hogan has not only read the entire manuscript several times and offered numerous insightful comments, but he has also run (and run and run) all the scripts associated with this book. I'd also like to thank Christina Palaia for her careful copyediting, helping to make my writing the best that it can be.

Lori Brady has been an awesome reviewer, has kept me honest, and has forced me to write clear text. David Schwinn and Bill Mell, both longtime reviewers, offered insightful comments and pointed out parts that were "boring." Alain Lissoir and Peter Costantini from Microsoft provided valuable feedback. Mary Gray from Microsoft has been a dedicated champion of this project and was invaluable in introducing me to key players on the WMI team. Travis Franklin, Karl Romike, Hal Lange, and Terry Brazzell all provided some really good feedback. Special mention must be made of Bob Wilton from Microsoft Product Support Services (PSS), for allowing me to use his WMIcheck utility, and of Gupreet Singh Jutla, also from Microsoft PSS, for allowing me to use his WMIScript_tocsv.exe utility. Chris Scoville from the Microsoft WMI Software Development Kit (SDK) team also gave me his WMI Code Creator tool. All of these utilities are in the tools directory on the companion CD, and I think you will enjoy using them. If you ever run into Bob, Gupreet, or Chris, be sure to thank him.

Finally, I must mention my wife, Teresa, who read this entire book at least three times (and she is not even a "computer person"). Thanks to everyone.

About This Book

Microsoft Windows Server 2003 marks a significant step forward in manageability, security, and stability. Network administrators and consultants, many of whom are the sole survivors of recent budget cuts, downsizing, and outsourcing, are left struggling to manage burgeoning task lists that never, ever seem to shrink. In a typical day, 5 to 10 tasks are completed—and 15 to 20 tasks are added. Although most of these tenacious networkers have heard of or have even been exposed to Microsoft Windows Management Instrumentation (WMI), they have little time to explore its power or to develop scripts to solve real-world problems. Indeed, one network administrator recently commented to me that scripting was basically useless because "if it takes me two hours to develop a script while I am facing a crisis, that is too long." Her solution was to call for lots of help and to go around and make changes manually. This situation is all too common and downright heartbreaking when you think about it. The right tool is right here...it is free...and it is very powerful—it is WMI.

As a senior consultant for Microsoft Corporation, I spend every week working with the world's largest companies. In every instance, the IT staff has heard of and wants to make more effective use of WMI. Questions, however, abound: Can I do this with WMI? Can I do that with WMI? Can I run this on multiple computers? What if the logged-on user does not have admin rights? Why does this script work on Windows Server 2003, but not on Microsoft Windows XP with Service Pack 2 installed? How can I find out everything I can do with WMI on the network?

Microsoft Windows Scripting with WMI: Self-Paced Learning Guide addresses these common questions and more.

Background

Windows Server 2003 makes significant changes to WMI. Dozens of new and exciting providers expose hundreds of new WMI classes and methods. In addition, many of the things you could do with the Active Directory directory service in Microsoft Windows 2000 Server have been removed. The result is that any WMI book based on Windows 2000 is simply out of date.

Network administrators and consultants need to go beyond simply developing a script that queries a single WMI class by using the Microsoft Scriptomatic. Although the Scriptomatic is useful for exploring WMI and can save you time by enabling you to cut and paste class property names, it simply does not substitute for deep, up-to-date knowledge of WMI.

Measuring, monitoring, and alerting are all tasks that WMI can easily perform; however, most network administrators and consultants relegate WMI to simply querying for basic information: How large is the hard disk? How much memory is installed? How fast is the processor?

Although these are all vital questions, WMI can do much more. The problem is that, until now, no book has been written in a clear, concise manner to assist IT professionals in gaining the vital skills required to leverage this flexible technology.

Editorial Objectives and Approach

Microsoft Windows Scripting with WMI: Self-Paced Learning Guide can equip readers with the tools to harness the power of WMI. Concepts are broken down into easy-to-complete, simple-to-understand lessons so that the reader can quickly gain the skills necessary to write custom scripts to manage, monitor, and control Windows Server 2003 networks.

The approach I take to teaching readers how to use WMI scripting to automate servers that run the Windows operating system is similar to the approach I use in my highly successful book *Microsoft Windows Scripting Self-Paced Learning Guide*. I take a topic, develop a WMI script that illustrates the essential learning point, and then move on to the next topic. Each topic I present is supported with one or more Microsoft Visual Basic Scripting Edition (VBScript) scripts that assist in developing the main point of the lesson. The scripts are real, complete, and fully functioning—not "scriptlets." Two lab exercises per chapter reinforce the material developed in the text.

This is a book about WMI—not VBScript. Therefore, coverage of VBScript is incidental to the coverage of WMI. I do discuss some advanced VBScript topics because they lend great power and flexibility to the scripts presented. If you are looking for a VBScript tutorial, you should get a copy of my *Microsoft Windows Scripting Self-Paced Learning Guide*. Indeed, the self-paced learning guide and this WMI book complement one another, and together they form the basis of a complete scripting library.

Microsoft Windows Scripting with WMI: Self-Paced Learning Guide assumes much of the knowledge presented in the self-paced learning guide. No information is duplicated.

Is This Book for Me?

Microsoft Windows Scripting with WMI: Self-Paced Learning Guide is aimed at several audiences, including the following:

- **Windows networking consultants**   Anyone who wants to standardize and automate the installation and configuration of Microsoft .NET Framework networking components
- **Windows network administrators**   Anyone who wants to automate the day-to-day management of Windows Server 2003 networks
- **Windows Help desk staff**   Anyone who wants to verify configuration of remotely connected desktops

- **Microsoft Certified Systems Engineers (MCSEs) and Microsoft Certified Trainers (MCTs)**   Although not a strategic core competency within the Microsoft Certified Professional (MCP) program, a few questions about scripting do come up from time to time on various exams

- **General technical staff**   Anyone who wants to collect information, configure settings on computers that run Windows XP, or implement management through WMI, Windows Script Host (WSH), or Web-Based Enterprise Management (WBEM)

- **Power users**   Anyone who wants to obtain maximum power and configurability of computers that run Windows XP either at home or in an unmanaged desktop workplace environment

Organization of the Book

This book is divided into six parts. Each section builds on the others to provide a thorough understanding of how to work with WMI from a scripting standpoint. The six parts of the book are discussed in the following subsections.

Part I: Getting Started with WMI

There are two chapters in Part I. In Chapter 1, "Introducing WMI," I provide a comprehensive introduction to WMI and discuss in a general manner where WMI came from, how classes are formed, and the WMI architecture. I close the chapter with a discussion of the WMI database, called the repository. In Chapter 2, "Configuring WMI," I discuss in detail how to tweak WMI. We look at the registry settings related to WMI, and you get your first look at the WMI Control Properties console.

- Chapter 1: Introducing WMI
- Chapter 2: Configuring WMI

Part II: WMI Queries and Events

Did you know WMI has its own query language? It is similar to structured query language (SQL) but is called WQL instead. WQL, which stands for WMI Query Language, is actually a subset of SQL but also includes enhancements. In Chapter 3, "Using Basic WMI Queries," we examine much of the WQL language. In addition, we look at two different methods available for executing scripts. We build upon this information in Chapter 4, "Using Advanced WMI Queries," where you see the power and flexibility of using special query strings such as the *ISA* operator. In Chapter 5, "Using WMI Events," you learn how to make your scripts respond to changes in the operating system or file system. If a new process starts, you can have your script perform a specific action. This adds an entirely new dimension to your code.

- Chapter 3: Using Basic WMI Queries
- Chapter 4: Using Advanced WMI Queries
- Chapter 5: Using WMI Events

Part III: Connect Server and Additional Privileges

Chapter 6, "Using the *SWbemLocator* Methods," introduces the rich programming model available from the *SWbemLocator* object. This is the way to make remote connections to computers on the network, and it even enables you to supply alternative credentials. It is a very rich model, so I have some tips and tricks that will enable you to mine this object easily. Chapter 7, "Requesting Additional Privileges for WMI," explores the WMI security model in detail and provides guidance on when to use each of the dozens of privilege strings that can be supplied to a WMI query.

- Chapter 6: Using the *SWbemLocator* Methods
- Chapter 7: Requesting Additional Privileges for WMI

Part IV: Classes

Classes provide the core functionality of WMI. But do you know how classes are organized? Most people do not realize that there is a pattern to the way the WMI classes are stored in the hierarchy. Once you recognize this pattern, which is discussed in each chapter in this section of the book, you will uncover new vistas in your scripting life.

- Chapter 8: Understanding WMI Classes
- Chapter 9: Using Win32 WMI Classes
- Chapter 10: Using System Hardware Classes
- Chapter 11: Using Operating System Classes
- Chapter 12: Using the Performance Counter Classes

Part V: Security and Troubleshooting

Everyone wants to talk about security—and for good reason. It does not make sense to have something that enables administrators to make changes to every workstation on the network if hackers can use the same tools to make changes to every workstation on the network. So, there is a balancing act between security and functionality. In Chapter 13, "Understanding WMI Security," we explore some of the security issues you might encounter while working with WMI and examine using WMI to make security configuration changes. This chapter resumes the discussion of the WMI security model begun in Chapter 7. Chapter 14, "Troubleshooting WMI," examines troubleshooting. Once you start using WMI for your critical applications, you must be able to troubleshoot and maintain WMI.

- Chapter 13: Understanding WMI Security
- Chapter 14: Troubleshooting WMI

Part VI: Appendixes

The appendixes of this book are designed to be used. In fact, I consult them on a regular basis. If you need to know which classes have the most methods or which classes have the most properties, these appendixes are your best source of information.

- Appendix A: Scripting API Methods and Properties
- Appendix B: WMI Security Constants
- Appendix C: WMI Security Privileges and Operations
- Appendix D: Computer System Hardware Classes
- Appendix E: Operating System Classes
- Appendix F: Performance Monitor Classes

About the Companion CD

The CD accompanying this book contains additional information and software components, including the following files:

- **Lab files**   The lab files contain starter scripts, some text files, and completed lab solutions for each of the 29 labs contained in this book. In addition, each script discussed in the book is contained in the folder corresponding to the chapter number.

- **eBooks**   The CD contains two eBooks: an electronic version of this book and an electronic version of my book *Microsoft Windows Scripting Self-Paced Learning Guide*. You can view the eBooks on-screen by using Adobe Acrobat or Adobe Reader.

- **Supplemental scripts**   In addition to the lab scripts and the scripts discussed in each chapter, a collection of supplemental scripts is also available. In some cases these scripts further illuminate a particular topic discussed in the book and are found in the corresponding chapter's numbered folder. In other cases they can be found in the supplemental scripts folder. Inside the supplemental scripts folder, you will find more than 900 WMI scripts that cover all properties of all *Win32* WMI classes in the *root\cimv2* namespace. If you do not know what all this means, you will by the time you are finished reading this book.

- **Utility scripts**   Thirty-two of my favorite utility scripts are in the Utility scripts folder on the companion CD. These scripts perform an incredible array of tasks. In some cases they are functions that draw a separator line on a page; in other cases they translate certain WMI messages into more presentable text. Many of these utility scripts are used in the labs to provide you with real-life examples of their employment in production scripting situations.

- **Tools**   The following tools are also included for your use:
    - Scriptomatic 2.0
    - WMICHK
    - WMI Code Creator
    - WMIScript_to_csv
    - WMI Administrative Tools
    - HTA Helpomatic
    - Primal Script Evaluation Version

Computer System Requirements

Be sure your computer meets the following system requirements for installation of the sample scripts and tools included on the companion CD.

- Minimum 233 megahertz (MHz) processor in the Intel Pentium/Celeron family or the AMD K6/Atholon/Duron family
- 128 megabytes (MB) of RAM
- 1.5 gigabytes (GB) of hard disk space available
- Display monitor capable of 800 × 600 resolution or higher
- CD-ROM drive or DVD-ROM drive
- Mouse or compatible pointing device
- Windows Server 2003 or Windows XP

Technical Support

Every effort has been made to ensure the accuracy of this book and the contents of the companion CD. Microsoft Press provides general support information for its books and companion CDs at the following Web site:

http://www.microsoft.com/learning/support/books

To search for book and CD corrections for this book by using the book's ISBN, go to:

http://www.microsoft.com/mspress/support/search.asp

If you have comments, questions, or ideas regarding this book or the companion CD, please send them to Microsoft Press using either of the following methods.

E-Mail	*mspinput@microsoft.com*
Postal Mail	Microsoft Press
	Attn: *Microsoft Windows Scripting with WMI: Self-Paced Learning Guide* Project Editor
	One Microsoft Way
	Redmond, WA 98052

Please note that Microsoft software product support is not offered through the above addresses.

Part I
Getting Started with WMI

Chapter 1
Introducing WMI

It seems that nearly everyone knows something about Windows Management Instrumentation (WMI); however, it also seems everyone knows something different. This chapter provides a foundation for the remainder of the book. First, we look at the Microsoft implementation of Web-Based Enterprise Management (WBEM). Next, we examine how the structure of the Common Information Model (CIM) affects our ability to work with WMI. Once you understand the organization of WMI, it is important to learn about the components that make up the WMI architecture—so we then take a quick look at various objects and providers. Finally, we discuss the key to the entire system: the WMI repository.

Before You Begin

To work through this chapter, you should be familiar with the following concepts:

- Fundamentals of reading and writing Microsoft Visual Basic Scripting Edition (VBScript)

- Basics of error handling

- Basics of Microsoft Windows Server operating systems administration

After you complete this chapter, you will be familiar with the following concepts:

- Fundamentals of WMI

- The Microsoft implementation of WBEM

- WMI architecture

- Managed providers and objects

- WBEM repository

> **Note** All the scripts used in this chapter are located on the CD that accompanies this book in the \Scripts\Chapter01 folder.

Defining WMI

Windows Management Instrumentation (WMI) is a tool that gives network administrators the ability to manage hundreds (or thousands) of computers in a safe, structured, systematic manner. WMI technology can be leveraged by complex, full-featured network management applications such as Microsoft Systems Management Server (SMS) or by a lone network administrator putting together a VBScript based on Scriptomatic.

Scriptomatic is a Microsoft scripting tool that assists you in writing WMI scripts and teaches you the fundamental concepts of WMI scripting. Scriptomatic can be downloaded from the following location: *http://www.microsoft.com/technet/scriptcenter/createit.mspx*.

> **The Basics of WMI**   The basics of WMI are covered in Chapters 8, 9, and 10 of *Microsoft Windows Scripting Self-Paced Learning Guide* (*http://www.microsoft.com/MSPress/books/ 6789.asp*). I won't repeat that information here because the learning guide is a complementary book that is great for reinforcing your VBScript skills and for supplementing your learning in this field.

Windows management, the first two words in WMI, tell you that the product is designed, implemented, and intended to be used to assist in managing Microsoft Windows networks. Most people understand what is involved in managing a Windows network, but the third word in WMI, *instrumentation*, confuses many.

Instrumentation, as used here, has its roots in the manufacturing industry. For example, tanks in paper mills have level indicators attached to them that tell the computers in the Wet End Control room the number of gallons of pulp in the tanks. The level is critical to operators for two reasons: knowing the level helps avoid overflowing a tank and running a tank dry, starving the paper machine of fiber. The indicators, sensors, and relays involved in such a system are called *instrumentation*. If the level indicators are programmed with some intelligence, they can automate much of the paper technician's tasks. As shown in Figure 1-1, when the tank begins to run low on pulp, the computer sends a signal to valve A to open and allow a greater flow of pulp into the tank. If the tank is filling too rapidly, the computer sends a signal to valve A to close or to throttle as appropriate.

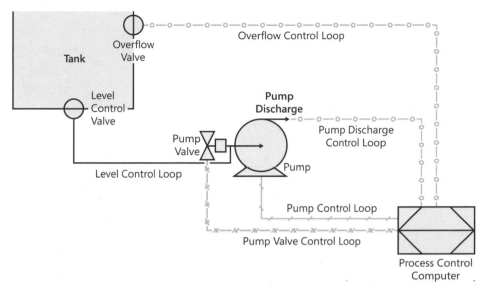

Figure 1-1 Instrumentation enabling a computer to control the level of pulp in a tank used in the paper industry

In the same way that instrumentation can help control the level of pulp in a tank, instrumentation can be used to control the behavior of applications. The tank scenario includes the following three operations:

- Query the level property of the tank.
- Evaluate the level.
- Execute open-valve or close-valve method.

These same types of operations are needed in controlling software: query, evaluate, and execute. We can apply the principles of instrumentation to a common network administration scenario: "What is going on with service *X*?"

Quick Check

Before you get too confused by all the new terms, take a few seconds to check your progress. Throughout this book, I use a Quick Check feature from time to time to help you reinforce your learning.

Q: What two concepts are expressed in the term *WMI*?

A: The two concepts expressed in the term *WMI* are management and instrumentation.

> Q: **What does instrumentation have to do with network administration?**
>
> A: Instrumentation enables applications to report on their health and to take corrective action if there is a problem.
>
> Q: **What are two broad categories of scripts that can be developed with WMI?**
>
> A: Two broad categories of scripts that can be developed with WMI are reporting and taking action based on results of reporting.

Querying and Starting a Service

The *Win32_Service* class can return the state of a service on a remote server. If you add logic based on the current state of a particular service, you can execute the *StopService* or the *StartService* method as appropriate. The following script, called QueryAndStartAService.vbs, does this. This script is in the Chapter01 scripts folder on the accompanying CD.

One thing to keep in mind, however, is that this script is not designed to handle the service if it is disabled. To add this capability to the script, you will need to use the changeStartMode method to set the service to manual, which you would do right after you retrieve the startMode of the service. Once you call the startService method, you capture the return code in a variable called errRTN. A return code of 0 means the operation was successful; anything else is an error. (Table 1-1 lists the potential return codes and their meaning. Error codes are talked about in the next section.) This script is in the Chapter01 scripts folder on the accompanying CD.

queryAndStartAService.vbs

```
objName = "'alerter'"
strComputer = "."
wmiNS = "\root\cimv2"
wmiQuery = "Select state,startmode from win32_service where Name = " & objName
Set objWMIService = GetObject("winmgmts:\\" & strComputer & wmiNS)
Set colItems = objWMIService.ExecQuery(wmiQuery)

For Each objItem in colItems
    Wscript.Echo ": " & objItem.state
    Wscript.Echo ": " & objItem.startmode
 If objItem.state <> "running" Then
 errRTN =objItem.startservice
 End If
 Wscript.echo errRTN
Next
```

A quick look at the queryAndStartAService.vbs script provides some interesting information. First, I assign the value " *'alerter'* " to the *objName* variable. This is the service I want to start. Note that the value must be contained inside single quotation marks that are then enclosed in double quotation marks. The double quotes in VBScript indicate that you are going to use everything inside the quotes as a string. A *string* is a type of data that is read but not interpreted by the scripting engine. In WMI, single quotes are used to pass a parameter, or a value, into the WMI query. *StrComputer* is assigned the value of ".", which is a shortcut name for the local machine. The *wmiNS* variable is used to hold the name of the WMI namespace to which you will connect. The *root\cimv2* namespace contains hundreds of very good WMI classes, and it is in this namespace that you find the *Win32_Service* class. These are the classes we will use to administer a server.

Defining the Query

The WMI query is contained in the variable called *wmiQuery*, and it uses a structured query language (SQL)–like language called WMI Query Language (WQL). In reality, WQL is a subset of SQL and is used in much the same manner. (Similarities and differences are covered in Chapter 3.) For now, we select two properties (*state* and *startmode*) from the *Win32_Service* class, but only if the name of the service happens to be *Alerter*. The name of the service is not case sensitive. (For more information on the basics of the WMI Query Language, refer to Chapter 9 of *Microsoft Windows Scripting Self-Paced Learning Guide* [Microsoft Press, 2004].)

The next step is to make the connection into WMI by using the moniker *winmgmts:*. The *winmgmts* moniker is not case sensitive, and, when using the *execQuery* method, the information that is returned is contained in a collection. Because you have a collection to work with, it is necessary to use the *for next* command to walk through the collection and perform the action defined inside the loop. *For next* is referred to as a "sandwich command" because *for* and *next* act like the slices of bread on the top and bottom of a traditional sandwich with the real meat (the good stuff, the action inside the loop) in between. This is the case here: *objItem* refers to one instance of an item that came back from the WMI query. It is used with the data inside the *for next* command, and *collItems* refers to the data that came back from the query into WMI.

Evaluating the State of the Service

If the state of the Alerter service is not equal to running, start the Alerter service by using the *StartService* method. The *StartService* method provides a return code for its attempted activity. To capture this return code, you can use a variable called *errRTN*, as demonstrated in the following code:

```
If objItem.state <> "running" Then
 errRTN =objItem.startservice
 End If
```

It is perfectly acceptable to call a method without capturing the return code (particularly if you have not scripted anything to handle the return code). In this case, you want to know whether WMI was able to start the Alerter service.

What Is a Return Code?

When a method is called in WMI, it returns with a number called a *return code* that is equal to the result of the method, For instance, a return code of 0 means the operation was successful. (Table 1-1 lists other return codes that come back if the operation is not successful.) I think of this in baseball terms: "no runs, no hits, no errors"—a perfect inning for a pitcher. The pitcher made no mistakes during that part of the game. The whole concept of a return code is to provide feedback on an operation. Imagine, for a moment, that you are an officer in the Navy and you tell an enlisted sailor to swab the deck. After you issue the order, you will be listening for the return code. In this case, the return code would be, "Aye, aye, sir," which in "sailor speak" means, "I understand and will carry out the order."

Capturing the Return Code

The return codes for most WMI methods can be found in the Platform software development kit (SDK). Although at first glance the SDK seems to cater to developers, it also contains a wealth of information for network administrators, help desk technicians, and consultants who might want to learn more about scripting in general or WMI specifically. In Lab 1, you download and install the SDK and explore the features of this comprehensive tool.

Table 1-1 lists the return codes from calling the *startService* method. A return code of 14 means the service is disabled, and, therefore, the script, as listed earlier, will fail. In Lab 4 (in Chapter 2), you modify this script to include additional logic to avoid a status of 14 in the return code. If you have not captured this information earlier, you will find it difficult to know what the problem is.

Table 1-1   Return Codes from the *StartService* Method of *Win32_Service*

Return Code	Description
0	Success
1	Not supported
2	Access denied
3	Dependent services running
4	Invalid service control
5	Service cannot accept control
6	Service not active

Table 1-1   Return Codes from the *StartService* Method of *Win32_Service*

Return Code	Description
7	Service request timeout
8	Unknown failure
9	Path not found
10	Service already running
11	Service database locked
12	Service dependency deleted
13	Service dependency failure
14	Service disabled
15	Service logon failure
16	Service marked for deletion
17	Service no thread
18	Status circular dependency
19	Status duplicate name
20	Status invalid name
21	Status invalid parameter
22	Status invalid service account
23	Status service exists
24	Service already paused

Using WMI as a Tool

As a tool, WMI has a number of parts, including management pieces, infrastructure pieces, security pieces, and consumer pieces. We examine the infrastructure pieces in Chapter 14 when we talk about troubleshooting. We talk about the security aspect when we look at security in Chapter 13. We have already been working with the consumer pieces—scripts, in this case. For now, let's look at the management pieces. The WMI Control console shown in Figure 1-2 is available when you add the WMI Control snap-in to a custom Microsoft Management Console (MMC). The WMI Control console provides you with access to important information such as the location of the WBEM repository and the version number of WMI running on the computer. This console enables you to target other computers and even to specify credentials for the connection. These two important features are not available when you access the tool from the Computer Management console Services And Applications node, which is permanently connected to the local machine with logged-on user credentials.

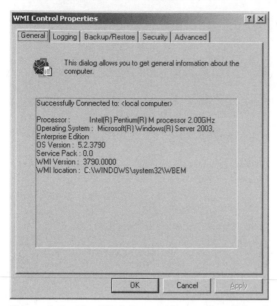

Figure 1-2   The WMI Control Properties dialog box, accessible from the WMI Control console

To add the WMI Control console to a custom MMC:

1. Click Start, click Run, and then type **mmc** in the Open box of the Run dialog box. Click OK.

2. On the custom console's (Console1) File menu, select Add/Remove Snap-In.

3. In the Add/Remove Snap-In dialog box, click Add.

4. In the Add Standalone Snap-In dialog box, select WMI Control (bottom of the list), and then click Add.

5. In the Change Managed Computer dialog box, select either Local Computer or Another Computer. If you choose Another Computer, you are given the opportunity to change the connection account.

6. Click Finish, click Close, and then click OK.

Implementing Microsoft WBEM

In some respects, WMI could be viewed as the Microsoft implementation of WBEM. If you know what WBEM is, this might be exciting. Perhaps a brief history lesson might be in order. In the early 1990s, a group called the Desktop Management Task Force (DMTF) got together to develop standards for managing desktop computers. This proved to be a real challenge because there were hundreds of different kinds of desktop computers with thousands of different types of components, all of which were manufactured in a very cost-sensitive, competitive industry. Eventually, it seemed that the industry was changing faster than the task force could even get proposals written (not to mention adopted), so the group decided to change its name to Distributed Management Task Force—and because it is a not-for-profit group, it was fortunate to be able to keep the same stationery, envelopes, T-shirts, coffee cups, and Web site by using the same acronym. The DMTF has created some pretty cool stuff, some of which is germane to this discussion:

- **Desktop Management Interface (DMI)**   A framework for tracking and managing desktop computers and laptop devices
- **Web-Based Enterprise Management (WBEM)**   The basis for WMI
- **Common Information Model (CIM)**   Vendor-neutral description of network equipment and environment. The CIM is famous for the schema that is used in WMI

You will never be asked what DMI stands for; neither do you really need to know what WBEM is or how the CIM is related. However, I mention these because you might want to visit the DMTF Web site, *http://www.dmtf.org/home,* which links to many very good white papers, and you will see these names appearing from time to time. If you see DMI, WBEM, or CIM, you can simply think to yourself "WMI" and you will be fine.

Describing Objects Using the CIM

The CIM is a way of describing the various components that make up a computer, network, or software package. In other words, the CIM is an abstract way to obtain and to process information. The two main parts of the CIM are the specification and the schema. The specification portion of the CIM describes how the data will be gathered and transported. In addition, it details the CIM metadata (*metadata* is data about data), which is called MetaSchema.

The existence of MetaSchema implies the existence of a schema. The CIM schema is composed of the following essential elements:

- Namespaces
- Providers
- Classes

The namespaces are the way in which the data is stored on the computer. CIM schema namespaces are hierarchical in much the same way as the Domain Name System (DNS) is a hierarchical namespace: the names have an additive property about them—and we have the tendency to move from the specific to the general or from the general to the specific. Data is stored in a repository that facilitates both storage and retrieval of the appropriate data. The hierarchical nature of namespaces enables us to navigate easily and to obtain the appropriate classes.

Working with Namespaces

Namespaces are used to organize the information with which you will be working. It is important to know where certain information is kept in the schema because you are not allowed to do a query between namespaces. For example, if you want to retrieve information about processes on a machine, you would use the *Win32_Process* class. To use this particular WMI class, you must make a connection to the *root\cimv2* namespace. A script called Win32_Process.vbs in the cimv2 folder on the accompanying CD lists all the processes and all the properties associated with the processes. A more practical approach, however, is to use the script called List-ProcessesByName.vbs. ListProcessesByName.vbs is a great tool to use when troubleshooting startup problems on a computer. I used it when I got a new laptop to determine why the computer was running 50 different processes when my old machine required 32 processes to do essentially the same thing. I still use this script prior to installing new software. When you run this script, you will find that a file called logfile.txt is created on your desktop.

ListProcessesByName.vbs

```
strComputer = "."
wmiNS = "\root\cimv2"
wmiQuery = "Select name, ExecutablePath from win32_process"
i = 0
Set objWMIService = GetObject("winmgmts:\\" & strComputer & wmiNS)
Set colItems = objWMIService.ExecQuery(wmiQuery)

For Each objItem in colItems
   message = message & vbcrlf &  objItem.name & vbtab & objItem.ExecutablePath
   i = i+1 ' counts the number of processes that are running
 Next

SubSpecialFolder
SubLogFile

' subs are below
Sub SubSpecialFolder
Dim objShell
Set objShell = CreateObject ("wscript.shell")
strFolder = objshell.SpecialFolders("Desktop")
End Sub


Sub SubLogFile
Dim objFSO             ' holds connection to file system object
Dim objFile             ' holds hook to the file to be used
Dim LogFile
Dim m1 ' holds message 1
m1 = "there are " & i & " processes running "
Const ForWriting = 2
Const ForAppending = 8
LogFile = strFolder & "\logFile.txt"
```

```
Set objFSO = CreateObject("Scripting.FileSystemObject")

    If objFSO.FileExists(LogFile) Then
        Set objFile = objFSO.OpenTextFile(LogFile, ForAppending)
        objFile.WriteBlankLines(1)
        objFile.Writeline " ** " & m1 & Now & message
        objFile.Close
    Else
        Set objFile = objFSO.CreateTextFile(LogFile)
        objfile.writeline " ** " & m1 & Now & message
        objFile.Close
    End If

End sub
```

You can use VBScript to obtain information about WMI. The following script, ListWMI-Namespace.vbs, initiates a query that will list all the namespaces that currently reside on the computer. Using this information, you can get a good idea of which groups of information you can work with and which you can view.

ListWMINamespace.vbs

```
strComputer = "."

Set objSwbemServices = GetObject("winmgmts:\\" & strComputer & "\root")
Set colNameSpaces = objSwbemServices.InstancesOf("__NAMESPACE")

For Each objNameSpace In colNameSpaces
    Wscript.Echo objNameSpace.Name
Next
```

The ListWMINamespace.vbs script makes a connection into the *root* namespace on the computer, and then uses the *instancesOf* method to list all the namespaces inside the current namespace (which is the *root* namespace). When you run the script, you receive output similar to the following:

```
SECURITY
CCM
RSOP
Cli
SecurityCenter
WMI
CIMV2
MSAPPS10
Policy
SmsDm
Microsoft
DEFAULT
directory
subscription
MSAPPS11
```

The namespaces are all off of the *root* namespace. That is, they are child namespaces just off of the *root* namespace. If you want to find out which namespaces are under each of these namespaces, you must connect to each namespace and then issue the same query. This process is known as a *recursive query* and is demonstrated in the following script.

recursiveListWmiNameSpace.vbs
```
strComputer = "."
Call EnumNameSpaces("root")

Sub EnumNameSpaces(strNameSpace)
    Wscript.Echo strNameSpace
    Set objSWbemServices = _
        GetObject("winmgmts:\\" & strComputer & "\" & strNameSpace)
    Set colNameSpaces = objSWbemServices.InstancesOf("__NAMESPACE")
    For Each objNameSpace In colNameSpaces
        Call EnumNameSpaces(strNameSpace & "\" & objNameSpace.Name)
    Next
End Sub
```

The results of running the recursive namespace script can be somewhat surprising. The following output is from a workstation running Microsoft Windows XP. You might see a couple of things normally, for instance, in the *root\CCM* namespace. This namespace is for the client connection manager software used by SMS 2003. Evidently, SMS is using WMI to assist in tracking the location of servers, messaging, and the policy that is created to determine how to manage the desktop computer. Another interesting namespace is the *root\SecurityCenter* namespace. As you might recall, the SecurityCenter was a feature introduced in Windows XP Service Pack 2. Any manipulation of settings or queries for information revealed by the SecurityCenter must take place inside this namespace.

The next level of inquiry might be to look for providers and classes that reside inside the namespace. The result of running this script is a list that looks similar to the following:

```
root
root\SECURITY
root\CCM
root\CCM\VulnerabilityAssessment
root\CCM\Events
root\CCM\invagt
root\CCM\SoftMgmtAgent
root\CCM\LocationServices
root\CCM\DataTransferService
root\CCM\Messaging
root\CCM\Policy
root\CCM\Policy\S_1_5_21_124525095_708259637_1543119021_179756
root\CCM\Policy\S_1_5_21_124525095_708259637_1543119021_179756\RequestedConfig
root\CCM\Policy\S_1_5_21_124525095_708259637_1543119021_179756\ActualConfig
root\CCM\Policy\S_1_5_21_2127521184_1604012920_1887927527_1098747
root\CCM\Policy\S_1_5_21_2127521184_1604012920_1887927527_1098747\RequestedConfig
root\CCM\Policy\S_1_5_21_2127521184_1604012920_1887927527_1098747\ActualConfig
root\CCM\Policy\DefaultUser
root\CCM\Policy\DefaultUser\RequestedConfig
```

```
root\CCM\Policy\DefaultUser\ActualConfig
root\CCM\Policy\Machine
root\CCM\Policy\Machine\RequestedConfig
root\CCM\Policy\Machine\ActualConfig
root\CCM\Policy\S_1_5_21_1960408961_484763869_854245398_500
root\CCM\Policy\S_1_5_21_1960408961_484763869_854245398_500\RequestedConfig
root\CCM\Policy\S_1_5_21_1960408961_484763869_854245398_500\ActualConfig
root\CCM\Policy\S_1_5_21_3410805860_1789667759_1435136519_500
root\CCM\Policy\S_1_5_21_3410805860_1789667759_1435136519_500\RequestedConfig
root\CCM\Policy\S_1_5_21_3410805860_1789667759_1435136519_500\ActualConfig
root\CCM\Policy\DefaultMachine
root\CCM\Policy\DefaultMachine\RequestedConfig
root\CCM\Policy\DefaultMachine\ActualConfig
root\CCM\SoftwareMeteringAgent
root\CCM\ContentTransferManager
root\CCM\Scheduler
root\RSOP
root\RSOP\User
root\RSOP\User\S_1_5_21_124525095_708259637_1543119021_179756
root\RSOP\User\S_1_5_21_2127521184_1604012920_1887927527_1098747
root\RSOP\User\ms_409
root\RSOP\User\S_1_5_21_1960408961_484763869_854245398_500
root\RSOP\User\S_1_5_21_1960408961_484763869_854245398_1004
root\RSOP\User\S_1_5_21_3410805860_1789667759_1435136519_500
root\RSOP\Computer
root\RSOP\Computer\ms_409
root\Cli
root\SecurityCenter
root\WMI
root\WMI\ms_409
root\CIMV2
root\CIMV2\ms_409
root\CIMV2\SMSSWUTemp
root\CIMV2\SMS
root\CIMV2\Applications
root\CIMV2\Applications\MicrosoftACT
root\CIMV2\Applications\MicrosoftIE
root\MSAPPS10
root\Policy
root\Policy\ms_409
root\SmsDm
root\Microsoft
root\Microsoft\HomeNet
root\DEFAULT
root\DEFAULT\ms_409
root\directory
root\directory\LDAP
root\directory\LDAP\ms_409
root\subscription
root\subscription\ms_409
root\MSAPPS11
```

Working with Providers

Providers are used to request information from WMI. They also can send instructions to WMI. From a direct scripting standpoint, you will never use the name of a provider in a WMI script. But as a network administrator or consultant, it is important to know about providers because they provide classes.

> **What Do Providers Provide?**   As a scripter, you will never actually use the name of a provider in a VBScript. However, it is important to be aware of which providers are installed on your computer because they provide the classes. Through the classes, you have access to properties and methods. Although you might never know which specific provider you are using, you will in fact be using a provider when you use properties and methods. By the same token, if a provider is not installed, you are not able to use the class it supplies.

As you explore the namespaces, it makes sense to use WMI to tell you something about the providers that reside in the namespaces. You can use the script listWMIproviders.vbs to iterate the providers in a particular namespace.

listWMIproviders.vbs
```
strComputer = "."
wmiNS = "\root\wmi"
Set objSWbemServices = _
    GetObject ("winmgmts:\\" & strComputer & wmiNS)
Set colWin32Providers = objSWbemServices.InstancesOf("__Win32Provider")

For Each objWin32Provider In colWin32Providers
    Wscript.Echo objWin32Provider.Name Next
```

The list of providers can give you insight into what you can use the namespace for in your script. The list of providers in the *root\wmi* namespace is as follows:

```
WMIEventProv
HiPerfCooker_v1
WMIProv EventTraceProv
SmonlogProv
```

If the list of providers is less than illuminating, you can always look up the provider in the Platform SDK. For instance, the SDK indicates that *HiPerfCooker_v1* is used to provide calculated performance counter data (this is where the term *cooked*, as opposed to *raw,* originates). An example of such cooked data is the percentage of time that a hard disk drive spends on write operations. To calculate this data, *HiPerfCooker* must determine how long the drive was in operation, how long the drive spent reading, and how long it spent writing. Based on this information, *HiPerfCooker* can give you a percentage of writes over a period of time. *HiPerf-Cooker* requires three raw data points to produce one cooked data point. We look at this provider more closely in Chapter 12.

Understanding Classes

Classes are the way that the CIM describes things. To describe a mouse (not the furry kind), you would list its features perhaps in terms of the number of buttons it has, whether it is for left-handed or right-handed users, whether it uses a PS/2 or universal serial bus (USB) interface, and so on. These are characteristics that typify a mouse used on computers running the Windows operating system, not other types of computers, so calling the whole class *mouse* might be a little too specific. Perhaps we could use a more generic term such as *pointing device* that includes features of other input devices as well. The DMTF did just that by creating a class called *CIM_pointingDevice*. If you look up this class in the Platform SDK, you will see that it has the following properties:

```
Availability
Caption
ConfigManagerErrorCode
ConfigManagerUserConfig
CreationClassName
Description
DeviceID
ErrorCleared
ErrorDescription
Handedness
InstallDate
IsLocked
LastErrorCode
Name
NumberOfButtons
PNPDeviceID
PointingType
PowerManagementCapabilities
PowerManagementSupported
Resolution
Status
StatusInfo
SystemCreationClassName
SystemName
```

The listing of pointing device properties is relatively generic. *CIM_PointingDevice* inherits from a class that is called *CIM_UserDevice*. In CIM terminology, this means that *CIM_userDevice* is a *superclass* to *CIM_PointingDevice*. The following properties were inherited from *CIM_UserDevice*:

```
Availability
Caption
ConfigManagerErrorCode
ConfigManagerUserConfig
CreationClassName
Description
DeviceID
ErrorCleared
ErrorDescription
InstallDate
IsLocked
LastErrorCode
Name
PNPDeviceID
PowerManagementCapabilities
PowerManagementSupported
Status
StatusInfo
SystemCreationClassName
SystemName
```

To complicate things a bit more, we customize the *CIM_PointingDevice* class so that it is more applicable to a Windows environment. In this regard, we call it *Win32_PointingDevice*, which has the following properties:

```
Availability
Caption
ConfigManagerErrorCode
ConfigManagerUserConfig
CreationClassName
Description
DeviceID
DeviceInterface
DoubleSpeedThreshold
ErrorCleared
ErrorDescription
Handedness
HardwareType
InfFileName
InfSection
InstallDate
IsLocked
LastErrorCode
Manufacturer
Name
NumberOfButtons
PNPDeviceID
PointingType
PowerManagementCapabilities
PowerManagementSupported
QuadSpeedThreshold
```

```
Resolution
SampleRate
Status
StatusInfo
Synch
SystemCreationClassName
SystemName
```

As you can see, the *Win32_PointingDevice* class has been customized and adapted to serve the needs of Windows environments more specifically. The Windows pointing device is a very rich implementation—adding nine additional properties—and therefore must have customized properties that are more germane to a Windows environment. If you wish to explore this evolution of class properties, I have summarized them in a Microsoft Excel spreadsheet called classcomparison.xls, which is included on the accompanying CD.

How does Microsoft extend the *CIM_PointingDevice* class? There are two answers. The technical answer is that the new class inherits all the properties of the *CIM_PointingDevice* class and then adds additional properties to support the richness of Windows-type pointing devices. The less technical answer is that you can simply create a new class called *Win32_PointingDevice*. This brings up a good point: both classes are in the *root\cimv2* namespace. Given the choice between two classes, one called *CIM_ something*, and one called *Win32_ something*, I always prefer to use classes with the Win32_ prefix because they have been customized for the Windows environment. Remember that the DMTF was technology neutral and, as such, developed a very generic CIM schema. We leverage this schema and call it WMI.

Implementing Programming Interfaces

The Microsoft implementation of WMI provides the following application programming interfaces (APIs):

- **COM API**   Provides support for WMI information through C++ development.

- **Scripting API**   Provides support for WMI information through VBScript, Microsoft Visual Basic, Microsoft JScript, and other languages that support Microsoft ActiveX.

- **WMI ADSI extension**   No longer available in Microsoft Windows Server 2003. Provides a way to manage computer objects returned from Active Directory directory service through WMI. The preferred way to do this in Windows Server 2003 is to use Active Directory Service Interfaces (ADSI).

- **WMI ODBC adapter**   Offers support for Open Database Connectivity (ODBC) applications to access the repository directly without going through the Component Object Model (COM) or ActiveX. This is not installed in Windows Server 2003, but is included in Windows XP, Microsoft Windows 2000, and even Microsoft Windows NT 4.0 with Service Pack 4 (SP4). An alternative way to do this in Windows Server 2003 is to use Microsoft Data Access Components (MDAC).

Using the WMI Architecture

The WMI architecture is the way everything is put together. Essentially, three pieces make up the WMI cosmos. As shown in Figure 1-3, these pieces work together to expose the WMI information to various applications, scripts, and programs. The management application talks to WMI through the different interfaces mentioned earlier. Remember, the application can be anything from SMS to a simple VBScript. The interface then retrieves the data from a variety of sources such as the registry or hardware. WMI stores the data using the CIM.

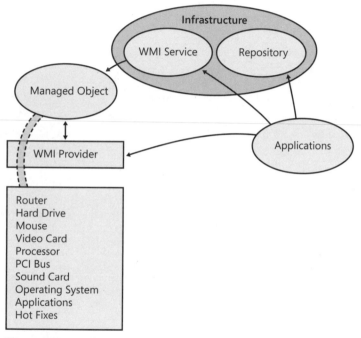

Figure 1-3   Putting together applications, providers, and the WBEM repository using the WMI architecture

Using Managed Objects and Providers

Managed objects are not really anything special; they are simply objects about which you can obtain information. In some instances, they are not really objects at all, but, rather, applications. The following types of objects can be managed using WMI providers:

- **Computer system hardware**   Examples include mouse, hard disk, memory, video card, keyboard

- **Operating system**   Examples include the desktop, drivers, COM, registry, processes

- **Installed applications**   Examples include Microsoft Office

- **WMI service management**   Examples include WMI settings

- **Performance counters**   Examples include formatted performance counters

Keep two things in mind regarding providers and objects. First, without a provider, you cannot access the properties of classes. In fact, without a provider, the class it supplies is either nonexistent or is inaccessible. Providers provide classes. In many respects it really is that simple. As mentioned earlier, you do not directly use a provider; rather, you use the provider indirectly through the supplied classes. At times, data is available in different formats, so the advantage of using a class that is supported by one of the special providers is that they make the data easier to consume. This is the case when you read performance data, as discussed earlier when I mentioned raw and cooked data. In other cases, the provider brings new functionality that otherwise is not available. The following sections discuss which providers are installed on a server that runs the Windows operating system.

WMI Infrastructure

The WMI infrastructure is part of the Windows operating system. It moves and stores the information about managed objects. Following are the two components of the WMI infrastructure:

- **Windows Management Instrumentation service**   Acts as the intermediary between providers, applications, and the repository.

- **WMI repository**   Stores information from providers and supplies data in response to queries. This is also known as the WBEM repository or, simply, the repository.

The Windows Management Instrumentation service can locate information and directs queries appropriately because each provider installed on the computer registers its location with the service. In addition, the provider also tells the management service about any additional functionality it can support, such as data modification or deletion. The Windows Management Instrumentation service also logs errors to the event logs. The Windows Management Instrumentation service provides the following additional functions:

- **Event notification support**   An *event* is something interesting that happened, such as a service starting or stopping or a file being created in a folder. Events are covered in detail in Chapter 5.

- **Query language support**   A *query* is a request for specific information; for example, how many disk drives are installed on the computer? The language that is used to submit these queries is called WMI Query Language (WQL), which is a subset of SQL. WQL is covered in detail in Chapters 3 and 4.

- **Security support**   WMI provides security support by identifying the user and impersonating that user. The provider can return information the user is allowed to see. The WMI infrastructure also provides security at the namespace level. A namespace is a logical grouping of classes and instances as discussed earlier. Security is discussed in more detail in Chapter 13.

- **Logging support**   WMI and the providers can create detailed tracing and error messsage files. This information can be valuable from a troubleshooting perspective. You can use the WMI Management console to configure this logging level. This is discussed in more detail in Chapter 14.

WMI Applications

WMI management applications talk to the WMI infrastructure. An application can simply submit a query to WMI to retrieve information such as how many disk drives are installed on the computer, or it can tell WMI to send an instruction to a managed device, such as an instruction for the device to tell how much free disk space is available on drive C. Most of the time, the management applications simply access information that is already stored in the repository.

WBEM Repository

The WBEM repository (or WMI repository) is essentially a database that contains stored data about your system. When the WMI service starts, it populates the WBEM repository with lots of data about your system. In some respects, you can think of the WBEM repository as a SQL server and each namespace as a database that is running on the SQL server. To continue the analogy, the classes in each namespace would be like tables, and the properties would be fields in the tables. The methods would be triggers or stored procedures resident on the tables.

Location

The location of the WBEM repository is generally the same in all newer versions of the Windows operating system (Windows 2000, Windows XP, and Windows Server 2003). It can be found at *%SystemRoot%*\system32\wbem\Repository. As shown in Figure 1-4, the WBEM folder contains more than just the repository. It is also where the backup folders, the logs, and much more are stored. Accessing this folder is the key to managing WMI.

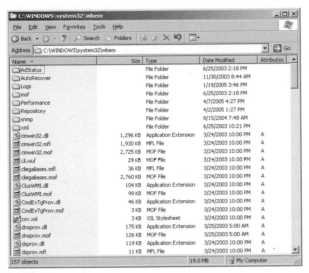

Figure 1-4   The WBEM folder

Retrieving from the Repository

When a WMI application receives a query, it submits the request to the appropriate provider. The provider must, of course, reside in the same namespace as the request. Once the WMI service receives the request, it will hand off the query to the appropriate provider.

Handing Off to a Provider

The provider receives the request, acts on the query as appropriate, and hands off as required. In this manner, it is an intermediary between the Common Information Model Object Manager (CIMOM) and the resource. The provider then requests the information from the resource. It acts like a concierge on behalf of the requesting application (which can be a simple VBScript) because it handles all the details of the query and then bundles the information and returns it to the requesting application. We cover this in more detail in Chapter 2.

Summary

In this chapter, we looked at the fundamentals of WMI. We examined classes, properties, providers, and namespaces and discussed the roles they perform in the WMI architecture. We looked at the WMI repository (also called the WBEM repository) and reviewed how applications can be written to interact with this database of system information. Finally, we examined how the handoff to the providers really works.

Quiz Yourself

Q: What is WMI?

A: WMI is the Microsoft implementation of WBEM, an industry-standard set of management and Internet-standard technologies.

Q: What does CIM stand for?

A: CIM stands for Common Information Model.

Q: How is the CIM used?

A: CIM is used to describe objects used within WMI. These form the basis of the CIM schema, which is used as the foundation for Windows-specific classes.

Q: What is the difference between a property and a method?

A: A property is used to describe something; for example, how much free space is on a hard disk. A method actually does something; for example, it formats the hard disk drive.

Q: Where is the WBEM repository located?

A: The WBEM repository is located in the *%SystemRoot%*\system32\wbem\Repository directory by default.

On Your Own

Lab 1 Installing and Configuring the Core Platform SDK

In this lab, you will download and install the Platform software development kit (SDK), along with the WMI Redistributable Components version 1.0. Feel free to take a look around and become familiar with the SDK. The SDK is covered in more detail in Lab 3, where you will practice configuring and using the various features of the SDK.

1. Open your Web browser, and navigate to *http://www.microsoft.com/downloads/ details.aspx?FamilyId=A55B6B43-E24F-4EA3-A93E-40C0EC4F68E5&displaylang=en*.

2. On the right-hand side of the screen, click Download Files Below.

3. Click PSDK-x86.exe. Depending on the version of the Windows operating system you are running and its security setting, you might be prompted multiple times by a security warning dialog box. Click the appropriate options to run Setup Wizard.

4. Walk through the pages of the Setup Wizard. (This takes about 15 minutes using a high-speed Internet connection.)

5. Once you have completed the installation of the Platform SDK, return to the download page and download and install WMI Redistributable Components version 1.0.

Lab 2 Online Install (Optional)

If you have not completed Lab 1, this lab is for information only. If you are not going to install the Platform SDK on more than one computer, doing an online install makes sense. If you need to install the SDK on multiple computers, or if Internet connectivity is unreliable or constrained, it makes sense to download the CAB files. *Do not* try to install the SDK on a computer that already has the Platform SDK installed on it.

1. Open your browser and navigate to *http://www.microsoft.com/downloads/ details.aspx?FamilyId=A55B6B43-E24F-4EA3-A93E-40C0EC4F68E5&displaylang=en.*

2. About halfway down the screen, under Related Downloads, choose Windows Server 2003 SP1 Platform SDK Full Download. The Windows Server 2003 SP1 Platform SDK Full Download page appears. Toward the bottom of the screen, under Files In This Download, are 16 CAB files and 1 extraction utility file. Download all 17 files and save them in a temporary directory.

3. Once the downloads have completed, open a CMD prompt and change to the temporary directory containing the files downloaded in step 3 from Lab 1.

4. Run the executable file and specify another temporary directory that will contain the extracted CAB files. If you saved the downloaded CAB files in the c:\TEMP directory and you want to extract the CAB files to the c:\TEMPSDK directory, the command line would look like the following:

```
C:\TEMP> PSDK-FULL.exe c:\TEMPSDK
```

5. Run Setup.exe from the c:\TEMPSDK directory.

6. Walk through the Setup Wizard.

7. Delete the temporary files as desired. You might want to copy the extracted files from the TEMPSDK directory to either a network share or a CD-ROM.

8. Once you have completed the installation of the core SDK, go back to the main page and download the WMI SDK. Click WMI SDK.

9. Click Install This SDK. The WMI SDK is 6.7 megabytes (MB) and requires 15.4 MB of disk space.

10. Walk through the Setup Wizard.

Lab 3 Navigating the SDK

In this lab, you will learn the basics of navigating your way around the Platform SDK documentation. Taking a few minutes to learn how to navigate the documentation properly will assist you in quickly finding the answers you're looking for when you need them.

1. Click Start, and then point to All Programs and Microsoft Platform SDK For Windows Server 2003 SP1. Click Platform SDK Documentation.

2. When launched, you are presented with two main windows: the Document window (located on the right) and the Navigation pane (located on the left).

3. Click the tabs at the bottom of the Navigation pane to get an idea of what each contains. The Search tab is the one you will use most often.

4. Click the Index tab. Notice there is an X in the upper-right corner. Click the X to close the Index pane. Close the Favorites pane as well.

5. To add the Favorites pane back to the pane view, on the View menu, choose Navigation, and then click Favorites.

6. Because the Platform SDK uses Microsoft Internet Explorer to display content, the Favorites are integrated with Internet Explorer. To separate the SDK articles from the rest of Internet Explorer Favorites, create a special folder. Open Internet Explorer; on the Favorites menu, choose Organize Favorites; and then select Create Folder. Name the folder SDK Articles. (You can also do this from the Favorites tab inside the SDK.) Click the Organize Favorites button.

7. Close Internet Explorer.

8. In the Search pane, in the Look For drop-down list, type **WMI providers**, and then click Search. In the Search Results pane, the bar will indicate the number of topics found, organized by rank.

9. Click the Location bar, and sort the results by book.

10. Above the document window, click the double-headed green arrow on the Standard toolbar. This brings the Contents pane to the foreground and synchronizes contents with the article currently in the document.

11. Each location in the Search Results pane corresponds to a book in the SDK. Scroll down the list of locations in the Search Results pane until you find a book called Windows Management Instrumentation SDK. This book was installed when you downloaded the WMI SDK.

12. Double-click the article titled "Managed Objects and Providers." It is ranked 14th and is the 7th article in the WMI SDK location.

13. Once the "Managed Objects and Providers" article appears in the document window, synchronize the contents with the double-headed green arrow. On the left side of the

Contents pane, you will see the article is located in the chapter called "WMI Architecture."

14.   Click the "WMI Architecture" chapter and, in the article that appears, you will see it links to a book on WMI infrastructure and one on WMI management applications, as well as the "Managed Objects and Providers" article.

15.   Use the back arrow (green arrow on the Standard toolbar) to go back to the "Managed Objects and Providers" article.

16.   Click the Favorites tab, and then click the Add To Favorites button near the top of the tab. The Add Favorite dialog box appears, giving you the opportunity to add the article to the folder you created in step 6.

17.   On the Standard toolbar, there is a text box that lists the topic's path. Hover the mouse over this, and the ScreenTip indicates the Uniform Resource Locator (URL). Right-click the white box and select Copy from the shortcut menu. (This looks weird because you have not selected anything yet, but don't let this confuse you.)

18.   Open Notepad and paste the URL you just copied. It will look like the following:

```
ms-help://MS.PSDKSVR2003SP1.1033/wmisdk/wmi/managed_objects_and_providers.htm
```

19.   Now you are going to play with the URL you have on the Clipboard. Close the SDK.

20.   Open the Platform SDK. Move the mouse over the white URL text box. Notice the pointer is an I-beam. Click in the middle of the box and it turns blue, indicating the box is selected. Paste the URL into this text box and press ENTER. The "Managed Objects and Providers" article appears.

21.   Because this is simply a URL, you can paste it into Internet Explorer, the Open box in the Run dialog box (click Run on the Start menu), or do other things you can do with URLs.

22.   On the CD that accompanies this book, there is a folder named "Chapter 1 Supplemental Material"; open the folder and peruse the SDK articles listed there. The file uses the URL properties discovered in step 18. Close your browser when you are finished reviewing the articles.

23.   Open the Lab1Starter.HTML file in Notepad. Examine the content of the file. Save the file with a new name (*StudentName*Lab1.html) in your workspace directory.

24.   Edit the second line of code, and then save the file. This line controls the title that appears at the top of the browser. Change the message to read Lab One. This is illustrated in the following code:

```
<html><head><title>
Lab One SDK References
</title></head>
```

25. The <h1> tag controls the heading that appears at the top of the page. Change it to read Lab One as well, as shown in the following line:

    ```
    <h1>Lab One SDK References</h1>
    ```

26. Now add one additional reference article. Look up __namespace in the SDK. Copy the URL location of the article that is called "__Namespace" (it should be the second article returned in the Search Results pane).

27. On the next-to-last line of the file, type **__Namespace** as shown in the following line:

    ```
    __Namespace
     </pre></font></div><html>
    ```

28. Add a hyperlink to the namespace article. Open the tag with <a href=" and then paste in the URL you copied in step 26. Make sure you close the URL with a closing quotation mark (") and a right angle bracket (>). It will look like the following:

    ```
    __Namespace
    <a href="ms-help://MS.PSDKSVR2003SP1.1033/wmisdk/wmi/__namespace.htm">
     </pre></font></div><html>
    ```

29. After the angle bracket, paste the URL again. Close the tag with </a>:

    ```
    <a href="ms-help://MS.PSDKSVR2003SP1.1033/wmisdk/wmi/__namespace.htm">ms-help://
    MS.PSDKSVR2003SP1.1033/wmisdk/wmi/__namespace.htm</a>
    ```

30. If the line wrapping is too confusing, refer to the solution file or to the __win32Provider line for a sample of what the line should look like.

31. Save the file and open it in Internet Explorer.

Chapter 2
Configuring WMI

Now that you have a common understanding of the fundamentals, you can learn how to fine-tune Windows Management Instrumentation (WMI) so it serves the exact needs of your organization. Whether you maintain a small workgroup of 10 computers or a large global network composed of 10 forests, you will certainly want to configure specific settings. In this chapter, I show you both the easy way and the hard way to do this—your perspective, of course, will be based on your network configuration. For instance, a nice graphical user interface (GUI) utility is perfect for a small network but is a major roadblock when configuring thousands of computers.

Before You Begin

To work through this chapter, you should be familiar with the following concepts:
- Elements of the basic WMI architecture
- Function and role of the Web-Based Enterprise Management (WBEM) repository
- Function and role of both the WMI providers and WMI objects

After you complete this chapter, you will be familiar with the following concepts:
- How to configure logging for WMI
- How to set the default namespace for WMI
- How to back up the WBEM repository
- How to restore the WBEM repository
- How to configure credentials for remote WMI connections
- How to configure service settings for the WMI service
- How to configure service settings for the WINMGMT service

 Note All the scripts used in this chapter are located on the CD that accompanies this book in the \Scripts\Chapter02 folder.

Understanding the WMI Control Snap-in

You can access the WMI Control snap-in in two ways. First, you can find it in the Computer Management console and, from there, you can access the configuration of WMI on the local computer. Second, you can add the WMI Control snap-in into a blank or custom Microsoft Management Console (MMC) and this enables you to change the target machine and the credentials used to make the connection into WMI. This dualistic approach can be disconcerting for those administrators who expect to be able to redirect the WMI Control console to target another computer because they are unable to access the Connect To Another Computer option on the Action menu from within the Computer Management console, as they can when they use the WMI Control snap-in. The Change Managed Computer dialog box, shown in Figure 2-1, is available from within the WMI Control snap-in.

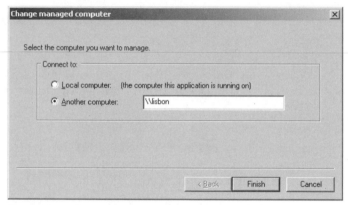

Figure 2-1   Targeting a remote computer with the WMI Control console

Configuring Logging

One of the most fundamental duties of a network administrator is configuring logging for a variety of activities. For instance, Microsoft Exchange Server administrators are often told by Microsoft Premier Support Services (PSS) to increase the amount of logging on a variety of interfaces. This can be a useful recommendation for WMI administrators (if there could ever be such a role). In this section, we examine the logging levels available as we explore the WMI configuration tool.

One of the really cool features of WMI is its logging capabilities. As shown in Figure 2-2, three levels of logging are available from the WMI Control tool. (As you will see later, these are the same levels available through the registry as well.) The levels are Disabled, Errors Only, and Verbose (Includes Extra Information For Microsoft Troubleshooting). Normally, you log using the Errors Only level unless you are having problems that need the additional logging supported by Verbose mode.

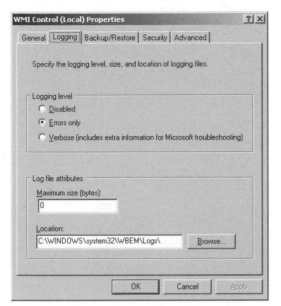

Figure 2-2   Three levels of error logging from the WMI Control console

When you change the logging level, the change takes place immediately. This is useful because you can avoid either cycling the service or rebooting the computer. It also enables you to increase the amount of logging while troubleshooting a problem and, after the problem is solved, you can reduce the logging level, all without interrupting services. Depending on the problem that is detected, you will find a newly created log file called Winmgmt.log in the *%SystemRoot%*\System32\WBEM\Logs directory. Diagnostic logging also is written in the Wbemcore.log file.

Quick Check

Q: How can you configure the WMI logging level?

A: You use the Logging tab of the WMI Control console.

Q: What are the three levels of logging that can be configured in the WMI Control console?

A: The three levels of logging that can be configured in the WMI Control console are Disabled, Errors Only, and Verbose.

Q: What is one reason you might configure Verbose logging?

A: Verbose logging is normally configured to aid troubleshooting a problem that needs diagnostic logging, such as in response to a PSS call.

WMI logging is dependent on the actual provider to supply the events and information to be logged. Not all providers write the same kind of data to the same logs. Additionally, not all

WMI providers are configured through the MMC snap-in. The following providers do not write to common WMI logs and they are not configurable through the MMC.

- Event log provider
- SNMP provider
- View provider
- Directory services provider

In addition to configuring the logging level, you can change the size of the log file by altering the default 65,536-byte size, and you can change the location of the logs from the default *%SystemRoot%*\\System32\WBEM\Logs location. As shown in Figure 2-2, the Logging tab easily exposes these two values. However, you probably will not have a very good reason to modify either value during normal operations. I recommend not moving the WMI logs from their default location because some applications expect to find the logs there, and if you move the logs, you would also have to reconfigure each application to access the new location. In addition, other administrators who need to troubleshoot WMI usually expect the logs to be in the default location as well.

If, however, you do decide to move the WMI log files to another location, keep in mind that the change does not take place immediately. You must cycle the WMI service for the change to take effect. If you do restart the WMI service, several dependencies could also be stopped and restarted, such as the Microsoft Windows Security Center, the Windows Firewall/Internet Connection Sharing (ICS), and, of course, the Systems Management Server (SMS) Agent Host.

When you make changes to these logging options through the GUI, the new values are written to the registry. Changes are reflected in the following registry keys:

```
HKEY_LOCAL_MACHINE\SOFTWARE\Microsoft\WBEM\CIMOM\Logging
HKEY_LOCAL_MACHINE\SOFTWARE\Microsoft\WBEM\CIMOM\Logging Directory
```

Backing Up the WMI Repository

"Oh, no! Not something else to back up," you might exclaim. Ah, yes, my friend, the WMI repository must be backed up on a regular basis. This is particularly important from a disaster recovery standpoint. As discussed in Chapter 1, the WMI repository contains valuable data about servers, workstations, and devices. To protect this information, you need to back it up periodically.

As shown in Figure 2-3, the only configurable options available to the network administrator are the location and the file name. Everything else is automatic and takes only a few seconds to complete on an average server. By default, the WMI repository is no longer backed up automatically every 30 minutes on computers running Microsoft Windows XP and Windows

Server 2003. So, you must back up the WMI repository if you customize it or if you install software that creates its own custom classes or installs its own custom providers. This is a change from earlier versions of WMI.

Figure 2-3   Specifying a name and location for WMI repository backup files

Restoring the WMI Repository

If you think backing up the WMI repository is easy, restoring it is even easier. Select the REC file (WMI recovery file) in the Open dialog box, as shown in Figure 2-4. Recovery begins immediately after you click Open. That's it. There is no prompt asking, "Are you sure you want to restore the WMI repository?" nor do you get "You are about to overwrite your current WMI repository with a previous recovery file. All current data will be lost. Are you sure you wish to continue?" No such warnings occur.

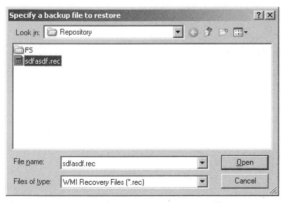

Figure 2-4   Restoring a WMI recovery file

Quick Check

Q: Where are the WMI log files stored?

A: The WMI log files can be found in the *%SystemRoot%*\System32\WBEM\Logs directory by default.

Q: How often should you back up the WMI repository?

A: You should back up the WMI repository on an as-needed basis—specifically, prior to making any changes you might wish to back out of later.

Q: What file extension is used for WMI backup files?

A: The WMI backups are stored as REC files (for *recovery*, perhaps).

It simply restores the previous backup file (called a WMI recovery file). For this reason, it is important that you do not restore a backup file that is very old because you could be restoring out-of-date data. If this is the case, you might simply need to delete the WMI repository and restart the WMI service, whereupon it will rebuild the repository with information stored in the registry *recovery* key (for more information on this, please refer to Chapter 14).

As the WMI recovery operation is taking place, a dialog box appears that tells you the WMI restore operation is in progress. To confirm the operation was successful, use the WMI Control console to reconnect with WMI. After you click OK in the WMI Control dialog box shown in Figure 2-5, close the WMI Control console dialog box, or else it will tell you that it is unable to connect to WMI because the computer is busy. Although this might seem like an error, it is not because the connection currently displayed is left over from the prerecovery WMI repository. (If you are unable to make a new connection at this point, however, you might have a more serious problem. You should review the troubleshooting information in Chapter 14.) Click Cancel, right-click the WMI Control node, and you will once again successfully connect.

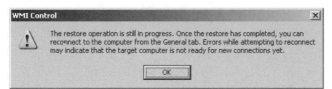

Figure 2-5   WMI Control dialog box indicating the restore operation is in progress

Why Back Up the WMI Repository?

Many network administrators never back up the WMI repository and, in fact, do not even know there is functionality to do so. Several good reasons exist, however, for performing a backup of the repository. For instance, if you are doing development work, remember that you are installing providers, classes, and the like into the repository. As you are developing, it makes sense to take snapshot backups along the way. They can be fast and easy ways to return to a previous state without having to delete a corrupt repository and rebuild it.

There are other reasons to back up the WMI repository as well. For instance, some applications install custom providers in the WMI repository and fail to add themselves to the *Autorecover MOF* registry key. To avoid manual recovery of the providers, you should back up the WMI repository.

Changing the Target of Operations

One of the nice things about being able to add the WMI Control snap-in into an MMC is how it enables you to change the target of operations. As shown in Figure 2-6, by using the snap-in in a blank or custom console you can easily change the target computer. This gives the network administrator a great deal of flexibility. For instance, you can connect to remote computers and perform all the normal administration tasks for WMI, such as the following:

- Configure logging level, log size, and log location
- Back up the WMI repository
- Restore the WMI repository
- Configure the default WMI namespace
- Configure namespace security

In addition, one of the easiest ways to check WMI security and health is simply to attempt to make a connection with the WMI Control console. If it connects successfully, the problem lies elsewhere. This is also a good way to test security because you have the capability to make the connection with alternative credentials.

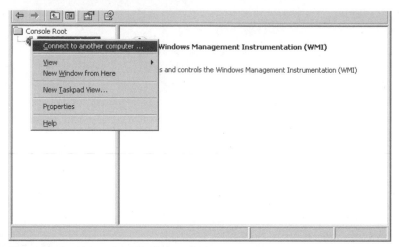

Figure 2-6   Using the MMC snap-in to connect to remote computers

Understanding Registry Settings

The WMI administrator needs to understand a number of registry settings, including settings that control the behavior of the Windows Script Host (WSH) and those that control the execution of WMI. You can define scripting configuration information in two locations: the current user or the machine level. By default, the current user settings override the local machine settings, but this is also configurable through the registry. The current user and machine level settings can be found under the *Settings* keys in the following locations:

```
HKEY_CURRENT_USER\Software\Microsoft\Windows Script Host\Settings
HKEY_LOCAL_MACHINE\SOFTWARE\Microsoft\Windows Script Host\Settings
```

Enabled

The *Enabled* key is a Boolean value that turns WSH off or on. When set to 1 (enabled), the scripts will run. When set to 0 (disabled), scripts will not run, and the error message shown in Figure 2-7 appears. The *Enabled* key can be added to either the user or the machine level. The locations of the *Enabled* key registry values are as follows:

```
HKEY_CURRENT_USER\Software\Microsoft\Windows Script Host\Settings\Enabled
HKEY_LOCAL_MACHINE\SOFTWARE\Microsoft\Windows Script Host\Settings\Enabled
```

Figure 2-7   An error message indicating that WSH has been disabled that appears when you attempt to execute a script

Several essential differences characterize the way Microsoft Windows 2000 implements this value as compared to Windows XP and Windows Server 2003. First, the key is not present by default in Windows XP and Windows Server 2003 as it is in Windows 2000. For all three platforms, the default value is 1 (enabled). To turn off the capability to run scripts in Windows XP and Windows Server 2003, you must add the *Enabled* value as a DWORD and set it equal to 0, as shown in Figure 2-8.

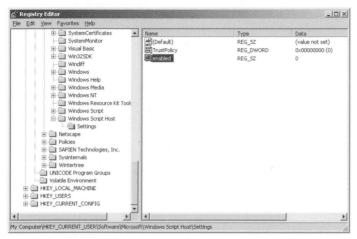

Figure 2-8   Turning off script processing in Windows XP and Windows Server 2003 by adding the *Enabled* value and setting it equal to 0

LogSecurityFailures

After you turn off WSH, you probably want to know if someone is trying to run scripts on the computer. In Windows 2000 and Windows XP prior to Service Pack 2 (SP2), you had to add the *LogSecurityFailures* value to change the value from the default of 0. With *LogSecurityFailures* enabled, when a script fails to execute, Event ID 1000 is logged from WSH. In Windows XP SP2, the default value is 1, which means security failures in script execution are written to the system log. (You might expect failures to be written to the security log, but because they originate from a system process, they go to the system log.) An example of the failure message is shown in Figure 2-9.

Keep in mind that the *LogSecurityFailures* value is stored as a REG_SZ string value, and the value enabling or disabling writing to the event log can be either 0 or 1, or true or false. Both types of Boolean values are accepted for this key. The registry locations for this value when specified for the user or machine level are as follows:

```
HKEY_CURRENT_USER\Software\Microsoft\Windows Script Host\Settings\LogSecurityFailures
HKEY_LOCAL_MACHINE\SOFTWARE\Microsoft\Windows Script Host\Settings\ LogSecurityFailures
```

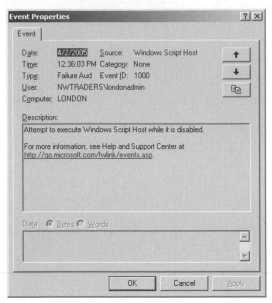

Figure 2-9   Event log security failure message

LogSecuritySuccesses

If you want to audit the execution of scripts on a computer in the event log, you can enable the *LogSecuritySuccesses* value. Just like the previous registry values examined in this section, it is not available by default in Windows XP or Windows Server 2003 and must be added manually. The default value for *LogSecuritySuccesses* is 0, which means it does not log the successful execution of scripts on the platform. If you want to log successes, add the *LogSecuritySuccesses* as a REG_SZ string value and set it equal to 1 or true. The registry locations for these values are as follows:

```
HKEY_CURRENT_USER\Software\Microsoft\Windows Script Host\Settings\LogSecuritySuccesses
HKEY_LOCAL_MACHINE\SOFTWARE\Microsoft\Windows Script Host\Settings\LogSecuritySuccesses
```

On a practical level, I do not think turning on logging of successes enables you to gain much useful information because the name of the script is not captured. An example of the information from Event ID 1001 is shown in Figure 2-10.

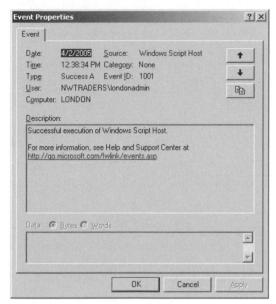

Figure 2-10   Logging Event ID 1001 from WSH

Remote

Sometimes it is advantageous to start a script on a remote computer. By default, this cannot be done in Windows XP and Windows Server 2003. Simply adding another value to the WSH settings section of the registry can resolve this. The value you add is called *Remote*, and it is a REG_SZ string value. As before, you might need to make the change in only one location, depending on your configuration. If you change the setting at the user level, the registry value looks like the following:

```
HKEY_CURRENT_USER\Software\Microsoft\Windows Script Host\Settings\Remote
```

If you need to control this setting at the machine level, add the *Remote* string value to the HKEY_LOCAL_MACHINE (HKLM) hive as shown here:

```
HKEY_LOCAL_MACHINE\SOFTWARE\Microsoft\Windows Script Host\Settings\Remote
```

Using the CIM Object Manager

In working with WMI, you need to be aware of the CIM Object Manager (CIMOM). As discussed in Chapter 1, two basic types of classes are available in WMI. The first is a static class, and, as you might guess, the second type is a dynamic class. For many operations, the dynamic classes are the most interesting. However, at times you must work with static classes. When you work with static classes, you are working with CIMOM.

CIMOM is a collection of application programming interfaces (APIs) that enables scripts and other applications to work with the static classes found in the Common Information Model (CIM) repository. Dynamic classes are generated by a provider, and they are not resident in the CIM repository; however, it is still necessary to use CIMOM when dealing with dynamic classes because the dynamic classes are based on the classes found in the repository. We discuss these classes in more detail in Chapter 9.

In Windows 2000, Windows XP, and Windows Server 2003, the role of CIMOM is performed by the WMI service. In Windows XP and Windows Server 2003, the WMI service, Winmgmt.exe, runs inside a generic service host process called Svchost.exe, which you see when you look at processes in Task Manager. In Windows 2000, the Winmgmt.exe service runs as a stand-alone service.

CIMOM acts like a gatekeeper in that all requests for data flow through it. CIMOM receives a request for information from your script or from an application and routes the request to the appropriate provider or retrieves the information directly from the CIM repository.

How does CIMOM know where to route the requests? When a provider is installed, it registers with CIMOM. This information is stored in the WMI repository. (Keep in mind that the CIM repository and the WMI repository are exactly the same thing. Another term you might see is *WBEM repository*, which is another name for the WMI repository. Three terms for the same object—this ought to tell you it is important.) When CIMOM receives a request for information, it looks up the provider that is able to service the request. For example, the Office_ExcelVersion.vbs script that follows retrieves important information about the version of Microsoft Excel that is installed on the computer. When CIMOM receives the request for the Excel version number, it needs to know which provider can supply this information. In this instance, the MS_VIEW_INSTANCE_PROVIDER supplies the *Office_ExcelVersion* class. The _VIEW_INSTANCE_PROVIDER is contained in Viewprov.dll. You will not have this class or provider unless you have the SMS 2003 client installed. If the provider is not present, the Office_ExcelVersion.vbs script will return a null value.

The *Set objWMIService* line in the script uses the *GetObject* method to make the connection into WMI. It does so by using the *winmgmts:* moniker (this is covered in detail in Chapter 3). Once you have established a connection into WMI, use the *ExecQuery* method to retrieve the requested information from the *Office_ExcelVersion* class. *ExecQuery* returns a collection, so it is necessary to use *For Next Each* to walk through the collection. The Office_ExcelVersion.vbs script simply uses *Wscript.echo* to output the properties contained in the *Office_ExcelVersion* class. A more interesting script might also return the name of the computer system and the name of the currently logged on user, and then perhaps write the output to either an Excel spreadsheet or to a database. Careful observation of the Office_ExcelVersion.vbs script reveals that at no time does it use the name of the MS_VIEW_INSTANCE_PROVIDER provider. This is not necessary (and would generate an error) because the CIMOM knows which providers provide which classes.

Office_ExcelVersion.vbs

```
strComputer = "."
wmiNS = "\root\cimv2"
wmiQuery = "Select * from Office_ExcelVersion"
Set objWMIService = GetObject("winmgmts:\\" & strComputer & wmiNS)
Set colItems = objWMIService.ExecQuery(wmiQuery)
For Each objItem in colItems

 wscript.echo "Build: " & objItem.Build
 wscript.echo "Name: " & objItem.Name
 wscript.echo "Path: " & objItem.Path
 wscript.echo "Version: " & objItem.Version
 wscript.echo " "
next
```

Once the information is collected, it is returned to the requesting application or script. Running a script on the local computer is really exciting—but, for extreme excitement, you need to talk to multiple machines. Network administrators rarely work with single computers, so the question often comes up, "How do I run this script against multiple machines?" This is the reason I defined the variable *strComputer* in the Office_ExcelVersion.vbs script. When you assign the value "." to the variable, you are telling Microsoft Visual Basic Scripting Edition (VBScript) to operate against the local machine. If you want to connect to a remote computer, you simply type in the name of a remote machine and (if you have permission, connectivity, and a few other things) the script will operate against the remote computer. Keep in mind that the script is actually running on the computer on which it is launched, but it targets the WMI query against the computer defined with the variable *strComputer*. (Because *strComputer* is a variable, I could have called it anything, but I like to call it *strComputer*, the variable used in Microsoft Scriptomatic. Scriptomatic is covered in Chapter 14.) From this high-level overview, you can see that the role of the provider is vital to the functionality (and extensibility) of WMI. Let's now examine the role of the provider in more detail.

Implementing Providers

Have you ever had the experience of being in a place where you did not speak the language? Recently, I was in Lisbon teaching a VBScript class to some of our partners. I do not speak Portuguese, but luckily my colleague, Luis, does, so I made sure I did not stray too far from him. Everyone in the class spoke English; however, a few times I had to call on Luis to explain in Portuguese a particularly difficult topic. (Actually, the topic was easy, but my explanation was making it difficult!) So, what does this have to do with WMI? In this story, Luis is the WMI provider. WMI providers act as intermediaries between CIMOM and resources. In the story, I am a resource, Luis is the provider, and the students in the class are the consumers (or applications, whichever you prefer).

Providers make it easy to retrieve information from WMI. Providers provide classes. (We look at classes in more detail later.) When you have a provider installed on your computer, it grants additional functionality to the consumer application that uses its services. In this manner, providers hide all the details involved in obtaining the information you need. You simply make the appropriate call and retrieve the desired information. An example can help clarify this: when I was in the Navy, we had an interface into the Engineering department called Damage Control Central (DC Central). DC Central was available 24 hours a day and was a single phone number we could call to learn the current status of all engineering functions, including the status of all boilers, how much fresh water we had, how much electricity was being produced, and so forth. If we did not have this interface, we would have had to make nearly a dozen different phone calls to obtain the same information. In WMI terms, DC Central was our engineering provider.

Each WMI provider installed on the server (or workstation) makes its presence known to WMI by making certain entries in the registry on the computer. Knowing where these registry entries reside is important for a couple of reasons. First, it makes it an easy task to retrieve these settings from the registry. Additionally, being able to look up the registry entries can be useful in a troubleshooting scenario. The registry settings are discussed in the section titled "Automatically Recovering Providers."

Configuring WMI Service Settings

When it comes to configuring WMI, you can use several settings. As discussed in the sidebar titled "Why Back Up the WMI Repository?" one reason for backing up the WMI repository is to be able to recover custom extensions that applications add to WMI.

Automatically Recovering Providers

The providers that are automatically backed up and automatically recovered are listed in the following registry key:

```
HKEY_LOCAL_MACHINE\SOFTWARE\Microsoft\WBEM\CIMOM\Autorecover MOFs
```

By using one of the following four methods, each discussed in the following subsections, you can ensure that the provider is automatically recovered in the event of a problem:

- Upon installation, the application lists itself in the *Autorecover MOF* key.
- You manually edit the *Autorecover MOF* key.
- You add the *#pragma autorecover* tag to the Managed Object Format (MOF) file.
- You use Mofcomp.exe with the *−autorecover* switch.

Initial Installation

On my system that runs Windows XP Service Pack 2, the following MOF files will be automatically recovered:

```
C:\WINDOWS\system32\WBEM\cimwin32.mof
C:\WINDOWS\system32\WBEM\cimwin32.mfl
C:\WINDOWS\system32\WBEM\system.mof
C:\WINDOWS\system32\WBEM\wmipcima.mof
C:\WINDOWS\system32\WBEM\wmipcima.mfl
C:\WINDOWS\system32\WBEM\regevent.mof
C:\WINDOWS\system32\WBEM\regevent.mfl
C:\WINDOWS\system32\WBEM\ntevt.mof
C:\WINDOWS\system32\WBEM\ntevt.mfl
C:\WINDOWS\system32\WBEM\secrcw32.mof
C:\WINDOWS\system32\WBEM\secrcw32.mfl
C:\WINDOWS\system32\WBEM\dsprov.mof
C:\WINDOWS\system32\WBEM\dsprov.mfl
C:\WINDOWS\system32\WBEM\msi.mof
C:\WINDOWS\system32\WBEM\msi.mfl
C:\WINDOWS\system32\WBEM\policman.mof
C:\WINDOWS\system32\WBEM\policman.mfl
C:\WINDOWS\system32\WBEM\subscrpt.mof
C:\WINDOWS\system32\WBEM\wmi.mof
C:\WINDOWS\system32\WBEM\wmi.mfl
C:\WINDOWS\system32\WBEM\scm.mof
C:\WINDOWS\system32\WBEM\fevprov.mof
C:\WINDOWS\system32\WBEM\fevprov.mfl
C:\WINDOWS\system32\WBEM\wmitimep.mof
C:\WINDOWS\system32\WBEM\wmitimep.mfl
C:\WINDOWS\system32\WBEM\wmipdskq.mof
C:\WTNDOWS\system32\WBEM\wmipdskq.mfl
C:\WINDOWS\system32\WBEM\wmipicmp.mof
C:\WINDOWS\system32\WBEM\wmipicmp.mfl
C:\WINDOWS\system32\WBEM\wmipiprt.mof
C:\WINDOWS\system32\WBEM\wmipiprt.mfl
C:\WINDOWS\system32\WBEM\wmipjobj.mof
C:\WINDOWS\system32\WBEM\wmipjobj.mfl
C:\WINDOWS\system32\WBEM\wmipsess.mof
C:\WINDOWS\system32\WBEM\wmipsess.mfl
C:\WINDOWS\system32\WBEM\krnlprov.mof
C:\WINDOWS\system32\WBEM\krnlprov.mfl
C:\WINDOWS\system32\WBEM\cli.mof
C:\WINDOWS\system32\WBEM\tscfgwmi.mof
C:\WINDOWS\system32\WBEM\tscfgwmi.mfl
C:\WINDOWS\system32\WBEM\licwmi.mof
C:\WINDOWS\system32\WBEM\licwmi.mfl
C:\WINDOWS\system32\WBEM\evntrprv.mof
C:\WINDOWS\system32\WBEM\hnetcfg.mof
C:\WINDOWS\system32\WBEM\sr.mof
C:\WINDOWS\system32\WBEM\CmdEvTgProv.mof
C:\WINDOWS\system32\WBEM\dgnet.mof
C:\WINDOWS\system32\WBEM\whqlprov.mof
C:\WINDOWS\system32\WBEM\ieinfo5.mof
C:\WINDOWS\SYSTEM32\WBEM\RSOP.MOF
C:\WINDOWS\SYSTEM32\WBEM\RSOP.MFL
C:\WINDOWS\SYSTEM32\WBEM\SCERSOP.MOF
C:\WINDOWS\SYSTEM32\WBEM\WSCENTER.MOF
C:\WINDOWS\MICROSOFT.NET\FRAMEWORK\V1.1.4322\ASPNET.MOF
C:\PROGRAM FILES\COMMON FILES\MICROSOFT SHARED\MSINFO\OINFOP11.MOF
```

```
C:\PROGRA~1\COMMON~1\MICROS~1\MSINFO\OINFOP11.MOF
C:\PROGRAM FILES\MICROSOFT ACT\ACTNAMESPACE.MOF
C:\PROGRAM FILES\MICROSOFT ACT\ACTCONTROLLER.MOF
C:\PROGRAM FILES\MICROSOFT ACT\ACTBROKER.MOF
C:\WINDOWS\system32\wbem\mof\good\msioff10.mof
C:\PROGRAM FILES\WMI TOOLS\EVIEWER.MOF
```

A review of the Autorecover information reveals that both MOF files and MFL files (language-specific MOF files) will be reloaded into the WBEM repository at detection of a failure. MOF files are used to define a provider to WMI and to specify which properties and methods are available through that provider. These text files are compiled and their information is written to the repository.

Manually Editing the *Autorecover MOF* Key

You might sometime install an application that supplies its own providers and the MOF files are not added to the *Autorecover MOF* key in the registry. If this is the case, a WMI automatic recovery operation will not load the MOF files into the repository. You can take several steps to protect against this eventuality. Probably the easiest thing to do is to add the appropriate MOF file to the *Autorecover MOF* registry key. This provides you with ease of recovery if the WBEM repository becomes corrupt.

Adding the *#pragma autorecover* tag to the MOF File

Another way to recover automatically from a repository corruption is to actually edit the MOF file that accompanies the offending application. This is an extremely easy operation because the MOF file is plaintext and can be edited using Notepad.exe. To do this, add the following command near the top of the MOF file:

```
#pragma autorecover
```

If you are wondering exactly where to place the *#pragma autorecover* command, examine the following few lines from the Eviewer.mof file, which is the last Autorecover file listed earlier. In this MOF file, the command is placed on the third line. In other files it might be on the second line. It does not really matter as long as the command is close to the top of the file. For consistency's sake, I prefer to make it the second line of the file. We examine MOF files in more detail in Chapter 13.

```
// Copyright (c) 1997-1999 Microsoft Corporation
#pragma namespace("\\root\\cimv2")
#pragma autorecover
```

The *#pragma autorecover* command tells WMI to write the name of the MOF file to the *Autorecover MOF* registry key. This happens when the MOF file is compiled and placed in the repository.

Using Mofcomp.exe

The fourth way to ensure automatic recovery of the MOF file is to use a special switch when using the Mofcomp.exe utility. If you think, judging from the name, the Mofcomp.exe utility might compile MOF files, you are very observant. That is exactly what the utility does. You might need to use Mofcomp.exe on any of the following occasions:

■ If you have written your own MOF file (don't laugh, you will be doing this later—it is not as hard as it sounds) and you want to actually use it, it needs to be compiled and placed in the WMI repository.

■ If you purchase an application, but the manufacturer does not by default enable instrumentation of the application.

■ If you need to recover a WMI provider that is not automatically recovered.

A lab in which you use the Mofcomp.exe utility is included in Chapter 14. For now, we are concerned only with the *–autorecover* switch. Usage of the *–autorecover* switch with Mofcomp.exe is illustrated in the following listing. In this example, I place Eviewer.mof into the *Autorecover MOF* registry location. A friendly "Done!" informs you that the operation was successful.

```
C:\>mofcomp -autorecover "C:\PROGRAM FILES\WMI TOOLS\EVIEWER.MOF"
Microsoft (R) 32-bit MOF Compiler Version 5.1.2600.2180
Copyright (c) Microsoft Corp. 1997-2001. All rights reserved.
Parsing MOF file: C:\PROGRAM FILES\WMI TOOLS\EVIEWER.MOF
MOF file has been successfully parsed
Storing data in the repository...
Done!
```

Exploring WMI Settings with WMI

Looking through the registry, clicking numerous tabs of overpopulated MMCs, and using strange utilities might sound like fun to some people, but I prefer to let VBScript do the work for me. After all, you might ask, why learn to script if you are not going to use that knowledge? See what you can find out about your WMI configuration by scripting. It just so happens, an entire class is devoted to WMI settings; it is appropriately called the *Win32_WMISetting* class. The script, WMISettings.vbs, returns a computer's current WMI configuration settings.

WMISettings.vbs

```
strComputer = "."
wmiNS = "\root\cimv2"
wmiQuery = "Select * from Win32_WMISetting"
Set objWMIService = GetObject("winmgmts:\\" & strComputer & wmiNS)
Set colItems = objWMIService.ExecQuery(wmiQuery)
For Each objItem in colItems

 wscript.echo "ASPScriptDefaultNamespace: " & objItem.ASPScriptDefaultNamespace
 wscript.echo "ASPScriptEnabled: " & objItem.ASPScriptEnabled
 wscript.echo "AutorecoverMofs: " & vbcrlf & vbtab &  _
```

```
        join(objItem.AutorecoverMofs, "" & vbcrlf & vbtab)
        wscript.echo "AutoStartWin9X: " & objItem.AutoStartWin9X
        wscript.echo "BackupInterval: " & objItem.BackupInterval
        wscript.echo "BackupLastTime: " & objItem.BackupLastTime
        wscript.echo "BuildVersion: " & objItem.BuildVersion
        wscript.echo "Caption: " & objItem.Caption
        wscript.echo "DatabaseDirectory: " & objItem.DatabaseDirectory
        wscript.echo "DatabaseMaxSize: " & objItem.DatabaseMaxSize
        wscript.echo "Description: " & objItem.Description
        wscript.echo "EnableAnonWin9xConnections: " & objItem.EnableAnonWin9xConnections
        wscript.echo "EnableEvents: " & objItem.EnableEvents
        wscript.echo "EnableStartupHeapPreallocation: " & objItem.EnableStartupHeapPreallocation
        wscript.echo "HighThresholdOnClientObjects: " & objItem.HighThresholdOnClientObjects
        wscript.echo "HighThresholdOnEvents: " & objItem.HighThresholdOnEvents
        wscript.echo "InstallationDirectory: " & objItem.InstallationDirectory
        wscript.echo "LastStartupHeapPreallocation: " & objItem.LastStartupHeapPreallocation
        wscript.echo "LoggingDirectory: " & objItem.LoggingDirectory
        wscript.echo "LoggingLevel: " & objItem.LoggingLevel
        wscript.echo "LowThresholdOnClientObjects: " & objItem.LowThresholdOnClientObjects
        wscript.echo "LowThresholdOnEvents: " & objItem.LowThresholdOnEvents
        wscript.echo "MaxLogFileSize: " & objItem.MaxLogFileSize
        wscript.echo "MaxWaitOnClientObjects: " & objItem.MaxWaitOnClientObjects
        wscript.echo "MaxWaitOnEvents: " & objItem.MaxWaitOnEvents
        wscript.echo "MofSelfInstallDirectory: " & objItem.MofSelfInstallDirectory
        wscript.echo "SettingID: " & objItem.SettingID
    wscript.echo " "
    next
```

Summary

In this chapter, we looked at the various settings you can configure for the WMI service in both Windows XP and Windows Server 2003. We looked at three methods for examining or making these configuration changes: through the MMC, through the registry, and through the *Win32_WMISetting* class. We also discussed making changes to logging detail levels and changing the logging location. We examined the effect of making logging-level changes and discussed how the changes take place immediately after the setting is modified. Changes to the logging location, however, require a service restart. We explored the methods for backing up the WMI repository and examined the contents of the *Autorecover MOF* key in the registry. Finally, we looked briefly at the *Win32_WMISetting* WMI class.

Quiz Yourself

Q: What is one difference between using the WMI Control console from the Computer Management console and using it in a custom MMC snap-in?

A: When added as an MMC snap-in, the WMI Control console enables you to redirect to additional computers and provides the opportunity for you to specify alternative credentials.

Q: When restoring the WMI repository using the WMI Control console, what is one important consideration?

A: When restoring the WMI repository using the WMI Control console, no warning message is displayed prior to restoration.

Q: Your WMI service detects a corrupt WBEM repository and performs an automatic recovery operation. However, you notice that one of your monitoring scripts no longer works. What is the first thing you should check?

A: The first thing you should check after an automatic recovery operation is the MOF files that are detailed in the following registry key:

`HKEY_LOCAL_MACHINE\SOFTWARE\Microsoft\WBEM\CIMOM\Autorecover MOFs`

Q: What are two methods you can use to ensure that a custom provider is automatically recovered?

A: One way to ensure that the provider is automatically recovered is to edit the MOF file and add the *#pragma autorecover* command. Another method is to compile the MOF file using Mofcomp.exe and specify the *–autorecover* switch.

On Your Own

Lab 4 Backing Up the WMI Repository

In this lab, you will back up the WMI repository. This is an extremely important procedure that is easy to perform. This backup of the WMI repository is essential if you change something—security settings, namespaces, or even classes and providers—in the repository and then need to quickly revert back.

1. Open a blank MMC by clicking Start and then choosing Run. Type **MMC** in the Open box in the Run dialog box, and click OK. A blank MMC appears.

2. From the File menu, choose Add/Remove Snap-In, and then click Add in the Add/Remove Snap-In dialog box.

3. Choose WMI Control from the list that appears, and click Add.

4. Select Local Computer, and then click Finish.

5. Click Close, and then click OK.

6. You now have the WMI Control console in a custom MMC. Save the MMC in the Administrative Tools folder by choosing Save from the File menu. Name the console WMI.msc, and then click OK.

7. Right-click the WMI Control (Local) icon in the left-hand pane and select Properties from the shortcut menu. Click the Backup/Restore tab and click Back Up Now.

8.   In the dialog box that appears, name the backup *yourname*.**rec**, and then click Open.

9.   A Backup In Progress dialog box appears for a few seconds and then closes.

10.   Click OK to close the WMI Control (Local) Properties dialog box.

11.   Open Windows Explorer and navigate to the *%SystemRoot%*\System32\WBEM\Repository directory. You should see the *yourname*.rec file. This indicates the backup was successful.

Lab 5 Restoring the WMI Repository

In this lab, you will restore the WMI repository by using the backup you made in Lab 4.

1.   Open the WMI.msc console you created in Lab 4. It should be available from the Administrative Tools folder if you saved it to the default location.

2.   Right-click WMI Control (Local) in the left-hand pane under Console Root, and click Properties.

3.   In the WMI Control (Local) Properties dialog box click the Backup/Restore tab, and click Restore Now.

4.   In the Specify A Backup File To Restore dialog box, select *yourname*.rec, which you created in Lab 4.

5.   After selecting the REC file, click Open. The restore operation begins immediately.

6.   The WMI Control dialog box appears stating, "The restore operation is still in progress. Once the restore has completed, you can reconnect to the computer from the General tab. Errors while attempting to reconnect may indicate that the target computer is not ready for new connections yet." Click OK.

7.   An error is displayed in the General tab of the WMI Control (Local) Properties dialog box. This error states, "Failed to connect to <*local computer*> because 'Target computer busy.' " Click OK.

8.   Notice you cannot click OK to make the error message go away. Click Cancel instead to close the error message.

9.   Go back to the WMI.msc console you created in Lab 4. Right-click WMI Control (Local), and select Properties.

10.   The message in the middle of the General tab indicates that you are successfully connected to <*local computer*>, indicating the restore was successful.

11.   Open the file WinMgmt.log, located at *%SystemRoot%*\System32\WBEM\Logs, and scroll down to the bottom of the file.

12.   Look for entries that indicate the core is being shut down. They look something like the following:

```
(Sun Feb 20 14:45:48 2005.77755977) : core is being shut down by WinMgmt, it returned
0x0
(Sun Feb 20 14:45:48 2005.77756037) : core is being resumed: it returned 0x0
```

These entries indicate WMI was shut down and then restarted so you could perform the restore operation.

13. Look at WbemCore.log as well. Examine the items logged there during the shutdown and restart of the services while the restore is taking place.

14. Do the restore one more time, but this time watch your computer clock, and start the restore just after a new minute starts. Make note of the exact time, click Restore | Reconnect, and then open the two logs. Again look at the bottom of each log and see what actually occurs during the restore operation.

15. Close the WMI.msc console tool.

Lab 6 Exploring WMI Settings via Script

In this lab, you will explore the *Win32_WMISetting* class and use it to report on the current configuration of your WMI service.

1. Look up the *Win32_WMISetting* class in the Platform software development kit (SDK). You can see from the article that this class contains the operational parameters for the WMI service.

2. Scroll through the article and see whether there are any methods you can use to configure WMI.

3. You will find there are no methods.

4. There are, however, 26 properties associated with this class. It is way too much typing if you want to echo out all the property values. You need to create a tool to help you.

5. Open the ListClassPropertiesIntoArray.vbs script, and examine the contents of the file. Notice you are pulling the *properties_* of the class.

6. Locate the line in the script that looks like the following:

```
strClass = "Win32_WmiSetting" 'Here is the Class Name
```

7. Change the code so that the value comes from an input box. If you are unfamiliar with the parameters available for the *inputbox* function, look it up in the Platform SDK. Supply a meaningful prompt, title, and, if you wish, even a default value. The new line will look something like the following:

```
strClass = inputbox("type in your class","ClassExplorer", "win32_") 'Here is the Class
    Name
```

8. Once that works, you can decide to clean up the code and place each of the three parameters in a variable. If so, complete the following steps. First, declare some variables, which go in the header section of the script. I used the following:

```
Dim StrPrompt, StrTitle, StrDefault ' used for InputBox Function
```

9. Next, supply values for each of the variables. These go in the reference section of the script and look something like the following:

```
StrPrompt = "Type in the class to explore"
StrTitle = "ClassExplorer"
StrDefault = "Win32_"
```

10. Now redo the *inputbox* function. This time, simply use the variables in order so it looks like the following:

```
strClass = inputbox(StrPrompt, StrTitle, StrDefault) 'Supply class to input box.
```

11. Save and run the script. An input box will pop up in which you can type the last part of the class name: **wmisetting**. You will retrieve an output of all the class properties.

12. If you wish, you can modify the line near the bottom of the script, which builds a single variable from each element in the array that contains all the properties in the class. The line looks like the following:

```
prop= prop  & Array1(b) & vbcrlf
```

13. You can modify it by adding a *Wscript.echo* command so that it writes some of the code for you. The line now looks like the following:

```
prop= prop  & "Wscript.echo objItem." & Array1(b) & vbcrlf
```

14. Save this script as StudentLab6a.vbs.

15. Run StudentLab6a.vbs and copy the output to the Clipboard.

16. Open WmiTemplate.vbs and paste the output from step 15 inside the *For Next* loop. The code looks like the following:

```
For Each objItem in colItems
Wscript.echo objItem.ASPScriptDefaultNamespace
Wscript.echo objItem.ASPScriptEnabled
Wscript.echo objItem.AutorecoverMofs
Wscript.echo objItem.AutoStartWin9X
Wscript.echo objItem.BackupInterval
Wscript.echo objItem.BackupLastTime
Wscript.echo objItem.BuildVersion
Wscript.echo objItem.Caption
Wscript.echo objItem.DatabaseDirectory
Wscript.echo objItem.DatabaseMaxSize
Wscript.echo objItem.Description
Wscript.echo objItem.EnableAnonWin9xConnections
Wscript.echo objItem.EnableEvents
Wscript.echo objItem.EnableStartupHeapPreallocation
Wscript.echo objItem.HighThresholdOnClientObjects
Wscript.echo objItem.HighThresholdOnEvents
Wscript.echo objItem.InstallationDirectory
Wscript.echo objItem.LastStartupHeapPreallocation
Wscript.echo objItem.LoggingDirectory
Wscript.echo objItem.LoggingLevel
```

```
Wscript.echo objItem.LowThresholdOnClientObjects
Wscript.echo objItem.LowThresholdOnEvents
Wscript.echo objItem.MaxLogFileSize
Wscript.echo objItem.MaxWaitOnClientObjects
Wscript.echo objItem.MaxWaitOnEvents
Wscript.echo objItem.MofSelfInstallDirectory
Wscript.echo objItem.SettingID
Next
```

Make sure you edit the line that contains the *wmiQuery*. Add the *wmiClass* name you are working with—here, it is *Win32_WMISetting*. Simply type the last part of the name: **wmisetting**. The completed line looks like the following:

```
wmiQuery = "Select * from win32_WmiSetting"
```

17. Save the script as StudentLab6a.vbs and then run it. The script should run successfully.

18. Turn off *On Error Resume Next* by placing a comment mark in front of it. Now run the script. A type mismatch error will appear. The following is the offending line:

```
Wscript.echo objItem.AutorecoverMofs
```

19. Go back to the Win32_WMISetting article in the Platform SDK and read what it has to say about this property. In fact, this article calls it a string (don't worry, I filed a bug report). However, I believe it is an array. How can you check for sure? Use the *isArray* function.

20. First, turn on *On Error Resume Next* again by removing the comment mark on that line. Then add some code just below the line that echoes out *AutorecoverMofs*. The modified line will look like the following:

```
Wscript.echo objItem.AutorecoverMofs
WScript.Echo IsArray(objItem.autorecovermofs) & " Is it an array?"
```

21. Run the script and you will see the answer:

```
True Is it an array?
```

22. Now that you know for sure that you are dealing with an array, you can use standard array techniques to retrieve information. Use the *join* function. If you are unfamiliar with this function, look it up in the Platform SDK.

23. Turn off the *isArray* line by placing a comment mark at the beginning of the line.

24. Modify the *Wscript.echo objItem.AutorecoverMofs* so that you use the *join* function to convert the array into a string. The modified line of code looks like the following:

```
Wscript.echo join(objItem.AutorecoverMofs, "," & vbcrlf)
```

25. Run the script and see all the MOF files that are automatically recovered.

26. Turn off *On Error Resume Next* and see if the script does this successfully. If it does not, compare it with the Lab6Bsolution.vbs script.

27. Save your work.

Part II
WMI Queries and Events

Chapter 3

Using Basic WMI Queries

Now that you are armed with an understanding of the structure of Windows Management Instrumentation (WMI), it is time to focus on the most fundamental WMI skill—performing queries. When you want to find the amount of free disk space on a server, you will use a query. When you want the server to respond to a specific error condition, you will use a query. If you want to find which WMI classes are base classes, you will use a query. As you can see, the query is foundational to the use of WMI in the enterprise space. You might also have noticed that there are three different types of WMI queries:

- Data query
- Event query
- Schema query

How to use each type of query is detailed in this chapter. This chapter also discusses the reasons you might use one type of query rather than another. Also covered are the features the queries have in common as well as the unique features of each type.

Before You Begin

To work through this chapter, you should be familiar with the following concepts:
- WMI default namespaces
- Basic elements of the WMI architecture
- Basic elements of reading and writing Microsoft Visual Basic Scripting Edition (VBScript)
- Collections and using *For Each Next*
- Arrays and manipulating collective data

After you complete this chapter, you will be familiar with the following concepts:
- The difference between a data query, an event query, and a schema query
- The basic syntax of a WMI Query Language (WQL) *Select* statement
- Using a WQL *Where* clause to limit the amount of returned data

- Using the _Class property in a WQL *Where* clause
- Using the WMI moniker

> **Note**   All the scripts used in this chapter are located on the CD that accompanies this book in the \Scripts\Chapter03 folder.

Understanding WQL

To query WMI, you must become familiar with WMI Query Language (WQL). If WQL reminds you of SQL, which stands for structured query language, it is for good reason. WQL is actually a subset of SQL—with some additions that make it more useful for returning information through WMI. When you perform a query using WMI, you have the ability to return prodigious amounts of information. This is compounded when the script runs against multiple machines. To deal with this, you need to know how to reduce the amount of information returned. Essentially, you can use the following four methods to specify the amount of data returned from a WMI query:

- Return everything from everything (basic *Select* statement)
- Return some things from everything (modified *Select* statement)
- Return everything from some things (modified *Where* clause)
- Return some things from some things (modified *Select* statement and *Where* clause)

As you can see, the means to control the WMI query consists of modifying either the *Select* statement or the *Where* clause. I cover each of these operations in this chapter. But before I do that, first we need to talk a little bit about the WMI moniker.

Using the Moniker

The WMI moniker is probably the most common means used to make a connection into WMI. The advantages of using the moniker are its simplicity, ease of use, and compact design. The disadvantage is its lack of flexibility and support for advanced queries.

The WMI moniker consists of the following three parts:

- Prefix
- Security
- Path

The Prefix

The prefix portion of the WMI moniker is the only part of the connection string that is mandatory. You use the *winmgmts://* prefix to connect into WMI. When you use this connection string, you use the *GetObject* method. You use *GetObject* over *CreateObject* when the WMI process is already running and resident in memory, so it is necessary only to make a connection to it instead of creating another instance of the service.

The Security

Two parts of the security settings can be specified in the moniker. The first part is the impersonation level. The second is the addition or subtraction of privilege strings. (Privilege strings are discussed in Chapter 7.)

Impersonation Levels

There are four impersonation levels that correspond to the Distributed Component Object Model (DCOM) security settings available on a computer. Table 3-1 lists the four impersonation levels and their associated registry settings.

Table 3-1   WMI Impersonation Levels

Moniker Impersonation Level	Description	Registry Value
Anonymous	Hides the credentials of the caller. Calls to WMI might fail with this impersonation level.	1
Identify	Allows objects to query the credentials of the caller. Calls to WMI might fail with this impersonation level.	2
Impersonate	Allows objects to use the credentials of the caller. This is the recommended impersonation level for Scripting API for WMI calls.	3
Delegate	Allows objects to permit other objects to use the credentials of the caller. This impersonation level works with Scripting API for WMI calls but might constitute an unnecessary security risk.	4

If you decide to specify the impersonation level of the script, it would look like the following:

```
Set objWMIService=GetObject("winmgmts:{ImpersonationLevel=Impersonate}")
```

Because Impersonate is the default impersonation level for WMI, the addition of the preceding line is redundant. If you want to keep your moniker nice and clean, yet feel the need to modify the impersonation level, you can do this easily by defining the impersonation level of the *SWbemSecurity* object. In practice, your code might look like the following:

```
Set objWMIService=GetObject("winmgmts:\\" & strComputer & wmiNS)
objWMIService.Security_.ImpersonationLevel = 4
```

In the preceding code, the first line contains the normal moniker to make the connection to WMI. Then you use *strComputer* and *wmiNS* to specify the target computers and target namespace, respectively. Because you have not specified an impersonation level, you are using the default Impersonate security setting. On the next line, use the handle that came back from the *GetObject* method that was assigned to *objWMIService* and define the *ImpersonationLevel* to be equal to 4, for Delegate (see Table 3-1). Obviously, you could define a constant and set it to a value of 4; then substitute the constant value for 4 in the script. *ImpersonationLevel* is a property of *Security_*. *Security_* is a property of the *SWbemSecurity* object. The *SWbemSecurity* object is used to read or set security settings for other WMI objects such as *SWbemServices*, which is actually the object created when you use *GetObject* and the WMI moniker.

The Path

The path portion of the WMI moniker connection string consists of two parts: the computer name and the WMI namespace. As you have seen in many scripts, the name of the local computer is often abbreviated as ".". It is also possible to leave the computer name out all together. The WMI namespace can also be omitted if you are using the default values, which are discussed in the next section.

Using the Defaults

A number of defaults are configured for WMI. Chapter 2 discusses these default values and examines ways to modify them. Often you can simply rely on the defaults and avoid a lot of extra typing. Following are a few default values:

- **Default computer name**   To operate the script against the local computer use ".", which means the computer is not specified.

- **Default impersonation level**   The default impersonation level is to impersonate the logged-on user using the Impersonate setting.

- **Default namespace**   The default namespace is *root\cimv2*.

Because several fields are optional in constructing a finely tuned WMI moniker, it should be rather obvious that clearly defined defaults are available for the optional fields. The defaults are stored in the following registry location: HKEY_LOCAL_MACHINE\SOFTWARE\ Microsoft\WBEM\Scripting. There are two keys. One is called *Default Impersonation Level*, and the other is called *Default Namespace*. The *Default Impersonation Level* is set to a default of 3, which means that WMI will impersonate the logged-on user. The *Default Namespace* is set to *root\cimv2*. The default computer is the local machine, so you do not need to specify a computer name if you are simply running against the local machine. In reality, these are useful defaults because they enable you to simplify your connection string to WMI. A default moniker is "*winmgmts:*". When using the *GetObject* method, you could simplify your connection string to the following:

```
Set objWMIService = GetObject("winmgmts:\\")
```

Understanding Data Queries

A *data query* is a query that retrieves basic WMI information. For example, if I want to know how much physical memory I have in my server, I make a query into *Win32_OperatingSystem* and ask for the *FreePhysicalMemory* property. Data queries are the most common types of queries used in WMI.

You can use WQL to perform data queries. The following script, Win32_Display-Configuration.vbs, which returns display adapter information, is typical of the data query. After making a connection into WMI using the moniker *winmgmts*, you use the *ExecQuery* method to run the query. The WMI query used in this example is the basic "tell me everything about everything" type of query.

Return Only the Data You Intend to Use

As you explore the WMI classes, properties, and methods, you are likely to be overwhelmed by the voluminous amount of data available. Most of the scripts you see on the Internet are the simple "Select * from *className*" variety. This is a completely valid approach if you are interested in obtaining all the information possible about a particular item.

One thing to keep in mind is that this approach consumes resources. On a workstation, it takes CPU time to retrieve the data; then it takes network resources to bring it across in packets; and finally, it takes CPU time on the workstation again to bring the data to the application. Additionally, if you are reading the output without further processing, you have a potentially long line of text to scroll through. It is better to be more selective.

For example, when I was in Navy boot camp, a sign in the dining hall said, "Take all you want, but eat all you take." We were allowed to fill our plates with as much food as we desired. But if we did not eat all of it, the drill instructor would gently assist us with our appetites (generally, he made us do push-ups until the food disappeared from our plates). So, when using data queries, do not be greedy—return only the information you plan on using.

Using the *Select* Statement

The *Select* statement is the most basic WQL command. It is one of three commands that can be used to retrieve data from WMI. Most of the time, when you need to retrieve data from WMI, you will use the *Select* statement, so it is important to understand it. Basically, you can perform the following four kinds of *Select* statements, which are discussed in the following subsections.

- Select everything from everything
- Select some things from everything
- Select everything from some things
- Select some things from some things

Select Everything from Everything

When you compose WQL statements, you have the opportunity to choose everything. This is represented by the asterisk (*).

As you look at the script called Win32_DisplayConfiguration.vbs, you can see it starts by specifying the namespace *root\cimv2*, which is the default namespace; in Microsoft Windows Server 2003 and Windows XP, it really is not necessary to specify this namespace. But it does not hurt and has the advantage of already being in the script WMITemplate.vbs, which is available on the accompanying CD. Also, it makes it easy to change namespaces later if required.

The *wmiQuery* is *Select *, which means you are selecting everything from the class that is called *Win32_DisplayConfiguration*. Look up *Win32_DisplayConfiguration* in the Platform software development kit (SDK) and you will see it has 15 properties and no methods. This class is derived from the *CIM_Setting* class, which defines only three properties—*caption*, *description*, and *settingID*—and no methods. The other dozen properties were defined by Microsoft Corporation in its implementation of WMI to describe the unique configuration of a Microsoft Windows–based display.

Win32_DisplayConfiguration.vbs

```
strComputer = "."
wmiNS = "\root\cimv2"
wmiQuery = "Select * from Win32_DisplayConfiguration"
Set objWMIService = getObject("winmgmts:\\" & strComputer & wmiNS)
Set colItems = objWMIService.ExecQuery(wmiQuery)
For Each objItem in colItems
 wscript.echo "BitsPerPel: " & objItem.BitsPerPel
 wscript.echo "Caption: " & objItem.Caption
 wscript.echo "Description: " & objItem.Description
 wscript.echo "DeviceName: " & objItem.DeviceName
 wscript.echo "DisplayFlags: " & objItem.DisplayFlags
 wscript.echo "DisplayFrequency: " & objItem.DisplayFrequency
 wscript.echo "DitherType: " & objItem.DitherType
```

```
wscript.echo "DriverVersion: " & objItem.DriverVersion
wscript.echo "ICMIntent: " & objItem.ICMIntent
wscript.echo "ICMMethod: " & objItem.ICMMethod
wscript.echo "LogPixels: " & objItem.LogPixels
wscript.echo "PelsHeight: " & objItem.PelsHeight
wscript.echo "PelsWidth: " & objItem.PelsWidth
wscript.echo "SettingID: " & objItem.SettingID
wscript.echo "SpecificationVersion: " & objItem.SpecificationVersion
wscript.echo " "
next
```

Select Some Things from Everything

One of the most basic ways you can reduce the amount of information returned by a query is to select only what is needed. The properties that you choose can be individually selected. The *Win32_ComputerSystem* class is a very rich class with more than 50 properties and three methods. (A sample script that lists all the properties is in the Cimv2 script folder. It is called Win32_ComputerSystem.vbs.) Clearly, this is a very good class to use to practice trimming down the amount of information returned.

For example, suppose I am doing inventory on my network. I want to know the make and model of the computers and the names of the users who are logged on to each computer. In this case, it certainly makes sense to return only those 3 properties as opposed to retrieving more than 50 properties. The following script, MakeModelUser.vbs, is essentially the same as the preceding Win32_DisplayConfiguration.vbs script we looked at earlier. The only differences are the name of the WMI class and a modification to the *Select* statement.

> **Tip** The important thing to realize is that you simply separate each property with a comma and there is no trailing comma after the last property. If you add one, the entire script will fail— no data is retrieved. The syntax is "Select *property name, property name, property name* from class name". The underscore (_) is used for line continuation. Because the query is broken in the middle of the query string in the following code listing, you also need to use the ampersand (&) to glue the line back together.

MakeModelUser.vbs

```
strComputer = "."
wmiNS = "\root\cimv2"
wmiQuery = "Select Manufacturer, Model, UserName" _
    & " from Win32_ComputerSystem"
Set objWMIService = getObject("winmgmts:\\" & strComputer & wmiNS)
Set colItems = objWMIService.ExecQuery(wmiQuery)
For Each objItem in colItems
wscript.echo "Manufacturer: " & objItem.Manufacturer
wscript.echo "Model: " & objItem.Model
wscript.echo "UserName: " & objItem.UserName
next
```

Where Is the *Where* Clause?

Modifying the *Select* statement is useful in limiting the data that is returned; similarly, you can also modify the *Where* clause. The *Where* clause is an optional part of the WMI query. It, too, can be very useful in reducing the amount of information that comes back from a WMI query. You can modify a *Where* clause in many ways, including the following:

- Filter on a property value by using a comparison operator

- Filter on a property if it is *NULL*

- Filter on a property if it is not *NULL*

- Filter on a property by making a compound comparison

Select Everything from Some Things

The first script in this section reverts back to the "select everything" type of statement. However, you can modify the amount of data returned by limiting the scope of the operation to only one instance. Do this by adding a *Where* clause to the query.

The *Win32_NetworkAdapter* class, also found in the *root\cimv2* namespace, can provide a wealth of information about the network adapter on your computer. Look it up in the Platform SDK (I'll wait). The *Win32_NetworkAdapter* class defines 35 properties and no methods. (It actually inherits two methods from *CIM_NetworkAdapter*, but they are not implemented. It also inherits 24 properties from *CIM_NetworkAdapter*.)

The interesting thing about most computers is the variety of items the device manager considers to be network adapters when queried. For example, my laptop has a built-in wired connection, a wireless connection, and a Bluetooth connection. I would expect it to have only three adapters. But there are others also: virtual network adapter, virtual private network (VPN) connection, cable peer connection. When I query the *Win32_NetworkAdapter* class, perhaps I am interested only in the wired connection. To return only information about the wired connection, I must modify the *Where* clause. This might sound easy, but in reality it can be rather cumbersome because of the funky names used by the device manager to identify the connections.

You can use any property you wish in the *Where* clause. Some potential candidates include *Caption*, *Description*, *DeviceID*, *Index*, *Name*, *Manufacturer*, *PNPDeviceID*, and even *MACAddress*. Some of these properties uniquely describe the adapter (*MACAddress*); others do not (*Manufacturer*). My personal preference is to use a property that uniquely identifies the adapter and at the same time is easy to type. If you like to rename your adapters that show up in Network Neighborhood, as shown in Figure 3-1, you have a very easy property to use. The trick, of course, is to find out what WMI actually calls the property once you change it. The way I found this information was to do the "everything from everything" query first (using the Win32_NetworkAdapter.vbs script in the cimv2 scripts folder). Then I did a *Find* command in the results for the name I had assigned to the adapter. It was then that I found the unique name was stored in the *NetConnectionID* property.

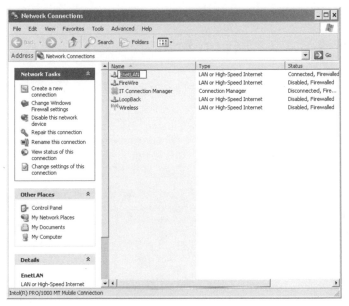

Figure 3-1   Uniquely identifying a network adapter

To use the *Where* clause, you choose a property and specify a value for the property. The modified Win32_NetworkAdapter.vbs script is called WiredNetworkAdapter.vbs, and it uses the fact that I named my network adapter enetLan. If yours still uses the default name, it would be called Local Area Connection or perhaps Wireless Network Connection. You can easily rename an adapter by right-clicking the computer icon in the Windows Network Connections window and choosing Rename from the Action menu. Using a short name helps you avoid typing a 20-character connection name.

WiredNetworkAdapter.vbs

```
strComputer = "."
wmiNS = "\root\cimv2"
wmiQuery = "Select * from Win32_NetworkAdapter where NetConnectionID = 'enetLan'"
Set objWMIService = getObject("winmgmts:\\" & strComputer & wmiNS)
Set colItems = objWMIService.ExecQuery(wmiQuery)
For Each objItem in colItems

 wscript.echo "AdapterType: " & objItem.AdapterType
 wscript.echo "AdapterTypeId: " & objItem.AdapterTypeId
 wscript.echo "AutoSense: " & objItem.AutoSense
 wscript.echo "Availability: " & objItem.Availability
 wscript.echo "Caption: " & objItem.Caption
 wscript.echo "ConfigManagerErrorCode: " & objItem.ConfigManagerErrorCode
 wscript.echo "ConfigManagerUserConfig: " & objItem.ConfigManagerUserConfig
 wscript.echo "CreationClassName: " & objItem.CreationClassName
 wscript.echo "Description: " & objItem.Description
```

```
wscript.echo "DeviceID: " & objItem.DeviceID
wscript.echo "ErrorCleared: " & objItem.ErrorCleared
wscript.echo "ErrorDescription: " & objItem.ErrorDescription
wscript.echo "Index: " & objItem.Index
wscript.echo "InstallDate: " & objItem.InstallDate
wscript.echo "Installed: " & objItem.Installed
wscript.echo "LastErrorCode: " & objItem.LastErrorCode
wscript.echo "MACAddress: " & objItem.MACAddress
wscript.echo "Manufacturer: " & objItem.Manufacturer
wscript.echo "MaxNumberControlled: " & objItem.MaxNumberControlled
wscript.echo "MaxSpeed: " & objItem.MaxSpeed
wscript.echo "Name: " & objItem.Name
wscript.echo "NetConnectionID: " & objItem.NetConnectionID
wscript.echo "NetConnectionStatus: " & objItem.NetConnectionStatus
wscript.echo "NetworkAddresses: " & objItem.NetworkAddresses
wscript.echo "PermanentAddress: " & objItem.PermanentAddress
wscript.echo "PNPDeviceID: " & objItem.PNPDeviceID
wscript.echo "PowerManagementCapabilities: " & objItem.PowerManagementCapabilities
wscript.echo "PowerManagementSupported: " & objItem.PowerManagementSupported
wscript.echo "ProductName: " & objItem.ProductName
wscript.echo "ServiceName: " & objItem.ServiceName
wscript.echo "Speed: " & objItem.Speed
wscript.echo "Status: " & objItem.Status
wscript.echo "StatusInfo: " & objItem.StatusInfo
wscript.echo "SystemCreationClassName: " & objItem.SystemCreationClassName
wscript.echo "SystemName: " & objItem.SystemName
wscript.echo "TimeOfLastReset: " & objItem.TimeOfLastReset

wscript.echo " "
next
```

In the preceding script, the *Where* clause looks like the following:

```
wmiQuery = "Select * from Win32_NetworkAdapter where NetConnectionID = 'enetLan'"
```

Comparison Operators

Note that the value supplied for the property *NetConnectionID* is ′ *enetLan* ′. The single quotes are required here or the query will fail. Other operators that can be used for this type of query are listed in Table 3-2.

Table 3-2   **Comparison Operators**

Operator	Meaning
=	Equal
<>	Not equal
<	Less than
>	Greater than
<=	Less than or equal to
>=	Greater than or equal to
!=	Not equal

The operators in Table 3-2 probably are familiar to you because they are basic algebra functions (now you know why you had to learn that stuff back in school). WQL also defines some additional operators: *IS, IS NOT, ISA, LIKE*. The meaning of these operators might not be as obvious, so I discuss them individually later.

Select Some Things from Some Things

When you modify both the *Select* statement and the *Where* clause, you can limit the retrieval to just the information needed to satisfy your requirements. You reduce the amount of information you have to process and the number of instances of the class with which you need to work.

The *Win32_NetworkProtocol* class represents a protocol and the associated network characteristics when it is installed on a computer running the Windows operating system. This class contains 22 properties and no methods. To retrieve just the information you are looking for, modify both the *Select* statement and the *Where* clause. The script SpecificNetworkProtocols.vbs illustrates the value of taking the time to craft a nice WMI query. The first time I ran the script, Win32_NetworkProtocol.vbs from the Scripts\Supplemental Scripts\cimv2 folder on the accompanying CD, it returned so much data I was unable to sort through it effectively. I was interested only in the quality of service property for the protocol. Once I modified the *Select* statement and limited the instances that were returned to only those that support quality of service, I was able to find the information I needed quickly. The *Name* property is the key value for this class. When using WQL, you do not need to select the key because it is automatically selected. This saves you some typing and still enables you to work with the *Name* property in the output section.

SpecificNetworkProtocols.vbs

```
strComputer = "."
wmiNS = "\root\cimv2"
wmiQuery = "Select Description, SupportsGuaranteedBandwidth, SupportsQualityofService" _
    & " from Win32_NetworkProtocol where SupportsQualityofService = 'true'"
Set objWMIService = getobject("winmgmts:\\" & strComputer & wmiNS)
Set colItems = objWMIService.ExecQuery(wmiQuery)
For Each objItem in colItems
 wscript.echo "Description: " & objItem.Description
 wscript.echo "Name: " & objItem.Name ' name is key value
 wscript.echo "SupportsGuaranteedBandwidth: " & objItem.SupportsGuaranteedBandwidth
 wscript.echo "SupportsQualityofService: " & objItem.SupportsQualityofService
 wscript.echo " "
next
```

IS Operator

The *IS* operator at first seems to be basically the same as the equality operator. This is not true, however, because it really is limited in its use in the WQL *Where* clause. The *IS* operator can be used only when the value you are comparing (called the *constant*) is *NULL*.

> **Null Is Not Zero**   *Null* means we do not really know the value, maybe because the data is missing, invalid, or just not supported on that platform. If we wanted to look at *FreeSpace* on partition 3 for a machine with two partitions, that value would come back as *NULL*. Clearly, the amount of free space is not zero. We could have zero free space on partition 2, but not on partition 3. Because we cannot connect to partition 3, we do not know how much free space is there. We can make comparisons against *NULL*, but it can be rather tricky at times to predict accurately what the outcome will be.

An example of using the *IS* operator is shown in the following script called NullMacAddress.vbs. In this script, I change the query from looking for a network adapter with a specific name to looking for a network adapter that does not have a Media Access Control (MAC) address, which could indicate adapters that are not currently initialized (that is, they have been disabled). I don't need to return *MACAddress* because it is a null value. Besides leaving out some additional details, *MACAddress* is left out as well. This script returns information from all instances of the *Win32_NetworkAdapter* class but only if the *MACAddress* is a null value. I am able to make the evaluation on the *MACAddress* property because it is included in the *Select* statement (I selected everything by doing *Select **).

NullMacAddress.vbs

```
strComputer = "."
wmiNS = "\root\cimv2"
wmiQuery = "Select * from Win32_NetworkAdapter where MACAddress IS null"
Set objWMIService = getObject("winmgmts:\\" & strComputer & wmiNS)
Set colItems = objWMIService.ExecQuery(wmiQuery)
For Each objItem in colItems
 wscript.echo "Description: " & objItem.Description
 wscript.echo "DeviceID: " & objItem.DeviceID
 wscript.echo "Index: " & objItem.Index
 wscript.echo "Installed: " & objItem.Installed
 wscript.echo "Manufacturer: " & objItem.Manufacturer
 wscript.echo "Name: " & objItem.Name
 wscript.echo "NetConnectionID: " & objItem.NetConnectionID
 wscript.echo "PNPDeviceID: " & objItem.PNPDeviceID
 wscript.echo "ProductName: " & objItem.ProductName
 wscript.echo "ServiceName: " & objItem.ServiceName
 wscript.echo "SystemName: " & objItem.SystemName
 wscript.echo "TimeOfLastReset: " & objItem.TimeOfLastReset
wscript.echo " "
next
```

Compound *Where* Clause

Let's trim the script even further and combine two operators, as shown in the following script, AdapterMicrosoft.vbs. This time I use the *IS NULL* operator and specify a value for the *Manufacturer* property as well. In this way, I find all the adapters that were made by Microsoft that have a *NULL MACAddress*. I limit the data returned to only the properties I specify in the *Select* statement. The modified query looks like the following:

```
"Select MACAddress, Manufacturer, Name, Description from Win32_NetworkAdapter" _
    & " where manufacturer = 'Microsoft' and MACAddress is null"
```

Note that I use a compound *Where* clause in this query. I want to know where the manufacturer is equal to Microsoft but only if the *MACAddress* is also *NULL*. This is a great technique for really focusing on the data that you are interested in retrieving.

AdapterMicrosoft.vbs

```
strComputer = "."
wmiNS = "\root\cimv2"
wmiQuery = "Select MACAddress, Manufacturer,  Name, Description from Win32_NetworkAdapter" _
    & " where manufacturer = 'Microsoft' and MACAddress is null"
Set objWMIService = getObject("winmgmts:\\" & strComputer & wmiNS)
Set colItems = objWMIService.ExecQuery(wmiQuery)
For Each objItem in colItems
 wscript.echo "Description: " & objItem.Description
 wscript.echo "Manufacturer: " & objItem.Manufacturer
 wscript.echo "Name: " & objItem.Name
 wscript.echo " "
next
```

Is Not Operator

The *IS NOT* operator works the same way the *IS* operator does. It must evaluate a null condition. However, there are problems with evaluating a null condition. In the following script, if you have groups without a description, the script completes successfully, but it returns groups both with descriptions and without descriptions.

Win32_GroupDescriptionNotNull.vbs

```
strComputer = "."
wmiNS = "\root\cimv2"
wmiQuery = "Select * from win32_group where Description is not Null"
Set objWMIService = getObject("winmgmts:\\" & strComputer & wmiNS)
Set colItems = objWMIService.ExecQuery(wmiQuery)

For Each objItem in colItems
    Wscript.Echo "Description: " & objItem.Description
    WScript.echo "Is description field null? " & IsNull(objItem.description)
    Wscript.Echo "Domain: " & objItem.Domain
    Wscript.Echo "LocalAccount: " & objItem.LocalAccount
    Wscript.Echo "Name: " & objItem.Name
    Wscript.Echo "SID: " & objItem.SID
    Wscript.Echo "SIDType: " & objItem.SIDType
    wScript.echo ""
Next
```

In the following WriteProcessesAndServicesToTxt.vbs script, I use the *IS NOT* operator to pull out processes and services that have a *NOT NULL* process ID. I do this because the *Win32_Process* class does not have a property that identifies the running status of a process. Whereas *Win32_Service* does implement this method, *Win32_Process* does not. So, I pull back a list of processes only if the process ID (PID) is not a null value. This does not filter out everything. I am looking for running processes, and the *IS NOT NULL* operator returns a lot of processes with a PID of 0. Zero, as you might recall from the earlier discussion, is not the same thing as *NULL*, and so these process IDs slip through the filter. To compensate for this, I use a simple *If (objItem2.ProcessID) > 0 then* construction. This helps achieve the desired result.

The other item that is of interest is the write to log file subroutine. For testing purposes, this is a really nice sub because it writes the output to a file on the desktop, making it easy to find. If you want to see what has changed in the services and processes running on a machine, run the script with two different output files and compare the results in Windiff.exe.

WriteProcessesAndServicesToTxt.vbs

```
strOut = "the following Processes are running " & vbcrlf
strOut2 = "the following Services are running " & vbcrlf
strComputer = "."
wmiNS = "\root\cimv2"
wmiQuery = "Select name, processID from win32_process where processID is not null"
wmiQuery2 = "Select name, processID from win32_Service where processID is not null"
Set objWMIService = getObject("winmgmts:\\" & strComputer & wmiNS)
Set colItems = objWMIService.ExecQuery(wmiQuery)
For Each objItem in colItems
    strOut = strOut & objItem.name & vbcrlf
Next

Set colItems2 = objWMIService.ExecQuery(wmiQuery2)
For Each objItem2 in colItems2
If (objItem2.ProcessID) > 0 then
    strOut2 = strOut2 & objItem2.name & vbtab & objItem2.processID & vbcrlf
End if
Next

subWriteToFile

Sub SubWriteToFIle
Dim objFSO, objFile, strDeskTop
Set strDesktop = CreateObject("wscript.shell")' holds instance of WshShell
strDesktop = strDesktop.specialFolders("desktop") ' recycle strDesktop here.
Set objFSO = CreateObject("scripting.filesystemobject")
Set objFILE = objFSO.openTextFIle(strDeskTop & "\" & "servicesOUT.txt", 8, True)
objFile.write strOut & vbcrlf & strOUT2
End sub
```

Understanding Event Queries

You can use WQL to query for events. "That's great!" you might exclaim, "But what is an event?" An *event* is something that happens on your computer system in response to some other action. For instance, if a file is deleted, a *file deletion* event is generated. If a file is created, a *file creation* event occurs. If a file is modified, a *file modification* event is created. These are in fact three of the main types of events. The listing of events in Table 3-3 can make it seem like there are many different kinds of events, but in reality *create*, *delete*, and *modify* events are repeated at class, instance, and namespace levels. The other events are *operation*, *method invocation*, *dropped event*, *queue overflow*, and *failure* events. In the labs in this chapter, you examine the appropriate use of events, and we come back to this topic in much more detail in Chapter 5.

Table 3-3   WMI Event Classes and Descriptions

Event Class	Event Description
__ClassCreationEvent	Notifies a consumer when a class is created.
__ClassDeletionEvent	Notifies a consumer when a class is deleted.
__ClassModificationEvent	Notifies a consumer when a class is modified.
__InstanceCreationEvent	Notifies a consumer when a class instance is created.
__InstanceOperationEvent	Notifies a consumer when any instance event occurs, such as creation, deletion, or modification of the instance. You can use this class in queries to get all events associated with an instance.
__InstanceDeletionEvent	Notifies a consumer when an instance is deleted.
__InstanceModificationEvent	Notifies a consumer when an instance is modified.
__NamespaceCreationEvent	Notifies a consumer when a namespace is created.
__NamespaceDeletionEvent	Notifies a consumer when a namespace is deleted.
__NamespaceModificationEvent	Notifies a consumer when a namespace is modified.
__ConsumerFailureEvent	Notifies a consumer when some other event is dropped because of a failure on the part of an event consumer.
__EventDroppedEvent	Notifies a consumer when some other event is dropped instead of delivered to the requesting event consumer.
__EventQueueOverflowEvent	Notifies a consumer when an event is dropped as a result of delivery queue overflow.
__MethodInvocationEvent	Notifies a consumer when a method call event occurs. This class is new in Windows XP.

So how does an event query work? Take a look at the MonitorProcessEvents.vbs script. Pay attention to two unique factors when using an event query. The first is the query. When performing an event query, specify the name of one of the types of events listed in Table 3-3. In the following MonitorProcessEvents.vbs script, we are interested in an *__instanceCreationEvent* because this permits notification when a new process is created. Also of interest in the query is the specification of the *TargetInstance*. The *TargetInstance* is where you specify the class you are monitoring for events. In the MonitorProcessEvents.vbs script, we are looking for *Win32_Process* creation events. Use the *ISA* operator to filter out only events that come from *Win32_Process*.

The second unique characteristic of event queries is the use of the *ExecNotificationQuery* method. This method tells WMI that the query is an event query, not a normal data type of query. Whereas you will often use the *ExecQuery* method for data queries, you need to use the

ExecNotificationQuery method for event queries to be able to receive the callback when an event occurs.

MonitorProcessEvents.vbs

```
strComputer = "."
wmiNS = "\root\cimv2"
objClass = "'Win32_Process'"
StrMessage = "A new " & objClass & " was created at : "
wmiQuery = "SELECT * FROM __InstanceCreationEvent " _
        & "WITHIN 10 WHERE TargetInstance ISA " & objClass

Set objWMIService = getObject("winmgmts:\\" & strComputer & wmiNS)
Set colItems = objWMIService.ExecNotificationQuery(wmiQuery)

Do
Set objItem = colItems.NextEvent
With objItem
    Wscript.Echo StrMessage & Now & vbcrlf & .TargetInstance.Name & vbtab & _
    .TargetInstance.CommandLine & vbtab & "PID: " & .TargetInstance.ProcessId
End with
Loop
```

You can also use event queries to check for changes in the state of a service. In the Monitor-ServiceChanges.vbs script, I use an *__InstanceModificationEvent* query to find changes in the state of services on the server. Because I am watching the *Win32_Service* class, any change to the state of the class triggers an event. This means any service that starts, stops, pauses, or undergoes any modification triggers an event. Clearly, on a busy server you would not want to monitor *Win32_Process* because processes change constantly on servers.

MonitorServiceChanges.vbs

```
strComputer = "."
wmiNS = "\root\cimv2"
objClass = "'Win32_Service'"
StrMessage = "A " & objClass & " was modified at : "
strMessage1 = "The Service is now: "
wmiQuery = "SELECT * FROM __InstanceModificationEvent " _
        & "WITHIN 10 WHERE TargetInstance ISA " & objClass

Set objWMIService = getObject("winmgmts:\\" & strComputer & wmiNS)
Set colItems = objWMIService.ExecNotificationQuery(wmiQuery)

Do
Set objItem = colItems.NextEvent
With objItem
    Wscript.Echo StrMessage & Now & vbcrlf & strMessage1 & _
    .TargetInstance.State & vbcrlf & .TargetInstance.Name & _
    vbtab & .TargetInstance.PathName & vbtab & "PID: " & _
    .TargetInstance.ProcessId
End with
loop
```

Understanding Schema Queries

You can use WQL to query for elements in the schema. Do not confuse the word *schema* as it is used here with the Microsoft Active Directory Schema. The word *schema* can also be used to describe the layout of the WMI classes and namespaces and their relationship to one another. Making schema queries has several benefits. Schema queries are an excellent source of information about WMI. In some fashion, you can liken a schema query to a query of SYStables in Microsoft SQL Server. You use WMI to find out about the technology. In another light, you can simply think of a schema query like any other WMI query–you ask WMI a question, and it responds with an answer. If you discover a class that is not documented, you can query the schema to obtain the information you need to enable you to use the class in your scripts.

You can also use schema queries to control the execution of a script: to specify "I want this operation to happen *only* if the following conditions are met." Clearly, using the schema to control execution of a script requires a superior knowledge of WMI, but the results can be dramatic.

Following are the four methods available for querying from the WMI schema:

- SELECT
- REFERENCES OF
- ASSOCIATORS OF
- ISA

Which method you use for a schema query depends on what you are looking for, as well as any other special needs you have. If you decide to use the *Select* statement, you need to use a special class called *Meta_Class* as the target of operation. When VBScript sees the WMI class *Meta_Class* in the *Select* statement, it recognizes the query as a schema query. In the script Meta_Class.vbs, which follows, we explore the use of this class.

SWbemObject

The object that comes back from the WMI query in the Meta_Class.vbs script is called *SWbemObject*. It is not really important to know this name, unless you want to look it up in the Platform SDK. If you intend to go very deep into understanding WMI, you need to know the official names of objects and understand how and when they are created. If, on the other hand, you only want to run WMI scripts and know enough to modify other people's scripts in an intelligent fashion, you don't need to know the names of objects. In fact, many very talented WMI scripters have never heard the word *SWbemObject* before, and their code is not necessarily poorer for it. In the Meta_Class.vbs script, I use the WMI moniker to execute a very general "select everything from *Meta_Class*" query.

Meta_Class.vbs

```
strComputer = "."
wmiNS = "\root\cimv2"
wmiQuery = "Select * from meta_Class"
Set objWMIService = getObject("winmgmts:\\" & strComputer & wmiNS)
Set colItems = objWMIService.ExecQuery(wmiQuery)

For Each objItem in colItems
WScript.Echo vbcrlf & "CLASS: " & objItem.Path_.Class & " has " & _
    objItem.properties_.count & " properties and " & _
    objItem.qualifiers_.count & " qualifiers" & vbcrlf & _
    funLine(objItem.Path_.Class)
WScript.Echo "PROPERTIES:"
        For Each b In objItem.properties_
        If IsArray(b) Then
        wscript.echo vbtab &  b.name & " is an array." & _
        vbcrlf & vbtab & "Values are: " & Join(b, ",")
        Else
        WScript.Echo vbtab & b.name
        End if
        Next
WScript.Echo "QUALIFIERS:"
        For Each a In objItem.qualifiers_
        If IsArray(a) Then
        wscript.echo vbtab & a.name & " is an array." & _
        vbcrlf & vbtab & "Values are: " & Join (a, ",")
        Else
        WScript.Echo vbtab & a.name & " = " & _
        objItem.qualifiers_.item(a.name)
        End if
        Next
Next

Function funLine(lineOfText)
Dim numEQs, separator, i
numEQs = Len(lineOfText) + 42
For i = 1 To numEQs
    separator = separator & "="
Next
 FunLine = separator
End function
```

Notice the use of *objitem.Path_.class*. You can use it to retrieve the *Class* property of the *Path_* property of the *SWbemObject*. An *SWbemObject* becomes available when you retrieve a WMI class definition or an instance of a WMI object. You can think of this process as making your connection into WMI. The WMI process is always running, and the *SWbemObject* is always available. Until you retrieve it for the application, you cannot use any properties or methods from the *SWbemObject* object.

SWbemObject Methods

The Meta_Class.vbs script uses only one method from *SWbemObject*. Many methods, detailed in Table 3-4, are available to the scripter. Familiarity and comfort in using these methods enable the enterprising network administrator to add a high level of flexibility and power to scripts.

Table 3-4   *SWbemObject* Methods

Method	Description
*Associators_*	Retrieves the associators of the object number
*AssociatorsAsync_*	Asynchronously retrieves the associators of the object
*Clone_*	Makes a copy of the current object
*CompareTo_*	Tests two objects for equality
*Delete_*	Deletes the object from WMI
*DeleteAsync_*	Asynchronously deletes the object from WMI
*ExecMethod_*	Executes a method exported by a method provider
*ExecMethodAsync_*	Asynchronously executes a method exported by a method provider
*GetObjectText_*	Retrieves the textual representation of the object (Managed Object Format syntax)
*Instances_*	Returns a collection of instances of the object (which must be a WMI class)
*InstancesAsync_*	Asynchronously returns a collection of instances of the object (which must be a WMI class)
*Put_*	Creates or updates the object in WMI
*PutAsync_*	Asynchronously creates or updates the object in WMI

SWbemObject Properties

A number of properties, listed in Table 3-5, are also available to an *SWbemObject*. Although these properties are particularly valuable during schema queries—pulling out the properties of a class—they can also be used in self-describing scripts. These properties are also extremely useful if you are working with a class you found in WMI that does not have any associated documentation.

Table 3-5   *SWbemObject* Properties

Property	Description
*Derivation_*	Contains an array of strings describing the derivation hierarchy
*Methods_*	An *SWbemMethodSet* object that is the collection of methods for this object
*Path_*	Contains an *SWbemObjectPath* object that represents the object path of the current class or instance
*Properties_*	An *SWbemPropertySet* object that is the collection of properties for this object

Table 3-5   *SWbemObject* Properties

Property	Description
Qualifiers_	An *SWbemQualifierSet* object that is the collection of qualifiers for this object
Security_	Contains an *SWbemSecurity* object used to read or change the security settings

SWbemObjectPath

When you use *objItem.Path_* to obtain the *Path* property in the Meta_Class.vbs script, you get back an *SWbemObjectPath* object. Instead of just a simple property, an entire object is returned, which enables you to examine more than just the *Path* property. Table 3-6 lists the properties available to an *SWbemObjectPath* object. The Meta_Class.vbs script uses the *Class* property to retrieve the name of the class being enumerated.

Table 3-6   *SWbemObjectPath* Properties

Property	Description
Authority	String that defines the *Authority* component of the object path
Class	Name of the class that is part of the object path.
DisplayName	String that contains the path in a form that can be used as a moniker display name.
IsClass	Boolean value that indicates whether this path represents a class.
IsSingleton	Boolean value that indicates whether this path represents a singleton instance.
Keys	An *SWbemNamedValueSet* object that contains the key value bindings.
Locale	String containing the locale for this object path.
Namespace	Name of the namespace that is part of the object path.
ParentNamespace	Name of the parent of the namespace that is part of the object path.
Path	Contains the absolute path. This is the default property.
Relpath	Contains the relative path.
Security_	Used to read or change the security settings.
Server	Name of the server.

Use of the *SWbemObjectPath* properties is relatively straightforward, and the object behaves in the manner you would expect. However, a few peculiarities exist, and these are illustrated in the script ObjectPathProperties.vbs.

To work with the *SWbemObjectPath* object, you first must retrieve an instance of an *SWbemObject*. I do this in the ObjectPathProperties.vbs script by making the query into WMI. When you use the *ExecQuery* command as shown in the following code, you retrieve an *SWbemObject*:

```
strComputer = "."
wmiNS = "\root\cimv2"
strClass = "'Win32_logicalDisk'"
wmiQuery = "Select * from meta_Class where __this ISA " & strClass
Set objWMIService = getobject("winmgmts:\\" & strComputer & wmiNS)
Set colItems = objWMIService.ExecQuery(wmiQuery)
```

Once you have this object, you can look at the object's path properties. This is where the quirkiness of the *SWbemObjectPath* object is revealed. This object works only on an *SWbem-Object*. Once you have returned the *SWbemObject* by using the WMI query, you can connect to the *SWbemObjectPath* object and retrieve the properties of the path. In the ObjectPathProperties.vbs script, I make the connection to the *SWbemObjectPath* object when I use the *Path_* property of the *SWbemObject* object. Once I have created the *SWbemObjectPath* object, I use a *With End With* statement to avoid some extra typing as I retrieve the properties of the *Path* object. This is illustrated in the following code:

```
With objItem.Path_
    strProperties = "displayname " & .displayname & vbcrlf
    strProperties = strProperties & "is class: " & .isClass & vbcrlf
    strProperties = strProperties & "is singleton: " & .IsSingleton & vbcrlf
    strProperties = strProperties & "namespace: " & .namespace & vbcrlf
    strProperties = strProperties & "parentNamespace: " & .parentNamespace & vbcrlf
    strProperties = strProperties & "path: " & .path & vbcrlf
    strProperties = strProperties & "relPath: " & .relpath & vbcrlf
    strProperties = strProperties & "server: " & .server & vbcrlf
    WScript.Echo "keys: " & .keys.count
End With
```

Once you have access to the *SWbemObjectPath* object, you can access any of the properties or methods directly. This is when using the *With End With* statement is so helpful—it avoids the confusion of the double label.

ObjectPathProperties.vbs

```
strComputer = "."
wmiNS = "\root\cimv2"
strClass = "'Win32_logicalDisk'"
wmiQuery = "Select * from meta_Class where __this ISA " & strClass
Set objWMIService = getobject("winmgmts:\\" & strComputer & wmiNS)
Set colItems = objWMIService.ExecQuery(wmiQuery)

For Each objItem in colItems
WScript.Echo "CLASS: " & objItem.path_.Class & " has " & _
    objItem.properties_.count & " properties and " & _
    objItem.qualifiers_.count & " qualifiers."
WScript.Echo "PROPERTIES:"
        For Each b In objItem.properties_
        If IsArray(b) Then
        wscript.echo b.name & " is an Array." & _
        vbcrlf & "The properties are: " & Join (b, ",")
        End if
        WScript.Echo vbtab & b.name
```

```
        Next
WScript.Echo "QUALIFIERS:"
      For Each a In objItem.qualifiers_
      If IsArray(a) Then
      wscript.echo vbtab & a.name & " is an array" & _
      vbcrlf & vbtab & "The Properties are: " & Join(a, ",")
      Else
      WScript.Echo vbtab & a.name & " = " & objItem.qualifiers_.item(a.name)
      End If
      Next
WScript.Echo "OBJECT PATH PROPERTIES: "
With objItem.Path_
    strProperties = "displayname " & .displayname & vbcrlf
    strProperties = strProperties & "is class: " & .isClass & vbcrlf
    strProperties = strProperties & "is singleton: " & .IsSingleton & vbcrlf
    strProperties = strProperties & "namespace: " & .namespace & vbcrlf
    strProperties = strProperties & "parentNamespace: " & .parentNamespace & vbcrlf
    strProperties = strProperties & "path: " & .path & vbcrlf
    strProperties = strProperties & "relPath: " & .relpath & vbcrlf
    strProperties = strProperties & "server: " & .server & vbcrlf
    WScript.Echo "keys: " & .keys.count
End With
WScript.Echo strProperties
Next
```

Summary

This chapter discussed the basics of performing WMI queries. In it we examined the use and the construction of the WMI moniker and looked at the different impersonation levels available to a VBScript. We looked at doing both data queries and schema queries. In relation to data queries, we examined modifying both the *Select* statement and the *Where* clause. In relation to schema queries, we looked at using the *Meta_Class* class. Finally, we examined the *SWbemObject* and the *SWbemObjectPath* objects.

Quiz Yourself

Q: **Which special class do you use to make schema queries?**

A: The special class you can use to make schema queries is the *Meta_Class* class.

Q: **Which method can you use to ensure you get a callback from an event query?**

A: The method you can use to ensure you get a callback from an event query is the *ExecuteNotificationQuery* method.

Q: **When you use the *IS* operator, what are you evaluating?**

A: When you use the *IS* operator, you are evaluating whether the evaluator is a null value.

On Your Own

Lab 7 Exploring *Win32_NTDomain*

In this lab, you will explore the *Win32_NTDomain* class. This is a new class for Windows XP and Windows Server 2003. Although this script can run on a workgroup computer running Windows XP, the most interesting information will be obtained when your workstation has access to the Microsoft Active Directory directory service. This script *will not* run on a computer running Microsoft Windows 2000 and earlier.

1. Open the WMI template script, and save it as StudentLab7.vbs. Notice that the full name of the WMI class is not listed.

2. Modify the *wmiQuery* line so that you are making a query into the *Win32_NTDomain* class. The modified line looks like the following:

   ```
   wmiQuery = "Select * from win32_NTDomain"
   ```

3. Open the script PropertyExplorer.vbs and run it. *Note:* If you are not using an Integrated Development Environment (IDE)–type script editor (such as PrimalScript), you will want to run these scripts from the command line Cscript scripting host, and not from the Wscript scripting host.

4. Type Win32_NTDomain in the input box. Make sure you clear the input box prior to entering the class name. The script runs when you click OK.

5. The output includes all the *Wscript.echo* statements needed for your lab solution.

6. Copy the *Wscript.echo* statements from the output of step 4 and paste them into the *For Next* loop in the WMI template. Make sure you delete all the *Wscript.echo* statements that are already in the WMI template.

7. Save and run the script.

Lab 8 Using Schema Queries

In this lab, you will use a schema query to obtain information about the properties and qualifiers of the *Win32_NTDomain* class. Because the information on the *cimTypes* is returned in the form of a coded decimal value, you will add a lookup routine to ensure you can understand the results. You might want to refer to the article in the SDK called "WbemCimtype-Enum" for details on all the *cimTypes*, their meanings, and their associated decimal values. *CimTypes* are used to describe the data type of a particular property value. You will use a dictionary to hold the results. As mentioned earlier, you can use this information to make using WMI in your scripts easier. Additionally, you can discover valuable information about classes that are not documented.

1. Open the WMI template script, and save it as StudentLab8.vbs.

2. Declare all the variables you will need to use for this script. You will need *dim a, b,* *statusCode,* and *objDictionary*.

3. Turn off *On Error Resume Next* while you are writing the script to ensure you see all the appropriate errors. Use the comment character to do this.

4. Edit the *wmiQuery* so that you are performing a schema query using the *Meta_Class* class. To limit the scope of the query, use *__this* and *ISA* while specifying the *Win32_NTDomain* class. Make sure you encase the Win32_NTDomain class name in single quotes. Your query will look something like the following:

    ```
    "Select * from meta_class where __this ISA 'win32_ntdomain'"
    ```

5. Delete all the *Wscript.echo* commands inside the *For Each Next* loop.

6. Use the *Properties_* property to count the number of properties associated with the *Win32_NTDomain* class.

7. Use the *Path_* property to print out the name of the class, and the *Qualifier_* property to count the number of qualifiers.

8. Use the *FunLine* function to underline the output. You can find this function in the script FunLineFunction.vbs. You will add the function later in the lab, but for now, you are simply calling the function. You can do this with a single *Wscript.echo* command as shown in the following code. Place this inside the *For Each Next* loop:

    ```
    WScript.Echo vbcrlf & "CLASS: " & objItem.path_.Class & " has " & _
        objItem.properties_.count & " properties and " & _
        objItem.qualifiers_.count & " qualifiers" & vbcrlf & _
        funLine(objItem.Path_.Class)
    ```

9. Use *Wscript.echo* to print out a line to separate the properties you are going to output.

10. Because the *Properties_* property is stored as an array, you need to use *For Each Next* to loop through the array. Because some of the properties might also be arrays, use *ISArray* to test each property to see if it is an array, prior to printing it out. If it is an array, use the *Join* command to enable a single print of the property. If it is not an array, print out the *cimType*, and use the *ISArray* property to see if the property has an array type. Your code might look something like the following:

    ```
    For Each b In objItem.properties_
    statusCode = CStr(b.cimtype)
            If IsArray(b) Then
            wscript.echo vbtab &  b.name & " is an array." & _
            vbcrlf & vbtab & "Values are: " & Join(b, ",")
            Else
            WScript.Echo vbtab & b.name & ":" & vbtab & "cimType: " & statusCode _
             & " is array? " & b.IsArray
            End if
            Next
    ```

11. Use *Wscript.echo* to print out a line to separate the qualifiers you are going to output. You might decide to do something like the following:

```
WScript.Echo "QUALIFIERS:"
```

12. Because the *Qualifiers_* are stored in an array, you need to use *For Each Next* to walk through the collection. Use the *ISArray* function to check whether the qualifier is an array. If it is, use the *Join* function to put it together into a single string. If it is not stored in an array, simply print the name of the qualifier. Following is the code to do this:

```
For Each a In objItem.qualifiers_
    If IsArray(a) Then
    wscript.echo vbtab & a.name & " is an array." & _
    vbcrlf & vbtab & "Values are: " & Join (a, ",")
    Else
    WScript.Echo vbtab & a.name & " = " & _
        objItem.qualifiers_.item(a.name)
    End if
    Next
```

13. Save the script.

14. Look over your code. Make sure you have declared all your variables.

15. To clean up the output, add the *FunLine* function. Open the script FunLineFunction.vbs, copy the entire function, and paste it at the bottom of your script. It contains the following code:

```
Function funLine(lineOfText)
Dim numEQs, separater, i
numEQs = Len(lineOfText) + 42
For i = 1 To numEQs
    separater = separater & "="
Next
 FunLine = separater
End Function
```

16. When you run the script, you will see output that looks similar to the following output (*Note*: I trimmed the output considerably):

```
CLASS: Win32_NTDomain has 27 properties and 4 qualifiers
========================================================
PROPERTIES:
    Caption:     cimType: 8 is array? False
    ClientSiteName:   cimType: 8 is array? False
QUALIFIERS:
    dynamic = True
    Locale = 1033
```

17. Now you want to add a lookup capability to translate the *cimType* output into something more readable. To do this, use the subroutine *subCreateDictionary* from the script SubDictionaryFromTxt.vbs. Open SubDictionaryFromTxt.vbs and copy everything from the *Sub* line to the *End Sub* line. Paste it at the bottom of your StudentLab8.vbs script.

18.   Save and run the script. There should be no errors.

19.   Under the line where you defined your *wmiQuery*, call the subroutine. You can simply type the name of the subroutine; you do not need to use the call command.

```
subCreateDictionary
```

20.   Save and run the script. This time you will get an error, unless you remembered to dim the *objDictionary* variable, which needs to be near the top with the other global variables because you need access to *objDictionary* from outside the subroutine.

21.   To make it easy to look up items in the dictionary, add a function that does the lookup for you. Call it *funLookUpCode*, and feed it a *statusCode* variable. The function simply looks up the *statusCode* as a dictionary item. You can place this function under the *Fun-Line* function. The code for this looks like the following:

```
Function funLookUpCode(statusCode)
    funLookUpCode = objDictionary.item(statusCode)
End Function
```

22.   Save your work. The script should run successfully.

23.   Now you can turn on the magic of the subroutine and function. To do this, make two changes. First, use the *cstr* function to convert the *cimType* value to a string to ensure ease of comparison in the dictionary and place it under the *For Each b In objItem.properties_* line of code. This line of code looks like the following:

```
statusCode = CStr(b.cimtype)
```

24.   The second change is to feed the *statuscode* variable into the new function. Modify the output line of the script so that the *cimType* printout now goes into the function instead of simply printing out the *b.cimtype* value. This modified line of code looks like the following:

```
Else
        WScript.Echo vbtab & b.name & ":" & vbtab & "cimType: " & funLookUpCode(status
Code) _
        & " is array? " & b.IsArray
```

25.   Save and run the script.

Chapter 4
Using Advanced WMI Queries

Chapter 4 covers a lot of ground. It discusses the various ways you can limit the amount of data returned from a basic data query and examines the use of schema queries to further your understanding of Windows Management Instrumentation (WMI). It discusses ways you can modify both the *Select* statement and the *Where* clause. In addition, it covers the use of the *Meta_Class* class and the *SWbemObject* and *SWbemObjectPath* objects. The third type of query, the event query, is covered in Chapter 5, where we will discuss how to use event-driven scripts to respond to various circumstances as they arise on your computer.

Before You Begin

To work through this chapter, you should be familiar with the following concepts:

- The basics of using both the *Select* statement and the *Where* clause to limit the data returned

- Use of the WMI moniker

- The differences between a data query, an event query, and a schema query

After you complete this chapter, you will be familiar with the following concepts:

- How to use the *ISA operator*

- *Associators of* and how to use *associators of* in a query

- How to use *references of* in a query

- How to use *SWbemSink*

- The new objects available in Microsoft Windows XP and Windows Server 2003

> **Note**   All the scripts used in this chapter are located on the CD that accompanies this book in the \Scripts\Chapter04 folder.

Using __Class

You can limit the amount of information returned based on the *__Class* property. In reality, *__Class* is not really a property; it is more of a pseudo property. *__Class* is used to refer to the class of the WMI object. In the data returned from a WMI query, you can use this well-known identifier in the *Where* clause to filter out objects that might be derived from a particular class.

Using *ISA*

No, I am not talking about Microsoft ISA (Internet Security and Acceleration) Server. In WMI, there is a command called *ISA*. The *ISA* operator (it does not need to be capitalized) can be used with data queries, schema queries, and event queries. In all three types of queries, if *ISA* is needed, it is found in the *Where* clause to limit the scope of the query to a particular class or a particular type of object. In the following script, ISA.vbs, I use the *ISA* operator to limit the scope of the query to the *Win32_ProductSoftwareFeatures* class. *ISA* is often paired with the *__This* property. The *__This* property identifies the target class of the query. When *ISA* is used in a schema query, it signals that the query will be applied to all subclasses of the *__This* target.

ISA.vbs

```
strComputer = "."
wmiNS = "\root\cimv2"
strClass = "'Win32_ProductSoftwareFeatures'"
wmiQuery = "Select * from meta_Class where __This ISA " & strClass
Set objWMIService = GetObject("winmgmts:\\" & strComputer & wmiNS)
Set colItems = objWMIService.ExecQuery (wmiQuery)

For Each objItem in colItems
WScript.Echo "CLASS: " & objItem.path_.Class & " has " & _
    objItem.properties_.count & " properties and " & _
    objItem.qualifiers_.count & " qualifiers."
WScript.Echo "PROPERTIES:"
        For Each b In objItem.properties_
        If IsArray(b) Then
        wscript.echo b.name & " is an Array." & _
        vbcrlf & "The properties are: " & Join (b, ",")
        End if
        WScript.Echo vbtab & b.name
        Next
        'WScript.Sleep 1000
WScript.Echo "QUALIFIERS:"
        For Each a In objItem.qualifiers_
        'WScript.Echo a.name
        If IsArray(a) Then
        wscript.echo vbtab & a.name & " is an array" & _
        vbcrlf & vbtab & "The Properties are: " & Join(a, ",")
        Else
        WScript.Echo vbtab & a.name & " = " & objItem.qualifiers_.item(a.name)
        End If
'WScript.Sleep 1000
        Next
Next
```

If you use the *ISA* operator in a data query, it retrieves embedded objects in the class hierarchy. The result will include both the instances of the class that has the embedded objects as well as the objects that are derived from the superclass. It is important to note that the instances of the class need not be derived from the superclass, but the embedded objects should be.

Scripting API Objects

In this section we will look at the scripting application programming interface (API) objects that exist for obtaining information from WMI. What's most important are the names of the objects that are returned when you perform different operations in the scripts. For example, if you submit an *ExecQuery* into WMI, a *SWbemServices* object is returned. Once you have the *SWbemServices* object, you are able to use it to perform a variety of tasks. Let's look at the *SWbemServices* object first.

SWbemServices

SWbemServices is used to perform many different operations against WMI namespaces. When you use the *winmgmts* moniker to make a connection into WMI, you are using an *SWbemServices* object, which comes back from the connection. When you use *ExecQuery* to return a collection of information from WMI, you are using the *ExecQuery* method from the *SWbemServices* object. Table A-1 (in Appendix A) lists all the methods available through *SWbemServices*. In Chapter 3, we looked at several of the methods of *SWbemServices* because it is used for the most basic types of WMI queries. In this chapter, we look at many of the other methods.

Using the *associators of* Command

The *associators of* command is used to bring back instances of classes that are associated with a particular source. The instances that are returned are called *endpoints*. An endpoint is returned for each association between it and the source object. *Associations* are the ways objects are related to one another. For example, one WMI class is called *Win32_NTDomain*. Another class is called *Win32_Group* and yet another is called *Win32_GroupInDomain*. The last class, as you might suspect, is a class that associates groups with domains. An example of using *associators of* is shown in the GroupsInDomain.vbs script.

GroupsInDomain.vbs

```
strComputer = "."
wmiNS = "\root\cimv2"
wmiQuery = "ASSOCIATORS OF {win32_ntdomain.name=""domain: nwtraders""}" _
    & " where assocClass =win32_groupInDomain"
Set objWMIService = GetObject("winmgmts:\\" & strComputer & wmiNS)
Set colItems = objWMIService.ExecQuery (wmiQuery)

For Each objItem in colItems
  With objItem
```

```
    Wscript.Echo .name
    WScript.echo vbtab & "sid type: " & .sidType & vbtab & .sid
      If .description = "" Then ' .description might be empty, but is not null
      else
      WScript.echo vbtab & .description
      End If
  End with
Next
```

When you use the *associators of* query, as in Figure 4-1, it is common to specify two classes, as shown in the script GroupsInDomain.vbs. I used both the *Win32_NTDomain* class and the *Win32_GroupInDomain* class.

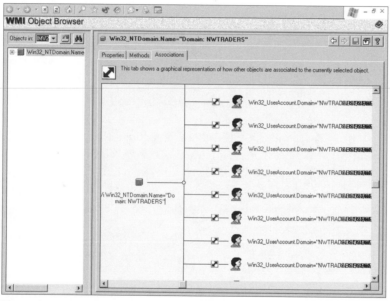

Figure 4-1   Associations of *Win32_NTDomain*

The first class identifies a specific domain, and the second class obtains the groups that reside in that domain. Some classes support an *associators of* query and do not require two classes because they are inherently associated with other classes. A good example is the *Win32_LogonSession* class, which is used to describe the logon session that is associated with a particular logged-on user. To do an *associators of* query with *Win32_LogonSession* you first must identify a particular logon session. Because you might not happen to know the name of a specific logon session off the top of your head, you can use the script ListLogonSessions.vbs first to obtain the information.

ListLogonSessions.vbs

```
strComputer = "."
wmiNS = "\root\cimv2"
wmiQuery = "Select * from win32_logonsession"
Set objWMIService = GetObject("winmgmts:\\" & strComputer & wmiNS)
Set colItems = objWMIService.ExecQuery (wmiQuery)
```

```
For Each objItem in colItems
Wscript.echo "AuthenticationPackage:"  & objItem.AuthenticationPackage
Wscript.echo "Caption:"  & objItem.Caption
Wscript.echo "Description:"  & objItem.Description
Wscript.echo "InstallDate:"  & objItem.InstallDate
Wscript.echo "LogonId:"  & objItem.LogonId
Wscript.echo "LogonType:"  & objItem.LogonType
Wscript.echo "Name:"  & objItem.Name
Wscript.echo "StartTime:"  & objItem.StartTime
Wscript.echo "Status:"  & objItem.Status
WScript.Echo ""
Next
```

The output from this script is not extremely helpful—but it returns enough information to get you started in your quest for a specific logon session. Following is a portion of the output.

```
AuthenticationPackage:Negotiate
Caption:
Description:
InstallDate:
LogonId:999
LogonType:0
Name:
StartTime:20050408181216.852140-240
Status:
```

A couple of interesting things are shown here. The *LogonType* property is returned as a zero (0). The software development kit (SDK) does not tell you what a *logonType* of 0 really is. The query does tell you that *logonID* 999 is associated with the *logonType* of 0. This is where the *associators of* query comes into play. In the script AssociatorsOfLogonSession.vbs you gain a powerful ally that can help you examine the users logged on to the computer. When you run the script AssociatorsOfLogonSession.vbs, you find that the logon ID 999 is used for the system process. You can extrapolate from this information that a logon type of 0 is a system logon.

AssociatorsOfLogonSession.vbs

```
strComputer = "."
wmiNS = "\root\cimv2"
wmiQuery = "ASSOCIATORS OF {win32_LogonSession.LogonId=""999""}"
Set objWMIService = GetObject("winmgmts:\\" & strComputer & wmiNS)
Set colItems = objWMIService.ExecQuery (wmiQuery)

For Each objItem in colItems
    Wscript.Echo "Name: " & objItem.name
    Wscript.Echo ": " & objItem.path_
Next
```

Using the *references of* Command

A *references of* type of query is used to return all association instances that refer to a particular source instance. As you can see in the script ReferencesOfLogonSession.vbs, association instances that refer to a logon session that has a *LogonID* property of 999 are returned. The instances that come back as a result of the *references of* query are intervening association instances rather than the actual endpoint instances. The *associators of* query retrieves the endpoint instances. Many times there is no difference in the information that is returned. In the scripts AssociatorsOfLogonSession.vbs and ReferencesOfLogonSession.vbs the returned results are equivalent. However, the difference in the way the output is formatted might influence whether you use a *references of* or *associators of* query. The other factor is whether you need returned an intervening association instance or an actual endpoint instance.

ReferencesOfLogonSession.vbs

```
strComputer = "."
wmiNS = "\root\cimv2"
intLogon = """999""}"
wmiQuery = "References of {win32_LogonSession.LogonId=" & intLogon
Set objWMIService = GetObject("winmgmts:\\" & strComputer & wmiNS)
Set colItems = objWMIService.ExecQuery (wmiQuery)

For Each objItem in colItems
    Wscript.Echo ": " & objItem.path_
Next
```

Modifying the *Where* clause

The *references of* query works similarly to the *Select* query examined in Chapter 3—you can make modifications to the *Where* clause. You can specify the following four keywords in the *Where* clause:

- *ClassDefsOnly*
- *requiredQualifier*
- *resultClass*
- *role*

ClassDefsOnly

ClassDefsOnly causes the query to come back with class definition objects rather than the actual association class instance. Don't let the terminology confuse you. A *ClassDefsOnly* clause does not cause the query to return something that actually tells you what the class does—it is not that kind of definition. When you run the query, what comes back could be described as a template of the class in memory. You do not see the template, but you do have a hook to the template. So, why would you be interested in doing such a thing? You can use the class definition object with the *SpawnDerivedClass_* method of the *SWbemObject* to create a class that is derived from the class definition object. This means that if I have a *Win32_LogonSession* class in memory, I can create a new instance of the class and modify it to meet my needs. The object that comes back from using *SpawnDerivedClass_* is a subclass of the current object.

requiredQualifier

The *requiredQualifier* keyword tells WMI that the association object that comes back from the query must include the specified qualifier. Only associated instances containing the specified qualifier are returned in the result set. In the script AssociatorsOfNetAdapterRequiredQualifier.vbs I do an *associators of* query to find items related to the network adapter on the computer. The *requiredQualifier* keyword goes into the *Where* clause. The really interesting thing about the AssociatorsOfNetAdapterRequiredQualifier.vbs script is the use of the *Path_* property inside the *For Each Next* loop. I need to use this so I can print out each of the classes associated with the network adapter. The problem is that all the classes do not have the same properties, but all the classes have a path.

AssociatorsOfNetAdapterRequiredQualifier.vbs

```
strComputer = "."
wmiNS = "\root\cimv2"
wmiQuery =
"ASSOCIATORS OF {win32_networkadapter.deviceID='1'} where requiredQualifier = locale"
Set objWMIService = GetObject("winmgmts:\\" & strComputer & wmiNS)
Set colItems = objWMIService.execquery(wmiQuery)
For Each objItem in colItems
    Wscript.Echo objItem.path_.relpath
Next
```

resultClass

When *resultClass* is used in the *Where* clause of a *references of* query, the object must belong to the specified class, or it must be derived from a specified class. This is useful when you need to filter out the results of a query based on the type of object being returned. In the script AssociatorsOfNetAdapterResultClass.vbs, I filter out everything associated with the network card and get back only the system drivers. I perform a query of all the properties of all the system drivers in the Win32_systemDriver.vbs script, which can be found in the Scripts\Supplemental Scripts\cimv2 folder on the accompanying CD. This script returns more than 4000 lines of information on my laptop. The Win32_NetworkAdapter.vbs script in the Scripts\ Supplemental Scripts\cimv2 folder returns more than 700 lines of information on my laptop because it picks up the virtual adapters, Bluetooth adapters, wireless adapters, and who knows what else. Rather than having to sort through nearly 4000 lines of information, it would be better simply to get the information I am looking for—that is, the drivers associated with my wired Ethernet card. The code to do this is shown in the AssociatorsOfNetAdapterResultClass.vbs script. Keep in mind that only the properties from the *Win32_SystemDriver* class are available—the properties from *Win32_NetAdapter* are not.

AssociatorsOfNetAdapterResultClass.vbs

```
strComputer = "."
wmiNS = "\root\cimv2"
wmiQuery =
"ASSOCIATORS OF {win32_networkadapter.deviceID='1'} where resultClass = Win32_SystemDriver"
Set objWMIService = GetObject("winmgmts:\\" & strComputer & wmiNS)
```

```
Set colItems = objWMIService.execquery(wmiQuery)
For Each objItem in colItems
 With objItem
  Wscript.Echo .path_.relpath
  WScript.Echo vbtab & .displayName & vbcrlf & vbtab & .pathName
 End with
Next
```

role

The last way to filter out *references of* queries in the *Where* clause is to use the *role* keyword. The *role* keyword is used to specify associations that fill a particular role.

Using the *ExecQuery* Method

You will use the *ExecQuery* method many times. Remember, methods do something, so you can use the *ExecQuery* method to retrieve a collection of objects from WMI. The objects are returned as an *SWbemObjectSet* collection. In this section, we examine the use of *ExecQuery*, the flags used to modify it, and the special considerations for working with an *SWbemObject-Set* collection.

Returning an *SWbemObjectSet* Collection

It is important to remember that the *ExecQuery* method returns an *SWbemObjectSet* collection. Because the *SWbemObjectSet* is a collection, you have to deal with the data returned as a collection rather than as a simple string value. This is true even if the query returns only a single instance. To work with the collection, use *For Each Next* in most cases because it is the simplest way to singularize an instance from within a collection.

Iflags

You can specify several flags with the *ExecQuery* method. A listing of the available *SWbemObjectIflags* is contained in Table A-2 in Appendix A. If no flags are specified, the default value for *Iflags* is the *wbemFlagReturnImmediately* flag, which tells WMI to return the call immediately. This is the opposite behavior of the *wbemFlagReturnWhenComplete* flag, which tells WMI to wait until the query is complete before returning any information. Control of this behavior is fundamentally tied to the way in which you anticipate utilizing your data or handling any errors that might arise during execution of your script. I discuss this in the following section on errors.

An example of using *Iflags* is shown in the script SystemBios.vbs. Note that you can specify the hexadecimal value codes directly in the *ExecQuery* statement. You could also define constants and assign values to them. What you cannot do is use the flag names directly in the script without the intervening step of creating them as constants.

SystemBios.vbs

```
strComputer = "."
wmiNS = "\root\cimv2"
wmiQuery = "Select * from win32_SystemBIOS"
Set objWMIService = GetObject("winmgmts:\\" & strComputer & wmiNS)
Set colItems = objWMIService.ExecQuery(wmiQuery,"wql",&h10 + &h20)
For Each objItem in colItems
    WScript.Echo "GroupComponent: " & objItem.GroupComponent
    WScript.Echo "PartComponent: " & objItem.PartComponent
    WScript.Echo
Next
```

Error Codes

WMI does not consider it an error for a query to return an empty result set. You might not think the query was successful, but as far as WMI is concerned, if it runs without errors, the query is fine. This is just one thing to keep in mind when evaluating error codes returned by the *ExecQuery* method. You must be aware of the peculiarities of any return flag you set. The *wbemFlagReturnImmediately* flag does not set the error object until an attempt to access the object set is made. This means you have to handle the error as part of the access mechanism. On the other hand, the *wbemFlagReturnWhenComplete* sets the error object when the *Exec-Query* method is actually called. This enables you to detect and handle the error much earlier in the script, which can be more efficient.

Using the *Get* Method

The *Get* method of the *SWbemServices* object retrieves a particular instance of an object. The object must reside in the namespace associated with the current *SWbemServices* object. The advantage of using the *Get* method is that you need not use the *For Each Next* statement to iterate through a collection as you must do with the *ExecQuery* method. The disadvantage of using the *Get* method is that you must be able to uniquely identify the instance to which you wish to connect. You must know the key property of the class you are using, and you must know the exact value being reported for that property. If you have this information, using the *Get* method is easy. If you do not know this information, writing a working script is an exercise in futility.

In the script ProxyServerInfo.vbs I connect to a computer identified by the variable *StrServer-Name*. As I am supplying values to the WMI query, I have to encase the computer name with three sets of quotation marks. You might wonder how I knew three sets of quotation marks were required, and the answer is simple—I just kept typing until the query worked. Additionally, whereas the value for the variable *strComputer* works for the moniker connection, it does not work as the key value for the *Get* method. Once the proxy server information is displayed, I call the *SetProxySetting* method. The interesting thing about the *SetProxySetting* method is that it requires two parameters to be supplied: the proxy name and the port to use for the proxy server.

> **Turning Off the Proxy Server**   If you call the *SetProxySetting* method and assign the values to *NULL*, you turn off the use of the proxy server .errRTN = objItem.SetProxySetting(null,null).

ProxyServerInfo.vbs

```
strComputer = "."
strServerName = """Mred.microsoft.com"""
wmiNS = "\root\cimv2"
wmiQuery = "win32_proxy.ServerName=" & strServerName
Set objWMIService = GetObject("winmgmts:\\" & strComputer & wmiNS)
Set objItem = objWMIService.get(wmiQuery)
    WScript.Echo "current proxy settings on: " & strServerName
    Wscript.Echo "ProxyPortNumber: " & objItem.ProxyPortNumber
    Wscript.Echo "ProxyServer: " & objItem.ProxyServer
'now call a method to change these settings

errRTN = objItem.SetProxySetting("myProxyServer","80")
subCheckError

Sub subCheckError
If errRTN = 0 Then
    WScript.Echo "New settings were accepted"
Else
    WScript.Echo "an error occurred. It was: " & errRTN
End If
End sub
```

wbemFlagUseAmendedQualifiers

Only one *Iflag* is used with the *Get* method and it's called *wbemFlagUseAmendedQualifiers*. The *wbemFlagUseAmendedQualifiers* flag is used to retrieve localized data from WMI. The base classes are language neutral and WMI allows multiple localized versions of the same class to be stored in the repository. The language-specific class information is stored in a child namespace under the same namespace that contains the language-neutral class. To retrieve this language-specific information, you must use the *wbemFlagUseAmendedQualifiers Iflag*.

SWbemLastError

The *SWbemLastError* object is used to check error objects for WMI operations. It has both properties and methods that are the same as the *SWbemObject* object. The difference is that these contain error information instead of class information.

The *SWbemLastError* object is used to inspect error information that is associated with a particular WMI call. If error information is not available, *SWbemLastError* object is created. If the *SWbemLastError* object is created, the error is returned and the status is reset. If you then attempt to create the object again, it will once again fail until additional errors are generated.

It is possible to create an asynchronous call to *SWbemLastError*, but it can be returned only by an *onCompleted* event from *SWbemSink*.

Three methods are used with the *SWbemLastError* object. These are listed in Table 4-1.

Table 4-1 *SWbemLastError* Methods

Method	Description
*Clone_*	Makes a copy of the current object
*CompareTo_*	Tests two objects for equality
*GetObjectText_*	Returns a text representation of the object in Managed Object Format (MOF) syntax

The *GetObjectText_* method is rather useful. It returns a MOF syntax description of a WMI object. The script DisplayMOF.vbs illustrates how to use this method. If you run this script, you will find that it gives you information similar to that found in the SDK—albeit not as easy to read. The MOF description of the class tells you data types, privileges required, key values, and much more.

DisplayMOF.vbs
```
strComputer = "."
wmiNS = "\root\cimv2"
wmiQuery = "win32_process"
Set objWMIService = GetObject("winmgmts:\\" & strComputer & wmiNS)
Set objItem = objWMIService.Get(wmiQuery)
objMOF = objItem.GetObjectText_
WScript.Echo(objMOF)
```

Although the *SWbemLastError* methods can be exciting, the properties are most useful to the scripter. Interestingly enough, there are only two properties, but they are very handy. The *Path_* property contains an *SWbemObjectPath* object, which we examine in detail in a later section. The *SWbemObjectPath* object gives you access to a number of useful properties such as keys and namespaces. The *Properties_* property of the *SWbemLastError* object contains an *SWbemPropertySet* object, which we examine later as well. The *SWbemPropertySet* object is exciting because it is a collection of other objects. The properties of *SWbemLastError* are listed in Table 4-2.

Table 4-2 *SWbemLastError* Properties

Property	Description
*Path_*	Contains an *SWbemObjectPath* object.
*Properties_*	The collection of properties of the *SWbemLastError* object. This is an *SWbemPropertySet* object.

SWbemObject

An *SWbemObject* object is used to represent either a class definition or an instance of a WMI object. Two different types of properties and methods can be used with *SWbemObject*: the generic properties and methods and the specific properties and methods of the underlying object as a dynamic automation property or method. The actual names and types of these properties and methods depend on the underlying WMI object.

The *SWbemObject* object is always in process, and you do not need to create an instance of this object prior to using it. Keep in mind that write operations affect the local copy of the object. Use the *Put_* method of the *SWbemObject* to actually modify an existing object. Changes are not written until you call *SWbemObject.Put_*.

Generic method and property names always end in a trailing underscore. This is so you can easily tell the difference between a dynamic WMI method or property and one from the underlying object.

Creating an Empty Class

You can create a new empty class to use with *SWbemObject* by using the *Get* method of the *SWbemService* object. The trick is to use an empty path parameter. When you do this, you get back an empty *SWbemObject* object, which becomes a class. You can then supply a class name for the *Class* property of the *SWbemObjectPath* object that comes back when you use the *Path_* call. Once you do this, you simply add properties to the new class by using the *Properties_* method. You can then use *GetObject* on the new class. The *SWbemObject* object that represents the class must use the *Put_* command to put it into the WMI repository.

SWbemObjectPath

The *SWbemObjectPath* object is used to work with the path of a WMI object. You can use it both to validate the path to an object and to construct the path to an object. Use the *CreateObject* command to create an instance of the *SWbemObjectPath* object. Once you have an instance of the *SWbemObjectPath* object, you have two methods and 13 properties available. The methods are listed in Table 4-3.

Table 4-3   *SWbemObjectPath* Methods

Method	Description
SetAsClass	Forces the path to address a WMI class
SetAsSingleton	Forces the path to address a singleton WMI instance

Complementing the two methods listed in Table 4-3 are 13 properties, which are detailed in Table A-3 in Appendix A. These properties can reveal a lot of information about the WMI object with which you are working. *Displayname*, *Path*, and *Relpath* are three properties I have found particularly useful.

The *Authority* property of the *SWbemObjectPath* object holds a string that represents the authority component of the object path. This authority string is the same as the *Authority* property associated with the *SWbemLocator ConnectServer* method. If the *Authority* property begins with the word *Kerberos*, you are using Kerberos authentication, and this parameter will contain a Kerberos principal name. If the *Authority* parameter has any other value, you are using NTLM authentication, and the field will possess an NTLM domain name. If the property is blank, the system will negotiate with Component Object Model (COM) to determine whether to use NTLM or Kerberos. This does not work for a WMI script running locally because it uses the default DCOM impersonation settings to impersonate the logged-on user.

IsSingleton

The *IsSingleton* property is a Boolean value that indicates whether the path object represents a singleton instance. A *singleton instance* in WMI is an instance of a class that can never have more than one instance. The property is read-only, so you cannot flip a bit and create the ability to have another instance of a singleton class.

Keys **Property**

The *Keys* property of the *SWbemObjectPath* object is actually a *SWbemNamedValueSet* object. To work with the *Keys* property of the *SWbemObjectPath* object, you have to do two things. First, you have to retrieve the property, which is simple enough. But next you have to treat the property as an *SWbemNamedValueSet* object. This is where things begin to get a little sticky because an *SWbemNamedValueSet* object is a collection of *SWbemNamedValue* objects.

An *SWbemNamedValue* object is called a single named value that belongs to the *SWbemNamedValueSet* collection object. You see, the *SWbemNamedValueSet* is actually a set of items, which is a collection. Additionally, because the items in the collection are *SWbemNamedValue* objects, you can use only the properties available to *SWbemNamedValue* objects. Only two properties are available in this context: *Name* and *Value*, both of which are self-explanatory.

You can use the methods and properties from *SWbemNamedValueSet* to provide additional information to WMI when you are making calls, or you can use the methods and properties to obtain information when receiving information from WMI. If you were making a call into an *SWbemServices* object, you would need to specify values for the *SWbemNamedValueSet* objects to enable WMI to make the proper connection. Additionally, if you want to receive the keys information about a class, you need to use *SWbemNamedValueSet* and *SWbemNamedValue* objects to specify the name of the key. You can add the extra information to the *SWbemNamedValueSet* object and send the object with the call as a parameter. You can use *CreateObject* when you do this. The *SWbemNamedValueSet* object has the methods listed in Table A-4 in Appendix A. The *SWbemNamedValueSet* object has only one property—the *Count* property.

Locale

The *Locale* property of the *SWbemObjectPath* object is used to identify the locale of the object path. When you use the *Locale* property, it is used as part of a standalone *SWbemObjectPath* object and it is both read and write. It can also be used to set the locale component of the WMI moniker. If you use the *Locale* property through an *SWbemObject.Property_* property, it is read-only, and it will report the value of the locale used in binding the namespace from the object that returned the property. All of the Microsoft locale identifiers are in the form of MS_*xxx*, such as MS_409 for American English. The system locale settings can be retrieved with Microsoft Visual Basic Scripting Edition (VBScript) by using the *GetLocale* function built into VBScript, but they report different numbers from the numbers reported by the *Locale* property (for example, 1033 for American English). In reality, the reported numbers are not different numbers but are different representations of the same number—1033 is base 10, and 409 is the same number in hexadecimal.

Namespace

The *Namespace* property of the *SWbemObjectPath* object holds the name of the namespace associated with the namespace part of the object path. You can use this property to see where in the WMI schema an object resides. This can assist you in creating scripts that do more than just work in the default namespace.

Security_

The *Security_* property of the *SWbemObjectPath* object is used to read or set the security components of an object path. It is not used to set the security attributes of the *SWbemObjectPath* object, but rather to set the security of the object path. It is used to represent the security components of the path for an *SWbemLocator* object. This property is an *SWbemSecurity* object. Notice that when you are working with this property, three different objects are involved: an *SWbemLocator* object, an *SWbemObjectPath* object, and an *SWbemSecurity* object. If you set the *Security_* property of an *SWbemObjectPath* object to *NULL*, it will grant unlimited access to everyone all the time.

SWbemObjectSet

An *SWbemObjectSet* object is a collection of *SWbemObject* objects. An *SWbemObjectSet* object is returned when you call any of the following methods from *SWbemObject,* the building blocks of WMI:

- *Associators_*
- *Instances_*
- *References_*
- *SubClasses_*

An *SWbemObjectSet* object is returned when you call any of the following methods from *SWbemServices*, the WMI service itself:

- *AssociatorsOf*
- *ExecQuery*

- *InstancesOf*
- *ReferencesTo*
- *SubClassesOf*

The *SWbemObjectSet* object does not support using an *Add* or *Remove* method. The only method is the *I* method, which returns an *SWbemObject* object from the collection. The two properties available are *Count* and *Security_*.

SWbemProperty

The *SWbemProperty* object is used to represent a single WMI property of a managed object. Although it does not have any methods, it does have some very useful properties. The properties are listed in Table A-5 in Appendix A.

CIMType

The *CIMType* property of the *SWbemProperty* object is returned as an integer that must be parsed to reveal useful information. When you retrieve the *CIMType* of an *SWbemProperty* object, it comes back as a *WbemCimTypeEnum* constant. You can look up the value in Table A-6 in Appendix A to determine the *CIMType* of an object.

Qualifiers_

The *Qualifiers_* property of the *SWbemProperty* object returns an *SWbemQualifierSet* object that is a collection of qualifiers for the property. This is a read-only property. The *SWbemQualifierSet* object is a collection of *SWbemQualifier* objects. Several methods can be used with an *SWbemQualifierSet* object, and these are listed in Table A-7 in Appendix A. Only one property is available with the *SWbemQualifierSet* object and that is the *Count* property.

SWbemQualifier

The *SWbemQualifier* objects are listed in Table A-8 of Appendix A. They are used to represent a single qualifier of a WMI class, instance, property, or method.

SWbemPropertySet

The *SWbemPropertySet* object is another one of those collection-type objects—it is a collection of *SWbemProperty* objects. It has three methods and one property. As you have observed in this chapter, most objects support the *Count* property at a minimum, as is the case here. You can add items to the collection by using the *Add* method, and you can retrieve items from the collection by using the *Item* method. The final method is the *Remove* method, which—you guessed it—removes an item from the collection. The collection of *SWbemProperty* objects that makes up an *SWbemPropertySet* collection is used to describe the properties of a single WMI class or a single instance of a WMI class.

SWbemSink

SWbemSink is used by client applications to receive the results of either an asynchronous operation or an event notification. If you need to perform an asynchronous WMI query, first you must create an instance of the *SWbemSink* object and then pass it as a parameter to the query. If you are creating an event notification script, the *SWbemSink* object is triggered when either a status update or a result is returned. Only one method is available with the *SWbemSink* object, the *Cancel* method. Four properties, listed in Table 4-4, can be used with this object.

Table 4-4   *SWbemSink* Properties

Event	Description
onCompleted	Triggered when an asynchronous operation is complete
onObjectPut	Triggered after an asynchronous put operation
onObjectReady	Triggered when an object provided by an asynchronous call is available
onProgress	Triggered to provide the status of an asynchronous operation

onCompleted

The *onCompleted* event of the *SWbemSink* object occurs when an asynchronous call completes. A script or application receiving this event is able to interpret the result of an asynchronous operation or determine the reason for failure from the error information. The *onCompleted* event contains three parameters: the result of the asynchronous method, an error object if the call fails, and an *objWbemAsyncContext* parameter that is in reality an *SWbemNamedValueSet* object that is passed to the original asynchronous call. This parameter can be used to identify the origin of the asynchronous call that trigged the event. Three errors can be returned as a result of an asynchronous call. These errors are listed in Table 4-5.

Table 4-5   *onCompleted* Error Messages

Error	Error Number	Meaning
wbemErrFailed	0x80041001	Unspecified error
wbemErrOutOfMemory	0x80041006	Not enough memory to complete the operation
wbemErrTransportFailure	0x80041015	Networking error occurred, preventing normal operation

Introducing New Objects in Windows XP and Windows Server 2003

Several new objects were added for Windows XP and for Windows Server 2003. Some of these objects, such as the *SWbemDateTime* object, make life easier by formatting data in a more usable fashion. In other cases, such as with the *SWbemRefresher* object, the object provides exciting new capabilities for scripts. All together, there are five new objects you can use in Windows XP and in Windows Server 2003 that were not available in earlier editions of the operating system

SWbemDateTime

The *SWbemDateTime* object is new in Windows XP and Windows Server 2003. This object is used to parse Common Information Model (CIM) datetime values. The datetime value is a fixed-length string that represents either a date or a time interval. The WMI datetime intervals have four trailing digits. The datetime does not allow the use of wildcards or padding to leave fields blank. It is capable of using either the VT_Date or a FILETIME value. *SWbemDateTime* can be formatted using a local time value or a Universal Time Coordinate (UTC) value. Any numeric field can have a wildcard value specified if the *IsInterval* property is set to false. A field that uses a wildcard must use asterisks in the entire field. Each property has a corresponding Boolean value. If the Boolean value is set to false, the value is interpreted as an interval rather than a specific number. If the interval is used in the CIM datetime value, the *isInterval* is also set to true. This is not the default behavior.

SWbemObjectEx

SWbemObjectEx provides some new and exciting functionality for the *SWbemObject*. Just like the *SWbemObject*, the methods of the *SWbemObjectEx* object can be used by all WMI objects. There are two just two methods: *GetText_* and *Refresh_*. The *GetText_* method returns a text file that shows the contents of an object in Extensible Markup Language (XML). *Refresh_* is used to refresh the data in an object. The *SystemProperties_* property is an *SWbemPropertySet* object that contains the collection of system properties that apply to *SWbemObjectEx*.

SWbemRefresher

The *SWbemRefresher* object is another container object that can be used to refresh the data for all objects that are added to the refresher object. Single instances and instance enumerators can be added or removed from the container. Sets of added objects are each represented by an *SWbemRefreshableItem* instance that can be treated as a collection. If the provider of the instance data is not a high-performance interface, you can still use the *SWbemRefresher* object to update the data when you use the refresh call. If the data is retrieved through a high-performance interface, you can use the *AutoReconnect* property to reestablish any broken connections to the data provider. If you need to carry out a refresh operation, you can use either the *Refresh* method from the *SWbemRefresher* object or you can use the *Refresh_* method from *SWbemObjectEx*.

Several methods are provided by the *SWbemRefresher* object. These methods are listed in Table A-9 in Appendix A.

In addition to the standard *Count* property, the *SWbemRefresher* object also defines the *AutoReconnect* property. When the *AutoReconnect* property is set to true, the refresher object automatically reconnects to a remote provider if the connection is broken. This works only if the provider is high performance. If the provider is not high performance, the *AutoReconnect* property has no effect on the *SWbemRefresher* object because it will never reconnect.

SWbemRefreshableItem

The *SWbemRefreshableItem* object is a single item in an *SWbemRefresher* object. You are able to obtain an *SWbemRefreshableItem* object by using either the *Add* or the *AddEnum* method of the *SWbemRefresher* object. One method is associated with the *SWbemRefreshableItem* object called the *Remove* method. It is used to remove an item from the refresher object.

There are also five properties associated with the *SWbemRefreshableItem* object. These properties are listed in the Table A-10 in Appendix A.

SWbemServicesEx

SWbemServicesEx extends the functionality of the *SWbemServices* object. There are two new methods in this object: the *Put* method and the *PutAsync* method. Both methods save an object to the namespace that is bound to the *SWbemServicesEx* namespace.

Summary

In this chapter, we examined many of the WMI objects available to you. First we looked at the *SWbemServices* object; then we worked our way through to the *SWbemServicesEx* object, which is new in Windows XP and Windows Server 2003. Knowing how to use these objects properly can greatly enhance the security and reliability of your scripts.

Quiz Yourself

Q: What is the *ISA* operator used for in a WMI script?

A: The *ISA* operator is used to filter out results based on the class of the object.

Q: Why would you need to use *wbemFlagUseAmendedQualifiers* in a WMI script?

A: You need to use *wbemFlagUseAmendedQualifiers* in a WMI script if you must access localization information.

Q: Name a new helper object in Windows XP and Windows Server 2003 that is capable of translating a UTC date format into something more understandable.

A: The new helper object in Windows XP and Windows Server 2003 called *SWbemDateTime* is capable of translating a UTC date format into a more easily understood format.

On Your Own

Lab 9 Working with the AutoDiscovery Process

In this lab, you will work with the *SWbemDateTime* object to incorporate it into a script to deliver a more readable date string. In doing so, you will look at the AutoDiscovery/AutoPurge (ADAP) status. ADAP is a process that runs regularly to convert Perfmon counters into WMI classes. Checking the status of ADAP is one of the first steps in troubleshooting these types of classes.

1. Open the WMITemplate script, and save it as StudentLab9.vbs.

2. Change the *wmiNS* value so that it points to *"\root\default"* namespace instead of the *root\cimv2* namespace. The modified *wmiNS* line will look like the following:

    ```
    wmiNS = "\root\default"
    ```

3. Modify the *wmiQuery* so that it selects everything from the *__AdapStatus* WMI class. The modified *wmiQuery* line will look like the following:

    ```
    wmiQuery = "Select * from __adapStatus"
    ```

4. Declare a variable to hold the *SWbemDateTime* object. You can simply call it *SWbemDateTime* if you wish.

5. Under the *GetObject* command that makes the WMI moniker connection, use the variable you declared in step 4 to hold an instance of the *SWbemDateTime* object. Use the *CreateObject* command because this object is not already in memory. Your line of code will look like the following:

    ```
    Set objSWbemDateTime = CreateObject("WbemScripting.SWbemDateTime")
    ```

6. Delete all the *Wscript.Echo* commands from inside the *For Each Next* loop. The loop will look like the following after you delete the *Wscript.Echo* commands:

    ```
    For Each objItem in colItems

    Next
    ```

7. Add a *With objItem End With* statement inside the *For Each Next* loop. The loop will now look like the following:

    ```
    For Each objItem in colItems
    With objItem

    End With
    Next
    ```

8. Turn off the *On Error Resume Next* statement. Save and run the script. You will not get any output, but you should not receive any errors either.

9. Assign the *.LastStartTime* property to the *Value* property of the *SWbemDateTime* object. Your command will look like the following:

```
objSWbemDateTime.Value = .LastStartTime
```

10. Use the *GetVarDate* method of the *SWbemDateTime* object to translate the UTC date into something readable. Use a variable called *strLastStart* to hold the translated timestamp.

```
strLastStart = "The last start time was: " & objSWbemDateTime.GetVarDate
```

11. Declare (dim) the *strLastStart* variable with the other variables at the top of the script.

12. Recycle the *Value* property of the *SWbemDateTime* object by assigning a new property to it. This time it is the *.LastStopTime* property from the *__AdapStatus* class.

```
objSWbemDateTime.Value =   .LastStopTime
```

13. Dim the *strLastStop* variable at the top of the script.

14. Use the *GetVarDate* method to translate the UTC date. Assign the value to the *strLastStop* variable.

15. Save and run the script. You should still see no output or errors.

16. Declare a new variable called *strStatus* to hold the *.Status* property. Assign the *.Status* property to the new variable:

```
strStatus = .Status
```

17. Add a single *Wscript.Echo* command under the *For Each Next* loop that prints out the values contained in the three variables. It will look something like the following:

```
WScript.Echo "ADAP Status: " & strStatus & strLastStart & strLastStop
```

18. Clean up the output a little. Dim a new variable called *myTab*.

19. Assign a carriage return and a tab to *myTab*. You can place this under the variable declaration. It will look like the following:

```
mytab = vbcrlf & vbtab
```

20. Put *myTab &* in front of each of the *"The last start"* and *"The last stop"* statements. It will look like the following:

```
With objItem
objSWbemDateTime.Value = .LastStartTime
strLastStart = myTab & "The last start time was: " &_ objSWbemDateTime.GetVarDate
objSWbemDateTime.Value =   .LastStopTime
strLastStop = myTab & "The last Stop time was:  " &_ objSWbemDateTime.GetVarDate
strStatus = .Status
End With
```

21. Now run the script. The output should be much nicer. As extra credit, look up _*__AdapStatus*_ in the SDK and see what the .*Status* property means. A table lists the values. You might want to create a function that translates this for you. I have included such a function in Lab9SolutionExtra.vbs.

22. If you want to see what the UTC time format actually looks like, add the following command directly under the *With objItem* command: *Wscript.Echo.LastStartTime*.

Lab 10 Using the *Get* Method for Inventory Types of Data

In this lab, you will use the *Get* method to obtain useful inventory types of data from WMI. You will connect to the *Win32_ComputerSystem* WMI class to retrieve this information.

1. Open the WMI template script, and save it as StudentLab10.vbs.

2. Locate the *Key* property of *Win32_ComputerSystem*. You can look it up in the SDK, use Wbemtest.exe, or use the GetClassKey.vbs script from the Lab10 folder on the accompanying CD. It should tell you that the *Name* property is the key.

3. Declare a new variable that holds the name of your computer by using the *Dim* command. Call the variable *strName*.

4. Delete the variable *colItems* because you will not need it in this script.

5. Turn off *On Error Resume Next* by inserting a single quote in front of it.

6. Under the *wmiNS= "\root\cimv2"* line, assign the name of your computer to the variable *strName*. Make sure you use a set of double quotes and single quotes as shown in the following code sample:

```
strName = "'TYPE_IN_YOUR_COMPUTER_NAME_HERE'"
```

7. Remove the *Select * from* section from the *wmiQuery*. Add *ComputerSystem.Name* after the *Win32_* Portion. Make it equal to *strName*. The modified line will look like the following:

```
wmiQuery = "win32_ComputerSystem.name=" & strName
```

8. Modify the *ExecQuery* line. Change the variable *colItems* to be *objItem*. Also, change the query type from an *ExecQuery* to a *Get*. The modified line looks like the following:

```
Set objItem = objWMIService.Get(wmiQuery)
```

9. Remove the *For Each Next* loop—but not the *Wscript.Echo* statements.

10. Echo out the value of the following properties: *Name*, *Manufacturer*, *Model*, *TotalPhysicalMemory*, and *UserName*.

11. Run the script. It should work fine. For even more fun, look up *FormatNumber* in the SDK and see how you can use it to clean up the output of the memory that is reported. You can also look up *Win32_ComputerSystem* in the SDK to see whether you want to report other properties.

Chapter 5
Using WMI Events

In Chapter 4, we looked at different ways to query Windows Management Instrumentation (WMI). We examined the various objects available to scripters and discussed how the application of the objects, methods, and properties can greatly enhance your scripting experience. In this chapter, we look at working with WMI events. By using events in your scripts, you enable WMI to respond to certain conditions when they arise on your computer.

Before You Begin

To work through this chapter, you should be familiar with the following concepts:

- The basics of writing WMI queries

- Use of various scripting objects available for WMI

- Use of WMI tools

After you complete this chapter, you will be familiar with the following concepts:

- The basics of event-driven scripts

- Use of the *NextEvent* keyword

- The different types of events

- How to create temporary events

Note All the scripts used in this chapter are located on the CD that accompanies this book in the \Scripts\Chapter05 folder.

Using *SWbemEventSource*

The *SWbemEventSource* object is used to retrieve events. Events are activities or occurrences that happen on a computer system. A process starts—it generates an event. A service pauses—it generates a different kind of event. A file is created, modified, deleted—all of which generate events. You can receive these events by using an event query in conjunction with the *ExecNotificationQuery* method of the *SWbemServices* object.

You get an *SWbemEventSource* object when you use the *ExecNotificationQuery* method to make an event query. Once you execute the query, you have access to the *NextEvent* method. Use the *NextEvent* method to receive events as they arrive in response to the query you performed. This might sound strange—it did to me at first. "Why am I doing a query to receive something in the future?" The key to understanding this is to realize that you are signing up for a subscription in the same way you subscribe to a magazine. The next time an issue of the magazine is published, you will receive it. The next time an event occurs that meets the criteria of your query, you will receive it. In the script MonitorForProcessDeletion.vbs in the next subsection, I use the variable *colItems* to hold what returns from executing the *ExecNotificationQuery*. This is shown in the following code, which is taken from the MonitorForProcessDeletion.vbs script.

```
Set objWMIService = GetObject("winmgmts:\\" & strComputer & wmiNS)
Set colItems = objWMIService.ExecNotificationQuery(wmiQuery)
```

NextEvent

You use the *NextEvent* method in a query to retrieve an event by using an event query. Only one parameter can be specified when you use the *NextEvent* method, and that is the timeout interval. This is an optional parameter, and it is specified in milliseconds. Use a *-1* to tell the call to wait forever, as shown in the following code.

```
Set objItem = colItems.NextEvent(-1)
```

> **Are You Seeing Timeout Errors When You Use *NextEvent*?**   If you see a timeout error, the event did not arrive within the timeout parameter you specified when you called the *NextEvent* method. You might consider increasing the timeout interval. One way to determine whether this will help (and to avoid a lot of experimentation) is to use the default *-1* parameter and incorporate the timer function from Microsoft Visual Basic Scripting Edition (VBScript). This will tell you rather quickly how much time you must specify for the timeout interval.

If the execution of *NextEvent* is successful, it returns an object that contains the requested event. If it is not successful, or if it times out, the command comes back with a null value and an error is raised. The error will be a *wbemErrTimedOut* error with a value of 0x80043001. This parameter is written to the *err* object if it is raised. In the MonitorForProcessDeletion.vbs script, you monitor running processes for the deletion of a process called Notepad.exe. To do this, you use the *ExecNotificationQuery* method to run the query. In the query, specify an *__InstanceDeletionEvent* (the double underscore is required), which means you will be notified only if the event that occurs is associated with an instance being deleted. The instance you are looking for is a *Win32_Process* (contained in the variable *objTGT*). The name of the target instance must be Notepad.exe as specified in the variable *objName*.

Once the query is executed, you use a *Do Loop* and wait for the next event to occur. You will not see any indication that the script is running, unless you are running it in a script editor. If you are, then you will notice a red "X" in the upper right portion of the editor indicating the script is running. If you launch an instance of notepad.exe and wait for a few seconds, you will still not see anything. However, if you then close Notepad.exe you will see the printout of the name, time, and Process ID. The script is still in a loop. It will continue to monitor for a process deletion event where the name of the process is notepad.exe. In your script editor go ahead and stop the running of the script. (Note: The MonitorForProcessDeletion.vbs script works on Microsoft Windows Server 2003.)

MonitorForProcessDeletion.vbs

```
strComputer = "."
objName = ""notepad.exe""
objTGT = ""win32_Process""
wmiNS = "\root\cimv2"

wmiQuery = "SELECT * FROM __InstanceDeletionEvent WITHIN 10 WHERE " _
        & "TargetInstance ISA " & objTGT & " AND " _
            & "TargetInstance.Name=" & objName
Set objWMIService = GetObject("winmgmts:\\" & strComputer & wmiNS)
Set colItems = objWMIService.ExecNotificationQuery(wmiQuery)

Do
    Set objItem = colItems.NextEvent
    Wscript.Echo "Name: " & objItem.TargetInstance.Name & " " & now
    Wscript.Echo "ProcessID: " & objItem.TargetInstance.ProcessId

Loop
```

Security_

It is not surprising that the *Security_* property is used to read or set the security settings of an *SWbemEventSource* object. This property is an *SWbemSecurity* object. We also use the *SWbem-Security* object to request additional privileges when performing operations such as loading or unloading drivers. In the MonitorForProcessDeletion.vbs script, we do not use the *SWbem-Security* object as no privileged operation is being conducted. It is mentioned here, so you will know you can retrieve a privilege object in an event driven query. The *SWbemSecurity* object is discussed in detail in Chapter 8.

Quick Check

   Q: Why would you use an *SWbemEventSource* object?

   A: You use the *SWbemEventSource* object to receive events from an event query.

   Q: Once you have created an *SWbemEventSource* object, which method is available to your script?

   A: Only one method is available from the *SWbemEventSource* object—the *NextEvent* method.

   Q: If you do not supply a parameter to the *NextEvent* method when you call it, how long will the script wait for an event to occur?

   A: If no parameter is supplied to the *NextEvent* method, the script will wait forever.

Working with *SWbemServices*

We discussed the *SWbemServices* object in more detail in Chapter 4. Now we examine two methods that are used when working with events: the *ExecNotificationQuery* method and the *ExecNotificationQueryAsync* method.

ExecNotificationQuery

Use the *ExecNotificationQuery* method of the *SWbemServices* object to execute a query that receives events. The nice thing about the *ExecNotificationQuery* method is that it returns immediately.

Several parameters need to be specified for the *ExecNotificationQuery* method to succeed. The first is obvious: you need to supply a query. What is not obvious is that everything else is optional. In the script MonitorFileCreationEvents.vbs, I use *ExecNotificationQuery* to look for events that meet the criteria contained in the variable *wmiQuery*. I look for creation events that occur when I monitor the directory C:\fso. I use the *FunFix* function to convert the directory name into acceptable form for WMI.

MonitorFileCreationEvents.vbs

```
strComputer = "."
wmiNS = "\root\cimv2"
objClass = ""cim_DirectoryContainsFile""
objGroup = ""Win32_Directory.Name="
strFolder = "C:\fso"
strFolder = funFix(strFolder)
StrMessage = "A new " & objClass & " was created: "
wmiQuery = "SELECT * FROM __InstanceCreationEvent " _
        & "WITHIN 10 WHERE TargetInstance ISA " & objClass & " AND " _
            & "TargetInstance.GroupComponent= " _
                & objGroup & strFolder

Set objWMIService = GetObject("winmgmts:\\" & strComputer & wmiNS)
Set colItems = objWMIService.ExecNotificationQuery(wmiQuery)
```

```
Do
Set objItem = colItems.NextEvent
    Wscript.Echo StrMessage & objItem.TargetInstance.PartComponent
Loop

Function funFix(strFolder)
funFix = """" & Replace(strFolder, "\", "\\\\") & """"
End function
```

ExecNotificationQueryAsync

The *ExecNotificationQueryAsync* method is used to receive events from a query in an asynchronous fashion. The results and the status messages are returned to the calling application through events that are delivered to the sink specified in the *objWbemSink* parameter. When you use an asynchronous query, the results do not come back immediately. To have a place to store the events until you are ready to use them, you have to create a sink, which is explained in the following paragraphs.

You can use this method to query any of the events built into WMI, such as the *__Instance-ModificationEvent*, or you can also use the *ExecNotificationQueryAsync* method to receive events from classes that are designed to provide events—such as the *Win32_IP4RouteTableEvent* class.

Two parameters must be specified to use the *ExecNotificationQueryAsync* method. The first is the name of an *objWbemSink*, and the second is the query. To specify the name of an *objWbemSink*, first you must create the sink by using a line of code that looks something like the following:

```
Set objSink = CreateObject("WbemScripting.SWbemSink","SINK_")
```

After the sink is created, you can then specify it as the first parameter of the *ExecNotification-QueryAsync* method. If you supply a value for the query language, it must be listed as *WQL*. You can also specify one of two flags. The first flag is the *wbemFlagSendStatus 0x80* flag, which causes the asynchronous call to send status updates to the *onProgress* event handler for the object sink. The second flag is the *wbemFlagDontSendStatus 0x0* flag, which prevents asynchronous calls from sending status updates to the *onProgress* event handler for the object sink.

Quick Check

Q: What are the two main types of event queries that you can perform from an *SWbem-Services* object?

A: The two main types of event queries that you can perform from an *SWbemServices* object are *ExecNotificationQuery* and *ExecNotificationQueryAsync*.

Q: What are the two parameters that must be supplied to *ExecNotificationQueryAsync*?

A: The two parameters that must be supplied to *ExecNotificationQueryAsync* are the name of an *objWbemSink* and the query.

The next parameter that can be specified is an *objWbemNamedValueSet* value. Although this is normally left blank, you can specify an object to represent context information that can be used by the provider that is servicing the request.

The last parameter is also optional, and it is an *SWbemNamedValueSet* object as well that is used to return information to the object sink to identify the source of the original call. This is used when you need to make multiple asynchronous calls that use the same sink. You can add this object by using the *Add* method. Once you add the object, you can obtain the source of the call by using the *Item* method.

Finally, you need to look at the return codes that come back once the *ExecNotificationQuery-Async* method has completed. Items that can be found in the *err* object are listed in Table 5-1.

Table 5-1   *ExecNotificationQueryAsync* Error Codes

Error	Number	Meaning
wbemErrAccessDenied	0x80041003	Current user is not authorized to view the result set.
wbemErrFailed	0x80041001	Unspecified error.
wbemErrInvalidParameter	0x80041008	Invalid parameter is specified.
wbemErrInvalidQuery	0x80041017	Query syntax is not valid.
wbemErrInvalidQueryType	0x80041018	Requested query language is not supported.
wbemErrOutOfMemory	0x80041006	Not enough memory to complete the operation.

In the script MonitorRegistryChangeEvents.vbs, I perform an asynchronous event-driven query by using the *ExecNotificationQueryAsync* method. I am monitoring a registry key for any changes by using the *RegistryKeyChangeEvent* class, which is supplied by the System Registry Provider and resides in the *root/default* namespace. Any change that occurs to the specified registry key generates an event. Because of the nature of the registry, I want these notifications to occur asynchronously, so I create a sink to store the events for a little while and use an asynchronous event query. Keep in mind that when you create a sink, you have to use the *Wscript* prefix in front of the *CreateObject* command.

To make the query easier to modify (without having to worry about single quotes, spacing, and helper words), I have included two functions that take the portions of the query and put them together for you. The *strEvent* variable holds the *Select* statement. You are choosing everything from the *RegistryKeyChangeEvent* class. You can modify this to examine a *Registry_TreeChangeEvent* or a *RegistryValueChangeEvent* as well. The *strHive* variable still monitors one of the major hives in the registry because *Hive* is the first parameter that needs to be supplied for these classes. The *strKeyPath* variable holds the path to a registry tree, key, or value—depending on which class you choose to use.

MonitorRegistryChangeEvents.vbs

```
strEvent = "SELECT * FROM RegistryKeyChangeEvent"
strHive = "HKEY_LOCAL_MACHINE"
strKeyPath = "SOFTWARE\Microsoft\Windows NT\CurrentVersion"

Set objwmiServices = GetObject("winmgmts:root/default")
Set objwmiSink = wscript.createObject("WbemScripting.SWbemSink", "SINK_")

objwmiServices.ExecNotificationQueryAsync objwmiSink, _
    funMakeStr(strEvent,strHive,StrKeyPath)
WScript.Echo "Monitoring for Registry Changes ..." & vbCrLf

While(true)
    WScript.Sleep 2000
Wend

Sub SINK_OnObjectReady(wmiObject, wmiAsyncContext)
    WScript.Echo "Registry Change occurred" & vbCrLf & _
                "----------------------------" & vbCrLf & _
                wmiObject.GetObjectText_()
End Sub

Function funMakeStr(strEvent,strHive,strKeyPath)
funMakeStr = strEvent & " Where Hive ="" & strHive & """"& _
    "And keyPath=" & funFixKeyPath(strKeyPath)
End Function

Function funFixKeyPath(strKeyPath)
funFixKeyPath = """" & replace(strKeyPath,"\","\\") & """"
End function
```

Quick Check

Q: When you use an *ExecNotificationQuery*, when does the script return?

A: When you use an *ExecNotificationQuery*, the script returns immediately.

Q: To use an *ExecNotificationQueryAsync* method, which object must be created to help with the query?

A: To use an *ExecNotificationQueryAsync* method, you must create an *objWbemSink* object.

Understanding Event Consumers

Event consumers are classes that already know how to respond to certain events that are triggered in response to particular activities. You can create an instance of one of these consumers and use the class to execute certain actions when the specified event occurs. When working with the standard event consumers, you must always put some common elements into place. These include the following:

- Create an instance of the consumer
- Create an event filter
- Create an event query
- Bind the filter to the consumer

Creating an Instance of the Consumer

The first step in working with a permanent event consumer is to create an instance of the consumer. You can do this using one of several methods. You can use a Managed Object Format (MOF) file, the WMI tools, or a script. Three ingredients are essential to creating an instance of the consumer:

- *Get*
- *SpawnInstance_ ()*
- *Put_*

Each consumer has its own peculiarities; in general, you will use code that looks like the following.

```
" create the active script consumer
set  objConsumerClass=objActiveScriptConsumer.get _ ("ActiveScriptEventConsumer")
set objconsumer=objconsumerclass.spawninstance_()
objconsumer.name="ToggleAlerter"
objconsumer.scriptfilename="c:\a\ToggleAlerterService.vbs"
objconsumer.scriptingengine="vbscript"
set consumerpath = objconsumer.put_
```

Creating an Event Filter

To create an event filter, you need to specify an event-driven query that is used to drive the subscription. This is the same type of query you used earlier with the notification query scripts. You specify the event system class you wish to monitor and the target class properties you are interested in tracking. Once you have defined the query, you use a *Get* statement to retrieve an "*__EventFilter*" you call *SpawnInstance_*, and finally you use a *Put_* statement to place the filter into the appropriate namespace. The following code illustrates this procedure.

```
"Create the event filter
eClass = "__instanceModificationEvent" "type of event to obtain
tClass = ""win32_service"" "wmi class to monitor
tName = ""Schedule"" "name property of target class
qQuery ="select * from " & eClass & " within 10 where targetInstance isa "_
    & tClass & " and targetinstance.name="
& tNameset objfilterclass=objActiveScriptConsumer.get("__EventFilter")
set objfilter=objfilterclass.spawninstance_()
objfilter.name="win32ServiceModification"
objfilter.querylanguage="wql"
```

```
objfilter.query=(qQuery)
set filterpath = objfilter.put_
```

Creating an Event Query

The event query you then create is a basic WMI query like the ones we have already examined. For more information on event queries, see Chapter 3.

Binding the Filter to the Consumer

Once you have created an instance of the desired consumer, crafted your event-driven query, and put your event filter into the appropriate WMI namespace, it is time to bind the filter to the consumer. As shown in Figure 5-1, you can use the WMI Event Registration tool to look at the event consumers that are installed on your computer. The WMI Event Registration tool is part of the WMI Administrative Tools, which can be found in the Tools folder on the accompanying CD.

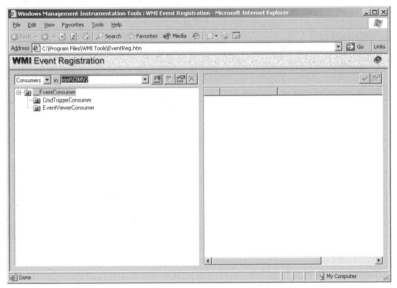

Figure 5-1   Using the event registration tool to view installed consumers

This might seem disappointingly simple after struggling through the two previous code samples. First, you get the _FilterToConsumerBinding_ system class. You assign the returned object to the *objBindingClass* variable. Next, you create a new instance of the *objBindingClass* by using the *SpawnInstance_* command. Then you wire up the connections by specifying the filter and the consumer. Once this is done, you use the *Put_* command to write the binding back to WMI, as shown in the following code:

```
"Do the binding
FTCB = "__filterToConsumerBinding"
set objbindingclass=objActiveScriptConsumer.get(FTCB)
set objbinding=objbindingclass.spawninstance_()
objbinding.filter=filterPath
objbinding.consumer=consumerpath
objbinding.put_
```

ActiveScriptEventConsumer

The *ActiveScriptEventConsumer* is used to execute a predefined script when an event is delivered to it. This consumer was first introduced in Microsoft Windows 2000, and it continues to be available in Windows Server 2003. The *ActiveScriptEventConsumer* class has a number of properties that can be specified. These properties are listed in Table 5-2. Two of the settings, the *Timeout* and *MaximumScripts* properties, can be applied to a running instance or can be applied as global values by specifying values of the *ScriptingStandardConsumerSetting* class.

Table 5-2   *ActiveScriptEventConsumer* **Properties**

Data Type	Property	Meaning
uint8	*CreatorSID*	Array that represents the secuirty identifier (SID) of the creator.
uint32	*KillTimeout*	Number of seconds the script is allowed to run. Default of 0 means no termination.
string	*MachineName*	Name of computer that receives the event.
uint32	*MaximumQueueSize*	Maximum queue in bytes.
string	*Name*	Key value. Unique ID for event consumer.
string	*ScriptFileName*	Name of the file from which the script is read.
string	*ScriptingEngine*	VBScript or Microsoft JScript. Cannot be a null value.
string	*ScriptText*	Text of the script. Must be a null value if *ScriptFileProperty* is not a null value.

The *ActiveScriptEventConsumer* class *CreatorSID* property is inherited from the *__EventConsumer* class, as is the *MachineName* property. The *ActiveScriptEventConsumer* class resides in the *root\subscription* namespace. If the text of the script is specified in the event consumer instance, the script has access to the event instance by using the script environment variable *TargetEvent*. When the script runs, it uses the localSystem account. As a security measure, only the local system administrator or a domain administrator is permitted to configure the scripting consumer. The access rights are not checked until run time.

After the consumer is configured, any user can trigger the event that causes the script to execute. If the script fails, error codes are returned. Scripts that use *MsgBox* will execute, but they will not display information on the screen because the script is not running under the Windows Script Host. In Windows 2000, the *ActiveScriptEventConsumer* is not compiled by default, and you must use Mofcomp.exe to compile the Scrcons.mof into a namespace. In

Microsoft Windows XP and Windows Server 2003, it is already compiled into the *root\ subscription* namespace. The Scrcons.mof file is located in the directory *%System-Root%*\System32\WBEM. The CreatePermanentEventRunScript.vbs script uses the *Active-ScriptEventConsumer*. We discussed the major concepts of this script earlier.

CreatePermanentEventRunScript.vbs

```
strcomputer = "mred" "name of target computer. Can not use "."
wmiNS = "\root\subscription"
eClass = "__instanceModificationEvent" "type of event to obtain
tClass = ""win32_service"" "wmi class to monitor
tName = ""Schedule"" "name property of target class
qQuery ="select * from " & eClass & " within 10 where targetInstance isa "_
    & tClass & " and  targetinstance.name=" & tName
set objActiveScriptConsumer=getobject("winmgmts:\\" & strcomputer & wmiNS)


"Create the event filter
set objfilterclass=objActiveScriptConsumer.get("__EventFilter")
set objfilter=objfilterclass.spawninstance_()
objfilter.name="win32ServiceModification"
objfilter.querylanguage="wql"
objfilter.query=(qQuery)
set filterpath = objfilter.put_


"Create the active script consumer
set  objConsumerClass=objActiveScriptConsumer.get("ActiveScriptEventConsumer")
set objconsumer=objconsumerclass.spawninstance_()
objconsumer.name="ToggleAlerter"
objconsumer.scriptfilename="c:\a\ToggleAlerterService.vbs"
objconsumer.scriptingengine="vbscript"
set consumerpath = objconsumer.put_


"Do the binding
FTCB = "__filterToConsumerBinding"
set objbindingclass=objActiveScriptConsumer.get(FTCB)
set objbinding=objbindingclass.spawninstance_()
objbinding.filter=filterPath
objbinding.consumer=consumerpath
objbinding.put_
```

Using *SMTPEventConsumer*

The *SMTPEventConsumer* can be used to send an e-mail message by using Simple Mail Transfer Protocol (SMTP) when an event is delivered to it. The *SMTPEventConsumer* is not compiled by default on a computer running Windows 2000. This means you need to use Mofcomp.exe to compile the file Smtpcons.mof into the namespace of your choosing. You might want to compile it into the *root\subscription* namespace because that is where it is compiled by default in Windows XP and Windows Server 2003. The file Smtpcons.mof is located in the directory *%SystemRoot%*\System32\WBEM. To compile the MOF file into the subscription namespace, you can use the following command:

```
Mofcomp -n:root\subscription smtpcons.mof
```

Keep in mind a few caveats when using the *SMTPEventConsumer*. The first one is most important: you must have an SMTP mail server accessible to the computer running the script because of the way the *SMTPEventConsumer* is implemented—it forwards the mail message to a mail server rather than installing its own server.

The second caveat is that you will not be able to send attachments with the *SMTPEvent-Consumer*. In addition, the mail message will need to be US-ASCII. Other than that, it is a great way to send e-mail alerts.

Understanding the New Event Consumers

LogFileEventConsumer

The *LogFileEventConsumer* is a standard event consumer that knows how to write to log files. That's right: this new class knows how to write customized strings to a text log file when an event is delivered to it. The strings are separated by an end-of-line sequence, such as a semicolon.

To use this class, you create an instance of the *LogFileEventConsumer* class, create an event filter, and then bind the filter to the consumer. You need to specify a file name to use for logging. The file need not exist (it is created automatically), but the path to the file must exist. The text that is written to the log file is defined in the *Text* property. This becomes a template for future log entries, and it is permissible to use parameters containing property names from the monitored class, for instance, "%freespace%" if you were tracking the *Win32_LogicalDisk* class.

NTEventLogEventConsumer

The *NTEventLogEventConsumer* class is used to write messages to the event log. It does this when it receives a message in response to the event filter bound to it. Because this is a standard event consumer, it follows the same pattern you have seen—that is, you first create an instance of the *NTEventLogEventConsumer* class by using the *SpawnInstance* method and putting the newly created instance of the class into the WMI namespace. Next, you create an instance of the event filter, and finally you bind the filter to the consumer. When you are creating a new instance of the class, you need to specify properties. The properties you use are listed in Table 5-3.

Table 5-3   *NTEventLogConsumer* Properties

Data Type	Property	Meaning
Uint16	Category	Event category. Not a null value.
Uint32	EventID	Event ID number. Not a null value.
Uint32	EventType	Type of event: *EventLog_Success*, *EventLog_Error_Type*, *EventLog_Warning_Type*, *EventLog_Information_Type*, *EventLog_Audit_Success*, *EventLog_Audit_Failure*

Table 5-3   *NTEventLogConsumer* Properties

Data Type	Property	Meaning
String Array	*InsertionStringTemplates*	Array of string templates used to write to the event log record.
String	*Name*	Name of the consumer. Key property.
String	*NameOfRawdataProperty*	Name of the event property containing data.
String	*NameOfUserSidProperty*	Name of the event property containing the SID.
Uint32	*NumberOfInsertionStrings*	Number of elements in the *InsertionStringTemplates*. Not a null value.
String	*SourceName*	Source name where the message is located. Not a null value.
String	*UNCServerName*	Name of the computer on which to log the event. If it is a null value, it is logged locally.

CommandLineEventConsumer

The *CommandLineEventConsumer* class is used to launch a process when it receives an event. The process is any executable that you want to launch. This can be a script, batch file, or EXE file. It is important to keep the process in a secure location that has an appropriate access control list (ACL) applied. The string used to specify the process to run can be a full path or a partial. If you specify a partial path, the current drive and directory are used, which can lead to unpredictable results. Two properties can be used to specify the executable: *ExecutablePath* and *CommandLineTemplate*. These two properties are not used together.

Working with Different Types of Events

The main barrier that most network administrators must face when working with eventing scripts is the sheer number of events that are available. There are four different kinds of events: class events, instance events, namespace events, and what I call eventing events (events that are related to events).

Class Events

There are three types of class events: the class creation event, the class deletion event, and the class modification event. The *__ClassCreationEvent* system class is used to represent an event that occurs when a class is created in a namespace. The *__ClassDeletionEvent* class represents an event that occurs in response to the deletion of a class in a namespace. The *__ClassModification-Event* system class is used to represent an event that occurs when a class is modified.

Instance Events

There are four types of instance events: the instance creation event, the instance operation event, the instance deletion event, and the instance modification event. When an instance of a class is created, you get an instance creation event. In the following script MonitorFor-ShareCreation.vbs, when a new share is created, it triggers an instance creation event and echoes out the name of the share, the path to the share, and the time the share was created.

MonitorForShareCreation.vbs

```
strComputer = "."
objTGT = ""win32_Share""
wmiNS = "\root\cimv2"

wmiQuery = "SELECT * FROM __InstanceCreationEvent WITHIN 10 WHERE " _
        & "TargetInstance ISA " & objTGT
Set objWMIService = GetObject("winmgmts:\\" & strComputer & wmiNS)
Set colItems = objWMIService.ExecNotificationQuery(wmiQuery)
Do
    Set objItem = colItems.NextEvent(-1)
    Wscript.Echo "A New Share was created at: " & Now & vbcrlf & _
    space(4) & "share name: " & objItem.TargetInstance.Name & vbcrlf & _
    space(4) & "share path: " & objItem.TargetInstance.Path
Loop
```

If you change the query from targeting the __*InstanceCreationEvent* class to monitoring __*InstanceDeletionEvent*, you get notification of shares that are being deleted, as shown in the MonitorForShareDeletion.vbs script that follows. This is the only change that is required—otherwise, the script works in the same manner and you are interested in the same properties in the *Win32_Share* class.

MonitorForShareDeletion.vbs

```
strComputer = "."
objTGT = ""win32_Share""
wmiNS = "\root\cimv2"

wmiQuery = "SELECT * FROM __InstanceDeletionEvent WITHIN 10 WHERE " _
        & "TargetInstance ISA " & objTGT
Set objWMIService = GetObject("winmgmts:\\" & strComputer & wmiNS)
Set colItems = objWMIService.ExecNotificationQuery(wmiQuery)
Do
    Set objItem = colItems.NextEvent(-1)
    Wscript.Echo "A Share was deleted at: " & Now & vbcrlf & _
    space(4) & "share name: " & objItem.TargetInstance.Name & vbcrlf & _
    space(4) & "share path: " & objItem.TargetInstance.Path
Loop
```

If you are concerned with changes to the shares on the server and not with the creation or deletion of shares, it would make sense to monitor for __*InstanceModificationEvent* events. Instead of selecting everything from the __*InstanceDeletionEvent* class, you can target your query onto the __*InstanceModificationEvent*. This system class informs you if something changes to a share on the server. If you add a description to a share, it triggers an event. If you change the number of users allowed to access the share, it triggers an event. If you delete the share, it triggers an __*InstanceDeletionEvent*.

Namespace Events

There are three types of namespace events: the namespace creation event, the namespace deletion event, and the namespace modification event. These events work in the same manner as do the instance events. By monitoring for namespace events, you can track the deployment of permanent event subscriptions as they make modifications to the namespace.

Eventing Events

There are four events that are related to event scripts: the consumer failed event, the event dropped event, the event queue overflow event, and the method invocation event. By monitoring eventing events, you can track the status of monitors.

Summary

In this chapter, we looked at the use of event-driven scripts. We examined the two ways you can write event-driven queries by using the *ExecNotificationQuery* and the *ExecNotificationQueryAsync* methods. We also discussed event consumers and the four types of events available through VBScript.

Quiz Yourself

Q: What is the difference between a class creation event and an instance creation event?

A: The difference between a class creation event and an instance creation event is that the instance creation event is generated when an individual item is created, whereas a class creation event is generated when a collection of items is created.

Q: When would you use *ExecNotificationQuery*?

A: You would use *ExecNotificationQuery* any time you wanted to subscribe to an event.

Q: Which three items must be created to use a permanent event subscription?

A: To use a permanent event subscription you must create an instance of the event consumer, an event filter, and a filter-to-consumer binder.

On Your Own

Lab 11 Creating a Video Change Notification Script

In this lab, you will create a script that provides notification when a change to the video settings on your workstation occurs.

1. Open the script WMITemplate.vbs, and save it as StudentLab11.vbs.

2. Turn off *On Error Resume Next.*

3. Declare a variable to hold the WMI class being monitored. Call it *objTGT.*

4. Above the *wmiQuery* line, assign the value of *objTGT* to be equal to *Win32_VideoController.* Make sure to embed double quotes as shown here:

    ```
    objTGT = ""Win32_VideoController""
    ```

5. Modify the *wmiQuery* so that it points to the *__InstanceModificationEvent* system class. For testing purposes, you will test within 10 seconds. The *TargetInstance* will be a *Win32_VideoController*, which you have assigned to *objTGT.* The modified query looks like the following:

    ```
    wmiQuery = "SELECT * FROM __InstanceModificationEvent WITHIN 10 WHERE " _
            & "TargetInstance ISA " & objTGT
    ```

6. Modify the *Set colItems* line so that you are doing an *ExecNotificationQuery* query instead of an *ExecQuery.*

7. Delete the *For Each Next* loop and everything inside it, including all the *Wscript.echo* commands. At this point nothing follows the *ExecNotificationQuery* line you just modified in step 6. Save your work, and then run the script. It should run without errors, but it will not do anything.

8. Add a *Do Loop* under the *ExecNotificationQuery.* On one line, type **Do**, insert a few blank lines under *Do*, and type **Loop**.

9. Under the *Do* command, set *objItem* to hold the next event that comes back. Your code will look like the following:

    ```
    Set objItem = colItems.NextEvent(-1)
    ```

10. Echo out a line that indicates the video settings were modified. Include a time stamp.

11. Echo out the *PreviousInstance.VideoModeDescription* property and the *TargetInstance.VideoModeDescription* property. This shows you what has changed. My code looks like the following:

     ```
     Wscript.Echo "Video Settings were Modified at: " & Now & vbcrlf & _
         space(4) & "Description: " & objItem.TargetInstance.Name & vbcrlf & _
         space(4) & "VideoModeDescription: "
     & objItem.TargetInstance.VideoModeDescription & vbcrlf & _
         Space(4) & "Previous Settings: " & objItem.PreviousInstance.VideoModeDescription
     ```

12. Save and run your script. Notice it does not appear to do anything. Change your video resolution and within a few seconds you should see something that looks like the following (depending on your video card and your screen resolution):

```
Video Settings were Modified at: 5/10/2005 11:37:40 PM
    Description: NVIDIA GeForce FX Go5200 32M/64M
    VideoModeDescription: 1280 x 1024 x 4294967296 colors
    Previous Settings: 1024 x 768 x 4294967296 colors
```

Lab 12 Expanding the Video Notification Script

In this lab, you will extend the script you created in Lab 11 to report on any modifications made to the video settings. You will do this by adding a subroutine that creates a dictionary to hold previous values of properties. Once an instance modification event is detected, you enter the subroutine and check for modifications.

1. Open and run the script Win32_VideoController.vbs. Note that there are more than 50 properties reported by this script. A change to any of these properties would cause an _InstanceModificationEvent_, yet the script in the previous lab checks for a change only in the _VideoModeDescription_ property. Close Win32_VideoController.vbs.

2. Open the script Lab12Starter.vbs and save it as StudentLab12.vbs.

3. Declare two variables to be used with the dictionary: _strProperty_ and _strPreProperty_, as shown here:

```
dim strProperty
dim strPreProperty
```

4. Create a dictionary object. Place the line that creates the dictionary under the _ExecNotificationQuery_ line. Assign the object to a variable called _objDictionary_. Make sure you declare _objDictionary_ under the other variables at the top of your script. The code to create the dictionary looks like the following:

```
Set objDictionary = CreateObject("scripting.dictionary")
```

5. Just above the _Loop_ command, add a command to enter the subroutine. This is simply the name of the subroutine. Call it _subGetModifiedProperty_, as shown here:

```
subGetModifiedProperty
```

6. Remove the two lines that print out the _VideoModeDescription_ associated with the _TargetInstance_ and the _PreviousInstance_. You can simply comment them out, as shown here:

```
" space(4) & "VideoModeDescription: "
& objItem.TargetInstance.VideoModeDescription & vbcrlf & _
"    Space(4) & "Previous Settings: " & objItem.PreviousInstance.VideoModeDescription
```

7. Remove the line continuation from the description line as shown here:

```
space(4) & "Description: " & objItem.TargetInstance.Name "& vbcrlf & _
```

8. At the bottom of your script, add the *Sub subGetModifiedProperty* command followed by an *End Sub* command on a separate line.

9. Under the *Sub subGetModifiedProperty* line, add a *For Each Next* structure that accesses the *Properties_* of the target instance. Add the name and value of each property to the dictionary. This will look like the following:

```
For Each strProperty In objItem.TargetInstance.properties_
objDictionary.add strProperty.name, strProperty.value
Next
```

10. Under the *Next* from the *For Each strProperty* command, evaluate the values from the previous instance against the values stored in the dictionary. If the values are not equal, echo out the changed properties. The code to do this is as follows:

```
For Each strPreProperty In objItem.previousInstance.properties_
    if objDictionary(strPreProperty.name) <> strPreProperty.value Then
    WScript.Echo " property modified: " & strPreProperty.name
    WScript.Echo vbtab & "Was: " & strPreProperty.value      & _
    " now: " & objDictionary(strPreProperty.name)
    End If
Next
```

11. Because you are continuing to monitor for events, you want to empty the dictionary so you can use it again on the next event. To do this, use the *RemoveAll* method as shown here:

```
objDictionary.removeAll
```

12. Save and run the script. Once again, it appears not to do anything. Change the color depth, and then you should see some information output. Change the color depth back to the original settings. Once again, you should see some output similar to the following:

```
Video Settings were Modified at: 5/11/2005 12:05:00 AM
    Description: NVIDIA GeForce FX Go5200 32M/64M
 property modified: CurrentBitsPerPixel
    Was: 32 now: 16
 property modified: CurrentNumberOfColors
    Was: 4294967296 now: 65536
 property modified: VideoModeDescription
    Was: 1024 x 768 x 4294967296 colors now: 1024 x 768 x 65536 colors
Video Settings were Modified at: 5/11/2005 12:05:21 AM
    Description: NVIDIA GeForce FX Go5200 32M/64M
 property modified: CurrentBitsPerPixel
    Was: 16 now: 32
 property modified: CurrentNumberOfColors
    Was: 65536 now: 4294967296
 property modified: VideoModeDescription
    Was: 1024 x 768 x 65536 colors now: 1024 x 768 x 4294967296 colors
```

Part III
Connect Server and Additional Privileges

Chapter 6

Using the *SWbemLocator* Methods

In Chapter 5, we covered a lot of material. We looked at the ways you can create scripts that respond to events and examined the different kinds of events, as well as the two main methods of performing event-driven queries. Along the way, we talked about permanent event consumers and discussed the main tasks involved in using them. In this chapter we look at the *SWbemLocator* methods used to connect into Windows Management Instrumentation (WMI). These methods give you more power and flexibility in scripting than using the simple WMI moniker does.

Before You Begin

To work through this chapter, you should be familiar with the following concepts:

- The basics of writing WMI queries

- The basic use of WMI classes, namespaces, and methods

- Use of basic Microsoft Visual Basic Scripting Edition (VBScript) commands and procedures

After you complete this chapter, you will be familiar with the following concepts:

- The use of the *SWbemLocator* object

- When to use the *SWbemLocator*

- Use of the *ConnectServer* method

- Specifying timeout values for the WMI connection

 Note All the scripts used in this chapter are located on the CD that accompanies this book in the \Scripts\Chapter06 folder.

Using the Locator Object

The *SWbemLocator* object offers a different way to make a connection into WMI. When you use the *SWbemLocator* object, the *SWbemServices* object returned is your connection into the specified namespace on either a local or a remote computer. Once you have made this connection, you can use any of the *SWbemServices* methods to accomplish the task at hand.

At first glance, it might seem that the *SWbemLocator* is rather lame—it has only one method: the *ConnectServer* method. It also has only one property: the *Security_* property. Do not allow this seeming lack of richness to fool you—this is the Swiss Army knife of WMI objects.

Using Alternate Credentials

One of the primary advantages of using the *SWbemLocator* object is the capability of specifying alternative credentials. The *ConnectServer* method of the *SWbemLocator* object is used to connect to the server that is specified as the first parameter. In the ConnectServer-Win32_NetworkProtocol.vbs script, the computer name is held in the *strComputer* variable, which is a remote computer named Acapulco. The computer specified has to be a remote computer if you are going to use alternate credentials. It can be any computer on the network that has WMI installed on it, including computers running Microsoft Windows 95 and Windows 98. The main consideration, of course, is that the class exists on the target computer. In the ConnectServerWin32_NetworkProtocol.vbs script, the variable *strUsr* holds the user name, and the variable *strPWD* contains the user's password. This is the security context used to connect to the *root\cimv2* namespace on the Acapulco server. The easiest way to specify these credentials is to use the *domain\username* form and to leave the authority parameter blank—the approach taken by the ConnectServerWin32_NetworkProtocol.vbs script.

ConnectServerWin32_NetworkProtocol.vbs

```
 strComputer = "acapulco" 'name of a remote computer
wmiNS = "\root\cimv2"
wmiClass = "win32_NetworkProtocol"
wmiWhere = " where name like '%TCP/IP%'"
wmiQuery = "Select * from " & wmiClass & wmiWhere
strUsr ="nwtraders\LondonAdmin"'Domain\Username
strPWD = "P@ssw0rd"'UserNames password

Set objLocator = CreateObject("WbemScripting.SWbemLocator")
Set objWMIService = objLocator.ConnectServer(strComputer, wmiNS, _
        strUsr, strPWD)
Set colItems = objWMIService.ExecQuery(wmiQuery)

For Each objItem in colItems
    With objItem
      msg = msg & "Caption: " & .Caption & vbcrlf
      msg = msg & "ConnectionlessService: " & .ConnectionlessService& vbcrlf
      msg = msg & "Description: " & .Description& vbcrlf
      msg = msg & "GuaranteesDelivery: " & .GuaranteesDelivery& vbcrlf
      msg = msg &  "GuaranteesSequencing: " & .GuaranteesSequencing& vbcrlf
```

```
        msg = msg &  "InstallDate: " & FunTime(.InstallDate)& vbcrlf
        msg = msg &  "MaximumAddressSize: " & .MaximumAddressSize& vbcrlf
        msg = msg &  "MaximumMessageSize: " & .MaximumMessageSize& vbcrlf
        msg = msg &  "MessageOriented: " & .MessageOriented& vbcrlf
        msg = msg &  "MinimumAddressSize: " & .MinimumAddressSize& vbcrlf
        msg = msg &  "Name: " & .Name& vbcrlf
        msg = msg &  "PseudoStreamOriented: " & .PseudoStreamOriented& vbcrlf
        msg = msg &  "Status: " & .Status& vbcrlf
        msg = msg &  "SupportsBroadcasting: " & .SupportsBroadcasting& vbcrlf
        msg = msg &  "SupportsConnectData: " & .SupportsConnectData& vbcrlf
        msg = msg &  "SupportsDisconnectData: " & .SupportsDisconnectData& vbcrlf
        msg = msg &  "SupportsEncryption: " & .SupportsEncryption& vbcrlf
        msg = msg &  "SupportsExpeditedData: " & .SupportsExpeditedData& vbcrlf
        msg = msg &  "SupportsFragmentation: " & .SupportsFragmentation& vbcrlf
        msg = msg &  "SupportsGracefulClosing: " & .SupportsGracefulClosing& vbcrlf
        msg = msg &  "SupportsGuaranteedBandwidth: " & .SupportsGuaranteedBandwidth& vbcrlf
        msg = msg &  "SupportsMulticasting: " & .SupportsMulticasting& vbcrlf
        msg = msg &  "SupportsQualityofService: " & .SupportsQualityofService& vbcrlf
    End With
Next
WScript.echo msg

Function FunTime(wmiTime)
 Dim objSWbemDateTime 'holds an swbemDateTime object. Used to translate Time
 Set objSWbemDateTime = CreateObject("WbemScripting.SWbemDateTime")
  objSWbemDateTime.Value= wmiTime
  FunTime = objSWbemDateTime.GetVarDate
End Function
```

Using *ConnectServer* in Different Ways

One reason the *ConnectServer* method is so flexible is the number of parameters that can be specified for it. The *ConnectServer* method connects to the namespace on a specific computer. Typically, this is either local or remote—and, of course, the target machine has to have WMI installed. The flexibility comes from all the different properties that can be used. If connecting locally, you will not be able to specify alternative credentials, so those parameters are padded out with commas. The other options are configurable for the context appropriate to the requisite situation. In the MSAcpi_ThermalZoneTemperature.vbs script, I use a cool class to tell about the temperature of my laptop. To use this class, you need to switch to the *root\wmi* namespace. You do this by using the *wmiNS* variable in the second position after the *ConnectServer* command.

MSAcpi_ThermalZoneTemperature.vbs

```
strComputer = "Mred"
wmiNS = "\root\wmi"
wmiQuery = "Select * from MSAcpi_ThermalZoneTemperature"

Set objLocator = CreateObject("WbemScripting.SWbemLocator")
Set objWMIService = objLocator.ConnectServer(strComputer, wmiNS)
Set colItems = objWMIService.ExecQuery(wmiQuery)
```

```
For Each objItem in colItems
With objItem
 wscript.echo "Active: " & .Active
 wscript.echo "ActiveTripPoint: " & join(.ActiveTripPoint, ",")
 wscript.echo "ActiveTripPointCount: " & .ActiveTripPointCount
 wscript.echo "CriticalTripPoint: " & .CriticalTripPoint
 wscript.echo "CurrentTemperature: " & .CurrentTemperature
 wscript.echo "InstanceName: " & .InstanceName
 wscript.echo "PassiveTripPoint: " & .PassiveTripPoint
 wscript.echo "Reserved: " & .Reserved
 wscript.echo "SamplingPeriod: " & .SamplingPeriod
 wscript.echo "ThermalConstant1: " & .ThermalConstant1
 wscript.echo "ThermalConstant2: " & .ThermalConstant2
 wscript.echo "ThermalStamp: " & .ThermalStamp
wscript.echo " "
End With
Next
```

Changing the Defaults

If you are going to use the *ConnectServer* method, it stands to reason you are going to be modifying the defaults. You do not have to specify the parameters for the *ConnectServer* method if you don't want to. You can use the default values as shown in the RunningNONautoServices-AndDescription.vbs script. You set *objLocator* to hold the *SWbemLocator* object that comes from the *CreateObject* command. Once you have the *SWbemLocator* object, you use the *ConnectServer* method. It is on this line that you specify the parameters. In the RunningNON-autoServicesAndDescription.vbs script, notice that no parameters are specified on the *Set objWMIService* line. I am using only the default values for each of the parameters available from the *ConnectServer* method. The default values for each of the parameters are listed in Table 6-1.

RunningNONautoServicesAndDescription.vbs

```
strProperty = "startMode, description"
strClass = "Win32_Service"
strState = "state = 'running' and startmode <> 'Auto'"

wmiQuery = "Select " & strProperty & " from " & strClass &_
            " where "& strState

Set objLocator = CreateObject("WbemScripting.SWbemLocator")
Set objWMIService = objLocator.ConnectServer
Set colItems = objWMIService.ExecQuery(wmiQuery)

For Each objItem in colItems
    With objItem
    Wscript.Echo "Name: " & .name & tab & "startMode: " & .startMode
    wscript.echo tab & .description
    End With
Next
```

Omitting Fields

Table 6-1 lists the parameters that can be specified for the *ConnectServer* method. The parameters must be specified in the order listed. If any are left out, you must pad out the connection string with commas—indicating the number of parameters not supplied.

Table 6-1   *ConnectServer* Parameters

Parameter	Default	Description
Server	"." for local machine.	Used for access to remote computer.
Namespace	*root\cimv2* in Microsoft Windows 2000, Windows XP, and Windows Server 2003.	The namespace in which to log on.
User	Current user.	The user name used with the connection; *domain\username* or universal principal name (UPN).
Password	Current security context.	The password used with the connection.
Locale	Current locale.	Localization code.
Authority	Operating system negotiates with Component Object Model (COM) to determine whether NTLM or Kerberos authentication is used.	Either Kerberos or NTLM. If domain is specified in *strUsername*, leave this blank.
SecurityFlags	0—the call returns only after the connection to the server is established.	Two values used: 0 and 128, which causes a timeout after 2 minutes.
objWbemNamedValueSet	Undefined.	An *SWbemNamedValueSet* object.

The first parameter that can be used is the name of the server to which you want to connect. If you do not specify a name for the computer, you will simply connect to the local machine. In the AssociatorsOfW32SystemDriver.vbs script, I am connecting to a remote computer named Acapulco. This is the only parameter specified for the *ConnectServer* method, after I create an instance of the *SWbemLocator* object. The query that is made is an associators type of query—in particular, I am interested in finding an association between the name of a particular system driver and the plug and play entity it is related to. The variable strDriver holds the name of a specific system driver on the Acapulco computer. The next script we will examine will produce a list of all the system drivers on the machine. From that listing you could easily find the name of the driver needed in the AssociatorsOfW32SystemDriver.vbs script.

I capture the name of the computer system in a variable called *strSYS* and print it out at the top of the output. The problem is that the computer name has a tendency to get buried in a mess of data. To preempt that eventuality, I decided to center the name of the computer system at the top of the output. I use two functions to accomplish this task. The first function gets the length of each service name, and the second function obtains the length of the computer name and compares it with the length of the longest description—arriving at the appropriate amount of space.

AssociatorsOfW32SystemDriver.vbs

```
strComputer = "acapulco"
strDriver = "'sysaudio'"
wmiQuery = "associators of {Win32_SystemDriver.Name="&strDriver&"}"_
    &" where assocClass=win32_SystemDriverPNPEntity role=Dependent"

Set objLocator = CreateObject("WbemScripting.SWbemLocator")
Set objWMIService = objLocator.ConnectServer(strComputer)
Set colItems = objWMIService.ExecQuery(wmiQuery)

For Each objItem in colItems
With objItem
    strSys = .systemName :funLen(.systemName)
    strMSG = strMSG & .service & vbcrlf :funLen(.service)
    strMSG = strMSG &  vbtab &.deviceID & vbcrlf:funLen(.deviceID)
    strMSG = strMSG & vbtab & .manufacturer & vbcrlf:funLen(.manufacturer)
    strMSG = strMSG & vbtab & .name & vbcrlf:funLen(.name)
End with
Next

WScript.echo Space(funCenter(intL)) & strSYS & vbcrlf & strMSG

'+++ Functions below +++
Function funLen(msg)
If Len(msg) > intL Then intL = Len(msg)
funLen = intL
End Function

Function funCenter(intL)'used to get space value used to center name
intL = (intL)/2 'gives 1/2 of longest line
intL = intL - (Len(strSYS)/2)'get 1/2 if sysName sub from intL
funCenter = intL
End function
```

To use the AssociatorsOfW32SystemDrivers.vbs script, you need to know the name of a running system driver. Use the RunningSystemDrivers.vbs script to obtain the actual name of the system driver you are interested in exploring. The RunningSystemDrivers.vbs script prints out a listing of each of the system drivers that are in a running state. It does this by using the *Win32_SystemDriver* class and printing out the *Name* and *Description* properties. To line up the description field on the right side of the printout, use a function that determines the length of the *Name* property and subtracts from a variable called *intD* that is fed to the space function to align the descriptions.

RunningSystemDrivers.vbs

```
strComputer = "."
vWhere = "state = 'running'"
wmiQuery = "Select name, description from win32_systemDriver where "& vWhere
```

```
Set objLocator = CreateObject("WbemScripting.SWbemLocator")
Set objWMIService = objLocator.ConnectServer(strComputer)
Set colItems = objWMIService.ExecQuery(wmiQuery)

For Each objItem in colItems
With objItem
intD = funTab(Len(.name))'obtain number of spaces required for alignment
   WScript.echo   .name & ": " & Space(intD) & .description
End with
Next

'#### tab output function below

Function funTab(funT)
Dim xfunT
xfunT = intL - funt
If xfunT<=0 Then 'catches a negative tab value
WScript.echo "******* intL Tab value should be: " & funT +1 'Tell you value for intL
funTab=1
else
funTab=xfunT
End if
End function
```

The namespace is the second parameter that can be specified. You can specify the name of the namespace that provides support for the class you want to use. If the class resides in the *root\cimv2* namespace, you can omit the namespace because this is the default in Windows 2000, Windows XP, and Windows Server 2003. If you are not working in the default namespace, you need to specify this value.

The next value you can specify is the user name. This is the name of the user whose credentials you want to use. It is best to specify this name in the *domain\username* format. If you leave this field blank, the script will use the current security context. It is important to note that you can specify alternative credentials only when you are making a remote connection. If you try to specify a different user name/password context with a local connection, the script will fail. If you are using Windows XP or Windows Server 2003, you can use the universal principal name (UPN) format for the user name.

After you specify the user name, the next field is the password. If you leave the password blank, you also need to leave the user name blank, and the connection will use the current security context. If you specify a user name, you also need to specify a password.

The field after the password is the locale settings. If you want to use the current locale, leave this field blank. If you need an alternative locale, you can specify it by using the Microsoft locale identifier for the desired language. For example, the code for U.S. English is MS_409. You can find code page identifiers on MSDN.

The authority field is used to specify a Kerberos principal name. A Kerberos principal name contains the word *Kerberos* followed by a colon and the name of the server to which you are connecting. In the W32DiskDriveUseKerberos.vbs script you can see this string contained in the variable *strAuth*. Because I am using Kerberos in the script, I can also use a UPN, as is shown in the *strUsr* variable. If you do not use a UPN, it is perfectly acceptable to use the *domain\username* form of supplying credentials.

W32DiskDriveUseKerberos.vbs

```
wmiNS = "\root\cimv2"
wmiQuery = "Select * from win32_DiskDrive"
strUsr ="londonadmin@nwtraders.msft"'Blank for current security. Domain\Username
strPWD = "P@ssw0rd"'Blank for current security.
strLocl = "MS_409" 'US English. Can leave blank for current language
strAuth = "kerberos:acapulco"'if specify domain in strUsr this must be blank
iFlag = "0" 'only two values allowed here: 0 (wait for connection) 128 (wait max two min)

Set objLocator = CreateObject("WbemScripting.SWbemLocator")
Set objWMIService = objLocator.ConnectServer(strComputer, wmiNS, _
    strUsr, strPWD, strLocl, strAuth, iFLag)
Set colItems = objWMIService.ExecQuery(wmiQuery)


For Each objItem in colItems
  wscript.echo "BytesPerSector: " & objItem.BytesPerSector
  wscript.echo "Capabilities: " & join(objItem.Capabilities)
  wscript.echo "Caption: " & objItem.Caption
  wscript.echo "Description: " & objItem.Description
  wscript.echo "DeviceID: " & objItem.DeviceID
  wscript.echo "Index: " & objItem.Index
  wscript.echo "InterfaceType: " & objItem.InterfaceType
  wscript.echo "Manufacturer: " & objItem.Manufacturer
  wscript.echo "MediaType: " & objItem.MediaType
  wscript.echo "Model: " & objItem.Model
  wscript.echo "Name: " & objItem.Name
  wscript.echo "Partitions: " & objItem.Partitions
  wscript.echo "PNPDeviceID: " & objItem.PNPDeviceID
  wscript.echo "SectorsPerTrack: " & objItem.SectorsPerTrack
  wscript.echo "Signature: " & objItem.Signature
  wscript.echo "Size: " & objItem.Size
  wscript.echo "Status: " & objItem.Status
  wscript.echo "SystemName: " & objItem.SystemName
  wscript.echo "TotalCylinders: " & objItem.TotalCylinders
  wscript.echo "TotalHeads: " & objItem.TotalHeads
  wscript.echo "TotalSectors: " & objItem.TotalSectors
  wscript.echo "TotalTracks: " & objItem.TotalTracks
  wscript.echo "TracksPerCylinder: " & objItem.TracksPerCylinder
  wscript.echo " "
Next
```

In addition, you can simply leave the user name blank, as well as the password, to use the current security context. If this field contains anything other than a Kerberos principal name, NT LAN Manager (NTLM) authentication will be used and this field should contain an NTLM domain name. The easiest way to use this field is to specify the domain name when you specify the user name and to leave this field blank. As shown in Figure 6-1, the RoutingTableNTLM.vbs script retrieves the routing table from a remote computer, which is the same as doing a route print locally on the machine.

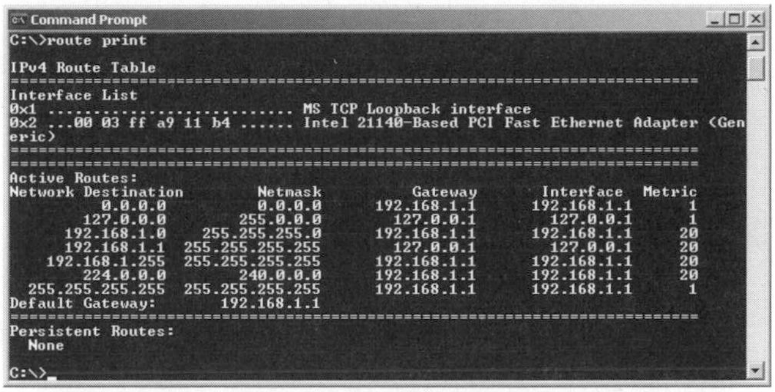

Figure 6-1   Routing table showing all the routes currently defined on the machine

In the RoutingTableNTLM.vbs script, I specify the use of NTLM authentication by using the phrase *NTLMDomain:domainname*. The domain name used is the domain you wish to use to do the authentication. To use the RoutingTableNTLM.vbs script, you must have a second computer in your domain. You must change the value of *strComputer* to be equal to that of the remote machine. If you do not have communication with the remote computer, the script will fail. WMI does not allow you to specify alternate credentials for a local connection, so it must be a remote physical machine.

RoutingTableNTLM.vbs

```
Const intMin = 3600'converts seconds to minutes
strComputer = "acapulco" 'A remote computer
wmiNS = "\root\cimv2"
wmiQuery = "Select * from win32_IP4RouteTable"
strUsr ="LondonAdmin"'Blank for current security. Domain\Username
strPWD = "P@ssw0rd"'Blank for current security.
strLocl = "MS_409" 'US English. Can leave blank for current language
strAuth = "NTLMDomain:nwtraders"'if specify domain in strUsr this must be blank
iFlag = "0" 'only two values allowed here: 0 (wait for connection) 128 (wait max two min)

Set objLocator = CreateObject("WbemScripting.SWbemLocator")
Set objWMIService = objLocator.ConnectServer(strComputer, wmiNS, _
    strUsr, strPWD, strLocl, strAuth, iFLag)
Set colItems = objWMIService.ExecQuery(wmiQuery)

For Each objItem in colItems
    WScript.Echo "Age in Minutes: " & int(objItem.Age/intMin)
    WScript.Echo "Caption: " & objItem.Caption
    WScript.Echo "Description: " & objItem.Description
    WScript.Echo "Destination: " & objItem.Destination
    WScript.Echo "InterfaceIndex: " & objItem.InterfaceIndex
    WScript.Echo "Mask: " & objItem.Mask
    WScript.Echo "Metric1: " & objItem.Metric1
    WScript.Echo "Metric2: " & objItem.Metric2
    WScript.Echo "Metric3: " & objItem.Metric3
    WScript.Echo "Metric4: " & objItem.Metric4
    WScript.Echo "Metric5: " & objItem.Metric5
    WScript.Echo "Name: " & objItem.Name
    WScript.Echo "NextHop: " & objItem.NextHop
    WScript.Echo "Protocol: " & objItem.Protocol
```

```
        WScript.Echo "Type: " & objItem.Type
        WScript.Echo

Next
```

Following the domain name field, you have the option of specifying a security flag. If you specify a value of 0 for this parameter, the call to *ConnectServer* will return only after the connection has been established. This can result in the call hanging indefinitely if the connection is not established. The only other value for this field is 128 (0x80). When you use this parameter, the call will wait two minutes before timing out. In the ProgramGroups.vbs script, I leave the authentication field blank because I am not assigning a value to the *strAuth* variable. I assign the value 128 to the *iFlag* variable. This causes the script to time out within two minutes of attempting a connection to a remote computer. The timeout value of two minutes does not mean the script will time out in two minutes. It means the connection attempt will timeout in two minutes if the remote computer is unavailable. In the ProgramGroups.vbs script below, the script has to do a lot of work to gather the available program groups installed on the machine. It will take four or five minutes depending on the speed of the computer, and the amount of information installed on the machine.

ProgramGroups.vbs

```
strComputer = "."
wmiNS = "\root\cimv2"
wmiQuery = "Select * from Win32_ProgramGroup"
strUsr =""'Blank for current security. Domain\Username
strPWD = ""'Blank for current security.
strLocl = "MS_409" 'U.S. English. Can leave blank for current language
strAuth = ""'if specify domain in strUsr, this must be blank
iFlag = "128" 'only two values allowed here: 0 (wait for connection), 128 (wait max two min)

Set objdictionary = CreateObject("scripting.dictionary")
Set objLocator = CreateObject("WbemScripting.SWbemLocator")
Set objWMIService = objLocator.ConnectServer(strComputer, wmiNS, _
    strUsr, strPWD, strLocl, strAuth, iFLag)
Set colItems = objWMIService.ExecQuery(wmiQuery)

For Each objItem in colItems
    If objdictionary.Exists(objItem.username) Then
    strGroup = strGroup & objItem.GroupName & vbcrlf & vbtab
    Else
    objDictionary.add objItem.UserName, strgroup
    strgroup = ""
    End if
Next

colItem = objDictionary.Items
colKeys = objDictionary.Keys
For i = 0 To objDictionary.Count -1
 Wscript.Echo "USER: " & colKeys(i) & vbcrlf &  vbtab & colItem(i)
next
```

The last property that you can specify is the *objWbemNamedValue* set, which is normally left blank. This field can contain an *SWbemNamedValueSet* object that can represent the context information to be used by the provider servicing the request. This information is dependent upon the provider.

When you attempt to make a connection into WMI, the connection could possibly result in an error. These errors are listed in Table 6-2.

Table 6-2   Error Messages

Error	Number	Meaning
wbemErrAccessDenied	0x80041003	The current or specified user name and password are not valid or authorized to make the connection.
wbemErrFailed	0x80041001	Unspecified error.
wbemErrInvalidNamespace	0x8004100E	The specified namespace does not exist on the server.
wbemErrInvalidParameter	0x80041008	An invalid parameter was specified, or the namespace could not be parsed.
wbemErrOutOfMemory	0x80041006	There is not enough memory to complete the operation.
wbemErrTransportFailure	0x80041015	A networking error occurred, preventing normal operation.

Error 0x80070005 is a COM access-denied error. When you make the connection into WMI on a computer running Windows 95 from a Windows NT-type of system, you need to pay attention to the credentials that are supplied. If the local system is supplying the user name and the password of a domain of which the machine is not a member, synchronous queries will take longer to process. If you supply the credentials in the connection, the logon will fail with an error indicating that the remote procedure call (RPC) server is unavailable. Whenever you see the RPC server unavailable error, you have failed to make the connection into WMI. If you are making a connection between different domains, you must supply both the domain name and the user name because pass-through authentication does not work.

Summary

In this chapter, we discussed using the *SWbemLocator* object. You saw that you can use the *ConnectServer* method from the *SWbemLocator* object to specify alternate parameters when making a connection into WMI. This includes specifying domain, name, and password for remote connections. It also enables you to connect to different WMI namespaces and to set a timeout value for the connection. In addition to these parameters, you can specify locale settings.

Quiz Yourself

Q: What is the default WMI namespace used by the *ConnectServer* method?

A: The default WMI namespace used by the *ConnectServer* method depends on the operating system because it uses the system defaults. On a server running Windows Server 2003, for example, the default WMI namespace is *root\cimv2*.

Q: To control the amount of time a script will spend waiting on a connection, which parameter can you specify?

A: The only parameter you can use to control the connection timeout value is the *iSecurity* flag.

Q: What are the two possible values you can specify for the *iSecurity* flag?

A: The two values you can specify for the *iSecurity* flag parameter are 0 and 128–0 means to wait forever, and 128 will cause a timeout after waiting two minutes.

On Your Own

Lab 13 Using the *ConnectServer* Method Locally

In this lab, you will use the *ConnectServer* method to develop a script that runs locally. As an extra bonus, the script you develop here will become a *ConnectServer* template that you can use to develop other scripts that need to use the *ConnectServer* method of the *SWbemLocator* object. You will make those changes in the next lab.

1. Open the wmiTemplate.vbs script, and save it as StudentLab13.vbs.

2. Turn off *On Error Resume Next*.

3. Declare variables to hold each of the seven parameters used for the *ConnectServer* method. Because you already have two variables you can use (*strComputer* and *wmiNS*), you need to add only five new variables: *strUsr*, *strPWD*, *strLocl*, *strAuth*, and *iFlag*. Place these variables under the *wmiNS* variable in the header section of your script.

4. Under the *wmiNS* = "\root\cimv2" line, add each of your new variables and assign them a value of "". The only exception to this is the *iFlag* variable, which does not permit a null value. For the *iFlag* variable, specify a value of 0. Your code will look like the following:

```
strUsr =""
strPWD = ""
strLocl = ""
strAuth = ""
iFlag = "0"
```

5. Because you will use this as a template in the future, add some comments describing the use of each parameter. Review this chapter if you need some hints. Once completed, your code might look something like the following:

```
strUsr =""'Blank for current security. Domain\Username
strPWD = ""'Blank for current security.
strLocl = "" 'MS_409 is U.S. English. Can leave blank for current language
strAuth = ""'if specify domain in strUsr, this must be blank
iFlag = "0"
'only two values allowed here: 0 (wait for connection), 128 (wait max two min)
```

6. Save your work. *Do not run this script*—you will get errors at this point.

7. Add code to create an *SWbemLocator* object. Place this line of code just above the *Set objWMIService* line. Assign it to a variable called *objLocator*. The *SWbemLocator* object has a program ID of *WbemScripting*. Your code to do this will look like the following:

```
Set objLocator = CreateObject("WbemScripting.SWbemLocator")
```

8. Declare the *objLocator* variable.

9. The *Set objWMIService* line of code is used to obtain a connection into WMI. You do not want to use the moniker here; rather, you are going to use the *ConnectServer* method. Use the variable and avoid some typing. Keep the *Set objWMIService* = part, and delete everything to the end of the line.

10. Use the *objLocator* object you created in step 7, and then use the *ConnectServer* method. Specify each of the seven parameters for this method. When done, your code will look like the following:

```
Set objWMIService = objLocator.ConnectServer(strComputer, wmiNS, _
strUsr, strPWD, strLocl, strAuth, iFlag)
```

11. Inside the *For Each Next* loop, comment out all the *Wscript.Echo* statements.

12. Add the last part of the WMI class name to the WMI query. You are going to look at *Win32_CurrentTime*, so the query will look like the following when you are done:

```
wmiQuery = "Select * from win32_currentTime"
```

13. Look up *Win32_CurrentTime* in the Platform SDK. Identify the properties that tell you the following: day, time, hour, minute, month, and year. Add them to the *Wscript.Echo* section of your script. The *Wscript.Echo* section will look like the following when you are done:

```
Wscript.Echo ": " & objItem.Day
    Wscript.Echo ": " & objItem.DayOfWeek
    Wscript.Echo ": " & objItem.Hour
    Wscript.Echo ": " & objItem.Minute
    Wscript.Echo ": " & objItem.Month
    Wscript.Echo ": " & objItem.Year
```

14. Save and run the script. You might want to modify the output so it is more readable. After a little bit of cleanup my script looks like the following:

```
Wscript.Echo objItem.Day & "/" & objItem.Month & "/"&objItem.Year _
    & " " & objItem.Hour & ":" & objItem.Minute
        Wscript.Echo "Day of the week is : " & objItem.DayOfWeek
```

15. Save the script.

Lab 14 Using Alternate Credentials in a Script

In this lab, you will write a script that uses alternate credentials to run against a remote machine. You must have either a second computer or a virtual machine you can communicate with to specify alternate credentials using the *ConnectServer* method. If you try to run this script against your local machine, it will fail. In the process of writing this script, you will develop a *ConnectServer* template script.

1. Open the SolutionLab13.vbs script, and save it as StudentLab14a.vbs.

2. Turn off *On Error Resume Next*.

3. On the *wmiQuery* line, delete the *CurrentTime* portion of the WMI class name. Ensure you do not delete the trailing quote. The line will look like the following:

```
"Select * from win32_"
```

4. Remove the *Wscript.Echo* section. Replace it with a couple of *Wscript.Echo* commands that echo out *objItem* as shown in the following code:

```
Wscript.Echo "" & objItem.
    WScript.echo "" & objItem.
```

5. Save your work.

6. Change the *wmiQuery* so it points to *Win32_LogicalDisk*. It will look like the following:

```
wmiQuery = "Select * from win32_logicalDisk"
```

7. Add two property names to the *Wscript.Echo* statements: *name* and *freespace*. The two commands will look like the following:

```
Wscript.Echo "" & objItem.name
    WScript.echo "" & objItem.freespace
```

8. Run the script.

9. So far, so good. Now tighten up the code a little more. Begin by using *With* and *End With*. To do so, you can use a lesser known feature of VBScript, the colon separator. This will give you real tight code in the worker section of the script. The colon acts like an end-of-line separator. You will use it on the *For Each* line. The modification looks like the following:

```
For Each objItem in colItems:with objitem
```

10. Using the *With* command enables you to erase the repetition of the *objItem* identifier in each of the output phrases. When working with large classes, this can save lots of typing. The revised *Wscript.Echo* statements now look like the following:

```
Wscript.Echo ": " & .name
    WScript.echo ": " &  .freespace
```

11. Conclude the *With* section by using *End With*. Place it before the final *Next* statement and use a colon to separate the two. The code looks like the following:

```
end with:Next
```

12. Run your script. You should get a listing of all the drives on your system and the associated free space.

13. To complete the transition to a template, erase the class name and the properties you added in steps 6 and 7. These were for testing. The completed template script will now look like the following:

```
Option Explicit
'On Error Resume Next
dim strComputer
dim wmiNS
dim wmiQuery
dim objWMIService
Dim objLocator
dim colItems
dim objItem
Dim strUsr, strPWD, strLocl, strAuth, iFlag 'connect server parameters
strComputer = "."
wmiNS = "\root\cimv2"
wmiQuery = "Select * from win32_"
strUsr =""'Blank for current security. Domain\Username
strPWD = ""'Blank for current security.
strLocl = "MS_409" 'U.S. English. Can leave blank for current language
strAuth = ""'if specify domain in strUsr, this must be blank
iFlag = "0"
'only two values allowed here: 0 (wait for connection), 128 (wait max two min)

Set objLocator = CreateObject("WbemScripting.SWbemLocator")
Set objWMIService = objLocator.ConnectServer(strComputer, wmiNS, _
    strUsr, strPWD, strLocl, strAuth, iFlag)
Set colItems = objWMIService.ExecQuery(wmiQuery)

For Each objItem in colItems:With objitem
    'Wscript.Echo ": " & .
    'WScript.echo ": " & .
end with:Next
```

14. Of course, the template script will not run because you have removed the class name and all associated properties. Save this with a name indicating that it is a *ConnectServer* template script.

Chapter 7

Requesting Additional Privileges for WMI

In Chapter 6, we looked at using the locator object to make a remote connection into Windows Management Instrumentation (WMI). We examined how the *ConnectServer* method enables us to specify alternative credentials when connecting remotely. This gives us the advantage of being able to run scripts with the fewest elevated privileges. To continue looking at the privileges required to work with WMI, in this chapter we examine the privilege structure.

Before You Begin

To work through this chapter, you should be familiar with the following concepts:

- The basics of writing WMI queries

- The use of the *ConnectServer* method

- The use of the moniker

After you complete this chapter, you will be familiar with the following concepts:

- The concept of least privilege in WMI

- Determining the privileges required for an operation

- The ways of specifying additional privileges

> **Note** All the scripts used in this chapter are located on the CD that accompanies this book in the \Scripts\Chapter07 folder.

Understanding Privileges

Privileged operations are those that require the specification of special access. The ability to elevate privileges and perform administrative operations is one of the changes made from earlier versions of the software. If I want to write a script that shuts down the server, I have to specify the *Shutdown* privilege. But what exactly does this mean? For one thing, it means a special privilege to shut down the server exists. Privileges are different from rights or access permissions; when you have specific privileges you are allowed to perform specific privileged operations. Users gain many privileges through group membership, but some privileges are specified individually.

The important thing to know about privileges is that unless you have the privilege you cannot use the privileged operation. For example, this means that I cannot specify a privilege in a script unless the user running the script already has the privilege. If the user has the privilege, why do we need to specify the privilege in the script? The idea is to operate with the least amount of privilege—we specify only the privileges the script needs to run.

Privileges give users the ability to do certain actions. For instance, a user might have the privilege to shut down the system, load a driver, or set the system time, each of which is a separate privilege.

Let's look at the concept of working with least privilege. If you visit a large city on vacation or for work, you will no doubt carry your wallet—which is loaded with privileges. Credit cards, identification papers, and cash are among the various privileges commonly found in a wallet. These privileges give you the ability to perform privileged operations—purchase items, drive vehicles, or gain entrance into buildings. If you are like most people, when you leave a hotel room, you lock up most of your privileges in the hotel safe and carry with you only the privileges you need to perform a few specific operations. For example, you might want to go out to eat, so you carry a credit card, identification, and your hotel room key. These are the least privileges you can carry to perform the intended operation; all the other privileges are safely locked up. Notice that you cannot carry privileges you do not possess. So, if you do not have a credit card, you cannot carry one. In a similar sense, if you do not possess the *Shutdown* privilege, you cannot specify it in your script.

The shift in the privilege structure in WMI occurs for the same reason you might leave items locked up in a hotel safe—to safeguard them. If a script that has the ability to perform elevated operations is compromised, it could have bad consequences. If a script that has permission only to read information from specific namespaces is compromised, the bad effect can be minimized. The network administrator using WMI to work on the network must understand which privileges are required to perform specific operations and how to invoke those privileges when required.

> Quick Check
>
> **Q: What is an example of a privileged operation?**
>
> A: One privileged operation is the *Shutdown* privilege.
>
> **Q: Why were some privileges removed from a basic running WMI query?**
>
> A: Some privileges were removed from basic running WMI scripts as a security measure. To perform certain privileged operations, the script writer must specifically request the privilege prior to using it.

Obtaining a Collection of Privileges

When you use the *Privilege* property on a WMI security object, you get back an object that represents a collection of privileges. This object is called an *SWbemPrivilegeSet*. You need access to the privilege set object so that you can work with privileges. You can obtain this collection at many different levels in a script. The following objects can receive privilege assignments:

- *SWbemServices*
- *SWbemObject*
- *SWbemObjectSet*
- *SWbemObjectPath*
- *SWbemLocator*

In each of these instances, you can add a privilege object by modifying the *Privileges* property of the *SWbemSecurity* object. The security object is created when you access the *Security_* property on any of the preceding objects. In the PrivilegesAtSWbemService.vbs script, I create an *SWbemPrivilegeSet* object on the *SWbemServices* object by using the *Privileges* command. This is done at the security object that is created by using the *Security_* command.

PrivilegesAtSWbemService.vbs
```
strComputer = "."
wmiNS = "\root\cimv2"
Set objWMIService = GetObject("winmgmts:\\" & strComputer & wmiNS)
set objWMISecurity = objWMIService.Security_.privileges
```

When you create a privilege object by using the WMI service object that comes back from using the moniker, you use the *Set* command to hold the object that is returned. Next, you assign a variable, and finally you specify the *Privilege* property on the security object of the WMI service object. It gets a little complicated because three different objects are at work here on a single line of code: an *SWbemService* object, an *SWbemSecurity* object, and an *SWbemPrivilegeSet* object. This is illustrated in the PrivilegesAtSWbemLocator.vbs script.

PrivilegesAtSWbemLocator.vbs

```
strComputer = "."
wmiNS = "\root\cimv2"
strUsr =""'Blank for current security. Domain\Username
strPWD = ""'Blank for current security.
strLocl = "MS_409" 'U.S. English. Can leave blank for current language
strAuth = ""'if specify domain in strUsr, this must be blank
iFlag = "0" 'only two values allowed here: 0 (wait for connection), 128 (wait max two min)

Set objLocator = CreateObject("WbemScripting.SWbemLocator")
Set objWMIService = objLocator.ConnectServer(strComputer, wmiNS, _
    strUsr, strPWD, strLocl, strAuth, iFlag)
Set objWMISecurity = objWMIService.Security_.privileges
```

The actual code used to create a security object for the locator object is exactly the same as the code used to create a security object for the moniker. You use the variable that contains the *SWbemLocator* object, and then you use *Security_* to create a security object. You add the *Privileges* property to the security object, and, voila, you have a privilege object.

Because it is a collection, it has the *Count* property and several methods. An *SWbemPrivilegeSet* object is a set of privilege override requests for a specific object. When an application programming interface (API) call is made using this object, the privilege set is attempted. Obtaining the privileges for any WMI object does not identify the privilege settings that are made on the initial connection into WMI or the privileges in effect when an object is delivered to a sink.

Representing a Single Privilege

SWbemPrivilege is an object that represents a single privilege. It has several properties. You are able to use these properties only after you have gotten the actual privilege object. To get a single privilege, you can retrieve the collection of privileges and iterate through it. This is what I do in the ListAllSWbemPrivileges.vbs script. I use the *Privileges* command at the security object to retrieve a collection of privileges. Once I have this collection I use *For Each Next* to walk through the collection. *ObjItem* is used to represent a single privilege, and it is here I can examine the properties of the privilege object. These properties are as follows:

- *DisplayName*
- *Identifier*
- *IsEnabled*
- *Name*

ListAllSWbemPrivileges.vbs

```
strComputer = "."
wmiNS = "\root\cimv2"
Set objWMIService = GetObject("winmgmts:\\" & strComputer & wmiNS)
set objWMISecurity = objWMIService.Security_.privileges 'creates swbemPrivilegeSet
For i = 1 To 27
objWMISecurity.add(i)
```

```
Next

WScript.echo "How Many Special Privileges? " & objWMISecurity.count

For Each objItem In objWMISecurity:With objItem
wscript.echo .identifier & vbtab & .name & vbtab & .displayname _
             & vbtab & .isenabled
end with:next
```

The *Name* property is a string that is used to uniquely identify a particular privilege. You can use this property when you need to refer to a specific privilege. This privilege controls whether a user can execute a particular method. If you need to read from the security event log, you need to specify the security privilege. The *Privilege* property itself is read-only.

Quick Check

Q: For what reason are privilege strings added to a script?

A: Privilege strings are added to a script to allow the script to execute special operations such as reading from the security log or loading a driver.

Q: Name one easy way to retrieve a single privilege property in a script.

A: One easy way to retrieve a single privilege property in a script is to retrieve the entire privilege collection and iterate through it.

Adding Additional Privileges

There are two ways to add additional privileges to a script. You can use the *Add* method or the *AddAsString* method. In most cases, which method you use is a matter of personal preference. In some instances, it might make more sense to use one method rather than the other, depending on where you actually want to specify the privilege. In this section, we examine using the *Add* method and the *AddAsString* method to provide additional privileges.

Adding a Privilege with *Add*

The *Add* method is used to add an *SWbemPrivilege* object to the collection. To use the *SWbem-Privilege* object to add objects, you need to use the *WbemPrivilegeEnum* constants. The software development kit (SDK) has a list of the *WbemPrivilegeEnum* constants, but they are not extremely useful in developing a Microsoft Visual Basic Scripting Edition (VBScript) script because they are not available to a VBScript even though they are defined in the WMI scripting type library, Wbemdisp.tlb. The listing of *WbemPrivilegeEnum* constants can be used directly with the *Add* method, or you can define your own constants and then use the numerical value of the constant later in the script. The BackupAppLog.vbs script illustrates this technique.

BackupAppLog.vbs

```
strComputer = "."
wmiNS = "\root\cimv2"
Const backup = 16
wmiQuery = "select name from Win32_NTEventlogFile where Name like "
strEventLog = "'%AppEvent.Evt'"
Set objWMIService = GetObject("winmgmts:\\" & strComputer & wmiNS)
Set colItems = objWMIService.execQuery(wmiQuery & strEventLog)
set objWMISecurity = objWMIService.Security_.privileges
objWMISecurity.add(backup)
subPrivileges

For Each objItem In colitems
errRTN = objItem.BackupEventLog("c:\fso\appLog.evt")
subError
next

Sub subPrivileges
WScript.echo objWMISecurity.count & " privilege exists"
For Each objItem In objWMISecurity:With objItem
wscript.echo .identifier & vbtab & .name & vbtab & .displayname _
           & vbtab & "is it enabled? " & .isenabled
end with:Next
End Sub

Sub subError
Select Case errRTN
Case 0
    wscript.echo"success!"
Case 8
    wscript.echo"Privilege missing"
Case 21
    wscript.echo"Invalid parameter"
Case 183
    wscript.echo"Archive file name already exists"
Case Else
    wscript.echo"unknown error occurred"
End Select
End sub
```

Adding a Privilege as a String

The *AddAsString* method requires you to use the privilege string. Privilege strings all begin with the prefix *se* and end with the modifier *privilege*. You cannot use a *WbemPrivilegeEnum* constant, nor can you use the numerical value of the constant directly when calling *AddAsString*. Use of *AddAsString* is illustrated in the ReadSecurityEventLog.vbs script. In this script, I make a connection into WMI by using the moniker. I define a constant called *Enable* that I set equal to *true* to make the code a little easier to read, though this certainly is not a requirement for using the *AddAsString* method. Once I have the connection into WMI, I use the *Security_.privileges.addAsString* method to add the *SeSecurityPrivilege* so I can read from the security event log. I have a variable called *strEventCode* set equal to a particular event ID–529. Event ID 529 is generated in response to a logon failure. Once the query is submitted, I use

For Each Next to walk through the collection and print out the time the event occurred and the message associated with the event.

ReadSecurityEventLog.vbs

```
strComputer = "."
strEventCode = "'529'"
wmiNS = "\root\cimv2"
wmiQuery = "SELECT * FROM Win32_NTLogEvent WHERE Logfile = 'security'"_
    & "AND EventCode = " & strEventCode
Const Enable = "true" 'true will turn on the privilege, FALSE turns OFF
Set objWMIService = GetObject("winmgmts:\\" & strComputer & wmiNS)
objWMIService.security_.Privileges.addASstring _
    "seSecurityPrivilege", Enable
Set colItems = objWMIService.ExecQuery(wmiQuery)

For Each objItem in colItems
    Wscript.Echo ": " & objItem.TimeGenerated
    Wscript.Echo ": " & objItem.message
Next
```

Using the *Item* Method

The *Item* method is used to access a specific privilege. To use the *Item* method you must specifically identify the privilege that you want to query. In the UseItem.vbs script I want to see if the script has the *Backup* privilege. To do this I specify *objWMISecurity.item(backup)*. *Backup* is a constant I set equal to 16, which is the value of the *WbemPrivilegeBackup* privilege. The UseItem.vbs script obtains a privilege object by using *objWMIService.security_.privileges*. Once I have the privilege object, I can work with it. In this script I verify the existence of the privilege—if the privilege exists, the *err* object will contain a 0 when the *Item* method is used. If the privilege does not exist, the *err* object will contain -2147217406, which translates into 80041002 when you send it into the *hex* function.

UseItem.vbs

```
Const backup=16
strComputer = "."
wmiNS = "\root\cimv2"
wmiQuery = "Select * from win32_Win32_NTEventlogFile"
Set objWMIService = GetObject("winmgmts:\\" & strComputer & wmiNS)
Set colItems = objWMIService.ExecQuery(wmiQuery)
Set objWMISecurity = objWMIService.security_.privileges
'objWMISecurity.add(backup)
objWMISecurity.item(backup)

WScript.echo hex(Err.Number)
```

Using the *DeleteAll* Method

The *DeleteAll* method is used to delete all the privileges that are associated with the current WMI session. To use the *DeleteAll* method you need to specify only the variable containing the security object by using the *DeleteAll* command. No special return code comes back from deleting all the privileges, so it is not necessary to capture a return code when calling *DeleteAll*. If an error occurs while you are deleting the privileges, it will appear on the standard error object.

In the script DeleteAllSWbemPrivileges.vbs I first add all the security privileges by using the *Add* method. I use a *For Next* loop to cycle through the 27 numbers representing all the privileges; in the middle of the loop I simply call the *Add* method. Once I have added all 27 privileges, I go into a subroutine that uses the *Count* method to tell me how many privileges are actually held. I print out a friendly message, allow the script to rest a little by using the *Sleep* command, and then call the *DeleteAll* method to remove the 27 privileges I just added. Once again I go into the *SubCount* to confirm the removal of all the privileges.

DeleteAllSWbemPrivileges.vbs

```
strComputer = "."
wmiNS = "\root\cimv2"
Set objWMIService = GetObject("winmgmts:\\" & strComputer & wmiNS)
set objWMISecurity = objWMIService.Security_.privileges
For i = 1 To 27
objWMISecurity.add(i)
Next

subCount
wscript.echo "wait while you delete Privileges":WScript.Sleep(1500)
objWMISecurity.deleteAll
subCount

Sub subCount 'uses count method to count privileges
WScript.echo "How Many Special Privileges? " & objWMISecurity.count
End sub
```

Removing a Specific Privilege

Sometimes you might add a privilege in one portion of a script and later need to remove the privilege in other portions of the script. To remove a single privilege you use the *Remove* method. In the RemovePrivilege.vbs script, I use the *Add* method to add a privilege. I go into a subroutine that counts the number of privileges currently held. Once I exit the subroutine, I pause script execution for a second and a half and then use the *Remove* method to delete the privilege previously added. The pause is not required to remove a privilege; it is merely added to make the script a bit more interesting as it runs. It enables you to watch as privileges are added and removed.

RemovePrivilege.vbs

```
Const backup=16
strComputer = "."
wmiNS = "\root\cimv2"
wmiQuery = "Select * from win32_Win32_NTEventlogFile"
Set objWMIService = GetObject("winmgmts:\\" & strComputer & wmiNS)
Set colItems = objWMIService.ExecQuery(wmiQuery)
Set objWMISecurity = objWMIService.security_.privileges
```

```
objWMISecurity.add(backup)

subcount
WScript.sleep 1500:WScript.echo "deleting privilege"
objWMISecurity.remove(backup)
subCount

Sub subcount
wscript.echo "There is: " & objWMISecurity.count & " privileges"
End sub
```

Finding the Most Common Privileges

There are 27 different privileges. These are listed in Appendix B. You might wonder which are the most important. Rather than give you an ambivalent "it depends" answer, I searched through every Managed Object Format (MOF) file for every WMI class in the *root\cimv2* namespace. The resulting list of operations and required privileges is contained in Appendix C. This list tells you exactly which privilege you need to perform which operation. In the meantime, three privileges seem to stand out as the most often required. Indeed, if a network administrator is required to perform a privileged operation, more than likely the privilege needed is one of the following: *Security*, *Loaddriver*, or *Shutdown*.

Using Privileges

You can work with the security privileges in several ways. Of course, you have been working with adding or requesting additional privileges, but you can also request the removal of privileges. If the operation you are attempting does not require a privilege you currently hold, you can request that the specific privilege be removed. You can use two methods to request additional privileges: make a request in the moniker or use *SWbemLocator*. Each is discussed in the following subsections.

In the Moniker

On those occasions when you use the moniker to make your WMI connection, you might also need to specify additional security privileges. I do not prefer this method because I think it is rather ugly; you can make your own decision about its usefulness. The fact that you do not have to define your own constant to use the security privilege is a key factor in using the security string in the moniker. But you have to use a specific form of the privilege string—drop the *se* prefix and the *privilege* suffix. By using this technique, the *SeBackupPrivilege* becomes simply the *Backup* privilege. To specify this privilege in the moniker, you must specify the impersonation level—in this case it is *ImpersonationLevel=impersonate*, which is the default impersonation level in Microsoft Windows 2000, Windows XP, and Windows Server 2003. Because this is the default impersonation level, most of the time it is left out of the scripting examples; however, it is required to be present if you wish to specify a privilege in the moniker.

The impersonation-level settings and the privilege specification are surrounded by curly braces ({ }); the privilege is enclosed in parentheses. When it is all put together, you have the *winmgmts* moniker, open curly brace, impersonation level, open parenthesis, privilege, close parenthesis, close curly brace, a couple of backslashes, and then the path portion of the moniker. This format is shown in the ClearEventLog.vbs script in which I use the *ClearEventLog* method from the *Win32_NTEventLogFile* class. To use this method I must specify the *Backup* privilege. When I call the *ClearEventLog* method, I have specified empty parentheses following the method name; this, however, is not required because I already have a connection to the specific event log. The Platform SDK states that the *ClearEventLog* method requires an input parameter that tells it which log file to clear. Because I have a connection to the specific event log, I can simply call the method without supplying any input parameters.

ClearEventLog.vbs

```
strComputer = "."
wmiNS = "\root\cimv2"
LogFile = "'application'"
wmiQuery = "Select * from win32_NTEventlogFile where " & _
"LogfileName = "& LogFile

Set objWMIService = GetObject("winmgmts:"&_
"{impersonationLevel=impersonate,(backup)}\\" & _
    strComputer & wmiNS)
Set colItems = objWMIService.ExecQuery(wmiQuery)
For Each objItem in colItems
rtnCode = objItem.ClearEventLog()
WScript.echo rtnCode
Next
```

Using *SWbemLocator*

If you use the *SWbemLocator* method to make a connection into WMI and you wish to perform privileged operations, you can add privileges by creating a security object and modifying the *Privilege* property. This works in exactly the same way as was discussed earlier because you are really performing the same operation—adding privileges at the *SWbemSecurity* level.

In the AddPrinterPort.vbs script, I define a constant called *LoadDriver*. I set this to 9, which is equivalent to the value of the *SeLoadDriverPrivilege* privilege string. To add a new printer port, I need to create a new instance of the *Win32_TcpIpPrinterPort* class; I do this by using *SpawnInstance* because there is no *AddPrinterPort* method for this class. Once I have a new copy of the *Win32_TcpIpPrinterPort* class, I set the values for the properties I am concerned with: *Name*, *Protocol*, *HostAddress*, *PortNumber*, and *SnmpEnabled*. Once I have assigned the values required for the new printer port, I use the *Put_* method to write it to WMI.

AddPrinterPort.vbs

```
strComputer = "."
wmiNS = "\root\cimv2"
wmiQuery = "win32_TcpIpPrinterPort"
strUsr =""'Blank for current security. Domain\Username
```

```
strPWD = ""'Blank for current security.
strLocl = "MS_409" 'U.S. English.
strAuth = ""'if specify domain in strUsr, this must be blank
iFlag = "0" '(wait for connection), 128 (wait max two min)
Const LoadDriver = 9 '9 is equal to SeLoadDriverPrivilege
Const TcpPORT = "111.111.111.111" 'IP address
Set objLocator = CreateObject("WbemScripting.SWbemLocator")
Set objWMIService = objLocator.ConnectServer(strComputer,_
    wmiNS, strUsr, strPWD, strLocl, strAuth, iFlag)
Set objWMISecurity =objWMIService.Security_.privileges
WScript.echo objWMISecurity.count 'debug
objWMISecurity.add(LoadDriver)
WScript.echo objWMISecurity.count 'debug
Set objItem = objWMIService.Get(wmiQuery).SpawnInstance_
objItem.Name = "IP_"& TcpPORT
objItem.Protocol = 1 '1 is raw, 2 is lpr
objItem.HostAddress = TcpPORT
objItem.PortNumber = "9100" 'default
objItem.SNMPEnabled = False
objItem.Put_
```

The other method for adding privileges when using *SWbemLocator* is to use the *AddAsString* method. The *AddAsString* method, examined earlier in this chapter, works exactly the same as creating a security object and modifying the *Privilege* property. In the script ChangeSystem-StartUp.vbs I use the *AddAsString* method to add the *SeSystemEnvironmentPrivilege* to enable me to modify the amount of time the computer displays the startup options when it first boots up. Of course, you can manually adjust this property in Control Panel by selecting System, clicking the Advanced tab, and selecting Settings in the Startup And Recovery section. Once you have navigated to this location, the Startup And Recovery dialog box appears, as shown in Figure 7-1.

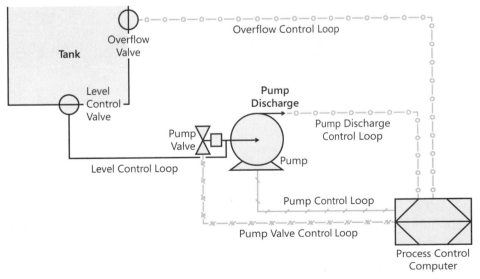

Figure 7-1 Manually setting startup delay times in the Startup And Recovery dialog box

ChangeSystemStartUp.vbs

```
strComputer = "mred" 'name of target computer
wmiNS = "\root\cimv2"
wmiQuery = "win32_ComputerSystem.name='" & strComputer & "'"
strUsr =""'Blank for current security. Domain\Username
strPWD = ""'Blank for current security.
strLocl = "MS_409" 'U.S. English. Can leave blank for current language
strAuth = ""'if specify domain in strUsr, this must be blank
iFlag = "0" 'only two values allowed here: 0 (wait for connection), 128 (wait max two min)

Set objLocator = CreateObject("WbemScripting.SWbemLocator")
Set objWMIService = objLocator.ConnectServer(strComputer, _
    wmiNS, strUsr, strPWD, strLocl, strAuth, iFlag)
Set objWMISecurity =objWMIService.Security_.privileges
Set objItem = objWMIService.get(wmiQuery)

WScript.echo objWMISecurity.count 'debug
objWMISecurity.addAsString("SeSystemEnvironmentPrivilege")
WScript.echo objWMISecurity.count 'debug
Set objItem = objWMIService.get(wmiQuery)
objItem.SystemStartupDelay=5
objItem.Put_

WScript.echo "SystemStartupDelay " & objItem.SystemStartupDelay
```

Quick Check

Q: **What are the two methods you can use to add privileges to a script?**

A: The two methods you can use to add privileges to a script are the *Add* method and the *AddAsString* method.

Q: **If you want to add privileges to a script that uses the moniker to connect into WMI, how do you specify this privilege?**

A: If you want to add privileges to a script that uses the moniker, you must specify the impersonation level settings and the privilege surrounded by curly braces ({ }); the privilege is enclosed in parentheses.

Summary

In this chapter, we looked at privileged operations in WMI. We examined the privileges required for some of the different WMI classes. We looked at ways of enumerating all privileges held by a script and discussed the different places in a script where privileges can be added. We looked at several methods for adding privileges, including the *Add* and *AddAsString* methods.

Quiz Yourself

Q: What is required to use the *Add* method for obtaining elevated privileges?

A: To use the *Add* method to obtain elevated privileges, you can either directly use the numeric value of one of the *WbemPrivilegeEnum* constants or define your own constant and set it equal to the integer.

Q: When adding a privilege as a string, how do you write the privilege?

A: When adding a privilege as a string, you write the privilege in the form of se*privilege-name*privilege.

Q: When adding a privilege in the moniker, in what form do you write the privilege?

A: When adding a privilege in the moniker, you drop the *se* prefix and the *privilege* suffix so you are left with only the privilege name.

On Your Own

Lab 15 Setting the Page File Size

In this lab, you will configure the initial size of your page file. This lab assumes you have a page file defined.

1. Open the WmiTemplate.vbs script, and save it as StudentCheckPageFile.vbs.

2. Edit the *wmiQuery* so that you are selecting just the name and the *InitialSize* from the *Win32_PageFileSetting* class:

```
wmiQuery = "Select InitialSize, name from win32_PageFileSetting"
```

3. Inside the *For Each Next* loop, add *InitialSize* and *Name* to two of the *objItem* objects, so they are echoed using *Wscript.Echo*. Add labels for the *Echo* commands. Remove the unused *objItem*. commands. The *For Each Next* loop will look like the following when you are finished:

```
For Each objItem in colItems
     Wscript.Echo "Name: " & objItem.Name
     Wscript.Echo "InitialSize: " & objItem.InitialSize
Next
```

4. Save and run the script. If you have a page file defined on your system, you will see it reported. Copy the name of your page file because you will need it for the next script.

5. Now you are going to create another script. Open the ConnectServerTemplate.vbs script, and save it as StudentLab15.vbs.

6. Declare a variable *strPageFile* and one called *objWMISecurity*.

7. In the reference section of your script, under *wmiNS*, assign the name of your page file retrieved in step 4 to the variable *strPageFile*. Make sure you enclose the name in single quotes padded with double quotes. On my computer it looks like the following:

```
strPageFile = "'c:\pagefile.sys'"
```

8. Modify the *wmiQuery* line to remove the *Select * from* portion. It will read simply *Win32_*. Choose the *Name* property of the *Win32_PageFileSetting* class and specify the page file you listed in step 7. Use this command with the *Get* method.

```
wmiQuery = "win32_PageFileSetting.name=" & strPageFile
```

9. Create a constant called *CreatePageFile* and set it equal to 14. You can place this line below the *iFlag = "0"* line. This code looks like the following:

```
Const CreatePagefile = 14
```

10. Under the *Set ObjWMIService* line (make sure you do not break the command because it continues to the next line) create a privilege set object by using the *Privileges* method on the *SWbemSecurity* object. This command looks like the following:

```
Set objWMISecurity=objWMIService.security_.privileges
```

11. Go to the bottom of the script and create a subroutine called *SubCheckPriv*. In this subroutine echo the count of the *objWMISecurity* object you just created. This code looks like the following:

```
Sub SubCheckPriv
WScript.echo "Privileges held: " & objWMISecurity.count
End sub
```

12. On the line below the one that creates the *objWMISecurity* object, first check for the number of privileges held, add the *CreatePageFile* privilege you defined with your constant, and finally check to ensure it was applied properly. These three lines of code look like the following:

```
SubCheckPriv
objWMISecurity.add(CreatePagefile)
SubCheckPriv
```

13. Delete the entire *For Each objItem in colItems Next* loop, as well as the two *Wscript.Echo* lines. The code you delete looks like the following:

```
For Each objItem in colItems
    Wscript.Echo "" objItem.
    WScript.echo "" objItem.
Next
```

14. Modify the *Set colItems* line so that you are setting *objItem* and using the *Get* method instead of the *ExecQuery* method. The revised line of code will look like the following:

```
Set objItem = objWMIService.get(wmiQuery)
```

15. Assign the *InitialSize* of your page file to *objItem*. Make sure the initial size is smaller than the maximum size or you will get an error. I set mine to 150 megabytes (MB) by using the following command:

```
objItem.InitialSize="150" 'size in MB
```

16. Use the *Put_* method to write the change to WMI. The command is a simple *objItem.Put_*.

17. Save and run your script. It should run without a problem.

18. Extra credit: Add a subroutine that checks the *err* object for errors. Check the *err.number* and *err.description*. Call this sub after issuing the *Put_* command.

Lab 16 Listing the Working Set

In this lab, you will add a privilege in the moniker. As you work through this lab, you will see the procedure to add the impersonation levels, the privilege strings, and the curly braces.

1. Open the WmiTemplate.vbs file, and save it as StudentLab16.vbs.

2. Declare a variable called *mytab*. You can use the colon separator on the same line, and assign *Space(2)* to be equal to *mytab*. It will look like the following:

```
Dim myTab:mytab=Space(2)
```

3. Turn off *On Error Resume Next* by remarking out the line.

4. Modify the *wmiQuery* line so that it selects *Name*, *MinimumWorkingSetSize*, and *MaximumWorkingSetSize* from the *Win32_Process* class if the *MinimumWorkingSetSize* is greater than zero. The query will look like the following:

```
wmiQuery = "Select name, MinimumWorkingSetSize," _
    &"MaximumWorkingSetSize from win32_process" _
    &" where MinimumWorkingSetSize >0"
```

5. Modify the *Set objWMIService* line so you add the *Debug* privilege. You will use the default Impersonate impersonation level. The line will look like the following:

```
Set objWMIService = GetObject("winmgmts:" _
& "{impersonationLevel=impersonate,(DeBug)}!\\" _
& strComputer & wmiNS)
```

6. Add the three properties you selected in the *wmiQuery* to the output section of your script. Delete the unused *Wscript.Echo* commands. Use *myTab* to space over the min and max working sets. The completed code will look like the following:

```
For Each objItem in colItems
    Wscript.Echo "name : " & objItem.name
    Wscript.Echo mytab & "MinimumWorkingSetSize: " & objItem.MinimumWorkingSetSize
    WScript.echo mytab & "MaximumWorkingSetSize " & objItem.MaximumWorkingSetSize
Next
```

7. Save and run the script.

Part IV
Classes

Chapter 8
Understanding WMI Classes

Classes provide the core functionality of Windows Management Instrumentation (WMI). But how are classes organized? Most people do not realize that there is a pattern to the way WMI classes are stored in the hierarchy. Once you recognize this pattern, you can open new vistas in your scripting life. You can achieve self-actualization as a seasoned IT pro. You can...OK, you get the idea.

Before You Begin

To work through this chapter, you should be familiar with the following concepts:
- The basics of WMI scripting
- The concept of WMI namespaces
- How WMI providers work

After you complete this chapter, you will be familiar with the following concepts:
- The use of WMI system classes
- The basics of namespace security
- How to set namespace security through scripting
- How to determine effective user rights into a WMI connection

> **Note** All the scripts used in this chapter are located on the CD that accompanies this book in the \Scripts\Chapter08 folder.

Using the System Classes

The system classes in WMI are all based on the Common Information Model (CIM) discussed in Chapter 1. As you might recall, the CIM classes are designed to be copied—like a book of patterns or templates. Some system classes always reside in every WMI namespace. These system classes are part of the core WMI functionality and are therefore not described in a Managed Object Format (MOF) file. If you create a new WMI namespace, these core system classes are copied there when the namespace is built. The core system classes are used to provide some basic functionality for WMI. They perform the following activities:

- Event and provider registration
- Security
- Event notification

If you are wondering how you will be able to identify a system class, it is actually very easy—all system classes are preceded with a double underscore (__). If you ever write your own WMI class, make sure you do not give it a name that is preceded by a double underscore because Mofcomp.exe ignores class names that begin with a double underscore. WMI reserves this naming convention for WMI system class names.

Abstract Base Classes

The abstract base classes are classes that can serve only as the basis for a new class. You cannot create an instance of an abstract class. If a class is an abstract class, the abstract qualifier is set. You never use these classes in creating another WMI class. The only class that could even be used to derive another class is the _NotifyStatus class, and if you need to do notification actions, you are better off using the _ExtendedStatus class instead because it has far more properties. The _SystemClass is used as the basis for all of the system classes that are not in the following list. You cannot directly derive a class from the _SystemClass, but that is not really an issue because if you are interested in the properties available from _SystemClass, you can derive a class from a system class already derived from _SystemClass. (The _PARAMETERS class shows up as all caps in the WMI namespaces, so I followed that convention.) The following are the abstract system base classes:

- _NotifyStatus
- _PARAMETERS
- _SecurityRelatedClass
- _SystemClass
- _SystemSecurity

Using System Classes as Base Classes

Some system classes built into WMI perform vital day-to-day functions behind the scenes. Most of these system classes stand alone—you cannot inherit properties from them, and you cannot use their methods. A few, indeed, a very small subset of system WMI classes, are willing to share their properties, methods, and events. These system classes can be used as base classes to enable you easily to create new event consumer types, event types, or error object types. Additionally, you can use the _Namespace system class to create a new namespace in

WMI. This might be useful if you were creating a number of new WMI classes used to manage a network. It might be a good idea to keep all these classes together in their own namespace. That way, if things get out of hand, you can easily delete the entire namespace and roll back to a previous level of functionality in your WMI infrastructure.

Identifying the Version of WMI

Most of the system classes are not usable as base classes for derived classes. This means you simply cannot use them when you are trying to derive additional classes. These are classes that seem to form core WMI functionality and would not make sense to be used as base classes. This does not prevent you from using the classes, however.

The __*CIMOMIdentification* class provides good troubleshooting information about WMI on your machine. It tells you when WMI was installed, the version that is currently running, and even the version that was used to create the database. You can use this class in your script just as you would use any other class. This is illustrated in the script CimomIdentification.vbs. Because there is only one instance of WMI running on a machine at a time, you can use the shorthand name @ to tell the script you want to retrieve the current running instance of WMI. This shortcut refers to the current instance of WMI, making it very easy to use the *Get* method instead of *ExecQuery* and having to loop the instance. To make the script a little easier to use, I build a single variable *strOut* to use for the output. This is better than having to use *Wscript.echo* many times to return the information retrieved from the query.

CimomIdentification.vbs

```
strComputer = "."
wmiNS = "\root\default"
wmiQuery = "__CIMOMIdentification=@"'only one instance of cimom
Set objWMIService = GetObject("winmgmts:\\" & strComputer & wmiNS)
Set objItem = objWMIService.get(wmiQuery)

With objItem
    strOut = "setupTime: " & .setupTime
    strOut = strOut & vbcrlf &"setupDate: " & .setupDate
    strOut = strOut & vbcrlf &"VersionCurrentlyRunning: " & .VersionCurrentlyRunning
    strOut = strOut & vbcrlf &"versionUsedToCreateDB: " & .versionUsedToCreateDB
    strOut = strOut & vbcrlf &"WorkingDirectory: " & .WorkingDirectory
end With

WScript.echo strOut
```

Working with System Security

Another useful base class is the __*SystemSecurity* class. Once again, this class is not usable as a base class for other classes, but it does provide valuable information. Several methods are exposed by the __*SystemSecurity* class. These methods enable you to set security access, get security permissions, and identify security privileges held by the user trying to make the WMI connection.

Displaying the Security Information

In the script DisplaySecurityDescriptor.vbs, I use the *GetSD* method from the __*SystemSecurity*
class to obtain the security descriptor of a WMI namespace to which I am connected. In this
case, I am connected to the *root\wmi* namespace, but the script works with any namespace
that exists on your computer. The interesting thing about this particular script is you can use
it to set the security descriptor on another namespace or on another machine. This is actually
the easiest way to set namespace security in WMI.

DisplaySecurityDescriptor.vbs
```
strComputer = "."
wmiNS = "\root\wmi"
wmiQuery = "__SystemSecurity=@"
Set objWMIService = GetObject("winmgmts:\\" & strComputer & wmiNS)
Set objItem = objWMIService.Get(wmiQuery)
intRTN = objItem.getSD(arrSD)
For I = 0 To UBound(arrSD)
intSD = intSD & arrSD(i)
    If I <> Ubound(arrSD) Then
      intSD = intSD & ","
       End If
Next
WScript.echo intSD
```

As shown in Figure 8-1, the Security tab can be accessed from the WMI Control Properties dialog box. Once you select the Security tab, the Security For dialog box appears. This enables
you to add users or modify security already in effect for groups or individuals.

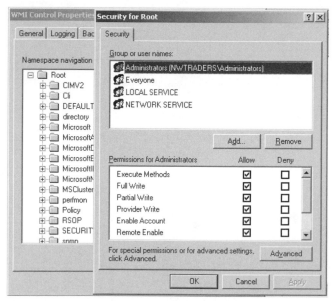

Figure 8-1   Manually setting security on namespaces in the WMI Security dialog box

Setting the Security Information

Once you have retrieved the security descriptor by using the DisplaySecurityDescriptor.vbs script, you can use the returned value to set the security on another WMI namespace—either on the same computer or on another computer—if the same users exist. The procedure is something like the following:

1. Use the WMI Control Properties dialog box to configure security on the namespace in the manner you wish it to be. Add users and grant rights as required.

2. Use the DisplaySecurityDescriptor.vbs script to retrieve the security descriptor.

3. Use the SetSecurityDescriptor.vbs script to set security on the target namespace or computer.

4. Open the WMI Control Properties dialog box on the target computer or in the namespace to ensure that rights are as expected.

Keep in mind the security descriptor is returned as an array data type. You have to use the *Array* command when you set it using the *SetSD* method. You can combine the two scripts, retrieve the security descriptor from one computer, and use it to set the security descriptor on another computer so that you are able to share the security descriptor value between the two computers and not have to type it in (or paste it in) as shown in the SetSecurityDescriptor.vbs script.

SetSecurityDescriptor.vbs

```
strComputer = "."
wmiNS = "\root\cimv2"
wmiQuery = "__SystemSecurity=@"
arSD= array(1,0,4,128,184,0,0,0,200,0,0,0,0,0,0,0,20,0,0,0,2,0,164,0,6,0,0,0,0,0,36,
0,35,0,0,0,1,5,0,0,0,0,0,5,21,0,0,0,182,68,228,35,192,133,56,93,22,192,234,50,248,
3,0,0,0,2,36,0,32,0,2,0,1,5,0,0,0,0,0,5,21,0,0,0,160,101,207,126,120,75,155,95,231,
124,135,112,149,89,0,0,0,18,24,0,63,0,6,0,1,2,0,0,0,0,0,5,32,0,0,0,32,2,0,0,0,18,
20,0,19,0,0,0,1,1,0,0,0,0,0,1,0,0,0,0,0,18,20,0,19,0,0,0,1,1,0,0,0,0,0,5,20,0,0,
0,0,18,20,0,19,0,0,0,1,1,0,0,0,0,0,5,19,0,0,0,1,2,0,0,0,0,0,5,32,0,0,0,32,2,0,0,
1, 2,0,0,0,0,0,5,32,0,0,0,32,2,0,0)
Set objWMIService = GetObject("winmgmts:\\" & strComputer & wmiNS)
Set colItems = objWMIService.Get(wmiQuery) ' note using Get not ExecQuery

WScript.Echo "Preparing to change the SD"

SubChangeSD

Sub SubChangeSD
errReturn = colItems.SetSD(arSD)
If Err <> 0 Then
   WScript.Echo "Method returned error " & errReturn
Else
WScript.Echo "SD was changed"
End If
End sub
```

Identifying the Caller's Rights

To identify the rights a user has in a namespace, you can use the *GetCallerAccessRights* method. All users have the right to call this method because it is required to enable them to determine whether they are allowed into the namespace. The rights are returned in hexadecimal and are additive. Table 8-1 lists the rights and the hexadecimal values that come back from the *Get-CallerAccessRights* method. Because the values are additive, if you had only the *WBEM_ENABLE* and the *WBEM_METHOD_EXECUTE* access rights, for instance, *GetCaller-AccessRights* would return 3.

Table 8-1   System Security Access Rights

Name	Value	Meaning
WBEM_ENABLE	0x1	Enables the account and grants the user read permissions; default access right for all users
WBEM_METHOD_EXECUTE	0x2	Allows the execution of methods
WBEM_FULL_WRITE_REP	0x4	Allows write to classes and instances except for system classes
WBEM_PARTIAL_WRITE_REP	0x8	Allows write to provider instances but not static classes or static instances to the repository
WBEM_WRITE_PROVIDER	0x10	Allows write to classes and instances to providers
WBEM_REMOTE_ACCESS	0x20	Allows remote operations granted by the permissions set by other bits
READ_CONTROL	0x20000	Allows read access to the security descriptors
WRITE_DAC	0x40000	Allows write access to discretionary access control lists (DACLs)

The script GetCallerRights.vbs uses the *ConnectServer* method of the *SWbemLocator* object. If you try to use this method with the moniker, the only thing that returns is a 0 (no problem, but no answer, either). The other thing that is a little strange about the GetCallerRights.vbs script is the use of an output variable. In the line *errRTN = objItem.GetCallerAccessRights(intRights)*, you use the variable *intRights* to hold the output from running the *GetCallerAccessRights* command. The variable *errRTN* holds the actual return code that comes back from running the command. In most instances, it should be 0 (no errors) because all users should have the ability to run *Get-CallerAccessRights*.

GetCallerRights.vbs

```
strComputer = "."
wmiNS = "\root\cimv2"
wmiQuery = "__SystemSecurity"
strUsr =""'Blank for current security. Domain\Username
strPWD = ""'Blank for current security.
strLocl = "MS_409" 'U.S. English. Can leave blank for current language
strAuth = ""'if specify domain in strUsr, this must be blank
iFlag = "0" 'only two values allowed here: 0 (wait for connection),
128 (wait max two min)
```

```
Set objLocator = CreateObject("wbemScripting.SwbemLocator")
Set objWMIService = objLocator.ConnectServer(strComputer, _
    wmiNS, strUsr, strPWD, strLocl, strAuth, iFlag)
Set objItem = objWMIService.get(wmiQuery)
errRTN = objItem.GetCallerAccessRights(intRights)

If errRTN = 0 then
WScript.Echo "Calling users rights: " & intRights
Else
WScript.echo "error occurred. It was: " & errRTN
End if
```

Quick Check

Q: When using the __CIMOMIdentification class to retrieve information about the version of WMI, what does __CIMOMIdentification=@ mean?

A: When using the __CIMOMIdentification class to retrieve information about the version of WMI, __CIMOMIdentification=@ means to use the current version of the installed instance of WMI.

Q: Why might you simply receive a zero when trying to retrieve the effective calling user rights by using the *GetCallerAccessRights* method from the __*SystemSecurity* class?

A: You might receive a zero when trying to retrieve the effective calling user rights by using the *GetCallerAccessRights* method from the __*SystemSecurity* class for one of three reasons: you are using the WMI moniker instead of the *SWbemLocator* method; you are echoing out the return code instead of the output variable value; or the caller has no rights.

Understanding the CIM Classes

There are many CIM classes. For example, there are 286 CIM classes in the *root\cimv2* namespace in a Microsoft Windows XP workstation installation. In many cases, CIM classes look exactly the same as Win32 classes. These are the base classes upon which WMI in Microsoft Windows is built. In this regard, they are organized in much the same way as the Win32 classes are. The interesting thing is the way they are used. If you run a script that queries *CIM_Card*, such as the script CIM_Card.vbs, you might see such information as the serial number and other data about the cards installed on the computer—provided the hardware maker supports the class.

CIM_Card.vbs

```
strComputer = "."
wmiNS = "\root\cimv2"
wmiQuery = "Select * from cim_card"
Set objWMIService = GetObject("winmgmts:\\" & strComputer & wmiNS)
Set colItems = objWMIService.ExecQuery(wmiQuery)

For Each objItem in colItems
   Wscript.echo "Caption:"  & objItem.Caption
Wscript.echo "CreationClassName:"  & objItem.CreationClassName
```

```
Wscript.echo "Depth:"  & objItem.Depth
Wscript.echo "Description:"  & objItem.Description
Wscript.echo "Height:"  & objItem.Height
Wscript.echo "HostingBoard:"  & objItem.HostingBoard
Wscript.echo "HotSwappable:"  & objItem.HotSwappable
Wscript.echo "InstallDate:"  & objItem.InstallDate
Wscript.echo "Manufacturer:"  & objItem.Manufacturer
Wscript.echo "Model:"  & objItem.Model
Wscript.echo "Name:"  & objItem.Name
Wscript.echo "OtherIdentifyingInfo:"  & objItem.OtherIdentifyingInfo
Wscript.echo "PartNumber:"  & objItem.PartNumber
Wscript.echo "PoweredOn:"  & objItem.PoweredOn
Wscript.echo "Removable:"  & objItem.Removable
Wscript.echo "Replaceable:"  & objItem.Replaceable
Wscript.echo "RequirementsDescription:"  & objItem.RequirementsDescription
Wscript.echo "RequiresDaughterBoard:"  & objItem.RequiresDaughterBoard
Wscript.echo "SerialNumber:"  & objItem.SerialNumber
Wscript.echo "SKU:"  & objItem.SKU
Wscript.echo "SlotLayout:"  & objItem.SlotLayout
Wscript.echo "SpecialRequirements:"  & objItem.SpecialRequirements
Wscript.echo "Status:"  & objItem.Status
Wscript.echo "Tag:"  & objItem.Tag
Wscript.echo "Version:"  & objItem.Version
Wscript.echo "Weight:"  & objItem.Weight
Wscript.echo "Width:"  & objItem.Width

Next
```

Close examination of the results will reveal that the query is actually fulfilled by the *Win32_BaseBoard* class. The output tells you this in the *CreationClassName* property value returned by the script. To verify the results, look at another script. In the Win32_Baseboard.vbs script, there are 29 properties. The *CIM_Card* class has only 27 properties. The output for CIM_Card.vbs returns values only for 27 properties—even though the query is actually serviced by the *Win32_BaseBoard* class. The two unique properties supplied by the *Win32_BaseBoard* class, *ConfigOptions* and *Product*, are returned only if the query is made directly against the *Win32_BaseBoard* class as shown in the Win32_Baseboard.vbs script. The *ConfigOptions* property is returned as an array, so you need to use the *Join* function to turn it into a string that you can easily print out.

Win32_Baseboard.vbs

```
strComputer = "."
wmiNS = "\root\cimv2"
wmiQuery = "Select * from win32_BaseBoard"
Set objWMIService = GetObject("winmgmts:\\" & strComputer & wmiNS)
Set colItems = objWMIService.ExecQuery(wmiQuery)

For Each objItem in colItems
Wscript.echo "Caption:"  & objItem.Caption
Wscript.echo "ConfigOptions:"  & JOIN (objItem.ConfigOptions)
Wscript.echo "CreationClassName:"  & objItem.CreationClassName
Wscript.echo "Depth:"  & objItem.Depth
Wscript.echo "Description:"  & objItem.Description
```

```
Wscript.echo "Height:" & objItem.Height
Wscript.echo "HostingBoard:"  & objItem.HostingBoard
Wscript.echo "HotSwappable:"  & objItem.HotSwappable
Wscript.echo "InstallDate:"  & objItem.InstallDate
Wscript.echo "Manufacturer:"  & objItem.Manufacturer
Wscript.echo "Model:"  & objItem.Model
Wscript.echo "Name:"  & objItem.Name
Wscript.echo "OtherIdentifyingInfo:"  & objItem.OtherIdentifyingInfo
Wscript.echo "PartNumber:"  & objItem.PartNumber
Wscript.echo "PoweredOn:"  & objItem.PoweredOn
Wscript.echo "Product:"  & objItem.Product
Wscript.echo "Removable:"  & objItem.Removable
Wscript.echo "Replaceable:"  & objItem.Replaceable
Wscript.echo "RequirementsDescription:"  & objItem.RequirementsDescription
Wscript.echo "RequiresDaughterBoard:"  & objItem.RequiresDaughterBoard
Wscript.echo "SerialNumber:"  & objItem.SerialNumber
Wscript.echo "SKU:"  & objItem.SKU
Wscript.echo "SlotLayout:"  & objItem.SlotLayout
Wscript.echo "SpecialRequirements:"  & objItem.SpecialRequirements
Wscript.echo "Status:"  & objItem.Status
Wscript.echo "Tag:"  & objItem.Tag
Wscript.echo "Version:"  & objItem.Version
Wscript.echo "Weight:"  & objItem.Weight
Wscript.echo "Width:"  & objItem.Width
Next
```

CIM Classes Are Really DMTF Classes

The CIM classes were devised by the Distributed Management Task Force (DMTF), and they form the basis of the WMI schema you use in the Windows operating system. In many cases, a CIM class is used as a basis for a Win32 class that performs a similar function within the schema. However, three-quarters of the CIM classes do not have a direct relation with a Win32 counterpart.

Consider the *MonitorResolution* Class

Suppose you are perusing the CIM classes and you run across the *CIM_MonitorResolution* class. You think it looks nice, and you whip out the cimMonitorResolution.vbs script. You are excited with the prospects of being able to utilize the information directly. When you run the script, what to your wondering eyes should appear? Nothing!

cimMonitorResolution.vbs

```
strComputer = "."
wmiNS = "\root\cimv2"
strFile = "'%boot.ini%'"
wmiQuery = "Select * from CIM_MonitorResolution"
Set objWMIService = GetObject("winmgmts:\\" & strComputer & wmiNS)
Set colItems = objWMIService.ExecQuery(wmiQuery)

For Each objItem in colItems
Wscript.echo "Caption:" & objItem.Caption
Wscript.echo "Description:"  & objItem.Description
```

```
Wscript.echo "HorizontalResolution:"  & objItem.HorizontalResolution
Wscript.echo "MaxRefreshRate:"  & objItem.MaxRefreshRate
Wscript.echo "MinRefreshRate:"  & objItem.MinRefreshRate
Wscript.echo "RefreshRate:"  & objItem.RefreshRate
Wscript.echo "ScanMode:"  & objItem.ScanMode
Wscript.echo "SettingID:"  & objItem.SettingID
Wscript.echo "VerticalResolution:"  & objItem.VerticalResolution
Next
```

To confirm your suspicions, you use the Windows Management Instrumentation Tester (Wbemtest.exe) and look up the *CIM_MonitorResolution* class in the *root/cimv2* namespace. The steps to do this are as follows:

1.   Click Start, click Run, and type **WbemTest.exe**.

2.   Click Connect.

3.   Change the namespace from *root\default* to *root\cimv2*, and then click Connect.

4.   Click Open Class, and type the name of the WMI class: **CIM_MonitorResolution**.

5.   Click Instances.

The window shown in Figure 8-2 confirms you have no instances of the *CIM_Monitor-Resolution* class implemented on your system.

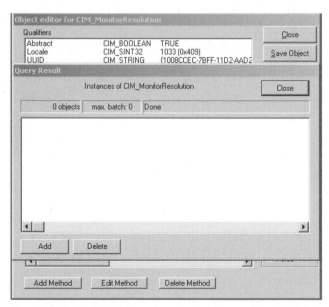

Figure 8-2   Determining whether instances of a class exist on the computer

If you want to see whether another class is using *CIM_MonitorResolution* as a base class and is inheriting all those wonderful properties, you can again turn to Wbemtest.exe. Open the *CIM_MonitorResolution* class as indicated in the preceding steps. Once it is open, click the Derived button on the right side of the screen, and the window shown in Figure 8-3 appears.

It is immediately obvious your investigation has come to an end—there are no derived classes. *CIM_MonitorResolution* is not implemented in any way, shape, or form on your system.

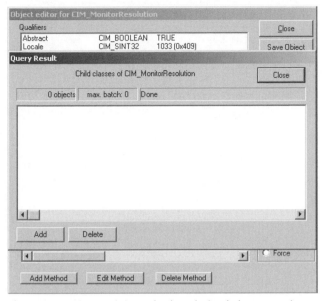

Figure 8-3   Determining whether derived classes are in use on a computer

Quick Check

Q: What tool can you use to determine quickly whether an instance of a class exists on your system?

A: The tool you can use to determine quickly whether an instance of a class exists on your system is the Windows Management Instrumentation Tester (Wbemtest.exe). It is always available on your computer.

Q: Why is it important to determine whether an instance of a class exists on your computer?

A: It is important to determine whether an instance of a class exists on your computer because, if there are no instances, you are not able to perform a query of that class.

Summary

In this chapter, we looked at the way WMI classes are put together. We examined abstract base classes and saw how they can be used in the formation of other WMI classes. We discussed the system classes that WMI uses as the building blocks of WMI, as well as those that are used to control the behavior of WMI. We determined which of these system classes you can use to build other classes as required. Finally, we examined the concept of instances.

Quiz Yourself

Q: **What is the difference between an abstract WMI class and a regular WMI class?**

A: The difference between an abstract WMI class and a regular WMI class is that an abstract WMI class cannot have any instances.

Q: **What does it mean for a WMI class to have instances?**

A: When a WMI class has instances, it means the class is active on the computer and you can query the properties of the class and use any methods it has implemented.

Q: **What does it mean if a WMI class does not have instances?**

A: If a WMI class does not have any instances, it might exist in the schema as an abstract concept, but it has not been implemented into reality. If the class does not have instances, you are not able to query against it.

Q: **You want to use the __*CIMOMIdentification* class to determine the version of WMI that is running. How can you use the *Get* method to retrieve this information?**

A: If you want to use the __*CIMOMIdentification* class to determine the version of WMI that is running using the *Get* method, you will need to use a query that specifies __*CIMOMIdentification=@*.

Q: **If you want to identify the security privileges a user has when making a WMI connection, which WMI class could you use?**

A: To determine the security privileges a user has when making a WMI connection, you could use the __*SystemSecurity* class.

On Your Own

Lab 17 Exploring Abstract Classes

In this lab, you will build a script that generates a list of abstract classes in a particular WMI namespace.

1. Open the ConnectorServerTemplate.vbs script from the Lab 17 folder. Save it as StudentLab17.vbs.

2. In the header section of the script, add some additional variables to be used in the script. You need five additional variables: *colClasses*, *strClass*, *a*, *strMsg*, and *strTab*.

3. Just under the variable declarations, make *strTab* equal to a carriage return line feed and a tab stop. Your code should look like the following:

```
strTab = VBcrlf & vbtab
```

4. At the bottom of the reference section where you assign values to the variables, just below the *iFlag="0"* line, assign the value for *strMsg*. It will print out a line that heads the list of abstract classes.

```
strMsg = "The following are abstract classes in the "_
    & wmiNS & " namespace"
```

5. Open the SeparatorLinefunction.vbs script, and copy the *FunLine* function from the bottom of that script. The function looks like the following:

```
Function funLine(lineOfText)
Dim numEQs, separator, i
numEQs = Len(lineOfText)
For i = 1 To numEQs
    separator = separator & "="
Next
 FunLine = lineOfText & vbcrlf & separator
End function
```

6. Go back to the StudentLab17.vbs script, and paste the *FunLine* function at the bottom of your script.

7. Now that you have the separator line function in place, go back to the *strMsg* line and use the function to underline the title of the report. The modified line of code looks like the following:

```
strMsg = funLine("The following are abstract classes in the "_
    & wmiNS & " namespace")
```

8. Set the *colClasses* variable to hold the collection of subclasses that comes back from using the *SubClassesOf* method of the *SWbemObject*. It looks like the following:

```
Set colClasses = objWMIService.SubclassesOf()
```

9. Change the *For Each objItem in ColItems* line to read *For Each strClass in colClasses*.

10. Delete all the *Wscript.echo* commands.

11. Save and run the script. At this point, you should not see any errors. If you do, you need to resolve them before continuing. (You can always look at the solution if you need to.)

12. Set the variable *objItem* equal to what comes back from using the *Get* method of the *SWbemObject* to get the *Class* property from *Path_*. This code looks like the following:

```
Set objItem = objWMIService.get(strClass.path_.class)
```

13. Use *For Each Next* to walk through the collection of qualifiers. Use the variable *a* as the counter. You get the collection of qualifiers by using the *Qualifiers_* property of *objItem* retrieved in the previous step. The code looks like the following:

```
For Each a In objItem.Qualifiers_
```

14. Use the *Instr* command to filter out the word *Abstract*. This will be part of an *If Then End If* command. It looks like the following:

```
If InStr(1,a.name,"abstract",1) Then
End If
```

15. You want to build an output variable so that the results come out in a single command. Use *strMSG*, which at this point contains the title. Now add it to itself, use *strTab*, and pick up the class name from the *Path* object. The line that does this goes between the *If Then* command you used for the *Instr* command.

```
strMsg= strMsg & strTab & objItem.path_.class
```

16. Make sure you have closed all the *For Next* loops you used. The bottom section of the code looks like the following:

```
For Each strClass in colClasses
  Set objItem = objWMIService.get(strClass.path_.class)
  For Each a In objItem.Qualifiers_
If InStr(1,a.name,"abstract",1) Then
strMsg= strMsg & strTab & objItem.path_.class
End if
Next
Next
```

17. Save and run the script. It should work just fine.

Lab 18 Examining WMI Classes

In this lab, you will use the Windows Management Instrumentation Tester (Wbemtest.exe) to examine several WMI classes.

1. Launch Wbemtest.exe from a command-prompt window.

2. Once Wbemtest.exe is running, you need to connect to a WMI namespace. Click Connect.

3. The Connect dialog box appears. Root\Default is highlighted as the default namespace. Unfortunately, setting a new default is not configurable. Change to the *root\cimv2* namespace, and click Connect. You can leave all the other parameters for the connection set to the default values.

4. Run the Lab17solution.vbs script to generate a list of abstract classes in the *root\cimv2* namespace.

5. Find *CIM_PhysicalMemory* on the list. This indicates it has the abstract qualifier set.

6. In Wbemtest.exe, click Open Class, and type in the **CIM_PhysicalMemory** class, and click OK.

7. The Object Editor For *CIM_PhysicalMemory* dialog box appears. In the upper pane, examine the qualifiers that are set for this class. The qualifier you are looking for is called *Abstract*. Is it present? It is. What is the value assigned to the qualifier? It is set to *True*.

8. Look through the properties of the class. They are enumerated in the middle pane.

9. Click Instances on the right side of the Object Editor dialog box. Are there any instances listed? No.

10. Close that dialog box, and click Derived. Are there any classes derived from *CIM_PhysicalMemory*? Yes. This indicates the class is used as a base class for *Win32_PhysicalMemory*.

11. Now you are going to explore two related classes in more detail. You can choose any association class from the earlier list and see if it has a class derived from it by using Wbemtest.exe. If you cannot find something, and your computer has a modem, you can use *CIM_PotsModem* and *Win32_PotsModem*.

12. Open the CompareClasses.vbs script. Run it, and type in **CIM_PotsModem,Win32_PotsModem**. This line needs to be exact because no error checking is included in the script to filter out the input. Basically, this script compares two classes that are derived from each other and prints out the unique properties.

13. Notice at the top of the output how many properties *CIM_PotsModem* has and how many properties *Win32_PotsModem* has (36 versus 79).

14. Open the script PropertyExplorer.vbs, and then open and make a copy of the WmiTemplate.vbs script.

15. Save the copy of the WmiTemplate.vbs script as StudentLab18A.vbs.

16. Go back to the PropertyExplorer.vbs script and run it. At the prompt, type **CIM_PotsModem**, and click OK. A list of 36 *Wscript.Echo* commands will be returned.

17. Copy all the *Wscript.Echo* commands, and paste them into the StudentLab18A.vbs script in the middle of the *For Next* loop. Replace the existing *Wscript.Echo* commands with this text.

18. Change the *wmiQuery* command so that it is selecting everything from *CIM_PotsModem*.

19. Run the script. It should run fine and return a decent amount of information.

20. Determine where the StudentLab18A.vbs script is getting its information. Examine the output for the *CreationClassName* property. You will see something that looks like the following:

```
CreationClassName:Win32_PotsModem
```

21. By using this class, you are really using only a subset of the *Win32_PotsModem* class.

22. Write another script that uses all of the available properties of the class. Open another copy of the WmiTemplate.vbs script, and save it as StudentLab18B.vbs.

23. Run the PropertyExplorer.vbs script. This time feed in *Win32_PotsModem*.

24. Copy all the *Wscript.Echo* commands from the output.

25. Go back to the StudentLab18b.vbs script, and replace the existing *Wscript.Echo* commands from the template with the ones copied from the output of the PropertyExplorer.vbs script.

26. Change the *wmiQuery* so that it is pointing to the *Win32_PotsModem* class.

27. Save and run the script. You should see quite a bit more information from this script.

28. If you look at the top of the script, you will see you have *On Error Resume Next* turned on. Turn off this command, and run the script. Now you will notice there is a problem—three, to be exact. Three of the properties are stored as an array.

29. Two of these properties are right next to one another: *DCB* and *Default*. Use the *Join* command so you can easily print out their values. The modified lines look like the following:

```
Wscript.echo "DCB:"  & join(objItem.DCB)
Wscript.echo "Default:"  & join(objItem.Default)
```

30. The third array property in this class is the *Properties* property. Again, use the *Join* command. The modified line of code now looks like the following:

```
Wscript.echo "Properties:"  & Join(objItem.Properties)
```

31. Run the script again. Look for the output of the *CreationClassName* property. See where it is pointing to: the *Win32_PotsModem* class.

This concludes this lab.

Chapter 9

Using Win32 WMI Classes

The Win32 Windows Management Instrumentation (WMI) classes can be categorized into five groups of related services and functionality: software application classes, service management classes, hardware classes, operating system classes, and performance counter classes. To a large extent, this is an arbitrary arrangement, but viewing classes in this manner enables us to grasp more quickly the scope of capabilities provided by these classes.

The Win32 classes have either been extended or customized for the Microsoft Windows environment. In nearly every instance, they are built upon an underlying Common Information Model (CIM) type of class. By understanding how these categories are put together, it becomes much easier to locate and use the appropriate class for your scripts. As you look at the way the classes are organized, you will see relations between the classes and the activities you are trying to perform. In addition, you will be able to leverage the information you have learned in the first part of the book. In this chapter, we look at two groups of classes—the software application classes and the WMI service management classes. In Chapter 10, we look at hardware classes; in Chapter 11, we look at the operating system classes; and in Chapter 12, we look at the performance counter classes.

Before You Begin

To work through this chapter, you should be familiar with the following concepts:
- The basics of the different types of classes
- The basics of WMI namespace organization
- How association classes work
- Base classes and schema inheritance

After you complete this chapter, you will be familiar with the following concepts:
- The classes provided by the Windows Installer provider
- How to install the Windows Installer provider in Microsoft Windows Server 2003
- How to change WMI configuration values by using a script

> **Note**   All the scripts used in this chapter are located on the CD that accompanies this book in the \Scripts\Chapter09 folder.

Working with Applications

For many network administrators, one of the most exciting groups of classes is the one supplied by the Windows Installer provider. Also known as the MSI provider, this provider works with applications that are configured to use the MSI software installation technology. The great thing about this provider is you can obtain lots of information about the applications installed on your computers, and you can even perform some of the same actions (such as installing software and patching software). The MSI provider exposes to WMI the same functions that a developer would use when creating MSI packages—because of this, there is a vast plethora of classes.

One of the more interesting classes available from the MSI provider is the *Win32_ShortCutAction* class. Although this class can be used to create shortcuts for an MSI software installation package, network administrators can use it to query and to retrieve some rather cool information about software shortcuts on a computer.

In the DisplayShortCuts.vbs script, I use the *Win32_ShortCutAction* class to return shortcut information. The results on my computer that runs Microsoft Windows XP were rather surprising. Because the script has to sort through a lot of data, it might take a minute or two to run, so don't get impatient. Once it comes back, on my computer it reported the following information near the bottom of a 2383-line printout:

```
ActionID:Shortcut5{EEC2DAFD-5558-40AC-8E9C-5005C8F810E8}
========================================================
Arguments:
Caption:Play the classic game of bowling with arcade-style action, 3D graphics, and sound.
Description:Play the classic game of bowling with arcade-
style action, 3D graphics, and sound.
Direction:
HotKey:
IconIndex:
Name:HYPERB~1|HyperBowl Plus! Edition
Shortcut:Shortcut5
ShowCmd:1
SoftwareElementID:
SoftwareElementState:
Target:[HYPERPATHDIR]\Hyperbowl.exe
TargetOperatingSystem:
Version:
WkDir:HYPERPATHDIR
ActionID:Shortcut6{EEC2DAFD-5558-40AC-8E9C-5005C8F810E8}
========================================================
Arguments:
Caption:Test your skills for quick thinking and strategy in this fast-paced game.
```

```
Description:Test your skills for quick thinking and strategy in this fast-paced game.
Direction:
HotKey:
IconIndex:
Name:RUSSIA~1|Russian Square Plus! Edition
Shortcut:Shortcut6
ShowCmd:1
SoftwareElementID:
SoftwareElementState:
Target:[DIR54]\RussSqr.exe
TargetOperatingSystem:
Version:
WkDir:DIR54
```

This information is interesting because it relates to Figure 9-1. When you launch Games from the Plus menu, a program switchboard appears. However, each of those links are viewed by the *Win32_ShortCutAction* class as shortcuts. This class seems to find shortcuts that are inside other programs—in addition to the standard shortcuts on the All Programs menu.

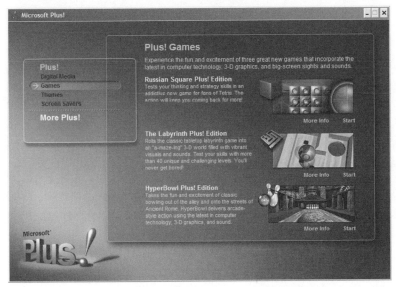

Figure 9-1   Shortcuts to games on the main menu for Microsoft Plus! Games

DisplayShortCuts.vbs

```
strComputer = "."
wmiNS = "\root\cimv2"
wmiQuery = "Select * from win32_ShortCutAction"
Set objWMIService = GetObject("winmgmts:\\" & strComputer & wmiNS)
Set colItems = objWMIService.ExecQuery(wmiQuery)

For Each objItem in colItems
Wscript.echo funLine("ActionID:"  & objItem.ActionID)
Wscript.echo "Arguments:"  & objItem.Arguments
Wscript.echo "Caption:"  & objItem.Caption
Wscript.echo "Description:"  & objItem.Description
```

```
Wscript.echo "Direction:"  & objItem.Direction
Wscript.echo "HotKey:"  & objItem.HotKey
Wscript.echo "IconIndex:"  & objItem.IconIndex
Wscript.echo "Name:"  & objItem.Name
Wscript.echo "Shortcut:"  & objItem.Shortcut
Wscript.echo "ShowCmd:"  & objItem.ShowCmd
Wscript.echo "SoftwareElementID:"  & objItem.SoftwareElementID
Wscript.echo "SoftwareElementState:"  & objItem.SoftwareElementState
Wscript.echo "Target:"  & objItem.Target
Wscript.echo "TargetOperatingSystem:"  & objItem.TargetOperatingSystem
Wscript.echo "Version:"  & objItem.Version
Wscript.echo "WkDir:"  & objItem.WkDir
Next


'### functions below ###
Function funLine(lineOfText)
Dim numEQs, separator, i
numEQs = Len(lineOfText)
For i = 1 To numEQs
    separator = separator & "="
Next
FunLine = lineOfText & vbcrlf & separator
End function
```

Working with Software Classes

Several classes are used to represent software. Use of these classes can assist in software inventory, audit, and version control. To work with these classes and the software, you must install them by using the Windows Installer.

Using the *Win32_SoftwareElement* Class

The *Win32_SoftwareElement* class provides very useful and interesting information. As shown in the LookForInstalledPrograms.vbs script, you can tailor your query to return just about any specific information desired. This is one script you do not want to run without filtering the data returned. The first time I ran this script on my workstation without the *Where* clause, I thought I had locked up the computer. It returned more than 60,000 lines of data, after eating up all my CPU time for nearly five minutes. (But, on the other hand, I did have Microsoft Virtual PC, Microsoft Word, Outlook, Media Player, Internet Explorer, and the Platform SDK open at the same time.)

In the LookForInstalledPrograms.vbs script, a couple of items are interesting. The first is the *FunFix* function, which is used to permit users of the script to type in the name of the program they are looking for instead of embedding the name in single quotes or using percent signs or whichever exact form is required to make the script work. So, the *FunFix* function adds a *Where* clause to the *wmiQuery* and uses the *Like* operator with the appropriate qualifiers.

The second thing that is interesting about the LookForInstalledPrograms.vbs script is the *FunTime* function used to translate the Universal Time Coordinate (UTC) time format into something more understandable. This function uses the *SWbemDateTime* object to perform the conversion. The use of a function keeps the details of creating the object, creating the variables, and using the methods out of the basic flow of the script. This promotes both readability and code re-use.

LookForInstalledPrograms.vbs

```vbs
strComputer = "."
wmiNS = "\root\cimv2"
strProg = funFix("Excel")
wmiQuery = "Select * from win32_SoftwareElement" & strProg
Set objWMIService = GetObject("winmgmts:\\" & strComputer & wmiNS)
Set colItems = objWMIService.ExecQuery(wmiQuery)

For Each objItem in colItems
Wscript.echo funLine("Attributes:"  & objItem.Attributes)
Wscript.echo "BuildNumber:"  & objItem.BuildNumber
Wscript.echo "Caption:"  & objItem.Caption
Wscript.echo "CodeSet:"  & objItem.CodeSet
Wscript.echo "Description:"  & objItem.Description
Wscript.echo "IdentificationCode:"  & objItem.IdentificationCode
Wscript.echo "InstallDate:"  & funTime(objItem.InstallDate)
Wscript.echo "InstallState:"  & objItem.InstallState
Wscript.echo "LanguageEdition:"  & objItem.LanguageEdition
Wscript.echo "Manufacturer:"  & objItem.Manufacturer
Wscript.echo "Name:"  & objItem.Name
Wscript.echo "OtherTargetOS:"  & objItem.OtherTargetOS
Wscript.echo "Path:"  & objItem.Path
Wscript.echo "SerialNumber:"  & objItem.SerialNumber
Wscript.echo "SoftwareElementID:"  & objItem.SoftwareElementID
Wscript.echo "SoftwareElementState:"  & objItem.SoftwareElementState
Wscript.echo "Status:"  & objItem.Status
Wscript.echo "TargetOperatingSystem:"  & objItem.TargetOperatingSystem
Wscript.echo "Version:"  & objItem.Version
Next


'##### functions are Below #####
Function funLine(lineOfText)
Dim numEQs, separator, i
numEQs = Len(lineOfText)
For i = 1 To numEQs
    separator = separator & "="
Next
 FunLine = lineOfText & vbcrlf & separator
End Function

Function funFix(strVar) 'adds in where clause
funFix = " where path like '%" & strVar & "%'"
End Function

Function FunTime(wmiTime) 'Used to translate Time
 Dim objSWbemDateTime 'holds an swbemDateTime object.
 Set objSWbemDateTime = CreateObject("WbemScripting.SWbemDateTime")
  objSWbemDateTime.Value=wmiTime
  FunTime = objSWbemDateTime.GetVarDate
End Function
```

Using the *Win32_SoftwareFeature* Class

The *Win32_SoftwareFeature* class provides some pretty cool information about the software installed on your computer. One of the more interesting properties is the date the software was last accessed. This information alone can be very valuable when it comes time to purchase software upgrades or determine whether having a program installed on a machine is cost effective. The SoftwareFeatures.vbs script illustrates using this class to retrieve this information. In this script, I once again use the *FunTime* function to translate the UTC time into a more readable format. I use the *FunLine* function to underline the first property I retrieve—the *Accesses* property. This separates the information retrieved into groupings of products. You could, of course, rearrange the properties or even add your header to print out with each software feature you retrieve.

SoftwareFeatures.vbs

```
strComputer = "."
wmiNS = "\root\cimv2"
strVar = funFix("word") 'the product looked for
wmiQuery = "Select * from win32_SoftwareFeature" & strVar
strUsr ="" 'Blank for current security. Domain\Username
strPWD = "" 'Blank for current security.
strLocl = "MS_409" 'U.S. English. Can leave blank for current language
strAuth = "" 'if specify domain in strUsr, this must be blank
iFlag = "0" 'only two values allowed here: 0 (wait for connection), 128 (wait max two min)

Set objLocator = CreateObject("WbemScripting.SWbemLocator")
Set objWMIService = objLocator.ConnectServer(strComputer, _
    wmiNS, strUsr, strPWD, strLocl, strAuth, iFlag)
Set colItems = objWMIService.ExecQuery(wmiQuery)

For Each objItem in colItems
Wscript.echo funLine("Accesses:"  & objItem.Accesses)
Wscript.echo "Attributes:"  & objItem.Attributes
Wscript.echo "Caption:"  & objItem.Caption
Wscript.echo "Description:"  & objItem.Description
Wscript.echo "IdentifyingNumber:"  & objItem.IdentifyingNumber
Wscript.echo "InstallDate:"  & funTime(objItem.InstallDate)
Wscript.echo "InstallState:"  & objItem.InstallState
Wscript.echo "LastUse:"  & funTime(objItem.LastUse)
Wscript.echo "Name:"  & objItem.Name
Wscript.echo "ProductName:"  & objItem.ProductName
Wscript.echo "Status:"  & objItem.Status
Wscript.echo "Vendor:"  & objItem.Vendor
Wscript.echo "Version:"  & objItem.Version
Next

'### functions below ###

Function FunTime(wmiTime)
If wmiTime <> Null then
 Dim objSWbemDateTime 'holds an swbemDateTime object. Used to translate Time
 Set objSWbemDateTime = CreateObject("WbemScripting.SWbemDateTime")
  objSWbemDateTime.Value= wmiTime
```

```
    FunTime = objSWbemDateTime.GetVarDate
End if
End Function


Function funLine(lineOfText)
Dim numEQs, separator, i
numEQs = Len(lineOfText)
For i = 1 To numEQs
    separator = separator & "="
Next
 FunLine = lineOfText & vbcrlf & separator
End Function


Function funFix(strVar) 'adds in where clause
funFix = " where description like '%" & strVar & "%'"
End Function
```

Understanding the MSI Installer Provider

The MSI provider is not installed by default on a computer running Windows Server 2003. Because the MSI installer provider contributes nearly 70 classes to the WMI installation, I recommend it be added as part of the normal Windows Server 2003 build. There are two ways to make sure the MSI Installer provider is installed on your system. As shown in Figure 9-2, you can access the Add/Remove Windows Components from Add Or Remove Programs. In the Windows Component Wizard, highlight (do not select the check box) Management And Monitoring Tools, and then click Details. In the Management And Monitoring Tools dialog box, select the WMI Windows Installer Provider check box, and then click OK twice. Once you do this, you must reboot the computer to complete the installation.

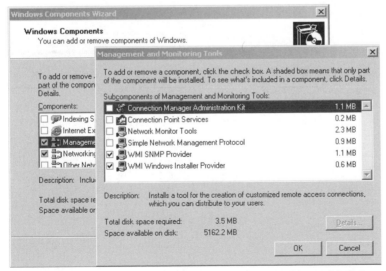

Figure 9-2   Adding WMI Windows Installer Provider from Add Or Remove Programs in Control Panel

If you want to confirm the WMI Windows Installer provider is installed on the computer prior to executing any queries that require its presence, you can write a quick program that queries for instances of installed providers. In the script FindMSIProvider.vbs, I perform such a query. By using the *Instr* function, I am able to filter out provider names that include the letters *MSI*. I specify the fourth parameter as 1 to perform a case-insensitive filter. Once I find the MSI provider, I might as well return some of the more exciting properties of the provider, such as the class ID and the hosting model. Keep in mind that although this script is currently only looking for the MSI provider, it can easily be altered to look for any other provider on a machine.

FindMSIProvider.vbs

```
strComputer = "."
wmiNS = "\root\cimv2"
strProv = "MSI"
Set objWMIService = _
    GetObject ("winmgmts:\\" & strComputer & wmiNS)
Set colItems = objWMIService.InstancesOf("__Win32Provider")

For Each objItem In colItems
With objItem
If InStr(1,.name, strProv,1) then
    WScript.echo .Name, .clsid _
    & vbcrlf & "hostingModel: " & .hostingModel

End If
End with
Next
```

Quick Check

Q: Is the MSI Installer provider installed by default on computers running Windows Server 2003?

A: The MSI Installer provider is not installed by default on computers running Windows Server 2003.

Q: You have a query that uses the *Win32_SoftwareElement* class to inventory software applications. It runs fine on computers running Microsoft Windows 2000 and Windows XP, but it fails on computers running Windows Server 2003. What must you do to correct the problem?

A: If you have a script that uses the *Win32_SoftwareElement* class that works on computers running Windows 2000 and Windows XP but not on those running Windows Server 2003, the first thing you must realize is the provider that supplies this class is the WMI Windows Installer provider. You should check by using Add Or Remove Programs on the computer running Windows Server 2003 to ensure that the WMI Windows Installer provider is installed.

Understanding WMI Service Management

Another grouping of WMI classes is used to assist us with the management of WMI. The main WMI class in this group is the *Win32_WMISetting* class. This class can retrieve some real nifty information about the way WMI is configured on your computer. Many of these properties are writable, so not only can you query the property, but you can also use the property to change the behavior of WMI. If you need to verify the default namespace, use the *ASPScriptDefault-Namespace* property. But if you need to change the default namespace, you can write a value to the same property. If you are concerned about the WMI logging level, query the *LoggingLevel* property. I illustrate using this class in the DisplayWMISettings.vbs script. This script can be a great starting place for WMI troubleshooting on a computer. The DisplayWMISettings.vbs script prints out most of the main properties related to WMI configuration on a computer.

DisplayWMISettings.vbs

```
strComputer = "."
wmiNS = "\root\cimv2"
wmiQuery = "win32_wmiSetting=@"
strUsr =""'Blank for current security. Domain\Username
strPWD = ""'Blank for current security.
strLocl = "MS_409" 'U.S. English. Can leave blank for current language
strAuth = ""'if specify domain in strUsr, this must be blank
iFlag = "0" 'only two values allowed here: 0 (wait for connection), 128 (wait max two min)

Set objLocator = CreateObject("WbemScripting.SWbemLocator")
Set objWMIService = objLocator.ConnectServer(strComputer, _
    wmiNS, strUsr, strPWD, strLocl, strAuth, iFlag)
Set objItem = objWMIService.get(wmiQuery)
With objItem
Wscript.echo "ASPScriptDefaultNamespace:" & .ASPScriptDefaultNamespace
Wscript.echo "ASPScriptEnabled:" & .ASPScriptEnabled
Wscript.echo "AutorecoverMofs:" & join(.AutorecoverMofs, vbcrlf)
Wscript.echo "AutoStartWin9X:" & .AutoStartWin9X
Wscript.echo "BackupInterval:" & .BackupInterval
Wscript.echo "BackupLastTime:" & FunTime(.BackupLastTime)
Wscript.echo "BuildVersion:" & .BuildVersion
Wscript.echo "Caption:" & .Caption
Wscript.echo "DatabaseDirectory:" & .DatabaseDirectory
Wscript.echo "DatabaseMaxSize:" & .DatabaseMaxSize
Wscript.echo "Description:" & .Description
Wscript.echo "EnableAnonWin9xConnections:" & .EnableAnonWin9xConnections
Wscript.echo "EnableEvents:" & .EnableEvents
Wscript.echo "EnableStartupHeapPreallocation:" & .EnableStartupHeapPreallocation
Wscript.echo "HighThresholdOnClientObjects:" & .HighThresholdOnClientObjects
Wscript.echo "HighThresholdOnEvents:" & .HighThresholdOnEvents
Wscript.echo "InstallationDirectory:" & .InstallationDirectory
Wscript.echo "LastStartupHeapPreallocation:" & .LastStartupHeapPreallocation
Wscript.echo "LoggingDirectory:" & .LoggingDirectory
Wscript.echo "LoggingLevel:" & .LoggingLevel
Wscript.echo "LowThresholdOnClientObjects:" & .LowThresholdOnClientObjects
Wscript.echo "LowThresholdOnEvents:" & .LowThresholdOnEvents
Wscript.echo "MaxLogFileSize:" & .MaxLogFileSize
Wscript.echo "MaxWaitOnClientObjects:" & .MaxWaitOnClientObjects
```

```
Wscript.echo "MaxWaitOnEvents:"  & .MaxWaitOnEvents
Wscript.echo "MofSelfInstallDirectory:"  & .MofSelfInstallDirectory
Wscript.echo "SettingID:"  & .SettingID
End with

'### functions below ####


Function FunTime(wmiTime)
If wmiTime <> Null Then
 Dim objSwbemDateTime 'holds an swbemDateTime object. Used to translate Time
 Set objSwbemDateTime = CreateObject("WbemScripting.SWbemDateTime")
  objSwbemDateTime.Value= wmiTime
  FunTime = objSwbemDateTime.GetVarDate
End if
End Function
```

Quick Check

Q: If you want to change the default WMI namespace on your workstation, how can you use a script to do this without editing the registry?

A: If you want to change the default WMI namespace on your workstation without editing the registry, you can do so by using the *ASPScriptDefaultNamespace* property of the *Win32_WMISetting* class.

Q: Because the *Win32_WMISetting* class does not expose any methods, how can you modify WMI settings?

A: You can modify many WMI settings by using the writable properties exposed by the *Win32_WMISetting* class.

Writing to the Properties

As interesting as reporting WMI configuration settings is, the real power comes when you decide to make changes. The *Win32_WMISetting* class follows normal WMI conventions in working with the read/write properties. You do not need to spawn a new instance of the class, but you will need to use the *Put_* method to write the changes back to the WMI database.

It is possible to use the *BackupInterval* property to configure an automatic backup of the WMI repository—the problem, though, is that this property is deprecated in Windows XP. This means that although you can use a script to set the property, it will not work on computers running Windows XP, but it will work on computers running Windows 2000 and earlier operating systems. For Windows XP, the capability of doing an automatic backup of the WMI repository was removed. Interestingly enough, when you set the *BackupInterval* property on computers that run Windows XP, it adds the HKLM\Software\Microsoft\WBEM\CIMOM\ Backup Interval Threshold registry key and even records the desired backup interval in minutes. A query of this property returns whichever value you set. But please keep in mind this does not work, although it appears to work and no errors are returned. The property is not marked as deprecated in the Managed Object Format (MOF) file, but it is, in fact, deprecated and it does not work. This means you must do a manual backup of the repository. You can find more information on this in Chapter 14.

The *BackUpLastTime* property also does not work on computers running Windows XP despite the fact you do a manual backup of the repository. This property was tied together with the *BackupInterval* property, and when that property was deprecated, so was the *BackUpLastTime* property. This property will never return any information on computers running Windows XP; it does, however, work on computers that run Windows 2000 and earlier.

Summary

In this chapter, we looked at two groups of Win32 classes: WMI management classes and classes provided by the WMI Windows Installer provider. The WMI Windows Installer provider is not installed by default on computers running Windows Server 2003, but it can easily be added by using Add Or Remove Programs. It is installed by default on earlier operating systems. Once the WMI MSI provider is installed, you gain access to nearly a hundred WMI classes that give you the capability to write scripts that install, patch, and inventory software in your Windows environment. You can use WMI to assist in managing WMI. Several classes fall into this category. The most important is the *Win32_WMISetting* class, but a few others warrant further exploration.

Quiz Yourself

Q: What is the main advantage of installing the WMI Windows Installer provider on a computer that runs Windows Server 2003?

A: The main advantage of installing the WMI Windows Installer provider on a computer that runs Windows Server 2003 is that it provides access to the software management classes. In this manner, you gain the opportunity to perform software installation, maintenance, and inventory.

Q: What is the main WMI management class?

A: The main WMI management class is *Win32_WMISetting*.

Q: How can you find out whether a WMI provider exists on a remote computer by using a script?

A: To find out whether a WMI provider exists on a remote computer, you can do an *InstancesOf* query and look for instances of the *__Win32Provider* system class.

On Your Own

Lab 19 Working with the *Win32_Product* Class

In this lab, you will use the *Win32_Product* class to obtain a list of applications installed on a computer. You will also use the class to obtain installation directory information about the products.

1. Open the ConnectServerTemplate.vbs file in the Lab 19 directory, and save it as StudentLab19.vbs.

2. For now, all the variables are declared. You simply need to modify the *wmiQuery* so that it points to *Win32_Product*. You are not using the *ExecQuery* method, so you want only the *ClassName* held here. The line will look like the following:

```
wmiQuery = "win32_Product"
```

3. Instead of using the *ExecQuery* method, use the *InstancesOf* method. Modify the *set colItems = objWMIService.ExecQuery(wmiQuery)* line to use *InstancesOf*. The modified line looks like the following:

```
Set colItems = objWMIService.instancesOf(wmiQuery)
```

4. Turn on two of the *Wscript.Echo* commands and have them print out the name and the version properties.

5. Save and run the script. You should see a printout of all the MSI-installed applications on your computer with their accompanying version information.

6. Now you want to obtain some file installation information. Not all of the applications provide this information. Additionally, doing an evaluation of *NULL* does not always work either. Instead, use the *Instr* function. All file installation directories will contain a backslash (\), so this is what you look for. If you find the backslash (\),you want to echo out the *InstallLocation* property inside a simple *For Next* loop. The completed code looks like the following:

```
If InStr(objItem.installLocation, "\") then
WScript.echo vbtab & objItem.InstallLocation
End if
```

7. Save and run the script. It should run without errors.

8. Now you want to clean up the output just a little bit. Instead of using two lines for the product name and the version name, move these items to a single line. The modified line will look like the following:

```
Wscript.Echo objItem.name & vbtab &objItem.version
```

9. Once you add or modify the two previously existing *Echo* commands, save and run the script. It should produce an adequate output.

Lab 20 Making Changes to WMI Settings

In this lab, you will use the write methods of the *Win32_WMISetting* class to change the default WMI namespace. This procedure works with other writable properties of the *Win32_WMISetting* class as well. As an added bonus, you will build two custom error handlers, examine Microsoft Visual Basic Scripting Edition (VBScript) data types, and, in short, have a lot of fun.

1. Open the ConnectServer.vbs file from the Lab 20 folder, and save it as StudentLab20.vbs.

2. The first thing you need to do is to modify the *wmiQuery* string so it points to the *Win32_WMISetting* class. Because WMI is already running, connect to the running instance of WMI. To do this, use the @ shorthand notation. The modified *wmiQuery* looks like the following:

   ```
   wmiQuery = "Win32_WMISetting=@"
   ```

3. Use the *Get* method to connect to the specific instance of *Win32_WMISetting*. This looks like the following:

   ```
   Set objItem = objWMIService.get(wmiQuery)
   ```

4. Delete the entire *For Each Next* section, including all the *Wscript.echo* commands.

5. To set the default WMI namespace, use the *ASPScriptDefaultNamespace* property and assign a value to it. You do so by using the equals sign. Do not "capture" the return code. This line of code looks like the following:

   ```
   objItem.ASPScriptDefaultNamespace ="root\wmi"
   ```

6. Use the *Put* command to put information into WMI. Because you are changing a specific value of a read/write property, you will want to write it back to the WMI repository. Use the *Put_* method as shown here:

   ```
   objItem.put_
   ```

7. Save and run the script. You should not see any errors. In fact, you will not see anything.

8. To see if the script worked, open the WMI Control Properties console: right-click My Computer, select Manage, click Services And Applications, click WMI Control to set the focus, right-click WMI Control, and click Properties. In the Advanced tab, you will see the default namespace—it should match *root\wmi*, which you specified in step 5.

9. If you see the same WMI namespace you specified earlier, you have it right so far. Change the WMI namespace back to the default by modifying the *ASPScriptDefault-Namespace* = "*root\wmi*" line to be *ASPScriptDefaultNamespace* = "*root\cimv2*". Run the script and confirm that the namespace, in fact, changed back.

10. Because you are not echoing out a return code, it makes sense to add an error handler. Use the error object, which is always in scope. Echo out the *Number*, *Description*, and

Source properties of the *err* object. (If you check the solution file you will see a different solution because we are not done with the error handler at this point.) This code looks like the following:

```
If Err.Number <> 0 Then
WScript.echo hex(Err.Number) & vbcrlf & Err.Description &_
    vbcrlf & Err.Source
End if
```

11. Run the script. Once again, you should not see any message. Save your script.

12. Use the WMI control tool to verify the changes took effect.

13. Declare a new variable called *strNS* to hold the desired WMI namespace.

14. In the reference section of the script, under the *wmiNS = "\root\cimv2"* line, add the line *strNS = "root\wmi"*.

15. Find the line where you are actually changing the WMI namespace. You have the namespace hard-coded right now. Change it to use the new *strNS* variable. The modified line of code looks like the following:

```
objItem.ASPScriptDefaultNamespace = strNS
```

16. Save and run the script.

17. Open the DisplayWMISettings.vbs script from the Lab 20 folder, and run it. Notice at the top the value of the *ASPScriptDefaultNamespace* property. It should read *root\wmi*, indicating you were successful in changing the default WMI namespace on the computer.

18. Add an error handler to indicate whether the operation was successful. Use the *Number*, *Description*, and *Source* properties of the *err* object. Use an *If Then Else End If* decision matrix. Make the evaluation on the value of *Err.Number* not being equal to 0. The error handler looks something like the following at this point:

```
If Err.Number<> 0 Then
WScript.echo Err.Number & vbtab & Err.Source & vbcrlf & Err.Description _
    & "occurred. The change did not occur"
    Else

End if
```

19. Run the script and see what happens. It should still work.

20. To enable the script to enter the error handler, you need to remove the comment mark from the *On Error Resume Next* statement at the top of the script. This enables the script to proceed past any errors that might be generated in script.

21. It works? Sweet! Now add to the error handler. In the *Else* condition, add code to indicate a successful completion of the script. Also, it would be nice to print out the new namespace, so echo out the value of *objItem.ASPScriptDefaultNamespace*. The code looks like the following inside the *Else End If*:

```
WScript.echo "The default wmi Namespace is now " & vbcrlf & _
    objItem.ASPScriptDefaultNamespace
```

22.   Save and run the script.

23.   There is one last little thing you need to do to complete the error handler: clear the error if it should occur. After the line that prints out that an error occurred and right before the *Else* condition, use the *Clear* method of the *err* object. It will simply look like *Err.Clear*. The code looks like the following:

```
If Err.Number<> 0 Then
WScript.echo Err.Number & vbtab & Err.Source & vbcrlf & Err.Description _
    & " occurred. The change did not occur"
    Err.clear
    Else
WScript.echo "The default wmi Namespace is now " & vbcrlf & _
    objItem.ASPScriptDefaultNamespace
End If
```

24.   Now that you have an error handler, test it to see how effective it is. Assign a numeric value for *strNS* in the reference section of the script, something like *strNS = 5*.

25.   Run the script. Do you get an error? No. The problem is that there is nothing that detects an invalid entry for the default WMI namespace. To this end, add a subroutine that both detects an invalid entry and ensures an entry that specifies the *root* type of namespace.

26.   Use the *vbscript VarType* function to detect the data type of the value supplied for *strNS*. If it is an integer, you will raise error 1031. If it is a string but does not have the word *root* with a backslash in it, you will raise error 1032. Both of these are standard VBScript errors. The code to do this looks like the following:

```
Sub subCheckNS
If VarType(StrNS) = vbInteger Then Err.Raise(1031)
If VarType(StrNS) = vbString Then
    If InStr(1,StrNS,"root\",1) = 0 Then Err.Raise(1032)
End If
End Sub
```

27.   To get an idea of the basic VBScript errors, you can look at the RaiseAbunchOfErrors.vbs script in the Lab 20 folder. This script simply walks through a whole lot of numbers, uses the *Err.Raise* method to raise the errors, and the *Err.Clear* method to clear the errors. In addition, it prints out the error numbers and descriptions. It does this while filtering out the word *unknown* (as in *unknown error*).

28.   Back in your StudentLab20.vbs script, move the original error handler into a subroutine. Call it *SubError*, and move it to the bottom of the script. It looks like the following when you're done:

```
Sub subError
If Err.Number<> 0 Then
WScript.echo Err.Number & vbtab & Err.Source & vbcrlf & Err.Description _
    & " occurred. The change did not occur"
    Err.clear
```

```
      Else
WScript.echo "The default wmi Namespace is now " & vbcrlf & _
      objItem.ASPScriptDefaultNamespace
End If
End sub
```

29. Finally, you will need to call *SubError* right after you use the *Put_* method to write to the database. This is where the error would most likely occur.

30. Now try to add the number 6 as a value for *strNS* and run the script. You should get the Invalid Number error 1031.

31. Try *cimv2* with no *root* in front of it for the value of *strNS* and run the script. You should get the Invalid Character error 1032. This means a string was supplied, but it did not contain the word *root*.

32. Try the value *"root\cimv2"* for *strNS* and run the script. It should work.

Chapter 10

Using System Hardware Classes

In the last chapter, we examined the five categories of Win32 Windows Management Instrumentation (WMI) classes. We saw how those classes can assist us in working with both WMI and with the Microsoft Windows operating system.

The system hardware classes are organized into nine different subcategories of classes that, when taken together, totally describe a computer system. Using these classes, you can find out all the information needed to manage and control a Microsoft Windows Server 2003–based system. In addition, numerous methods enable you to perform useful tasks on your server.

Before You Begin

To work through this chapter, you should be familiar with the following concepts:

- The basics of performing WMI queries
- The use of the WMI moniker
- The use of the *ConnectServer* method
- The basics of event-driven queries
- The basics of conducting privileged operations

After you complete this chapter, you will be familiar with the following concepts:

- The use of the system hardware classes
- The organization of the WMI hardware classes

 Note All the scripts used in this chapter are located on the CD that accompanies this book in the \Scripts\Chapter10 folder.

Using Cooling Device Classes

The cooling device classes are used to represent items related to cooling on servers and workstations. Four classes are found in this category:

- *Win32_Fan*

- *Win32_HeatPipe*

- *Win32_TemperatureProbe*

- *Win32_Refrigeration*

Of the four classes, the two that are most interesting are the *Win32_Fan* class and the *Win32_TemperatureProbe* class.

Working with *Win32_Fan*

The *Win32_Fan* class is derived from the *cim_fan* class in the *root\cimv2* namespace. The *Win32_Fan* class inherits three methods from *cim_fan*—however, none of these methods are implemented by WMI. The *cim_fan* class is an abstract class, which means it is used as the basis for the development of other WMI classes. You can, of course, write a script that uses *cim_fan*, and it will work, but there is really no reason to do this because both *cim_fan* and *Win32_Fan* have the same number of properties and methods. The *Win32_Fan* class might not return any information on your system because we have to retrieve information from the hardware. If the hardware vendor has not provided information to the class, the script returns an error.

The interesting thing about the *Win32_Fan* class (and *cim_fan*, for that matter) is the three methods that are defined. The methods are not implemented, which means the schema defines the methods but WMI does not implement them. The strange thing about this class is the way the key value is expressed. The key property is the *DeviceID*, but rather than being a normal device ID 0 or something similar, it is *root\cimv2* 0. This was discovered using the Get-ClassKey.vbs script that is located in the UtilityScripts subdirectory on the accompanying CD. If the GetWin32_Fan.vbs script fails, it is possible the class is not populated on your system. If the GetClassKey.vbs script does not return a key value, you can use Wbemtest.exe to see if there is an instance of the class on your system.

GetWin32_Fan.vbs

```
strComputer = "."
wmiNS = "\root\cimv2"
wmiQuery = "Win32_Fan.deviceID='root\cimv2 0'"
Set objWMIService = GetObject("winmgmts:\\" & strComputer & wmiNS)
Set objItem = objWMIService.get(wmiQuery)

 wscript.echo "ActiveCooling: " & objItem.ActiveCooling
 wscript.echo "Availability: " & objItem.Availability
 wscript.echo "Caption: " & objItem.Caption
 wscript.echo "ConfigManagerErrorCode: " & objItem.ConfigManagerErrorCode
 wscript.echo "ConfigManagerUserConfig: " & objItem.ConfigManagerUserConfig
 wscript.echo "CreationClassName: " & objItem.CreationClassName
 wscript.echo "Description: " & objItem.Description
 wscript.echo "DesiredSpeed: " & objItem.DesiredSpeed
 wscript.echo "DeviceID: " & objItem.DeviceID
```

```
wscript.echo "ErrorCleared: " & objItem.ErrorCleared
wscript.echo "ErrorDescription: " & objItem.ErrorDescription
wscript.echo "InstallDate: " & objItem.InstallDate
wscript.echo "LastErrorCode: " & objItem.LastErrorCode
wscript.echo "Name: " & objItem.Name
wscript.echo "PNPDeviceID: " & objItem.PNPDeviceID
wscript.echo "PowerManagementCapabilities: " & objItem.PowerManagementCapabilities
wscript.echo "PowerManagementSupported: " & objItem.PowerManagementSupported
wscript.echo "Status: " & objItem.Status
wscript.echo "StatusInfo: " & objItem.StatusInfo
wscript.echo "SystemCreationClassName: " & objItem.SystemCreationClassName
wscript.echo "SystemName: " & objItem.SystemName
wscript.echo "VariableSpeed: " & objItem.VariableSpeed
```

Probing the *Win32_TemperatureProbe* Class

The *Win32_TemperatureProbe* class is derived from the *CIM_TemperatureSensor* class. In fact, just like *Win32_Fan*, it has no specific properties that are not derived. The two methods that are defined are not implemented. Most of the information that the *Win32_TemperatureProbe* class displays is reported to it from the computer's system management BIOS (SMBIOS). If the computer's SMBIOS does not report to WMI, you are not provided the information and the script will error out. If you are interested in the system BIOS on your computer in particular, you might find useful the *Win32_SMBiosMemory* class, the *Win32_BIOS* class, and the *Win32_SystemBios* class, which are discussed later in the "Motherboard, Controller, and Port Classes" section.

The GetWin32_TemperatureProbe.vbs script uses the *Get* method to make a connection to the key property (*DeviceID*), which has a value of '*root\cimv2 0*' just like the *Win32_ Fan* class did. All of the temperature-related properties (such as tolerance) are reported in tenths of degrees centigrade. The *CurrentReading* property does not report because of the problems involved in retrieving the real-time value from the SMBIOS tables. If the GetWin32_TemperatureProbe.vbs script fails, you can use Wbemtest.exe to open the *Win32_TemperatureProbe* class to see if there are any instances of the class represented on your system. If there are not, your hardware maker does not provide the information to WMI.

GetWin32_TemperatureProbe.vbs
```
strComputer = "."
wmiNS = "\root\cimv2"
wmiQuery = "Win32_TemperatureProbe.DeviceID='root\cimv2 0'"
Set objWMIService = GetObject("winmgmts:\\" & strComputer & wmiNS)
Set objItem = objWMIService.get(wmiQuery)
With objItem
 wscript.echo "Accuracy: " & .Accuracy
 wscript.echo "Availability: " & .Availability
 wscript.echo "Caption: " & .Caption
 wscript.echo "ConfigManagerErrorCode: " & .ConfigManagerErrorCode
 wscript.echo "ConfigManagerUserConfig: " & .ConfigManagerUserConfig
 wscript.echo "CreationClassName: " & .CreationClassName
 wscript.echo "CurrentReading: " & .CurrentReading
 wscript.echo "Description: " & .Description
```

```
wscript.echo "DeviceID: " & .DeviceID
wscript.echo "ErrorCleared: " & .ErrorCleared
wscript.echo "ErrorDescription: " & .ErrorDescription
wscript.echo "InstallDate: " & .InstallDate
wscript.echo "IsLinear: " & .IsLinear
wscript.echo "LastErrorCode: " & .LastErrorCode
wscript.echo "LowerThresholdCritical: " & .LowerThresholdCritical
wscript.echo "LowerThresholdFatal: " & .LowerThresholdFatal
wscript.echo "LowerThresholdNonCritical: " & .LowerThresholdNonCritical
wscript.echo "MaxReadable: " & .MaxReadable
wscript.echo "MinReadable: " & .MinReadable
wscript.echo "Name: " & .Name
wscript.echo "NominalReading: " & .NominalReading
wscript.echo "NormalMax: " & .NormalMax
wscript.echo "NormalMin: " & .NormalMin
wscript.echo "PNPDeviceID: " & .PNPDeviceID
wscript.echo "PowerManagementCapabilities: " &.PowerManagementCapabilities
wscript.echo "PowerManagementSupported: " & .PowerManagementSupported
wscript.echo "Resolution: " & .Resolution
wscript.echo "Status: " & .Status
wscript.echo "StatusInfo: " & .StatusInfo
wscript.echo "SystemCreationClassName: " & .SystemCreationClassName
wscript.echo "SystemName: " & .SystemName
wscript.echo "Tolerance: " & .Tolerance
wscript.echo "UpperThresholdCritical: " & .UpperThresholdCritical
wscript.echo "UpperThresholdFatal: " & .UpperThresholdFatal
wscript.echo "UpperThresholdNonCritical: " & .UpperThresholdNonCritical
End with
```

Examining the Input Device Classes

Only two classes are used to represent input devices:

- *Win32_Keyboard*
- *Win32_PointingDevice*

Working with the *Win32_Keyboard* Class

Win32_Keyboard is derived from *CIM_Keyboard*. Both classes have 23 properties and two methods. The two methods (*Reset* and *SetPowerState*) are not implemented. If you want to use the *Get* method to connect to the *Win32_Keyboard* class, you need to use the *DeviceID* property. The problem with using the *Get* method here is that the *DeviceID* property is not the most intuitive property around, and you will end up with a value something like the following: ACPI\PNP0303\4&1D6F7EAE&0. You can easily obtain this value by using the GetClass-Key.vbs script from the UtilityScripts folder. You could also find this value by simply running the following Win32_Keyboard.vbs script. You need to decide if it is worth the trouble of using *ExecQuery* to return "all instances of keyboards" on your computer and then using *For Next* to walk through the results or of changing the script to look something like the

GetWin32_Keyboard.vbs script (in the Chapter10 folder) and potentially having to edit the
DeviceID property.

Win32_Keyboard.vbs

```
strComputer = "."
wmiNS = "\root\cimv2"
wmiQuery = "Select * from Win32_Keyboard"
Set objWMIService = GetObject("winmgmts:\\" & strComputer & wmiNS)
Set colItems = objWMIService.ExecQuery(wmiQuery)
For Each objItem in colItems

 wscript.echo "Availability: " & objItem.Availability
 wscript.echo "Caption: " & objItem.Caption
 wscript.echo "ConfigManagerErrorCode: " & objItem.ConfigManagerErrorCode
 wscript.echo "ConfigManagerUserConfig: " & objItem.ConfigManagerUserConfig
 wscript.echo "CreationClassName: " & objItem.CreationClassName
 wscript.echo "Description: " & objItem.Description
 wscript.echo "DeviceID: " & objItem.DeviceID
 wscript.echo "ErrorCleared: " & objItem.ErrorCleared
 wscript.echo "ErrorDescription: " & objItem.ErrorDescription
 wscript.echo "InstallDate: " & objItem.InstallDate
 wscript.echo "IsLocked: " & objItem.IsLocked
 wscript.echo "LastErrorCode: " & objItem.LastErrorCode
 wscript.echo "Layout: " & objItem.Layout
 wscript.echo "Name: " & objItem.Name
 wscript.echo "NumberOfFunctionKeys: " & objItem.NumberOfFunctionKeys
 wscript.echo "Password: " & objItem.Password
 wscript.echo "PNPDeviceID: " & objItem.PNPDeviceID
 wscript.echo "PowerManagementCapabilities: " & objItem.PowerManagementCapabilities
 wscript.echo "PowerManagementSupported: " & objItem.PowerManagementSupported
 wscript.echo "Status: " & objItem.Status
 wscript.echo "StatusInfo: " & objItem.StatusInfo
 wscript.echo "SystemCreationClassName: " & objItem.SystemCreationClassName
 wscript.echo "SystemName: " & objItem.SystemName
wscript.echo " "
next
```

Working with the *Win32_PointingDevice* Class

Generally speaking, when you use the *Win32_PointingDevice* class, you are concerned with
mouse devices. *Win32_PointingDevice* is a good example of a situation in which Microsoft
extended the class to make it more applicable to a Windows environment. The
Win32_PointingDevice.vbs script tells you everything there is to know about a mouse on a
computer running the Windows operating system. This script provides some useful inven-
tory-type data.

Win32_PointingDevice.vbs

```
strComputer = "."
wmiNS = "\root\cimv2"
wmiQuery = "Select * from Win32_PointingDevice"
Set objWMIService = GetObject("winmgmts:\\" & strComputer & wmiNS)
Set colItems = objWMIService.ExecQuery(wmiQuery)
```

```
For Each objItem in colItems

    wscript.echo "Availability: " & objItem.Availability
    wscript.echo "Caption: " & objItem.Caption
    wscript.echo "ConfigManagerErrorCode: " & objItem.ConfigManagerErrorCode
    wscript.echo "ConfigManagerUserConfig: " & objItem.ConfigManagerUserConfig
    wscript.echo "CreationClassName: " & objItem.CreationClassName
    wscript.echo "Description: " & objItem.Description
    wscript.echo "DeviceID: " & objItem.DeviceID
    wscript.echo "DeviceInterface: " & objItem.DeviceInterface
    wscript.echo "DoubleSpeedThreshold: " & objItem.DoubleSpeedThreshold
    wscript.echo "ErrorCleared: " & objItem.ErrorCleared
    wscript.echo "ErrorDescription: " & objItem.ErrorDescription
    wscript.echo "Handedness: " & objItem.Handedness
    wscript.echo "HardwareType: " & objItem.HardwareType
    wscript.echo "InfFileName: " & objItem.InfFileName
    wscript.echo "InfSection: " & objItem.InfSection
    wscript.echo "InstallDate: " & objItem.InstallDate
    wscript.echo "IsLocked: " & objItem.IsLocked
    wscript.echo "LastErrorCode: " & objItem.LastErrorCode
    wscript.echo "Manufacturer: " & objItem.Manufacturer
    wscript.echo "Name: " & objItem.Name
    wscript.echo "NumberOfButtons: " & objItem.NumberOfButtons
    wscript.echo "PNPDeviceID: " & objItem.PNPDeviceID
    wscript.echo "PointingType: " & objItem.PointingType
    wscript.echo "PowerManagementCapabilities: " & objItem.PowerManagementCapabilities
    wscript.echo "PowerManagementSupported: " & objItem.PowerManagementSupported
    wscript.echo "QuadSpeedThreshold: " & objItem.QuadSpeedThreshold
    wscript.echo "Resolution: " & objItem.Resolution
    wscript.echo "SampleRate: " & objItem.SampleRate
    wscript.echo "Status: " & objItem.Status
    wscript.echo "StatusInfo: " & objItem.StatusInfo
    wscript.echo "Synch: " & objItem.Synch
    wscript.echo "SystemCreationClassName: " & objItem.SystemCreationClassName
    wscript.echo "SystemName: " & objItem.SystemName
wscript.echo " "
next
```

Mass Storage Classes

Six classes are used to represent mass storage classes. By using these classes, you have access to properties that can describe nearly every possible configuration available to a computer running the Windows operating system. No methods are available in this grouping of classes, but there are a few writable properties. The main use of these classes is for reporting purposes. Following are the mass storage classes:

- *Win32_AutoChkSetting*

- *Win32_CDROMDrive*

- *Win32_DiskDrive*

- *Win32_FloppyDrive*

- *Win32_PhysicalMedia*
- *Win32_TapeDrive*

Checking the Autocheck Settings

The *Win32_AutoChkSetting* class displays information related to a check disk operation that is scheduled as a result of a potential problem on the hard disk drive. This class does not tell you if you need to do a disk check; rather, it tells you what will happen if an automatically scheduled disk check is scheduled. The most interesting property of this class is the *UserInputDelay* property. This property determines how long before the Autocheck will run, unless you press the space bar. This property is writable, so if the default value is too short or too long, you can change it by writing to the property. The technique for making this change is illustrated in the SetAutoCheckSetting.vbs script. To set the property you make the connection into WMI, connect to the class, and assign a value to the property. The Win32_AutoChkSetting.vbs script in the Chapter10 folder on the accompanying CD reports all the properties.

SetAutoCheckSetting.vbs
```
strComputer = "."
wmiNS = "\root\cimv2"
wmiQuery = "select * from win32_autoChkSetting"
Set objWMIService = GetObject("winmgmts:\\" & strComputer & wmiNS)
Set colItems = objWMIService.execQuery(wmiQuery)
For Each objItem in colItems
objItem.UserInputDelay = 15
 objItem.Put_
Next
```

Examining the *Win32_CDROMDrive* Class

The *Win32_CDROMDrive* class describes the removable storage device of the same name. This class can provide numerous properties, as shown in the Win32_CDROMDrive.vbs script in the Chapter10 folder on the accompanying CD. This class does not do some things very well. For instance, it will not tell you if a drive is writable. A property called *Capabilities* that is stored as an array indicates what the CD-ROM drive is capable of. Capability 4 means it supports writing; however, I have never seen a CD-ROM drive report back that it supports writing. Usually something silly such as "supports removable media" (capability 7) comes back, along with "random access" (capability 3). The *Win32_CDROMDrive* class does not have a property that tells you if the device supports DVD either.

You are not stuck with only the information provided directly by the class. You can modify the output to suit your needs. The CDDriveInfo.vbs script includes a technique for doing this. You rely upon the fact that most of the time manufacturers display drive information in the caption property of the *Win32_CDROMDrive* class. If you are looking for DVD drives, you use the *Instr* command to pull out the drive that is displaying that information.

CDDriveInfo.vbs

```
strComputer = "."
wmiNS = "\root\cimv2"
wmiQuery = "Select * from Win32_CDROMDrive"
Set objWMIService = GetObject("winmgmts:\\" & strComputer & wmiNS)
Set colItems = objWMIService.ExecQuery(wmiQuery)
For Each objItem in colItems
 wscript.echo "Caption: " & objItem.Caption

if instr(1,objItem.caption,"DVD",1) <> 0 then
    WScript.echo "this drive is a DVD player"
End If

wscript.echo "Drive: " & objItem.Drive
wscript.echo "SystemName: " & objItem.SystemName
Next
```

Examining the Disk Drive

There is absolutely nothing exciting about the *Win32_DiskDrive* class. It reports 49 properties, none of which are writable, and the only two methods (inherited) are not implemented. That said, there is nothing wrong with this class. If you need to inventory your hard disk drives, this is the class for you. If you need to find out how many sectors, heads, or types of interfaces your computer is using for storage, fire up the script editor and write your query. You can, of course, use the Win32_DiskDrive.vbs script. It reports all the properties of every hard disk drive on the system. You can find it in the Chapter10 folder on the accompanying CD.

Examining the Floppy Drive

Of course, you have to have a floppy drive on your computer to use this class. The *Win32_FloppyDrive* class provides detailed information about a floppy drive. It can give you the size and device ID, as well as the make and, in some instances, the model of the floppy drive. No methods or writable properties are available for this class. The Win32_FloppyDrive.vbs script in the Chapter10 folder on the accompanying CD provides an example of using the *Win32_FloppyDrive* class.

Working with Tapes

The *Win32_PhysicalMedia* class provides lots of good information about the tape that goes into your tape drive. It also reports on other removable media. Although the *Capabilities* property theoretically is able to report on removable media from a CD-ROM drive, you are better off using the *Win32_CDROMDrive* class to provide this information. The Win32_PhysicalMedia.vbs script in the Chapter10 folder on the accompanying CD provides an example of using the *Win32_PhysicalMedia* class.

Using the *Win32_TapeDrive* Class

The *Win32_TapeDrive* class is another reporting class. It has 40 properties and two inherited methods, which are not implemented. The 40 properties describe nearly every conceivable piece of information about a tape drive: Does it support hardware compression, and if so, what method does it use? How much space is devoted to the end-of-tape warning? Does it need cleaning? Inquiring minds want to know these things, and this information is very useful if you need to do a backup drive inventory. The Win32_TapeDrive.vbs script uses this class. The *Capabilities* and the *CapabilityDescriptions* properties work hand in hand with one another. The *CapabilityDescriptions* property translates the values retrieved from the *Capabilities* property. Several WMI classes do this, although most do not. When you find one, it is a real treat.

Win32_TapeDrive.vbs

```
strComputer = "."
wmiNS = "\root\cimv2"
wmiQuery = "Select * from Win32_TapeDrive"
Set objWMIService = GetObject("winmgmts:\\" & strComputer & wmiNS)
Set colItems = objWMIService.ExecQuery(wmiQuery)
For Each objItem in colItems

 wscript.echo "Availability: " & objItem.Availability
 wscript.echo "Capabilities: " & objItem.Capabilities
 wscript.echo "CapabilityDescriptions: " & objItem.CapabilityDescriptions
 wscript.echo "Caption: " & objItem.Caption
 wscript.echo "Compression: " & objItem.Compression
 wscript.echo "CompressionMethod: " & objItem.CompressionMethod
 wscript.echo "ConfigManagerErrorCode: " & objItem.ConfigManagerErrorCode
 wscript.echo "ConfigManagerUserConfig: " & objItem.ConfigManagerUserConfig
 wscript.echo "CreationClassName: " & objItem.CreationClassName
 wscript.echo "DefaultBlockSize: " & objItem.DefaultBlockSize
 wscript.echo "Description: " & objItem.Description
 wscript.echo "DeviceID: " & objItem.DeviceID
 wscript.echo "ECC: " & objItem.ECC
 wscript.echo "EOTWarningZoneSize: " & objItem.EOTWarningZoneSize
 wscript.echo "ErrorCleared: " & objItem.ErrorCleared
 wscript.echo "ErrorDescription: " & objItem.ErrorDescription
 wscript.echo "ErrorMethodology: " & objItem.ErrorMethodology
 wscript.echo "FeaturesHigh: " & objItem.FeaturesHigh
 wscript.echo "FeaturesLow: " & objItem.FeaturesLow
 wscript.echo "Id: " & objItem.Id
 wscript.echo "InstallDate: " & objItem.InstallDate
 wscript.echo "LastErrorCode: " & objItem.LastErrorCode
 wscript.echo "Manufacturer: " & objItem.Manufacturer
 wscript.echo "MaxBlockSize: " & objItem.MaxBlockSize
 wscript.echo "MaxMediaSize: " & objItem.MaxMediaSize
 wscript.echo "MaxPartitionCount: " & objItem.MaxPartitionCount
 wscript.echo "MediaType: " & objItem.MediaType
 wscript.echo "MinBlockSize: " & objItem.MinBlockSize
 wscript.echo "Name: " & objItem.Name
 wscript.echo "NeedsCleaning: " & objItem.NeedsCleaning
 wscript.echo "NumberOfMediaSupported: " & objItem.NumberOfMediaSupported
```

```
    wscript.echo "Padding: " & objItem.Padding
    wscript.echo "PNPDeviceID: " & objItem.PNPDeviceID
    wscript.echo "PowerManagementCapabilities: " & objItem.PowerManagementCapabilities
    wscript.echo "PowerManagementSupported: " & objItem.PowerManagementSupported
    wscript.echo "ReportSetMarks: " & objItem.ReportSetMarks
    wscript.echo "Status: " & objItem.Status
    wscript.echo "StatusInfo: " & objItem.StatusInfo
    wscript.echo "SystemCreationClassName: " & objItem.SystemCreationClassName
    wscript.echo "SystemName: " & objItem.SystemName
wscript.echo " "
next
```

Motherboard, Controller, and Port Classes

There are 50 classes used to represent the motherboard, controller, and port classes. These classes can tell you information about processors, the BIOS, memory, and can even indicate whether your laptop supports Bluetooth, for example. There are too many classes to list here, but they are included in the "Motherboard, Controller, and Port Classes" section of Appendix D. No real methods are exposed by these classes. However, some cool classes are in this group. We look at a couple of them in this section, beginning with the *Win32_PortConnector* class.

Reporting with Port Classes

The Port classes can provide vital information about the input/output capabilities of your machine. The *Win32_PortConnector* at first glance seems rather trite. It was not until I started looking at the descriptions that I began to get rather excited. In particular, the *ExternalReferenceDesignator* property can report useful information such as whether the laptop has a wireless card, Bluetooth, or infrared capabilities. The PortConnector.vbs script uses this class to query a subset of the properties available from the *Win32_PortConnector* class (the Win32_PortConnector.vbs script in the Chapter10 folder on the accompanying CD prints out all the properties). The *ConnectorType* property is an array, so you use the *Join* function to convert it into a string so you can easily print it out. The *ConnectorType* property is stored as an array because it first reports the configuration type, and the second element of the array indicates whether the port is male or female. On my laptop, the parallel port reports the following information:

```
ConnectorType:23,3
ExternalReferenceDesignator:PARALLEL PORT
PortType:3
Tag:Port Connector 0
```

A *ConnectorType* of 23 means that it is a parallel port. The second element, 3, means it is a female type of connector. The *PortType* of 3 shown in the preceding report means it is a parallel Extended Capabilities Port (ECP), and the tag of *Port Connector 0* is a unique identifier of a port connection on the computer system. The next port is *Port Connector 1*, and then *Port Connector 2*, with each port on the system receiving its own unique identifier. The Platform software development kit (SDK) includes tables that enable you to look up the meanings of these various properties.

PortConnector.vbs

```
strComputer = "."
wmiNS = "\root\cimv2"
wmiQuery = "Select * from win32_PortConnector"
strUsr =""'Blank for current security. Domain\Username
strPWD = ""'Blank for current security.
strLocl = "MS_409" 'U.S. English. Can leave blank for current language
strAuth = ""'if specify domain in strUsr, this must be blank
iFlag = "0" 'only two values allowed here: 0 (wait for connection), 128 (wait max two min)
Set objLocator = CreateObject("WbemScripting.SWbemLocator")
Set objWMIService = objLocator.ConnectServer(strComputer, _
    wmiNS, strUsr, strPWD, strLocl, strAuth, iFLag)
Set colItems = objWMIService.ExecQuery(wmiQuery)

For Each objItem in colItems
Wscript.echo "ConnectorType:"  & join(objItem.ConnectorType, ",")
Wscript.echo "ExternalReferenceDesignator:" &_ objItem.ExternalReferenceDesignator
Wscript.echo "PortType:"  & objItem.PortType
Wscript.echo "Tag:"  & objItem.Tag
WScript.echo ""
Next
```

Networking Device Classes

Three classes are used to represent networking devices. These are extremely powerful and flexible classes. By using these classes, you can describe the network adapter, including its protocol settings, security configuration, and hardware descriptions. The logic of these classes is as follows: the adapter class describes the network adapter itself—the physical piece of hardware. The network adapter configuration class is used to describe and to set the protocol configuration on a specific network adapter. To this end, the adapter configuration class contains 41 methods, providing the intrepid network administrator a Swiss army knife for dealing with network configuration issues. The adapter setting class is used to match a network adapter with its configuration settings—it is an association class. An example of using this class is the Win32_NetworkAdapterSetting.vbs script in the cimv2 folder on the accompanying CD. The networking device classes are as follows:

- *Win32_NetworkAdapter*

- *Win32_NetworkAdapterConfiguration*

- *Win32_NetworkAdapterSetting*

Working with the Network Adapter Class

The *Win32_NetworkAdapter* class is used to describe the network adapter you might have installed on your computer. It contains 36 properties and two methods (inherited), which are not implemented. Basically, you use this class to tell you everything you need to know about the network adapter. *Win32_NetworkAdapter* is related to many other classes on the computer, as shown in Figure 10-1. Some of these classes are in the networking category; others are not.

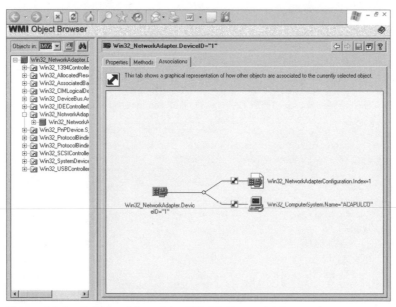

Figure 10-1   Relationships of the *Win32_NetworkAdapter* class

The *Win32_NetworkAdapter* class does not allow you to make any changes to the network adapter—for that you use the *Win32_NetworkAdapterConfiguration* class. In the Win32_NetworkAdapter.vbs script, I use a variable *Where* clause to filter out information on network adapters that contain the name Intel. I do this to remove information about remote access server (RAS) adapters, infrared adapters, parallel cable connections, virtual private network (VPN) adapters, and even virtual machine adapters. On my laptop, I have two real network cards: a wired card and a wireless card. Both happen to be made by Intel, so that is the name that shows up in the caption. If your network card is made by some other company, you need to substitute that name in the *strWhere* assignment. If you want to see all the network adapters regardless of manufacturer, modify the *wmiQuery* line so it looks like the following:

```
wmiQuery = "Select * from Win32_NetworkAdapter"
```

Win32_NetworkAdapter.vbs

```
strComputer = "."
wmiNS = "\root\cimv2"
strWhere = "caption like '%intel%'"
wmiQuery = "Select * from Win32_NetworkAdapter where " & strWhere
Set objWMIService = GetObject("winmgmts:\\" & strComputer & wmiNS)
Set colItems = objWMIService.ExecQuery(wmiQuery)
For Each objItem in colItems:With objItem
 wscript.echo funLine("Caption: " & .Caption)
 wscript.echo "AdapterType: " & .AdapterType
```

```
wscript.echo "AdapterTypeId: " & .AdapterTypeId
wscript.echo "AutoSense: " & .AutoSense
wscript.echo "Availability: " & .Availability
wscript.echo "ConfigManagerErrorCode: " & .ConfigManagerErrorCode
wscript.echo "ConfigManagerUserConfig: " & .ConfigManagerUserConfig
wscript.echo "CreationClassName: " & .CreationClassName
wscript.echo "Description: " & .Description
wscript.echo "DeviceID: " & .DeviceID
wscript.echo "ErrorCleared: " & .ErrorCleared
wscript.echo "ErrorDescription: " & .ErrorDescription
wscript.echo "Index: " & .Index
wscript.echo "InstallDate: " & .InstallDate
wscript.echo "Installed: " & .Installed
wscript.echo "LastErrorCode: " & .LastErrorCode
wscript.echo "MACAddress: " & .MACAddress
wscript.echo "Manufacturer: " & .Manufacturer
wscript.echo "MaxNumberControlled: " & .MaxNumberControlled
wscript.echo "MaxSpeed: " & .MaxSpeed
wscript.echo "Name: " & .Name
wscript.echo "NetConnectionID: " & .NetConnectionID
wscript.echo "NetConnectionStatus: " & .NetConnectionStatus
wscript.echo "NetworkAddresses: " & .NetworkAddresses
wscript.echo "PermanentAddress: " & .PermanentAddress
wscript.echo "PNPDeviceID: " & .PNPDeviceID
wscript.echo "PowerManagementCapabilities: " & .PowerManagementCapabilities
wscript.echo "PowerManagementSupported: " & .PowerManagementSupported
wscript.echo "ProductName: " & .ProductName
wscript.echo "ServiceName: " & .ServiceName
wscript.echo "Speed: " & .Speed
wscript.echo "Status: " & .Status
wscript.echo "StatusInfo: " & .StatusInfo
wscript.echo "SystemCreationClassName: " & .SystemCreationClassName
wscript.echo "SystemName: " & .SystemName
wscript.echo "TimeOfLastReset: " & .TimeOfLastReset & vbcrlf
end with:Next


'### functions below ###
Function funLine(lineOfText)
Dim numEQs, separator, i
numEQs = Len(lineOfText)
For i = 1 To numEQs
    separator = separator & "="
Next
 FunLine = lineOfText & vbcrlf & separator
End function
```

Using the Adapter Configuration Class

The *Win32_NetworkAdapterConfiguration* class is one of the largest WMI classes in existence. It contains 60 properties and 41 methods. Fortunately, the methods are implemented in a straightforward manner, so once you know how to set two or three of them, you know how to work with all 41 methods. The frustrating thing for beginning scripters is that many of the properties of the *Win32_NetworkAdapterConfiguration* class are stored as arrays. This means you have to deal with them using standard array techniques: use the *Join* function, use *For Each Next*, or print out a specific element. I prefer to use the *Join* function because it is quick and easy. But it brings up a special issue: you will get an error if you try to join a property that is *NULL*. The solution is illustrated in the Win32_NetworkAdapterConfiguration.vbs script—use the *isNull* function that is also built into Microsoft Visual Basic Scripting Edition (VBScript). The following code illustrates using this procedure:

```
If not isNull(.DefaultIPGateway) then
 wscript.echo "DefaultIPGateway: " & join(.DefaultIPGateway, ",")
 End if
```

This effectively traps a type mismatch error that occurs when you try to use *Join* with a null property. The properties are *NULL* if the adapter is not in use. On my laptop, I am currently using the wired network connection. It reports all the normal Transmission Control Protocol/Internet Protocol (TCP/IP) configuration settings. The wireless adapter is not in use and reports very little—most of the properties are *NULL*.

Win32_NetworkAdapterConfiguration.vbs

```
strComputer = "."
wmiNS = "\root\cimv2"
strWhere = "caption like '%intel%'" 'the name of your enet or wireless card
wmiQuery = "Select * from Win32_NetworkAdapterConfiguration where " &_ strWhere
Set objWMIService = GetObject("winmgmts:\\" & strComputer & wmiNS)
Set colItems = objWMIService.ExecQuery(wmiQuery)
For Each objItem in colItems:With objItem
 wscript.echo funLine("Caption: " & .Caption)
 wscript.echo "ArpAlwaysSourceRoute: " & .ArpAlwaysSourceRoute
 wscript.echo "ArpUseEtherSNAP: " & .ArpUseEtherSNAP
 wscript.echo "DatabasePath: " & .DatabasePath
 wscript.echo "DeadGWDetectEnabled: " & .DeadGWDetectEnabled
 If not isNull(.DefaultIPGateway) then
 wscript.echo "DefaultIPGateway: " & join(.DefaultIPGateway, ",")
 End if
 wscript.echo "DefaultTOS: " & .DefaultTOS
 wscript.echo "DefaultTTL: " & .DefaultTTL
 wscript.echo "Description: " & .Description
 wscript.echo "DHCPEnabled: " & .DHCPEnabled
 wscript.echo "DHCPLeaseExpires: " & .DHCPLeaseExpires
 wscript.echo "DHCPLeaseObtained: " & .DHCPLeaseObtained
 wscript.echo "DHCPServer: " & .DHCPServer
 wscript.echo "DNSDomain: " & .DNSDomain
 wscript.echo "DNSDomainSuffixSearchOrder: " & .DNSDomainSuffixSearchOrder
 wscript.echo "DNSEnabledForWINSResolution: " &_ .DNSEnabledForWINSResolution
 wscript.echo "DNSHostName: " & .DNSHostName
 If Not IsNull(.DNSServerSearchOrder) then
 wscript.echo "DNSServerSearchOrder: " & join(.DNSServerSearchOrder, ",")
 End if
 wscript.echo "DomainDNSRegistrationEnabled: " & .DomainDNSRegistrationEnabled
 wscript.echo "ForwardBufferMemory: " & .ForwardBufferMemory
 wscript.echo "FullDNSRegistrationEnabled: " & .FullDNSRegistrationEnabled
 If Not IsNull(.GatewayCostMetric) then
 wscript.echo "GatewayCostMetric: " & join(.GatewayCostMetric, ",")
```

```
      End if
      wscript.echo "IGMPLevel: " & .IGMPLevel
      wscript.echo "Index: " & .Index
      If Not IsNull(.IPAddress) then
      wscript.echo "IPAddress: " & join(.IPAddress, ",")
      End if
      wscript.echo "IPConnectionMetric: " & .IPConnectionMetric
      wscript.echo "IPEnabled: " & .IPEnabled
      wscript.echo "IPFilterSecurityEnabled: " & .IPFilterSecurityEnabled
      wscript.echo "IPPortSecurityEnabled: " & .IPPortSecurityEnabled
      If Not IsNull(.IPSecPermitIPProtocols) then
      wscript.echo "IPSecPermitIPProtocols: " & _
      join(.IPSecPermitIPProtocols, ",")
      End If
      If Not IsNull(.IPSecPermitTCPPorts) then
      wscript.echo "IPSecPermitTCPPorts: " & join(.IPSecPermitTCPPorts, ",")
      End If
      If Not IsNull(.IPSecPermitUDPPorts) then
      wscript.echo "IPSecPermitUDPPorts: " & join(.IPSecPermitUDPPorts, ",")
      End If
      If Not IsNull(.IPSubnet) then
      wscript.echo "IPSubnet: " & join(.IPSubnet, ",")
      End if
      wscript.echo "IPUseZeroBroadcast: " & .IPUseZeroBroadcast
      wscript.echo "IPXAddress: " & .IPXAddress
      wscript.echo "IPXEnabled: " & .IPXEnabled
      wscript.echo "IPXFrameType: " & .IPXFrameType
      wscript.echo "IPXMediaType: " & .IPXMediaType
      wscript.echo "IPXNetworkNumber: " & .IPXNetworkNumber
      wscript.echo "IPXVirtualNetNumber: " & .IPXVirtualNetNumber
      wscript.echo "KeepAliveInterval: " & .KeepAliveInterval
      wscript.echo "KeepAliveTime: " & .KeepAliveTime
      wscript.echo "MACAddress: " & .MACAddress
      wscript.echo "MTU: " & .MTU
      wscript.echo "NumForwardPackets: " & .NumForwardPackets
      wscript.echo "PMTUBHDetectEnabled: " & .PMTUBHDetectEnabled
      wscript.echo "PMTUDiscoveryEnabled: " & .PMTUDiscoveryEnabled
      wscript.echo "ServiceName: " & .ServiceName
      wscript.echo "SettingID: " & .SettingID
      wscript.echo "TcpipNetbiosOptions: " & .TcpipNetbiosOptions
      wscript.echo "TcpMaxConnectRetransmissions: " & _ .TcpMaxConnectRetransmissions
      wscript.echo "TcpMaxDataRetransmissions: " & .TcpMaxDataRetransmissions
      wscript.echo "TcpNumConnections: " & .TcpNumConnections
      wscript.echo "TcpUseRFC1122UrgentPointer: " & .TcpUseRFC1122UrgentPointer
      wscript.echo "TcpWindowSize: " & .TcpWindowSize
      wscript.echo "WINSEnableLMHostsLookup: " & .WINSEnableLMHostsLookup
      wscript.echo "WINSHostLookupFile: " & .WINSHostLookupFile
      wscript.echo "WINSPrimaryServer: " & .WINSPrimaryServer
      wscript.echo "WINSScopeID: " & .WINSScopeID
      wscript.echo "WINSSecondaryServer: " & .WINSSecondaryServer & vbcrlf
      end with:Next

      '### functions below####
      Function funLine(lineOfText)
      Dim numEQs, separator, i
```

```
numEQs = Len(lineOfText)
For i = 1 To numEQs
    separator = separator & "="
Next
 FunLine = lineOfText & vbcrlf & separator
End function
```

Power Classes

Seven WMI classes are used to describe items related to power on a system that runs the Windows operating system. The most interesting are the ones related to laptop batteries. By using these classes, you can retrieve information about the status of portable batteries, how much run time is left on them, and the chemistry used in those batteries. We examine two of the battery classes in this section because they are the most useful from a network administrator perspective. Scripts related to the remaining classes are on the accompanying CD in the cimv2 folder. Additional information on these classes can be obtained by referring to the Platform SDK. The power classes are as follows:

- *Win32_AssociatedBattery*
- *Win32_Battery*
- *Win32_CurrentProbe*
- *Win32_PortableBattery*
- *Win32_PowerManagementEvent*
- *Win32_UniterruptiblePowerSupply*
- *Win32_VoltageProbe*

Batteries Are Included

If the target of your script is a portable computer, you might be able to retrieve some really technical information about the battery. The reason I say you *might* be able to retrieve this information is because, of the last three laptops I have had, only one correctly reported this information.

In the Win32_Battery.vbs script, I retrieve some rather interesting information about the battery. If the battery is fully charged, the *BatteryStatus* property reports 3. Most other times it reports 2, which means the status is unknown. The property *DesignVoltage* reports in millivolts, so in the Win32_Battery.vbs script, I divide the number by 1000 to report in volts. Estimated run time reports in minutes, so I divide the number by 60 to report in hours. If the laptop is using electricity, this property reports a very large number and is essentially meaningless. If the laptop is using battery power, this value is constantly changing based upon current running conditions of the machine, becoming more accurate the closer you are to running out of power. Two properties in this class are deprecated: *BatteryRechargeTime* and

ExpectedBatteryLife—I left these properties out of the Win32_Battery.vbs script because they do not report meaningful information.

Win32_Battery.vbs

```
strComputer = "."
wmiNS = "\root\cimv2"
wmiQuery = "Select * from Win32_Battery"
Set objWMIService = GetObject("winmgmts:\\" & strComputer & wmiNS)
Set colItems = objWMIService.ExecQuery(wmiQuery)
For Each objItem in colItems:With objItem
 wscript.echo "Availability: " & .Availability
 wscript.echo "BatteryStatus: " & .BatteryStatus
 wscript.echo "Caption: " & .Caption
 wscript.echo "Chemistry: " & .Chemistry
 wscript.echo "ConfigManagerErrorCode: " & .ConfigManagerErrorCode
 wscript.echo "ConfigManagerUserConfig: " & .ConfigManagerUserConfig
 wscript.echo "CreationClassName: " & .CreationClassName
 wscript.echo "Description: " & .Description
 wscript.echo "DesignCapacity: " & .DesignCapacity
 wscript.echo "DesignVoltage: " & .DesignVoltage/1000
 wscript.echo "DeviceID: " & .DeviceID
 wscript.echo "ErrorCleared: " & .ErrorCleared
 wscript.echo "ErrorDescription: " & .ErrorDescription
 wscript.echo "EstimatedChargeRemaining: " & .EstimatedChargeRemaining
 wscript.echo "EstimatedRunTime: " & .EstimatedRunTime/60
 wscript.echo "ExpectedLife: " & .ExpectedLife
 wscript.echo "FullChargeCapacity: " & .FullChargeCapacity
 wscript.echo "InstallDate: " & .InstallDate
 wscript.echo "LastErrorCode: " & .LastErrorCode
 wscript.echo "MaxRechargeTime: " & .MaxRechargeTime
 wscript.echo "Name: " & .Name
 wscript.echo "PNPDeviceID: " & .PNPDeviceID
 If not IsNull(.PowerManagementCapabilities)then
 wscript.echo "PowerManagementCapabilities: " & Join(.PowerManagementCapabilities)
 End if
 wscript.echo "PowerManagementSupported: " & .PowerManagementSupported
 wscript.echo "SmartBatteryVersion: " & .SmartBatteryVersion
 wscript.echo "Status: " & .Status
 wscript.echo "StatusInfo: " & .StatusInfo
 wscript.echo "SystemCreationClassName: " & .SystemCreationClassName
 wscript.echo "SystemName: " & .SystemName
 wscript.echo "TimeOnBattery: " & .TimeOnBattery
 wscript.echo "TimeToFullCharge: " & .TimeToFullCharge & vbcrlf
end with:next
```

Using Portable Batteries

The *Win32_PortableBattery* class has a great deal of overlap with the *Win32_Battery* class. The difference is the portable battery class is specifically designed to work with portable computers, whereas the *Win32_Battery* class is not. One inconvenience is that you will probably need to use both classes to retrieve meaningful information about your portable computer. Generally, the maker of the laptop publishes information in one or the other class, but not in both. However, you can often pick up information from the other class. In the Win32_PortableBattery.vbs script, *Chemistry* reports a number 6 on my laptop. The Platform SDK tells me that 6 indicates a lithium-ion battery.

Win32_PortableBattery.vbs

```
strComputer = "."
wmiNS = "\root\cimv2"
wmiQuery = "Select * from Win32_PortableBattery"
Set objWMIService = GetObject("winmgmts:\\" & strComputer & wmiNS)
Set colItems = objWMIService.ExecQuery(wmiQuery)
For Each objItem in colItems

 wscript.echo "Availability: " & objItem.Availability
 wscript.echo "BatteryStatus: " & objItem.BatteryStatus
 wscript.echo "CapacityMultiplier: " & objItem.CapacityMultiplier
 wscript.echo "Caption: " & objItem.Caption
 wscript.echo "Chemistry: " & objItem.Chemistry
 wscript.echo "ConfigManagerErrorCode: " & objItem.ConfigManagerErrorCode
 wscript.echo "ConfigManagerUserConfig: " & objItem.ConfigManagerUserConfig
 wscript.echo "CreationClassName: " & objItem.CreationClassName
 wscript.echo "Description: " & objItem.Description
 wscript.echo "DesignCapacity: " & objItem.DesignCapacity
 wscript.echo "DesignVoltage: " & objItem.DesignVoltage
 wscript.echo "DeviceID: " & objItem.DeviceID
 wscript.echo "ErrorCleared: " & objItem.ErrorCleared
 wscript.echo "ErrorDescription: " & objItem.ErrorDescription
 wscript.echo "EstimatedChargeRemaining: " & objItem.EstimatedChargeRemaining
 wscript.echo "EstimatedRunTime: " & objItem.EstimatedRunTime
 wscript.echo "ExpectedLife: " & objItem.ExpectedLife
 wscript.echo "FullChargeCapacity: " & objItem.FullChargeCapacity
 wscript.echo "InstallDate: " & objItem.InstallDate
 wscript.echo "LastErrorCode: " & objItem.LastErrorCode
 wscript.echo "Location: " & objItem.Location
 wscript.echo "ManufactureDate: " & objItem.ManufactureDate
 wscript.echo "Manufacturer: " & objItem.Manufacturer
 wscript.echo "MaxBatteryError: " & objItem.MaxBatteryError
 wscript.echo "MaxRechargeTime: " & objItem.MaxRechargeTime
 wscript.echo "Name: " & objItem.Name
 wscript.echo "PNPDeviceID: " & objItem.PNPDeviceID
 wscript.echo "PowerManagementCapabilities: " & objItem.PowerManagementCapabilities
 wscript.echo "PowerManagementSupported: " & objItem.PowerManagementSupported
 wscript.echo "SmartBatteryVersion: " & objItem.SmartBatteryVersion
 wscript.echo "Status: " & objItem.Status
 wscript.echo "StatusInfo: " & objItem.StatusInfo
 wscript.echo "SystemCreationClassName: " & objItem.SystemCreationClassName
 wscript.echo "SystemName: " & objItem.SystemName
 wscript.echo "TimeOnBattery: " & objItem.TimeOnBattery
 wscript.echo "TimeToFullCharge: " & objItem.TimeToFullCharge
wscript.echo " "
next
```

Quick Check

Q: Which class can be used to display information about writable CD-ROM devices on a computer?

A: To display information about writable CD-ROM devices on a computer, you can use the *Win32_CDROMDrive* class, but you need to filter out the word *DVD* from the *Caption* property.

Q: You are trying to retrieve information about the battery on your laptop computer, but the query is coming back blank. What could be the problem?

A: If you are trying to retrieve information about the battery on your laptop computer but the query is coming back blank, there could be two potential problems: the laptop maker chose not to report battery information to WMI, or the laptop is currently running on house electricity and not on battery power.

Printing Classes

There are nine printing classes. By using a combination of these classes, the network administrator can bring a sense of order to the printing environment. The *Win32_DriverForDevice* class relates printers and their drivers. The *Win32_Printer* class is the main class in this group; weighing in at 86 properties and nine methods, it is certainly the heavyweight in this division. The *Win32_TCPIPPrinterPort* class does not have any methods, but you can create a new instance of the class, which gives you the ability to create printer ports anyway. In this section, we will look at four of the nine printer-related classes. Information on the other classes can be found in the Platform SDK. The printer classes are as follows:

- *Win32_DriverForDevice*
- *Win32_Printer*
- *Win32_PrinterConfiguration*
- *Win32_PrinterController*
- *Win32_PrinterDriver*
- *Win32_PrinterDriverDll*
- *Win32_PrinterSetting*
- *Win32_PrintJob*
- *Win32_TCPIPPrinterPort*

Finding Drivers Used for Print Devices

The *Win32_DriverForDevice* association class relates a *Win32_Printer* to a *Win32_PrintDriver*. Using a direct query to this class provides you with a list of all the printers and their drivers.

This can be used by a network administrator to detect out-of-date print drivers on the network. The Win32_DriverForDevice.vbs script uses the *Win32_DriverForDevice* class to produce a list of printers and the drivers that are loaded for each printer. The *Antecedent* property of this class comes from the *Win32_Printer DeviceID* property, and the *Dependent* property comes from the *Win32_PrintDriver Name* property. These key values are used to link the two classes together in the *Win32_DriverForDevice* class.

Win32_DriverForDevice.vbs

```
strComputer = "."
wmiNS = "\root\cimv2"
wmiQuery = "Select * from Win32_DriverForDevice"
Set objWMIService = GetObject("winmgmts:\\" & strComputer & wmiNS)
Set colItems = objWMIService.ExecQuery(wmiQuery)
For Each objItem in colItems:With objItem
 wscript.echo "Printer: " & .Antecedent
 wscript.echo "Driver: " & .Dependent & vbcrlf
end with:next
```

Printing Information on Printers

The main class in the printing group is the *Win32_Printer* class. You use this class to return information about the printer such as the printer capabilities, number of pages printed, and sizes of paper the printer can handle. The use of the *Win32_Printer* class is illustrated in the Win32_Printer.vbs script.

Win32_Printer.vbs

```
strComputer = "."
wmiNS = "\root\cimv2"
wmiQuery = "Select * from Win32_Printer"
Set objWMIService = GetObject("winmgmts:\\" & strComputer & wmiNS)
Set colItems = objWMIService.ExecQuery(wmiQuery)
For Each objItem in colItems

 wscript.echo "Attributes: " & objItem.Attributes
 wscript.echo "Availability: " & objItem.Availability
 wscript.echo "AvailableJobSheets: " & objItem.AvailableJobSheets
 wscript.echo "AveragePagesPerMinute: " & objItem.AveragePagesPerMinute
 wscript.echo "Capabilities: " & join(objItem.Capabilities, ",")
 wscript.echo "CapabilityDescriptions: " & join(objItem.CapabilityDescriptions, ",")
 wscript.echo "Caption: " & objItem.Caption
 wscript.echo "CharSetsSupported: " & objItem.CharSetsSupported
 wscript.echo "Comment: " & objItem.Comment
 wscript.echo "ConfigManagerErrorCode: " & objItem.ConfigManagerErrorCode
 wscript.echo "ConfigManagerUserConfig: " & objItem.ConfigManagerUserConfig
 wscript.echo "CreationClassName: " & objItem.CreationClassName
 wscript.echo "CurrentCapabilities: " & objItem.CurrentCapabilities
 wscript.echo "CurrentCharSet: " & objItem.CurrentCharSet
 wscript.echo "CurrentLanguage: " & objItem.CurrentLanguage
 wscript.echo "CurrentMimeType: " & objItem.CurrentMimeType
 wscript.echo "CurrentNaturalLanguage: " & objItem.CurrentNaturalLanguage
 wscript.echo "CurrentPaperType: " & objItem.CurrentPaperType
 wscript.echo "Default: " & objItem.Default
```

```
wscript.echo "DefaultCapabilities: " & objItem.DefaultCapabilities
wscript.echo "DefaultCopies: " & objItem.DefaultCopies
wscript.echo "DefaultLanguage: " & objItem.DefaultLanguage
wscript.echo "DefaultMimeType: " & objItem.DefaultMimeType
wscript.echo "DefaultNumberUp: " & objItem.DefaultNumberUp
wscript.echo "DefaultPaperType: " & objItem.DefaultPaperType
wscript.echo "DefaultPriority: " & objItem.DefaultPriority
wscript.echo "Description: " & objItem.Description
wscript.echo "DetectedErrorState: " & objItem.DetectedErrorState
wscript.echo "DeviceID: " & objItem.DeviceID
wscript.echo "Direct: " & objItem.Direct
wscript.echo "DoCompleteFirst: " & objItem.DoCompleteFirst
wscript.echo "DriverName: " & objItem.DriverName
wscript.echo "EnableBIDI: " & objItem.EnableBIDI
wscript.echo "EnableDevQueryPrint: " & objItem.EnableDevQueryPrint
wscript.echo "ErrorCleared: " & objItem.ErrorCleared
wscript.echo "ErrorDescription: " & objItem.ErrorDescription
wscript.echo "ErrorInformation: " & objItem.ErrorInformation
wscript.echo "ExtendedDetectedErrorState: " & objItem.ExtendedDetectedErrorState
wscript.echo "ExtendedPrinterStatus: " & objItem.ExtendedPrinterStatus
wscript.echo "Hidden: " & objItem.Hidden
wscript.echo "HorizontalResolution: " & objItem.HorizontalResolution
wscript.echo "InstallDate: " & objItem.InstallDate
wscript.echo "JobCountSinceLastReset: " & objItem.JobCountSinceLastReset
wscript.echo "KeepPrintedJobs: " & objItem.KeepPrintedJobs
wscript.echo "LanguagesSupported: " & objItem.LanguagesSupported
wscript.echo "LastErrorCode: " & objItem.LastErrorCode
wscript.echo "Local: " & objItem.Local
wscript.echo "Location: " & objItem.Location
wscript.echo "MarkingTechnology: " & objItem.MarkingTechnology
wscript.echo "MaxCopies: " & objItem.MaxCopies
wscript.echo "MaxNumberUp: " & objItem.MaxNumberUp
wscript.echo "MaxSizeSupported: " & objItem.MaxSizeSupported
wscript.echo "MimeTypesSupported: " & objItem.MimeTypesSupported
wscript.echo "Name: " & objItem.Name
wscript.echo "NaturalLanguagesSupported: " & objItem.NaturalLanguagesSupported
wscript.echo "Network: " & objItem.Network
wscript.echo "PaperSizesSupported: " & join(objItem.PaperSizesSupported, ",")
wscript.echo "PaperTypesAvailable: " & objItem.PaperTypesAvailable
wscript.echo "Parameters: " & objItem.Parameters
wscript.echo "PNPDeviceID: " & objItem.PNPDeviceID
wscript.echo "PortName: " & objItem.PortName
wscript.echo "PowerManagementCapabilities: " & objItem.PowerManagementCapabilities
wscript.echo "PowerManagementSupported: " & objItem.PowerManagementSupported
wscript.echo "PrinterPaperNames: " & objItem.PrinterPaperNames
wscript.echo "PrinterState: " & objItem.PrinterState
wscript.echo "PrinterStatus: " & objItem.PrinterStatus
wscript.echo "PrintJobDataType: " & objItem.PrintJobDataType
wscript.echo "PrintProcessor: " & objItem.PrintProcessor
wscript.echo "Priority: " & objItem.Priority
wscript.echo "Published: " & objItem.Published
wscript.echo "Queued: " & objItem.Queued
wscript.echo "RawOnly: " & objItem.RawOnly
wscript.echo "SeparatorFile: " & objItem.SeparatorFile
wscript.echo "ServerName: " & objItem.ServerName
```

```
    wscript.echo "Shared: " & objItem.Shared
    wscript.echo "ShareName: " & objItem.ShareName
    wscript.echo "SpoolEnabled: " & objItem.SpoolEnabled
    wscript.echo "StartTime: " & objItem.StartTime
    wscript.echo "Status: " & objItem.Status
    wscript.echo "StatusInfo: " & objItem.StatusInfo
    wscript.echo "SystemCreationClassName: " & objItem.SystemCreationClassName
    wscript.echo "SystemName: " & objItem.SystemName
    wscript.echo "TimeOfLastReset: " & objItem.TimeOfLastReset
    wscript.echo "UntilTime: " & objItem.UntilTime
    wscript.echo "VerticalResolution: " & objItem.VerticalResolution
    wscript.echo "WorkOffline: " & objItem.WorkOffline
wscript.echo " "
next
```

Printing the Print Jobs

The *Win32_PrintJob* class is used to describe a print job. As you can imagine, on a busy print server, this class gets heavy use. With this particular class, keep in mind each instance of a print job lives only until the print job is completed. Once the print job is finished, the *Win32_PrintJob* class can no longer report on it. If you run the Win32_PrintJob.vbs script on a computer that has no jobs in the print spooler, the script reports back no information. This class basically provides a snapshot in time of print jobs.

Win32_PrintJob.vbs

```
strComputer = "."
wmiNS = "\root\cimv2"
wmiQuery = "Select * from Win32_PrintJob"
Set objWMIService = GetObject("winmgmts:\\" & strComputer & wmiNS)
Set colItems = objWMIService.ExecQuery(wmiQuery)
For Each objItem in colItems

 wscript.echo "Caption: " & objItem.Caption
 wscript.echo "DataType: " & objItem.DataType
 wscript.echo "Description: " & objItem.Description
 wscript.echo "Document: " & objItem.Document
 wscript.echo "DriverName: " & objItem.DriverName
 wscript.echo "ElapsedTime: " & objItem.ElapsedTime
 wscript.echo "HostPrintQueue: " & objItem.HostPrintQueue
 wscript.echo "InstallDate: " & objItem.InstallDate
 wscript.echo "JobId: " & objItem.JobId
 wscript.echo "JobStatus: " & objItem.JobStatus
 wscript.echo "Name: " & objItem.Name
 wscript.echo "Notify: " & objItem.Notify
 wscript.echo "Owner: " & objItem.Owner
 wscript.echo "PagesPrinted: " & objItem.PagesPrinted
 wscript.echo "Parameters: " & objItem.Parameters
 wscript.echo "PrintProcessor: " & objItem.PrintProcessor
 wscript.echo "Priority: " & objItem.Priority
 wscript.echo "Size: " & objItem.Size
 wscript.echo "StartTime: " & objItem.StartTime
 wscript.echo "Status: " & objItem.Status
 wscript.echo "StatusMask: " & objItem.StatusMask
```

```
wscript.echo "TimeSubmitted: " & objItem.TimeSubmitted
wscript.echo "TotalPages: " & objItem.TotalPages
wscript.echo "UntilTime: " & objItem.UntilTime
wscript.echo " "
next
```

Working with Printer Ports

The *Win32_TCPIPPrinterPort* class seems modest in comparison to some of the other printer classes—17 properties, no methods—but this is a lean, mean, streamlined WMI class carefully crafted to meet the most exacting needs of network administrators. All the essential printer port properties can be reported by running the Win32_TCPIPPrinterPort.vbs script. If you need to create a new printer port on a server, spawn a new instance of the class, make your changes, and use the *Put_* method to write it back to the WMI repository.

Win32_TCPIPPrinterPort.vbs

```
strComputer = "."
wmiNS = "\root\cimv2"
wmiQuery = "Select * from Win32_TCPIPPrinterPort"
Set objWMIService = GetObject("winmgmts:\\" & strComputer & wmiNS)
Set colItems = objWMIService.ExecQuery(wmiQuery)
For Each objItem in colItems

 wscript.echo "ByteCount: " & objItem.ByteCount
 wscript.echo "Caption: " & objItem.Caption
 wscript.echo "CreationClassName: " & objItem.CreationClassName
 wscript.echo "Description: " & objItem.Description
 wscript.echo "HostAddress: " & objItem.HostAddress
 wscript.echo "InstallDate: " & objItem.InstallDate
 wscript.echo "Name: " & objItem.Name
 wscript.echo "PortNumber: " & objItem.PortNumber
 wscript.echo "Protocol: " & objItem.Protocol
 wscript.echo "Queue: " & objItem.Queue
 wscript.echo "SNMPCommunity: " & objItem.SNMPCommunity
 wscript.echo "SNMPDevIndex: " & objItem.SNMPDevIndex
 wscript.echo "SNMPEnabled: " & objItem.SNMPEnabled
 wscript.echo "Status: " & objItem.Status
 wscript.echo "SystemCreationClassName: " & objItem.SystemCreationClassName
 wscript.echo "SystemName: " & objItem.SystemName
 wscript.echo "Type: " & objItem.Type
wscript.echo " "
next
```

Telephony Classes

Two telephony classes are used to describe modems:

- *Win32_POTSModem*
- *Win32_POTSModemToSerialPort*

Although many computer users in the United States are not using dial-up modems on a regular basis for Internet access, in other parts of the world, dial-up Internet access is still the standard. These two classes provide rich modem information. Lots of computers still use modems, so the technology is not obsolete yet. For instance, many servers use modems to send faxes and pages and to make remote server connections. Additionally, in many countries, modem communication is one of the few types of remote access actually available and is used routinely to connect offices. The classes in this category are really straightforward, and no methods are implemented in either class. The Win32_PotsModem.vbs script and the Win32_PotsModemToSerialPort.vbs script are included in the Chapter10 folder on the accompanying CD.

Video and Monitor Classes

There are six video and monitor classes. Of these, two are obsolete, and one has been removed from Microsoft Windows XP and Windows Server 2003. The two obsolete classes (*Win32_DisplayConfiguration* and *Win32_DisplayControllerConfiguration*) still work and return information, but they should not be relied upon. The *Win32_VideoConfiguration* class that was removed from Windows XP and Windows Server 2003 still works for computers that run Microsoft Windows 2000. The six video and monitor classes are as follows:

- *Win32_DesktopMonitor*
- *Win32_DisplayConfiguration* (obsolete)
- *Win32_DisplayControllerConfiguration* (obsolete)
- *Win32_VideoConfiguration* (removed from Windows XP and Windows Server 2003)
- *Win32_VideoController*
- *Win32_VideoSettings*

Displaying the Display

In the Windows XP and Windows Server 2003 realms, you will want to work with only three video classes: *Win32_DesktopMonitor*, *Win32_VideoController*, and *Win32_VideoSettings*. Of course, the obsolete classes mostly still work, but they are being replaced, so it is important to begin migration to using other WMI classes. The most important of these WMI classes is the *Win32_DesktopMonitor* class, which contains 28 WMI properties, including important properties that provide information such as whether the screen is locked and what the display resolution is. The Win32_DesktopMonitor.vbs script displays all 28 of these properties.

Win32_DesktopMonitor.vbs

```
strComputer = "."
wmiNS = "\root\cimv2"
wmiQuery = "Select * from Win32_DesktopMonitor"
Set objWMIService = GetObject("winmgmts:\\" & strComputer & wmiNS)
Set colItems = objWMIService.ExecQuery(wmiQuery)
```

```
For Each objItem in colItems

    wscript.echo "Availability: " & objItem.Availability
    wscript.echo "Bandwidth: " & objItem.Bandwidth
    wscript.echo "Caption: " & objItem.Caption
    wscript.echo "ConfigManagerErrorCode: " & objItem.ConfigManagerErrorCode
    wscript.echo "ConfigManagerUserConfig: " & objItem.ConfigManagerUserConfig
    wscript.echo "CreationClassName: " & objItem.CreationClassName
    wscript.echo "Description: " & objItem.Description
    wscript.echo "DeviceID: " & objItem.DeviceID
    wscript.echo "DisplayType: " & objItem.DisplayType
    wscript.echo "ErrorCleared: " & objItem.ErrorCleared
    wscript.echo "ErrorDescription: " & objItem.ErrorDescription
    wscript.echo "InstallDate: " & objItem.InstallDate
    wscript.echo "IsLocked: " & objItem.IsLocked
    wscript.echo "LastErrorCode: " & objItem.LastErrorCode
    wscript.echo "MonitorManufacturer: " & objItem.MonitorManufacturer
    wscript.echo "MonitorType: " & objItem.MonitorType
    wscript.echo "Name: " & objItem.Name
    wscript.echo "PixelsPerXLogicalInch: " & objItem.PixelsPerXLogicalInch
    wscript.echo "PixelsPerYLogicalInch: " & objItem.PixelsPerYLogicalInch
    wscript.echo "PNPDeviceID: " & objItem.PNPDeviceID
    wscript.echo "PowerManagementCapabilities: " & objItem.PowerManagementCapabilities
    wscript.echo "PowerManagementSupported: " & objItem.PowerManagementSupported
    wscript.echo "ScreenHeight: " & objItem.ScreenHeight
    wscript.echo "ScreenWidth: " & objItem.ScreenWidth
    wscript.echo "Status: " & objItem.Status
    wscript.echo "StatusInfo: " & objItem.StatusInfo
    wscript.echo "SystemCreationClassName: " & objItem.SystemCreationClassName
    wscript.echo "SystemName: " & objItem.SystemName
wscript.echo " "
next
```

Controlling the Video

The *Win32_VideoController* class has 59 properties and no methods, which makes it the largest video class on the system. In many respects, the video controller actually has the most impact on video performance. Properties such as *CurrentRefreshRate*, *MaxRefreshRate*, and *AdapterRAM* are most important to video performance. When working with the *Win32_VideoController* class, you need to keep in mind the associations that are set up between the controller card and each of the video settings. The number of these potential instances of the class can be very confusing. This is shown in Figure 10-2.

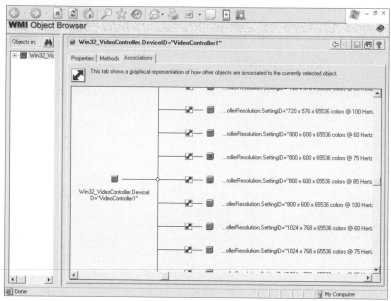

Figure 10-2   Video controller instances

It is the wise network administrator who understands these principles and who keeps tabs on these properties. The Win32_VideoController.vbs script illustrates using this class to monitor video performance.

Win32_VideoController.vbs

```
strComputer = "."
wmiNS = "\root\cimv2"
wmiQuery = "Select * from Win32_VideoController"
Set objWMIService = GetObject("winmgmts:\\" & strComputer & wmiNS)
Set colItems = objWMIService.ExecQuery(wmiQuery)
For Each objItem in colItems

 wscript.echo "AcceleratorCapabilities: " & objItem.AcceleratorCapabilities
 wscript.echo "AdapterCompatibility: " & objItem.AdapterCompatibility
 wscript.echo "AdapterDACType: " & objItem.AdapterDACType
 wscript.echo "AdapterRAM: " & objItem.AdapterRAM
 wscript.echo "Availability: " & objItem.Availability
 wscript.echo "CapabilityDescriptions: " & objItem.CapabilityDescriptions
 wscript.echo "Caption: " & objItem.Caption
 wscript.echo "ColorTableEntries: " & objItem.ColorTableEntries
 wscript.echo "ConfigManagerErrorCode: " & objItem.ConfigManagerErrorCode
 wscript.echo "ConfigManagerUserConfig: " & objItem.ConfigManagerUserConfig
 wscript.echo "CreationClassName: " & objItem.CreationClassName
 wscript.echo "CurrentBitsPerPixel: " & objItem.CurrentBitsPerPixel
 wscript.echo "CurrentHorizontalResolution: " & objItem.CurrentHorizontalResolution
 wscript.echo "CurrentNumberOfColors: " & objItem.CurrentNumberOfColors
 wscript.echo "CurrentNumberOfColumns: " & objItem.CurrentNumberOfColumns
 wscript.echo "CurrentNumberOfRows: " & objItem.CurrentNumberOfRows
 wscript.echo "CurrentRefreshRate: " & objItem.CurrentRefreshRate
 wscript.echo "CurrentScanMode: " & objItem.CurrentScanMode
```

```
      wscript.echo "CurrentVerticalResolution: " & objItem.CurrentVerticalResolution
      wscript.echo "Description: " & objItem.Description
      wscript.echo "DeviceID: " & objItem.DeviceID
      wscript.echo "DeviceSpecificPens: " & objItem.DeviceSpecificPens
      wscript.echo "DitherType: " & objItem.DitherType
      wscript.echo "DriverDate: " & objItem.DriverDate
      wscript.echo "DriverVersion: " & objItem.DriverVersion
      wscript.echo "ErrorCleared: " & objItem.ErrorCleared
      wscript.echo "ErrorDescription: " & objItem.ErrorDescription
      wscript.echo "ICMIntent: " & objItem.ICMIntent
      wscript.echo "ICMMethod: " & objItem.ICMMethod
      wscript.echo "InfFilename: " & objItem.InfFilename
      wscript.echo "InfSection: " & objItem.InfSection
      wscript.echo "InstallDate: " & objItem.InstallDate
      wscript.echo "InstalledDisplayDrivers: " & objItem.InstalledDisplayDrivers
      wscript.echo "LastErrorCode: " & objItem.LastErrorCode
      wscript.echo "MaxMemorySupported: " & objItem.MaxMemorySupported
      wscript.echo "MaxNumberControlled: " & objItem.MaxNumberControlled
      wscript.echo "MaxRefreshRate: " & objItem.MaxRefreshRate
      wscript.echo "MinRefreshRate: " & objItem.MinRefreshRate
      wscript.echo "Monochrome: " & objItem.Monochrome
      wscript.echo "Name: " & objItem.Name
      wscript.echo "NumberOfColorPlanes: " & objItem.NumberOfColorPlanes
      wscript.echo "NumberOfVideoPages: " & objItem.NumberOfVideoPages
      wscript.echo "PNPDeviceID: " & objItem.PNPDeviceID
      wscript.echo "PowerManagementCapabilities: " & objItem.PowerManagementCapabilities
      wscript.echo "PowerManagementSupported: " & objItem.PowerManagementSupported
      wscript.echo "ProtocolSupported: " & objItem.ProtocolSupported
      wscript.echo "ReservedSystemPaletteEntries: " & objItem.ReservedSystemPaletteEntries
      wscript.echo "SpecificationVersion: " & objItem.SpecificationVersion
      wscript.echo "Status: " & objItem.Status
      wscript.echo "StatusInfo: " & objItem.StatusInfo
      wscript.echo "SystemCreationClassName: " & objItem.SystemCreationClassName
      wscript.echo "SystemName: " & objItem.SystemName
      wscript.echo "SystemPaletteEntries: " & objItem.SystemPaletteEntries
      wscript.echo "TimeOfLastReset: " & objItem.TimeOfLastReset
      wscript.echo "VideoArchitecture: " & objItem.VideoArchitecture
      wscript.echo "VideoMemoryType: " & objItem.VideoMemoryType
      wscript.echo "VideoMode: " & objItem.VideoMode
      wscript.echo "VideoModeDescription: " & objItem.VideoModeDescription
      wscript.echo "VideoProcessor: " & objItem.VideoProcessor
   wscript.echo " "
   next
```

Summary

In this chapter, we looked at the system hardware grouping of WMI classes. This category of
WMI classes includes cooling device, pointing device, keyboard, storage device, motherboard,
networking, video, and printer classes. These classes form the basis for managing computer
hardware from the WMI perspective. Many of these classes include methods that enable you
to perform hardware configuration. Classes such as *Win32_NetworkAdapterConfiguration*
expose dozens of methods that enable you to configure the hardware in nearly every conceiv-

able way—remotely, securely, and by using an easily written VBScript. Some of the other classes in this category enable you to perform hardware manipulation, but you first have to create a new instance of the class and then make the changes. Classes such as *Win32_TCPIPPrinterPort* fall into this group.

Quiz Yourself

Q: You have been getting a number of calls from users who indicate their keyboards do not seem to work properly. This issue has been traced back to various regional settings used on some of the computers. What is one property of the keyboard that can be used to see if the keyboard malfunction is a regional settings issue?

A: To tackle the problem of various regional settings used on some computers and their impact on keyboard configuration, you can use the *Layout* property of the *Win32_Keyboard* class. This property reports the language setting as an integer. U.S. English is reported as 409.

Q: You are trying to create a list of computers on the network that have video cards with more than 32 megabytes (MB) of video random access memory (RAM). Which class and property can be used to return this information?

A: To determine the amount of video RAM on a computer, you can use the *Win32_VideoController* class and look at the *AdapterRAM* property.

Q: You need to find out which portable computers on the network have built-in wireless network adapters. Which WMI class can retrieve this information for you?

A: To find which portable computers on the network have built-in wireless network adapters, you can use the *Win32_PortConnector* class and write a filter to pull the information from the *ExternalReferenceDesignator* property.

On Your Own

Lab 21 Hardware Inventory

In this lab, you will create a script that performs a basic hardware inventory scan of some of the more important subsystems: networking, processor, memory, disk drive, and port configuration. You might use a script like this to plan a hardware upgrade.

1. Open the wmiTemplate.vbs script, and save it as StudentLab21.vbs.

2. Turn off the *On Error Resume Next* statement by remarking it out.

3. Define three more variables to be used to hold queries: *wmiQuery1*, *wmiQuery2*, *wmiQuery3*. Place them next to the *wmiQuery* variable.

4. Do the same thing for the *objItem* and the *colItems* variables. When you are done, the variables look like the following:

```
dim strComputer
dim wmiNS
dim wmiQuery, wmiQuery1, wmiQuery2, wmiQuery3
dim objWMIService
dim colItems, colItems1, colItems2, colItems3
dim objItem, objItem1, objItem2, objItem3
```

5. In the reference section of the script, define four WMI queries: *wmiQuery*, *wmiQuery1*, *wmiQuery2*, and *wmiQuery3*. All four queries will be *Select * From* queries. The classes you will use are the following: *Win32_Processor*, *Win32_NetworkAdapter*, *Win32_Physical-Memory*, and *Win32_DiskDrive*. The queries look like the following when you are done:

```
wmiQuery = "Select * from win32_Processor"
wmiQuery1 = "Select * from win32_networkAdapter"
wmiQuery2 = "Select * from win32_PhysicalMemory"
wmiQuery3 = "Select * from win32_DiskDrive"
```

6. You need only one connection into WMI, so leave the *Set ObjWmiService* line of code alone.

7. Now you need to execute the four WMI queries. To do this, use all four *Set colItems* commands. You will need to modify the first *Set colItems* command and copy it three times. Use *colItems1* through *3* and *wmiQuery1* through *3*. It should look like the following when you are done:

```
Set colItems = objWMIService.ExecQuery(wmiQuery)
Set colItems1 = objWMIService.ExecQuery(wmiQuery1)
Set colItems2 = objWMIService.ExecQuery(wmiQuery2)
Set colItems3 = objWMIService.ExecQuery(wmiQuery3)
```

8. Copy the *For Each Next* block and paste it three times under the original one. Now you need to modify each one to use *objItem1*, *objItem2*, or *objItem3*. When you are done, it looks like the following:

```
For Each objItem in colItems
    Wscript.Echo ": " & objItem.
    Wscript.Echo ": " & objItem.
    Wscript.Echo ": " & objItem.
    Wscript.Echo ": " & objItem.
    Wscript.Echo ": " & objItem.
    Wscript.Echo ": " & objItem.
Next
For Each objItem1 in colItems1
    Wscript.Echo ": " & objItem1.
    Wscript.Echo ": " & objItem1.
    Wscript.Echo ": " & objItem1.
    Wscript.Echo ": " & objItem1.
    Wscript.Echo ": " & objItem1.
    Wscript.Echo ": " & objItem1.
Next
For Each objItem2 in colItems2
```

```
        Wscript.Echo ": " & objItem2.
        Wscript.Echo ": " & objItem2
        Wscript.Echo ": " & objItem2
        Wscript.Echo ": " & objItem2.
        Wscript.Echo ": " & objItem2.
        Wscript.Echo ": " & objItem2.
    Next
    For Each objItem3 in colItems3
        Wscript.Echo ": " & objItem3.
        Wscript.Echo ": " & objItem3.
        Wscript.Echo ": " & objItem3.
        Wscript.Echo ": " & objItem3.
        Wscript.Echo ": " & objItem3.
        Wscript.Echo ": " & objItem3.
    Next
```

9. The first WMI query, *wmiQuery*, uses the *Win32_Processor* class. You are interested in three properties: *Caption*, *CurrentClockSpeed*, and *L2CacheSize*. Delete all the unused *Wscript.Echo* commands. Modify the first *For Each Next* block as shown here:

```
For Each objItem in colItems
    Wscript.Echo ": " & objItem.Caption
    Wscript.Echo ": " & objItem.CurrentClockSpeed
    Wscript.Echo ": " & objItem.L2CacheSize
Next
```

10. The second WMI query, *wmiQuery1*, uses the *Win32_NetworkAdapter* class. You are interested in two properties: *Caption* and *MaxSpeed*. Delete the unused *Wscript.Echo* commands. Once you make the change to the second *For Each Next* loop, the code looks like the following:

```
For Each objItem1 in colItems1
    Wscript.Echo ": " & objItem1.Caption
    Wscript.Echo ": " & objItem1.MaxSpeed
Next
```

11. The third WMI query, *wmiQuery2*, uses the *Win32_PhysicalMemory* class. You are interested in two properties: *DeviceLocator* and *Capacity*. Delete the unused *Wscript.Echo* commands. The modified *For Each Next* loop looks like the following:

```
For Each objItem2 in colItems2
    Wscript.Echo ": " & objItem1.DeviceLocator
    Wscript.Echo ": " & objItem1.Capacity
Next
```

12. The last WMI query, *wmiQuery3*, uses the *Win32_DiskDrive* class. You are interested in two properties: *Name* and *Size*. Delete the unused *Wscript.Echo* commands. The modified *For Each Next* loop looks like the following:

```
For Each objItem3 in colItems3
    Wscript.Echo ": " & objItem1.Name
    Wscript.Echo ": " & objItem1.Size
Next
```

13. Save and run the script; it should run fine. Now, you want to go back and dress up the display. To do so, use the *SeparatorLine* function. Add the *SeparatorLine* function to the *Name*, *Caption*, *DeviceLocator*, and *Caption* properties in each of the four groupings.

14. Copy the function from the SeparatorLine.vbs script in the Chapter10\Lab21 folder, and paste it at the bottom of the script. Now run the script; it should work fine.

15. The last cleanup step is to add the property names in front of the colon (:) in each *Wscript.Echo* command. The first *For Each Next* loop looks like the following:

```
For Each objItem in colItems
    Wscript.Echo funLine("Caption: " & objItem.Caption)
    Wscript.Echo "CurrentClockSpeed: " & objItem.CurrentClockSpeed
    Wscript.Echo "L2CacheSize: " & objItem.L2CacheSize
Next
```

16. Make sure you have completed each of the four *For Each Next* loops, and then save and run the script. It should run fine.

Chapter 11

Using Operating System Classes

In Chapter 10, we examined the nine different categories of system hardware Microsoft Windows Management Instrumentation (WMI) classes. In this chapter, we look at the operating system classes. There are 21 groups of operating system classes available for the enterprising network administrator. Classes in this category enable you to query and set screen savers, work with the file system, create scheduled tasks, and much more. A useful overview of the operating system classes is contained in Appendix E.

Before You Begin

To work through this chapter, you should be familiar with the following concepts:

- The basics of using the WMI moniker
- The basics of using the *ConnectServer* method
- Use of WMI methods
- The basics of WMI providers

After you complete this chapter, you will be familiar with the following concepts:

- The organization of the operating system classes
- The use of operating system classes to manage Microsoft Windows environments

> **Note** All the scripts used in this chapter are located on the CD that accompanies this book in the \Scripts\Chapter11 folder.

Using the COM-Related Classes

The Component Object Model (COM) category represents both COM and Distributed Component Object Model (DCOM) settings and classes as well as settings for client applications. There are 7 instance classes and 10 association classes in this group. These classes are documented in Appendix E, Table E-1. There are no methods in any of these classes, but the properties described by them can be very useful to the network administrator.

Using the *Win32_ClassicComClass*

COM classic—got to love that name. The *Win32_ClassicComClass* is one of the most basic WMI COM classes that we will examine. The basic script called Win32_ClassicComClass.vbs is located in the cimv2 folder on the accompanying CD. This script returns everything about every COM class on my computer. When I run it, it takes nearly 5 minutes to complete and returns more than 32,000 lines of information—a bit more reading than I want to do. So, I modified the Win32_ClassicComClass.vbs script so that it searches for information related to WMI only.

The first change I made for ease of maintenance and ease of use was to modify the WMI query to use a variable to contain the *Where* clause. You could change the script further to use an input box. The *Where* clause uses a WMI feature that exists only in Microsoft Windows XP and Windows Server 2003—the *LIKE* operator. By using a percent sign (%) before and after the word you're searching for, in this case *WMI*, you direct WMI to come back with information that contains the letters *WMI*. The last pretty cool modification I made was to use a function to put the *Where* clause together. You have to change only the term, or the word you are searching for among the COM classes—and, like magic, the answer is returned by the Classic-ComClassWMI.vbs script as listed here.

ClassicComClassWMI.vbs

```
strComputer = "."
wmiNS = "\root\cimv2"
strWhere = funQuery("wmi")
wmiQuery = "Select * from Win32_ClassicCOMClass" & strWhere

Set objWMIService = GetObject("winmgmts:\\" & strComputer & wmiNS)
Set colItems = objWMIService.ExecQuery(wmiQuery)
For Each objItem in colItems
 wscript.echo "Caption: " & objItem.Caption
 wscript.echo "ComponentId: " & objItem.ComponentId
 wscript.echo "Description: " & objItem.Description
 wscript.echo "Name: " & objItem.Name & vbcrlf
Next

Function funQuery(strwmi)
funQuery = " where caption like " & "'%" & strwmi & "%'"
End function
```

Examining the Desktop

The desktop classes are used to describe the various configuration settings available for the Windows desktop. Four classes are in this category. There are no methods, but there are two fairly large classes—the *Win32_TimeZone* class with 24 properties, and the *Win32_Desktop* class with 21 properties. The most useful class might be the *Win32_Environment* class because it contains three properties that are writable and enables the network administrator to modify Windows environment strings. The fourth class in this category, *Win32_UserDesktop*, is an association class that relates a particular user on a system to specific desktop settings. The four desktop-related classes are as follows:

- *Win32_Desktop*
- *Win32_Environment*
- *Win32_TimeZone*
- *Win32_UserDesktop*

Listing the Drivers on a System

The drivers category is used to describe both the virtual device drivers and the system drivers that form the base operating system. Only two classes are in this category:

- *Win32_DriverVXD*
- *Win32_SystemDriver*

Examining System Drivers

If you are working with a particular driver, and you need to find out more about it, the easiest way is to write a script that uses the *Win32_SystemDriver* class. In the Win32_SystemDriver-Specific.vbs script, I use a *Where* clause to limit the data returned to only the drivers specified in the input box. To use this script, you need not know the specific driver name because you can use the *LIKE* operator to make a fuzzy match. The *Where* clause is contained inside a function called *FunFix*, which adds limiting parameters in the search. Using the function in this manner enables you simply to type the name of the driver you are looking for in the input box.

Win32_SystemDriverSpecific.vbs

```
strComputer = "."
wmiNS = "\root\cimv2"
strWhere =funfix(InputBox("what driver are you looking for"))
wmiQuery = "Select * from Win32_SystemDriver" & strWhere
Set objWMIService = GetObject("winmgmts:\\" & strComputer & wmiNS)
Set colItems = objWMIService.ExecQuery(wmiQuery)
For Each objItem in colItems

 wscript.echo "AcceptPause: " & objItem.AcceptPause
 wscript.echo "AcceptStop: " & objItem.AcceptStop
 wscript.echo "Caption: " & objItem.Caption
 wscript.echo "CreationClassName: " & objItem.CreationClassName
 wscript.echo "Description: " & objItem.Description
 wscript.echo "DesktopInteract: " & objItem.DesktopInteract
 wscript.echo "DisplayName: " & objItem.DisplayName
 wscript.echo "ErrorControl: " & objItem.ErrorControl
 wscript.echo "ExitCode: " & objItem.ExitCode
 wscript.echo "InstallDate: " & objItem.InstallDate
 wscript.echo "Name: " & objItem.Name
 wscript.echo "PathName: " & objItem.PathName
```

```
wscript.echo "ServiceSpecificExitCode: " & objItem.ServiceSpecificExitCode
wscript.echo "ServiceType: " & objItem.ServiceType
wscript.echo "Started: " & objItem.Started
wscript.echo "StartMode: " & objItem.StartMode
wscript.echo "StartName: " & objItem.StartName
wscript.echo "State: " & objItem.State
wscript.echo "Status: " & objItem.Status
wscript.echo "SystemCreationClassName: " & objItem.SystemCreationClassName
wscript.echo "SystemName: " & objItem.SystemName
wscript.echo "TagId: " & objItem.TagId & vbcrlf
Next

Function FunFix (strwhere)
funFix = " where name like '%" & strwhere & "%'"
End function
```

Exploring the File System

Nineteen classes are used to describe and manipulate the Windows file system. These classes enable you to retrieve information on directories and quotas and represent the drive in a logical manner. The 19 classes are listed in Appendix E, Table E-4. Some of these classes are ripe for exploration. For example, the *Win32_Directory* class has 31 properties and 14 methods. Something in this class might be useful to network administrators. *Win32_LogicalDisk* is used to represent the logical configuration of a disk drive, and it has 40 properties and 5 methods—it, too, can be useful to network administrators.

Working with Directories

Three classes are specifically related to directories: *Win32_Directory*, *Win32_SubDirectory*, and *Win32_DirectorySpecification*. The most powerful class in this group is *Win32_Directory*.

Getting the *Win32_Directory* Class

When you work with many of the WMI classes related to the file system, you must replace the normal single backslash (\) with a double backslash (\\). This substitution must be made everywhere a backslash is normally used. In the Get_Win32_Directory.vbs script, I connect to a specific folder called C:\A. To make this connection, I use the notation *c:\\a*. The *Win32_Directory* class has only one key—the *Name* property, as shown in Figure 11-1. Because the class has only one key, you need not repeat the name of the property in the query.

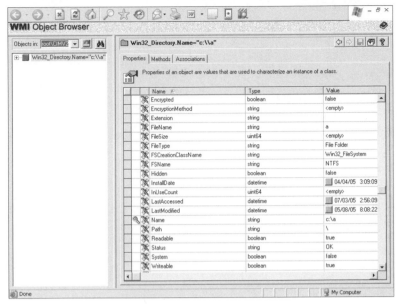

Figure 11-1   *Win32_Directory* properties

Note   The WMI query is held in the variable called *wmiQuery* as shown here:

```
wmiQuery = "Win32_Directory='c:\\a'"
```

When you run the Get_Win32_Directory.vbs script, it will work fine as long as there is a directory called A on the C drive. This line of code is exactly the same as the following:

```
wmiQuery = "Win32_Directory.name='c:\\a'"
```

In my mind, the choice is simply a matter of personal preference. Normally, I do specify the name of the property to aid in readability. It is very confusing to people who do not understand this shortcut method of notation—particularly because it is not a very well-documented shortcut!

Get_Win32_Directory.vbs

```
strComputer = "."
wmiNS = "\root\cimv2"
wmiQuery = "Win32_Directory='c:\\a'"
Set objWMIService = GetObject("winmgmts:\\" & strComputer & wmiNS)
Set objItem = objWMIService.get(wmiQuery)
With objItem
 msg = "AccessMask: " & .AccessMask
 msg = msg  & vbcrlf & "Archive: " & .Archive
 msg = msg  & vbcrlf & "Caption: " & .Caption
 msg = msg  & vbcrlf & "Compressed: " & .Compressed
 msg = msg  & vbcrlf & "CompressionMethod: " & .CompressionMethod
 msg = msg  & vbcrlf & "CreationClassName: " & .CreationClassName
 msg = msg  & vbcrlf & "CreationDate: " & .CreationDate
```

```
    msg = msg  & vbcrlf &   "CSCreationClassName: " & .CSCreationClassName
    msg = msg  & vbcrlf &   "CSName: " & .CSName
    msg = msg  & vbcrlf &   "Description: " & .Description
    msg = msg  & vbcrlf &   "Drive: " & .Drive
    msg = msg  & vbcrlf &   "EightDotThreeFileName: " & .EightDotThreeFileName
    msg = msg  & vbcrlf &   "Encrypted: " & .Encrypted
    msg = msg  & vbcrlf &   "EncryptionMethod: " & .EncryptionMethod
    msg = msg  & vbcrlf &   "Extension: " & .Extension
    msg = msg  & vbcrlf &   "FileName: " & .FileName
    msg = msg  & vbcrlf &   "FileSize: " & .FileSize
    msg = msg  & vbcrlf &   "FileType: " & .FileType
    msg = msg  & vbcrlf &   "FSCreationClassName: " & .FSCreationClassName
    msg = msg  & vbcrlf &   "FSName: " & .FSName
    msg = msg  & vbcrlf &   "Hidden: " & .Hidden
    msg = msg  & vbcrlf &   "InstallDate: " & .InstallDate
    msg = msg  & vbcrlf &   "InUseCount: " & .InUseCount
    msg = msg  & vbcrlf &   "LastAccessed: " & .LastAccessed
    msg = msg  & vbcrlf &   "LastModified: " & .LastModified
    msg = msg  & vbcrlf &   "Name: " & .Name
    msg = msg  & vbcrlf &   "Path: " & .Path
    msg = msg  & vbcrlf &   "Readable: " & .Readable
    msg = msg  & vbcrlf &   "Status: " & .Status
    msg = msg  & vbcrlf &   "System: " & .System
    msg = msg  & vbcrlf &   "Writeable: " & .Writeable
    End With

    WScript.echo msg
```

Understanding Job Objects

Fourteen classes are used to describe and instrument named job objects. These classes are supplied by the job object provider (called *NamedJobObjectProv* in the registration with *__Win32Provider*), which is installed by default in Windows XP and Windows Server 2003. The provider and the classes live in the *root\cimv2* namespace. Previous versions of the Windows operating system do not contain the job object provider; therefore, these classes will not work. These must be named job objects because unnamed job objects cannot be instrumented.

Identifying Named Job Objects

A job object is a kernel object that is used by the operating system to treat a group of processes as a single entity for the purpose of managing the resources and the life cycle of those processes. You can work only with named job objects, so you must identify any named job objects that are running on your system. To do this, use the *Win32_NamedJobObject* class. On my laptop, the Win32_NamedJobObject.vbs script retrieves only one named job object—but at least I know how many instances of *Win32_NamedJobObject* reside on my computer.

Win32_NamedJobObject.vbs

```
strComputer = "."
wmiNS = "\root\cimv2"
wmiQuery = "Select * from Win32_NamedJobObject"
Set objWMIService = GetObject("winmgmts:\\" & strComputer & wmiNS)
Set colItems = objWMIService.ExecQuery(wmiQuery)
For Each objItem in colItems

 wscript.echo "BasicUIRestrictions: " & objItem.BasicUIRestrictions
 wscript.echo "Caption: " & objItem.Caption
 wscript.echo "CollectionID: " & objItem.CollectionID
 wscript.echo "Description: " & objItem.Description
wscript.echo " "
next
```

Identifying Resources Used by Job Objects

Once you have identified the presence of a job object on your computer, you might want to see which resources the object is consuming. To do this, use the *Win32_NamedJobObjectActgInfo* class, which provides the name of the job object, the number of processes in the job object, and the amount of memory, page faults, and other performance-related information. The Win32_NamedJobObjectActgInfo.vbs script uses this class.

Win32_NamedJobObjectActgInfo.vbs

```
strComputer = "."
wmiNS = "\root\cimv2"
wmiQuery = "Select * from Win32_NamedJobObjectActgInfo"
Set objWMIService = GetObject("winmgmts:\\" & strComputer & wmiNS)
Set colItems = objWMIService.ExecQuery(wmiQuery)
For Each objItem in colItems
With objItem
 wscript.echo "ActiveProcesses: " & .ActiveProcesses
 wscript.echo "Caption: " & .Caption
 wscript.echo "Description: " & .Description
 wscript.echo "Name: " & .Name
 wscript.echo "OtherOperationCount: " & .OtherOperationCount
 wscript.echo "OtherTransferCount: " & .OtherTransferCount
 wscript.echo "PeakJobMemoryUsed: " & .PeakJobMemoryUsed
 wscript.echo "PeakProcessMemoryUsed: " & .PeakProcessMemoryUsed
 wscript.echo "ReadOperationCount: " & .ReadOperationCount
 wscript.echo "ReadTransferCount: " & .ReadTransferCount
 wscript.echo "ThisPeriodTotalKernelTime: " & .ThisPeriodTotalKernelTime
 wscript.echo "ThisPeriodTotalUserTime: " & .ThisPeriodTotalUserTime
 wscript.echo "TotalKernelTime: " & .TotalKernelTime
 wscript.echo "TotalPageFaultCount: " & .TotalPageFaultCount
 wscript.echo "TotalProcesses: " & .TotalProcesses
 wscript.echo "TotalTerminatedProcesses: " & .TotalTerminatedProcesses
 wscript.echo "TotalUserTime: " & .TotalUserTime
 wscript.echo "WriteOperationCount: " & .WriteOperationCount
 wscript.echo "WriteTransferCount: " & .WriteTransferCount & vbcrlf
End with Next
```

Working with Memory Devices and Page Files

The six classes in this category are used to describe virtual memory and physical memory objects. Two classes are obsolete and one is deprecated. The deprecated class, *Win32_PageFile*, can still be used, but its functionality has been replaced by the newer classes in this group. The *Win32_PageFileElementSetting* class is an association class that relates a page file to its settings and utilization. The *Win32_PageFileSetting* class is used to make setting and configuration changes on the page file or to report the settings that have been defined. *Win32_PageFileUsage* reports on how a page file is being utilized. We delve into the *Win32_PageFileSetting* class in the following subsection. A listing of all the classes in this category is as follows:

- *Win32_PageFileElementSetting*

- *Win32_PageFileSetting*

- *Win32_PageFileUsage*

- *Win32_LogicalMemoryConfiguration* (obsolete)

- *Win32_PageFile* (deprecated)

- *Win32_SystemLogicalMemoryConfiguration* (obsolete)

Setting the Page File

The *Win32_PageFileSetting* class does not have any methods, but it has several properties that are read/write. If you want to change the initial size of the page file, do not call the *Setpagefile* method; rather write a new value to the *InitialSize* property. In the Change_PageFileSetting.vbs script, I use the *Get* method to connect to a specific page file—the default Pagefile.sys. I perform a query to list the properties of the page file, and then I change the initial size of the page file to 19 megabytes (MB). Once I assign a value to this property, I have to use the *Put_* method to write it back to the database. Then I echo out the new value of the property to confirm the setting was accepted.

Change_PageFileSetting.vbs
```
strComputer = "."
wmiNS = "\root\cimv2"
wmiQuery = "Win32_PageFileSetting='c:\pagefile.sys'"
Set objWMIService = GetObject("winmgmts:\\" & strComputer & wmiNS)
Set objItem = objWMIService.get(wmiQuery)

 wscript.echo "Caption: " & objItem.Caption
 wscript.echo "Description: " & objItem.Description
 wscript.echo "InitialSize: " & objItem.InitialSize
 wscript.echo "MaximumSize: " & objItem.MaximumSize
 wscript.echo "Name: " & objItem.Name
 wscript.echo "SettingID: " & objItem.SettingID

WScript.Echo "let's change the initial size"
objItem.initialSize = 19
```

```
objItem.put_
WScript.Echo "the new size is now: " & objItem.initialsize
```

Using the Multimedia Audiovisual Class

One class is in the multimedia audiovisual category: the *Win32_CodecFile* class is used to describe various codecs that are located on a computer running the Windows operating system. *Win32_CodecFile* is derived from *Win32_DataFile* and, as a result, inherits 14 methods. Unfortunately, these methods have very little to do with installed codecs on your computer because they are methods that enable you to work with file system objects in a generic fashion. The Win32_CodecFile.vbs script (in the cimv2 folder on the companion CD) prints out all the properties associated with a codec, for every codec installed on your computer.

Retrieving a Single Codec

You could easily modify the script to look for the presence of one critical codec. This is what I did in GetWin32_CodecFile.vbs. When retrieving a single codec file, you need to use the double backslash as discussed earlier. The other rather unusual characteristic of this script is the requirement to supply the file path in double double quotation marks—this means we end the query with three sets of closing double quotation marks as shown in the *wmiQuery* line. Single quotation marks that are normally used to supply a value to WMI do not work in this situation—and to use double quotation marks to supply a value, you need to use two sets (double double quotation marks) because the first set is interpreted as the string terminator.

GetWin32_CodecFile.vbs

```
strComputer = "."
wmiNS = "\root\cimv2"
wmiQuery = "Win32_CodecFile=""C:\\WINDOWS\\system32\\MSAUD32.ACM"""
Set objWMIService = GetObject("winmgmts:\\" & strComputer & wmiNS)
Set objItem = objWMIService.get(wmiQuery)
With objItem
 wscript.echo "AccessMask: " & .AccessMask
 wscript.echo "Caption: " & .Caption
 wscript.echo "Compressed: " & .Compressed
 wscript.echo "CompressionMethod: " & .CompressionMethod
 wscript.echo "CreationClassName: " & .CreationClassName
 wscript.echo "CreationDate: " & .CreationDate
 wscript.echo "CSCreationClassName: " & .CSCreationClassName
 wscript.echo "CSName: " & .CSName
 wscript.echo "Description: " & .Description
 wscript.echo "Encrypted: " & .Encrypted
 wscript.echo "EncryptionMethod: " & .EncryptionMethod
 wscript.echo "Extension: " & .Extension
 wscript.echo "FileName: " & .FileName
 wscript.echo "FileSize: " & .FileSize
 wscript.echo "FileType: " & .FileType
 wscript.echo "FSCreationClassName: " & .FSCreationClassName
 wscript.echo "FSName: " & .FSName
 wscript.echo "Group: " & .Group
```

```
wscript.echo "Hidden: " & .Hidden
wscript.echo "InstallDate: " & .InstallDate
wscript.echo "LastAccessed: " & .LastAccessed
wscript.echo "LastModified: " & .LastModified
wscript.echo "Manufacturer: " & .Manufacturer
wscript.echo "Name: " & .Name
wscript.echo "Path: " & .Path
wscript.echo "System: " & .System
wscript.echo "Version: " & .Version
wscript.echo "Writeable: " & .Writeable
End With
```

Working with Networking

Ten classes are used to describe networking on a computer running the Windows operating system. These classes enable the network administrator to work with Internet Protocol (IP) routing tables, the network client, connections, protocols, and domain information. One of the more interesting networking classes, *Win32_NTDomain*, retrieves information you would not normally expect to get back from WMI—Active Directory directory service configuration information. When a client machine is a member of an Active Directory domain, two instances are reported for this class. The first instance is specific to the workstation and reports back in the form *Domain: computername*. The second instance reports back in the form: *Domain: domainname*. Note that the space is required between the colon following the domain and the name of the instance you are trying to retrieve. In the GetWin32_NTDomain.vbs script, I use this feature of the class to retrieve information about the Active Directory configuration by connecting specifically to the domain instance. With this class, you can supply the value inside single quotation marks.

GetWin32_NTDomain.vbs

```
strComputer = "."
wmiNS = "\root\cimv2"
wmiQuery = "Win32_NTDomain='Domain: nwtraders'"
Set objWMIService = GetObject("winmgmts:\\" & strComputer & wmiNS)
Set objItem = objWMIService.get(wmiQuery)
With objItem
 wscript.echo "Caption: " & .Caption
 wscript.echo "ClientSiteName: " & .ClientSiteName
 wscript.echo "CreationClassName: " & .CreationClassName
 wscript.echo "DcSiteName: " & .DcSiteName
 wscript.echo "Description: " & .Description
 wscript.echo "DnsForestName: " & .DnsForestName
 wscript.echo "DomainControllerAddress: " & .DomainControllerAddress
 wscript.echo "DomainControllerAddressType: " & .DomainControllerAddressType
 wscript.echo "DomainControllerName: " & .DomainControllerName
 wscript.echo "DomainGuid: " & .DomainGuid
 wscript.echo "DomainName: " & .DomainName
 wscript.echo "DSDirectoryServiceFlag: " & .DSDirectoryServiceFlag
 wscript.echo "DSDnsControllerFlag: " & .DSDnsControllerFlag
```

```
       wscript.echo "DSDnsDomainFlag: " & .DSDnsDomainFlag
       wscript.echo "DSDnsForestFlag: " & .DSDnsForestFlag
       wscript.echo "DSGlobalCatalogFlag: " & .DSGlobalCatalogFlag
       wscript.echo "DSKerberosDistributionCenterFlag: " & .DSKerberosDistributionCenterFlag
       wscript.echo "DSPrimaryDomainControllerFlag: " & .DSPrimaryDomainControllerFlag
       wscript.echo "DSTimeServiceFlag: " & .DSTimeServiceFlag
       wscript.echo "DSWritableFlag: " & .DSWritableFlag
       wscript.echo "InstallDate: " & .InstallDate
       wscript.echo "Name: " & .Name
       wscript.echo "NameFormat: " & .NameFormat
       wscript.echo "PrimaryOwnerContact: " & .PrimaryOwnerContact
       wscript.echo "PrimaryOwnerName: " & .PrimaryOwnerName
       wscript.echo "Roles: " & .Roles
       wscript.echo "Status: " & .Status
End with
```

Using Operating System Events

Fourteen classes represent operating system events. These classes can be used to respond to various events that arise on servers or workstations that run the Windows operating system. If a process starts up or shuts down, it generates the appropriate event. The event classes are listed in Appendix E, Table E-9. In some cases, these event classes duplicate functionality that could be achieved by using one of the standard event classes we discussed in Chapter 5. Other classes offer new and exciting functionality that simply is not available elsewhere. All of the classes are easier to use and make for a cleaner, more straightforward solution than if you were to try to achieve similar functionality using the generic event queries. An example of this is the *Win32_ProcessStartup* class, which enables you to write a script that responds to the startup event of a process. You can achieve similar results by using a query that looks for instance creation events if the instance is a *Win32_Process*, but that query is more difficult to write and to understand. To illustrate the ease of use of operating system event classes, look at the MonitorProcessStartUp.vbs script.

MonitorProcessStartUp.vbs

```
strComputer - "."
wmiNS = "\root\cimv2"
wmiQuery = "SELECT * FROM Win32_ProcessStartTrace"
Set objWMIService = GetObject("winmgmts:\\" & strComputer & wmiNS)
Set colItems = objWMIService.ExecNotificationQuery(wmiQuery)
       WScript.Echo "Waiting for process to start ..."
   Do
       Set objItem = colItems.NextEvent
       With objItem
           Wscript.Echo "StartedProcess Name: " & .ProcessName
           Wscript.Echo "Process ID: " & .ProcessId
           Wscript.Echo "Time Generated: " & .Time_Created
           WScript.Echo "SID: " & Join(.SID)
           WScript.Echo "Session ID: " & .sessionID
       End With
   Loop
```

Examining Operating System Settings

There are 31 classes in the operating system settings group. Of these classes, the majority are association classes. Of the 31, only 9 are actual instance classes. Table E-10 in Appendix E details all the operating system settings classes. These classes are used to retrieve configuration information and to make changes to the way computers running the Windows operating system behave. One class represents startup commands and other configuration information. The most important class in this group is appropriately called *Win32_OperatingSystem*. This class has been expanded in Windows XP and Windows Server 2003. In addition to including many properties, it also has four methods.

One of the instance classes that is useful is the *Win32_LoadOrderGroup* class, which provides information about the order in which system services are loaded on system startup; hence the order in which these services will start. You can use this to determine dependencies. This can be interesting from an academic perspective, but on the other hand, the information can be used to optimize system startup or system shutdown. In the Win32_LoadOrderGroup.vbs script, I obtain a list of system services and the order in which they start up.

Win32_LoadOrderGroup.vbs

```
strComputer = "."
wmiNS = "\root\cimv2"
wmiQuery = "Select * from Win32_LoadOrderGroup"
Set objWMIService = GetObject("winmgmts:\\" & strComputer & wmiNS)
Set colItems = objWMIService.ExecQuery(wmiQuery)
For Each objItem in colItems

 wscript.echo "Caption: " & objItem.Caption
 wscript.echo "Description: " & objItem.Description
 wscript.echo "DriverEnabled: " & objItem.DriverEnabled
 wscript.echo "GroupOrder: " & objItem.GroupOrder
 wscript.echo "Name: " & objItem.Name
 wscript.echo "Status: " & objItem.Status & vbcrlf
next
```

Employing the Process Classes

Three WMI classes are used to work with processes:

- *Win32_Process*
- *Win32_Thread*
- *Win32_ProcessStartUp*

The *Win32_Process* class and the *Win32_Thread* class are instance classes that represent actual processes and threads running on the system. The *Win32_ProcessStartUp* class is rather unusual. It is used to pass information to *Win32_Process*. We look at how it is used in the following subsection.

Configuring Application Startup

In the ConfigureAndLaunchApp.vbs script, I use both the *Win32_Process* class and the *Win32_ProcessStartUp* class to configure and launch an application on a computer. I use the *Create* method from the *Win32_Process* class to launch the application, but to configure the way the application is actually started, I use the *Win32_ProcessStartUp* class to set the startup parameters.

In this type of script, the first thing you need to do is get the *Win32_ProcessStartUp* class. Do this by using the *Get* method. Next, get the *Win32_Process* class. Once you have these two classes, use the *SpawnInstance_* method to create a new instance of the *Win32_ProcessStartUp* class. This enables you to specify the startup parameters.

Specifying Window Parameters

Once you have created a new process startup object, you can assign some parameters to it. In the ConfigureAndLaunchApp.vbs script, I use three properties: *x*, *y*, and *ShowWindow*. The *x* and *y* properties are used to assign the starting position offset location for a new window that is created when the application launches. This value is measured in pixels.

The *ShowWindow* property indicates how the window will appear once the application is launched. A value of 1 means to launch in a normal window. A value of 2 means to activate the window but show it in a minimized state. The application must support the different window styles, or it will ignore the property.

Using the *Create* Method

After you have specified the startup parameters for the application, it is time to use the *Create* method of the *Win32_Process* class to actually launch the process. The first thing you see when working with this method is that it requires you to capture the return code. Even if you have no intention of using it, you must catch the return. Once you have created the variable to catch the return code, you supply the parameters. The first parameter is the process you wish to create, and the next value is the current drive and directory for the process. If you specify the value as *NULL*, it uses the process that is created and inherits the same path and directory from the calling process. The value you supply for this parameter must be able to be resolved. You can use a Universal Naming Convention (UNC) path or hard code an absolute value. Using the *Win32_ProcessStartUp* class, you can specify environmental variables in addition to the directory information used for this class. The next parameter is the variable you use to hold the *Win32_ProcessStartUp* object. Last, you specify the variable that will hold the process ID that is generated by creating the new process. When you run ConfigureAndLaunchApp.vbs, you will need to verify the path to Wordpad.exe on your system.

ConfigureAndLaunchApp.vbs

```
strComputer = "."
wmiNS = "\root\cimv2"
wmiQuery = "win32_ProcessStartUP"
wmiQuery1="win32_process"

strCommand = "c:\Program Files\Windows NT\Accessories\wordpad.exe" 'application you want to
launch.
Set objWMIService = GetObject("winmgmts:\\" & strComputer & wmiNS)
Set objProcessSU = objWMIService.Get(wmiQuery)'Process Startup object
Set objProcess = objWMIService.Get(WmiQuery1) 'Get win32_process class
Set objConfig = objProcessSU.SpawnInstance_ 'Create instance processSU
objConfig.ShowWindow = 1 'normal window
objConfig.x = 5
objConfig.y = 5
errRTN = objProcess.Create(strCommand, Null, objConfig, procID)
SubERR


Sub subERR
If errRTN <> 0 Then
WScript.echo "An error occurred while launching " & strcommand &_
    vbcrlf & "the error was: " & errRTN
End If
End sub
```

Working with the Registry

Only one class is used to represent the registry—*Win32_Registry*. This class is used to describe
the registry or to represent registry settings such as size. It is not used to read or modify registry values. If you want to work directly with the registry values, you need to use the *strRegistry*
provider. In the GetWin32_Registry.vbs script, I connect to the registry on the computer. The
Win32_Registry class does not have any methods—but it does have one writable property that
can be used to propose the size of the registry. In most instances, the *ProposedSize* property
and the *MaximumSize* property should be reported as the same unless you have recently
changed the proposed size.

Modifying the Registry Size

To modify the registry size or, more correctly, to change the proposed maximum size of the
registry, you assign a new value for the *ProposedSize* property and then use the *Put_* method to
write it to the database. This looks like the following:

```
objItem.ProposedSize = 6
   objItem.Put_
```

In the GetWin32_Registry.vbs script, these two lines are in the script, but they are commented
out—it is not up to me to modify the maximum size of the registry on your computer. Keep in

mind that this is a proposed maximum size—and it takes effect only after a reboot, if allowed by the operating system. This is one of the changes in Windows XP and Windows Server 2003 that was made to reduce the likelihood of misconfiguration—the value supplied here is only a proposal. If the operating system detects an entry (such as one that is smaller than the current registry size), it will write to the event log and politely ignore your suggestion.

GetWin32_Registry.vbs

```
strComputer = "."
wmiNS = "\root\cimv2"
strPath = "'Microsoft Windows XP Professional|C:\WINDOWS|\Device\Harddisk0\Partition1'"
wmiQuery = "Win32_Registry.name=" & strPath
WScript.echo wmiquery
Set objWMIService = GetObject("winmgmts:\\" & strComputer & wmiNS)
Set objItem = objWMIService.get(wmiQuery)

 wscript.echo "Caption: " & objItem.Caption
 wscript.echo "CurrentSize: " & objItem.CurrentSize
 wscript.echo "Description: " & objItem.Description
 wscript.echo "InstallDate: " & FunTime(objItem.InstallDate)
 wscript.echo "MaximumSize: " & objItem.MaximumSize
 wscript.echo "Name: " & objItem.Name
 wscript.echo "ProposedSize: " & objItem.ProposedSize
 wscript.echo "Status: " & objItem.Status
wscript.echo " "
' objItem.ProposedSize = 6
' objItem.Put_
WScript.echo "New proposal: " & objItem.ProposedSize

Function FunTime(wmiTime)
Dim objSWbemDateTime 'holds an swbemDateTime object. Used to translate Time
 Set objSWbemDateTime = CreateObject("WbemScripting.SWbemDateTime")
  objSWbemDateTime.Value= wmiTime
  FunTime = objSWbemDateTime.GetVarDate
End Function
```

Leveraging the Scheduler Job Classes

There are two scheduler job classes—well, maybe only one scheduler job class and then a local time class. You need to use these two classes together—they are grouped together. Let's look at the *Win32_LocalTime* class first. The local time class inherits all 10 of its properties from the *Win32_CurrentTime* abstract class. There are no instances of the *Win32_CurrentTime* class on a computer, so to work with the properties, you use the *Win32_LocalTime* class, which has exactly the same 10 properties as the *Win32_CurrentTime* class. The other class that inherits from *Win32_CurrentTime* is the *Win32_UTCTime* class, which displays time values in Universal Time Coordinate (UTC) format.

> ## What Is UTC?
>
> Universal Time Coordinate (UTC) is a way of formatting time values to include time zone information. It has effectively replaced Greenwich Mean Time (GMT) for many computer-based activities. UTC uses time offset numbers in the range of +720 to -720. A UTC time value with a time offset number of 0 is the same as GMT 0 or the current time in Greenwich, England. Of course, 0 is easy. If you divide 720 by 24, you get 30. If you know that Charlotte, North Carolina, in the United States is -5, and you multiply -5 by 30, you get -150 for the UTC offset. The problem is that an offset of -150 does not represent the time in Charlotte but that of somewhere in the middle of the Atlantic Ocean. Remember, the GMT values go to -12, not to -24. Therefore, you need to divide 720 by 12 to get 60. This makes UTC even easier to work with. The UTC for Charlotte, North Carolina, in the United States is -300.

Marking Time

Simply reporting the time values is rather boring and, frankly, is more complicated than using the built-in Microsoft Visual Basic Scripting Edition (VBScript) functions *NOW* and *DateTime*. The GetWin32_LocalTime.vbs script on the accompanying CD reports the *Win32_LocalTime* properties. One of the more interesting tasks you can perform using the *Win32_LocalTime* class is to create a custom timer—an alarm clock. You can use an event-driven script, and when the instance modification event that matches the values you specify for the *Win32_LocalTime* properties occurs, you trigger the event. The event, of course, can be anything you desire. In the MonitorTime.vbs script, you create an instance modification event script that simply prints out the current date and time, with a message that the event occurred. As you query from *InstanceModificationEvent* class which is an intrinsic provider, we do not need to specify a polling interval and therefore we do not use the WITHIN operator as is done with non-provider scripts. In this script, you use three variables to hold the hour, minute, and seconds properties—this becomes the time at which you want the event to trigger. After you make a connection into WMI, use the *ExecNotificationQuery* method of the *SWbemServices* object and put the script into a loop while you wait for the next event to occur.

In the MonitorTime.vbs script, I supply three properties for *Win32_LocalTime*. If I did not supply the property for the second property, the event would fire 60 times during the minute. As this script currently stands, it will fire an event once every day, each day of the year, at 12:55. The hour property is supplied in the 24-hour clock format—meaning the 12:55 event will occur 5 minutes before 1:00 in the afternoon. If you want to try out the MonitorTime.vbs script, modify the *intHour* and the *intMinute* values to a time that is a minute or two in the future from the current time. An example of this would be intHour = "8" for 8:00 AM, and intHour="20" for 8:00 PM. If you want the script to trigger at 8:15 in the morning, then it would be intHour="8" intMinute ="15". Because this is an event-driven script and it uses *Do Loop*, it will run forever. You need to manually stop the script once the event fires.

MonitorTime.vbs

```
strComputer = "."
objTGT = "'Win32_LocalTime'"
wmiNS = "\root\cimv2"
intHour = "12"
intMinute = "55"
intSecond = "0"
wmiQuery = "SELECT * FROM __InstanceModificationEvent WHERE " _
        & "TargetInstance ISA " & objTGT & "AND TargetInstance.Hour="&intHour _
        & "And TargetInstance.Minute = "&intMinute _
        & " And targetInstance.second="&intSecond
Set objWMIService = GetObject("winmgmts:\\" & strComputer & wmiNS)
Set colItems = objWMIService.ExecNotificationQuery(wmiQuery)
Do
    Set objItem = colItems.NextEvent
    Wscript.Echo  "Event triggered at " & now
Loop
```

Working with the Job Scheduler

The *Win32_ScheduledJob* class is used to interact with the AT command job scheduler on computers that run Microsoft Windows NT 4 Service Pack 4 or later. It does not work if the computer runs Microsoft Windows 95 or Windows 98. Two task schedulers run on Windows 2000 and later: the command-line scheduler AT, and the Scheduled Tasks Wizard. These two separate job schedulers do not communicate with one another. *Win32_ScheduledJob* talks only to AT and knows only about AT.

The Scheduled Tasks Wizard does know about AT and can display information about jobs created by *Win32_ScheduledJob*. Figure 11-2 shows five jobs in the Scheduled Tasks folder. Four of these jobs were scheduled by the ScheduleNoteToRun.vbs script. One of the scheduled jobs shown was created by the Scheduled Tasks Wizard. When you look at the jobs in the Scheduled Tasks folder, you cannot tell where the jobs came from (except that three of the jobs are named with the default AT prefix).

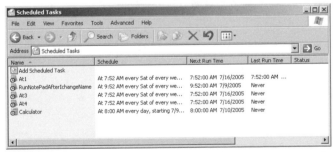

Figure 11-2   Scheduled Tasks folder displaying the status of scheduled jobs

If you were to run the *Win32_ScheduledJob.vbs* script (which is located on the accompanying CD), it would not report the job created by the Scheduled Tasks Wizard. It would report all the other scheduled jobs, including the one you renamed. In previous versions of the Windows operating system, it was possible to alter a job created by using the AT command in the Scheduled Tasks Wizard. If you were to do this, it would break the jobs that had been scheduled by AT. As shown in Figure 11-3, these jobs are now in read-only mode. You can view the settings, but you cannot make any changes to the jobs unless you do it by using a script or the AT command interface.

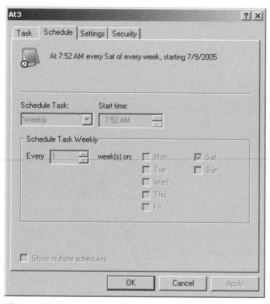

Figure 11-3 Read-only status of AT jobs

ScheduleNoteToRun.vbs

```
strComputer = "."
wmiNS = "\root\cimv2"
wmiQuery = "win32_ScheduledJob"
objJob = "notepad.exe"
Set objWMIService = GetObject("winmgmts:\\" & strComputer & wmiNS)
Set objitem = objWMIService.Get(wmiQuery)
errRTN = objitem.Create _
    (objJob, "********075200.000000-300", True , 32, , , JobID)

If errRTN <> 0 Then
Wscript.Echo " error: " & errRTN
Else
WScript.echo "New Job created. " & objJob & vbcrlf & " job id: " & jobID
End if
```

Using the Security Classes

There are 22 security-related classes. These classes are listed in Table E-14 in Appendix E. Security classes are often used in tandem because of the way the Windows security model works. (If you would like to find more information about the Windows Security model, go to *http://www.microsoft.com/security*.) When you retrieve the security settings on a folder, WMI returns several objects, each containing information that must be parsed separately. Access masks (read, write, etc.)—what most people think of when considering security on a folder— are but a very small part of the overall security model. We explore these settings when we examine the *Win32_LogicalFileSecuritySetting* class later. In addition to access control masks, you can work with trustees, security identifiers (SIDs), and other objects separately or in conjunction with other security objects.

Security in most operating systems is complicated, as it is in the Windows world—but luckily you have WMI to assist you. We cover some of the nuances of using security classes in Chapter 13, but for now, we look at an example of using the *Win32_LogicalFileSecuritySetting* class.

Reading Security on a Folder

In the GetSecurityDescriptorOnFolder.vbs script, I first specify the value for the variable *strFolder*—in this case, I use the cimv2Scripts folder, but it can be any folder you can access. Remember to include the double backslash that is used to separate parts of folder names in WMI. Next, I build the query and assign it to the *wmiQuery* variable. I concatenate the *Win32_LogicalFileSecuritySetting* with *strFolder*. Then I make the connection into WMI and go into the *SubGetDacl* subroutine. Once in the subroutine, I execute the query by using the *Get* method, and then use the *GetSecurityDescriptor* method to retrieve the security descriptor from the folder. I use the variable *wmiSecurityDescriptor* to hold the security descriptor representation that is returned from the *GetSecurityDescriptor* method. It is not a real object; rather, the format that returns is based on the *Win32_SecurityDescriptor* abstract class, which is used to represent the security structure of the folder. The discretionary access control list (DACL) is returned as an array of DACLs. I then walk through this array and retrieve the access mask, trustee information, and the SIDs associated with these entries. As with other methods in WMI, you have to capture the return code or else the call to the method fails.

Quick Check

Q: When you read the security descriptor for a file or a folder using the *Win32_LogicalFileSecuritySetting* class, how are access control masks retrieved?

A: When you read the security descriptor for a file or a folder using the *Win32_LogicalFileSecuritySetting* class, the access control masks are retrieved as a *Win32_Ace* array.

Q: When you use *Win32_ScheduledJob* to create a scheduled job, how is the time of the job determined?

A: When you use *Win32_ScheduledJob* to create a scheduled job, the time of the job is determined by using the UTC time format.

GetSecurityDescriptorOnFolder.vbs

```
strComputer = "."
strFolder = "'c:\\CIMv2Scripts'"
wmiQuery = "win32_LogicalFileSecuritySetting=" & strFolder
Set objWMIService = GetObject ("winmgmts:\\" & strComputer)
subGetDacl

'### subs are below ###
Sub subGetDacl
set objItem = objWMIService.Get(wmiQuery) 'use get method to get the folder
errRTN = objItem.GetSecurityDescriptor(wmiSecurityDescriptor)
subErr 'check for errors in retrieving the SID.
colDacl = wmiSecurityDescriptor.DACL ' Retrieve DACL
For each intAce in colDacl
    wscript.echo "Access Mask: "      & strAccessMask(intAce.AccessMask)
    wscript.echo "ACE Type: "         & intAce.AceType
Set intTrustee = intAce.Trustee ' Get Win32_Trustee object from ACE object
    wscript.echo "Trustee Domain: "  & intTrustee.Domain
    wscript.echo "Trustee Name: "    & intTrustee.Name
intSID = intTrustee.SID ' Get SID as array from Trustee object
    For i = 0 To UBound(intSID) - 1
        strsid = strsid & intSID(i) & ","
    Next
    strsid = strsid & intSID(i)
    wscript.echo "Trustee SID: {"     & strsid & "}" & vbcrlf
Next
End sub


Sub subErr
If Err <> 0 Then
    WScript.Echo "GetSecurityDescriptor failed" & vbcrlf & Err.Number & vbcrlf _
& Err.Description
    WScript.Quit
Else
    WScript.Echo "GetSecurityDescriptor succeeded"
End If
End Sub


Function strAccessMask(inMask)
Dim strPerm
    If inMask AND 1 Then strPerm = strPerm & "File List Dir, "
    If inMask AND 2 Then strPerm = strPerm & "File Add File, "
    If inMask AND 4 Then strPerm = strPerm & "File Add Sub, "
    If inMask AND 8 Then strPerm = strPerm & "File Read Ext Attr, "
    If inMask AND 16 Then strPerm = strPerm & "File Write Ext Attr, "
    If inMask AND 32 Then strPerm = strPerm & "File Traverse, "
    If inMask AND 64 Then strPerm = strPerm & "File Delete Child, "
    If inMask AND 128 Then strPerm = strPerm & "File Read Attrrib, "
    If inMask AND 256 Then strPerm = strPerm & "File Write Attrib, "
    If inMask AND 65536 Then strPerm = strPerm & "Delete, "
    If inMask AND 131072 Then strPerm = strPerm & "Read Control, "
    If inMask AND 262144 Then strPerm = strPerm & "Write DAC, "
    If inMask AND 524288 Then strPerm = strPerm & "Write Owner, "
```

```
    If inMask AND 1048576 Then strPerm = strPerm & "Synchronize, "
strAccessMask = strPerm
End Function
```

Using the Service Classes

Two classes are in this group: *Win32_BaseService* and *Win32_Service*. Each class contains 10 methods. *Win32_BaseService* has 22 properties, and *Win32_Service* has 25 properties. In 22 cases, the properties are identical; three unique properties are defined in *Win32_Service*: *Checkpoint*, *ProcessID*, and *WaitHint*. This makes sense because *Win32_BaseService* is used to describe a service that starts when the Windows operating system starts. These are very low-level types of services that do not belong to any particular user; rather, they are owned by the system. All of these base services are controlled by the Service Control Manager and can be found in the registry. This registry-based database of services is also owned and controlled by the Service Control Manager. There might be times when a network administrator or consult-ant is called upon to modify the start order or to change some parameter for one of these sys-tem base services, but it is extremely rare. In the old days, this entailed hacking the registry; in the 21st century, you use WMI.

Creating a Service

In the CreateAService.vbs script, I use the *Win32_Service* class to install Notepad as a service. There are several problems with this approach—not the least of which is that Notepad will not run as a service. But because I do not have an uninstalled service lying around for us to prac-tice with, I use Notepad. If the script runs without errors, it was successful. Another problem with this approach is that when you try to run as a service an application that is not designed as a service, it raises security concerns. This is one reason for the disappearance of the Resource Kit utility called Srvany.exe—it enabled you to treat an application as a service. From a security perspective, a service must be designed as a service from the ground up, and specific coding recommendations exist for doing this.

In the CreateAService.vbs script, I first use *Win32_Service*, and then I call the *Create* method to create a new service. The *Create* method from *Win32_Service* can take up to a dozen parame-ters, some of which are integers; others are strings, Booleans, and arrays. To keep the parame-ters straight, I tried to follow the Hungarian notation when I created the variable names. Additionally, by using variables for each parameter, I understand better what the actual *Create* command is trying to do, which can greatly facilitate troubleshooting. If the command errors out, it will more than likely simply say "Type Mismatch" and point to the line where you include the *Create* command. This doesn't help you identify the real error because you might need to examine up to a dozen parameters. This method requires you to capture the return code; if you do not, the error displayed might warn that you cannot use parentheses when calling a subroutine. This error is shown in Figure 11-4.

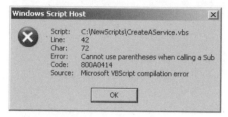

Figure 11-4   An error message that has nothing to do with a subroutine but that is caused by not capturing the return code

To avoid the bogus error, echo out the return code from the operation. You are, of course, looking for a zero here. Any number other than zero indicates an error. The errors you might see are many and vary from "The Service Already Exists" to "Access Denied." A complete listing of the return codes are in the Platform software development kit (SDK).

CreateAService.vbs

```
strComputer = "Acapulco"
wmiNS = "\root\cimv2"
wmiQuery = "win32_service"
strName = "notepad"
strDisplay = "notepad"
strPath="c:\windows\System32\notepad.exe"
intErr = 0 'do not notify user if error
strStartMode = "Manual"
bolDesk = False


Set objWMIService = GetObject("winmgmts:\\" & strComputer & wmiNS)
Set objItem = objWMIService.get(wmiQuery)
errRTN=objItem.create(strName,strDisplay,strPath,,intErr,strStartMode,bolDesk)
WScript.Echo(errRTN)
```

Deleting a Service

Because you created a bogus service, it would be nice to be able to delete the silly thing. This is much easier than creating the service. You use the *Delete* method of the *Win32_Service* class. The only trick to this operation is that you have to connect directly to the service by using the *Get* method. You supply the *Name* property because it is the key property for this class. You need to know the name of the service you are trying to delete, which is no problem because it is easily found in the Services console. As in the CreateAService.vbs script, you must capture the return code from the operation. So, when you run the DeleteAService.vbs script, you delete the Notepad service, and your computer no longer has a Notepad service.

DeleteAService.vbs

```
strComputer = "."
wmiNS = "\root\cimv2"
strServiceName = "'notepad'"
wmiQuery = "win32_service.name=" & strServiceName
Set objWMIService = GetObject("winmgmts:\\" & strComputer & wmiNS)
```

```
Set objItem = objWMIService.get(wmiQuery)

errRTN=objItem.delete("notepad")
WScript.Echo(errRTN)
```

Working with Shares

There are 11 share-related operating system classes. Eight of these are association classes, and only three are instance classes. Following are the three instance classes:

- *Win32_Share*
- *Win32_ServerConnection*
- *Win32_ServerSession*

Each of these classes is interesting and can provide some valuable information to the network administrator who is trying to get a handle on hundreds of shares that can be created on a workstation or a server. As you have seen in recent years, controlling shares is also a big security concern. Two of the classes, *Win32_ServerConnection* and *Win32_ServerSession*, provide very similar information. The difference is that *Win32_ServerConnection* provides you with the name of a share to which the connection is made and it gives you the number of users and the number of files open on the connection. The *Win32_ServerSession* class does not provide this information.

Reporting Connections to the Servers

In the Win32_ServerConnection.vbs script, I report on connections that are made to the server. The *Win32_ServerConnection* class can provide information on the number of connections, the shares in use, the users who are making the connection, and even the operating system the client machine is using to make the connection.

I begin by making a connection into WMI by using the moniker. I then use the *ExecQuery* method of the *SWbemServices* object to bring back every instance of a server session connected to the machine. I then report the values of each property by using *Wscript.Echo*.

Win32_ServerConnection.vbs
```
strComputer = "."
wmiNS = "\root\cimv2"
wmiQuery = "Select * from Win32_ServerSession"
Set objWMIService = GetObject("winmgmts:\\" & strComputer & wmiNS)
Set colItems = objWMIService.ExecQuery(wmiQuery)
For Each objItem in colItems

  wscript.echo "ActiveTime: " & objItem.ActiveTime
  wscript.echo "Caption: " & objItem.Caption
  wscript.echo "ClientType: " & objItem.ClientType
  wscript.echo "ComputerName: " & objItem.ComputerName
  wscript.echo "Description: " & objItem.Description
```

```
wscript.echo "IdleTime: " & objItem.IdleTime
wscript.echo "InstallDate: " & objItem.InstallDate
wscript.echo "Name: " & objItem.Name
wscript.echo "ResourcesOpened: " & objItem.ResourcesOpened
wscript.echo "SessionType: " & objItem.SessionType
wscript.echo "Status: " & objItem.Status
wscript.echo "TransportName: " & objItem.TransportName
wscript.echo "UserName: " & objItem.UserName
wscript.echo " "
next
```

Starting with the Start Menu

The Start menu group of classes contains four instance classes and three association classes. The *Win32_ProgramGroup* class, one of the instance classes, is deprecated and is not recommended for use by scripters. The *Win32_LogicalProgramGroup* is designed to take the place of the *Win32_ProgramGroup* class. An overview of the classes in this category is in Appendix E. The instance classes in this category are as follows:

- *Win32_LogicalProgramGroupItem*

- *Win32_ProgramGroupOrItem*

- *Win32_LogicalProgramGroup*

- *Win32_ProgramGroup* (deprecated)

In the Win32_LogicalProgramGroup.vbs script, I report on the program groups installed on the computer that are assigned to the All Users user. These are program groups that are available to any user who logs on to the computer. Controlling such program group assignments is a big concern of administrators who are working with Terminal Services or workstations with shared users. The *InstallDate* property is reported in a UTC date format; use the *FunTime* function to translate it into a more palatable format.

Win32_LogicalProgramGroup.vbs

```
strComputer = "."
wmiNS = "\root\cimv2"
wmiQuery = "Select * from Win32_LogicalProgramGroup " _
    & "where username = 'All Users'"
Set objWMIService = GetObject("winmgmts:\\" & strComputer & wmiNS)
Set colItems = objWMIService.ExecQuery(wmiQuery)
For Each objItem in colItems
 wscript.echo "Caption: " & objItem.Caption
 wscript.echo "Description: " & objItem.Description
 wscript.echo "GroupName: " & objItem.GroupName
 wscript.echo "InstallDate: " & funTime(objItem.InstallDate)
 wscript.echo "Name: " & objItem.Name
 wscript.echo "Status: " & objItem.Status
 wscript.echo "UserName: " & objItem.UserName & vbcrlf
Next
```

```
Function FunTime(wmiTime)
 Dim objSWbemDateTime 'holds an swbemDateTime object.
 Set objSWbemDateTime = CreateObject("WbemScripting.SWbemDateTime")
  objSWbemDateTime.Value= wmiTime
  FunTime = objSWbemDateTime.GetVarDate
End Function
```

Monitoring Storage

The WMI storage group of classes continues to evolve as more classes are added. Eleven classes are in this category, most dealing with shadow storage or user quotas. One new and exciting class is available in Windows Server 2003: the *Win32_Volume* class. It is a mega class that has 42 properties and 9 methods. The methods are not lame methods, either; they are awesome, exciting methods such as *Defrag*, *Format*, *Chkdsk*, and *AddMount*. The Windows storage team has done an awesome job by adding these methods, enabling the network administrator to perform nearly every conceivable kind of storage management task from a WMI script.

Using the *Win32_Volume* Methods

The *DefragAnalysis* method of the *Win32_Volume* class is a very useful class from a trouble-shooting and maintenance perspective. The only bad thing about this class is that it is available only in Windows Server 2003 and later. It is not available in Windows XP. Using the method is a little strange. Keep in mind the *DefragAnalysis* method requires two output variables. The first output variable is used to contain the evaluation of the drive condition—does the disk drive need to be defragmented? The second output variable is used to hold the details of the defrag analysis report. In reality, what is contained in the second output variable is not a mere report; rather, it is a *Win32_DefragAnalysis* object. You use the properties of the *Win32_DefragAnalysis* class to retrieve the report results. The NeedADefrag.vbs script illustrates how to call the *DefragAnalysis* method.

NeedADefrag.vbs

```
strComputer = "."
wmiNS = "\root\cimv2"
wmiQuery = "Select * from win32_Volume where DriveType ='3'"

Set objWMIService = GetObject("winmgmts:\\" & strComputer & wmiNS)
Set colItems = objWMIService.ExecQuery(wmiQuery)

For Each objItem in colItems
    Wscript.Echo "Beginning analysis of: " & objItem.DriveLetter
objItem.DefragAnalysis defrag,objitem1
    SubEvalDefrag
Next

Sub SubEvalDefrag
If defrag = 0 then
 WScript.echo "this disk does not need defragmentation"
```

```
    Else
      WScript.echo defrag
    End if

    Wscript.Echo "AverageFileSize: " & objitem1.AverageFileSize
    Wscript.Echo "FilePercentFragmentation: " & _ objitem1.FilePercentFragmentation
    Wscript.Echo "FragmentedFolders: " & objitem1.FragmentedFolders
    Wscript.Echo "TotalExcessFragments: " & objitem1.TotalExcessFragments
    Wscript.Echo "MFTPercentInUse: " & objitem1.MFTPercentInUse
    Wscript.Echo "TotalPageFileFragments: " & _ objitem1.TotalPageFileFragments
End Sub
```

Understanding User Classes

For many administrators, a surprising group of WMI classes is the user classes group. Using the power of WMI, you can retrieve reams of extremely valuable information about users and their activities on systems.

Working with Logon Sessions

In the Win32_LogonSession.vbs script, I return information regarding the authentication package used to authenticate the user, the type of logon, and the time in which the authentication took place. Because the time is returned in UTC format, I use the *FunTime* function to translate the time into a more readable format.

Win32_LogonSession.vbs

```
strComputer = "."
wmiNS = "\root\cimv2"
wmiQuery = "Select * from Win32_LogonSession"
Set objWMIService = GetObject("winmgmts:\\" & strComputer & wmiNS)
Set colItems = objWMIService.ExecQuery(wmiQuery)
For Each objItem in colItems

 wscript.echo "AuthenticationPackage: " & objItem.AuthenticationPackage
 wscript.echo "Caption: " & objItem.Caption
 wscript.echo "Description: " & objItem.Description
 wscript.echo "InstallDate: " & objItem.InstallDate
 wscript.echo "LogonId: " & objItem.LogonId
 wscript.echo "LogonType: " & objItem.LogonType
 wscript.echo "Name: " & objItem.Name
 wscript.echo "StartTime: " & funTime(objItem.StartTime)
 wscript.echo "Status: " & objItem.Status
wscript.echo " "
Next

Function FunTime(wmiTime)
 Dim objSWbemDateTime 'holds an SWbemDateTime object. Used to translate Time
 Set objSWbemDateTime = CreateObject("WbemScripting.SWbemDateTime")
  objSWbemDateTime.Value= wmiTime
  FunTime = objSWbemDateTime.GetVarDate
End Function
```

Working with User Accounts

The *Win32_UserAccount* class has a number of properties that can help you. This class can report whether an account is locked out, whether it is a local account or a domain account, and even whether the password is set to expire. As an added bonus, you can also retrieve the SID for a user. The Win32_UserAccount.vbs script demonstrates how to use this class.

Win32_UserAccount.vbs

```
strComputer = "."
wmiNS = "\root\cimv2"
wmiQuery = "Select * from Win32_UserAccount"
Set objWMIService = GetObject("winmgmts:\\" & strComputer & wmiNS)
Set colItems = objWMIService.ExecQuery(wmiQuery)
For Each objItem in colItems
 wscript.echo "AccountType: " & objItem.AccountType
 wscript.echo "Caption: " & objItem.Caption
 wscript.echo "Description: " & objItem.Description
 wscript.echo "Disabled: " & objItem.Disabled
 wscript.echo "Domain: " & objItem.Domain
 wscript.echo "FullName: " & objItem.FullName
 wscript.echo "InstallDate: " & objItem.InstallDate
 wscript.echo "LocalAccount: " & objItem.LocalAccount
 wscript.echo "Lockout: " & objItem.Lockout
 wscript.echo "Name: " & objItem.Name
 wscript.echo "PasswordChangeable: " & objItem.PasswordChangeable
 wscript.echo "PasswordExpires: " & objItem.PasswordExpires
 wscript.echo "PasswordRequired: " & objItem.PasswordRequired
 wscript.echo "SID: " & objItem.SID
 wscript.echo "SIDType: " & objItem.SIDType
 wscript.echo "Status: " & objItem.Status
wscript.echo " "
next
```

Leveraging the Windows NT Event Log

Five operating system classes are used to work with the event log. Two of the classes are instance classes: *Win32_NTEventLogFile* and *Win32_NTLogEvent*. I admit, the class names are a little confusing. The way I keep them straight is to remember that the word *file* in the class name *Win32_NTEventLogFile* refers to the physical log file used for the event log, not the events stored in the log. The script Win32_NTEventLogFile.vbs, found in the Chapter11 folder on the companion CD, reports all the properties of the *Win32_NTEventLogFile* class. Let's look at the methods of this class.

Backing Up Event Log Files

The *Win32_NTEventLogFile* class has 16 methods. This isn't as exciting as it might at first sound because the class inherits *CIM_DataFile*, and the 14 methods that come from there are more generic file methods (such as *Copy*) and are not specifically designed for working with event logs. However, two of the methods, *ClearEventLog* and *BackupEventLog*, are very useful.

Many administrators prefer to write scripts to perform their event log maintenance because the scripts can be more flexible than are the settings provided by using Event Viewer.

In the BackupEventLogCreateFileName.vbs script, I use the *BackupEventLog* method to back up the event log. If the backup is successful, the log file is cleared. In the process, I create a file name for the event log. The particular log file I am working with in the script is the application log, but you can perform the same operation on the system log, security log, or whichever event log file you happen to have on your computer. The *ClearEventLog* and *BackupEventLog* methods have been around since Windows NT 4 Service Pack 4.

In the *wmiQuery* string, you specify the name of the log file you want to back up. The *strLog* variable contains the actual name of the log. In this case, I specify the *LogFileName* property as *application*. You need to enclose this name in single quotes when it is passed to the query.

When you call the *BackupEventLog* method, you need to tell it the path and the name of the file that will be created for the backup. To do this, use two variables that are concatenated: *strLog-Folder* and *strFile*. Do this to create the file name dynamically. Assign the value of the folder in the reference section of the script, but the *strFile* variable will obtain its value in the subroutine that creates the file name.

In the *SubCreateFileName* subroutine, I make a WMI query to obtain the domain name; I obtain this property from the *Win32_ComputerSystem* class. I also obtain the computer name, but because *Name* is the key value and, therefore, automatically selected, I don't need to select *name, domain* in the *Select* statement. I glue these two properties together, pick up the log file name from the value of *strLog*, obtain the date, replace back slashes with underscores, put it all together, and this becomes the file name. You are allowed to perform this operation once a day. You could add additional logic to delete the log if you needed to back up twice a day or append a letter to the end indicating sequence of operation. You could use the *FileExists* method from the *FileSystemObject* to do this.

If the backup of the event log is successful, you clear the event log by using the *ClearEventLog* method.

BackupEventLogCreateFileName.vbs

```
strComputer = "."
wmiNS = "\root\cimv2"
strLOG = "'application'"
strMSG = " The Application event log could not be backed up."
wmiQuery = "Select * from win32_NTEventLogFile where LogFileName=" & strLOG
strLogFolder = "C:\fso\"

subCreateFileName

Set objWMIService = GetObject("winmgmts:" _
    & "{impersonationLevel=impersonate,(Backup)}!\\" & _
        strComputer & wmiNS)
Set colItems = objWMIService.ExecQuery(wmiQuery)
For Each objItem in colItems
```

```
    errBackupLog = objItem.BackupEventLog(strLogFolder & strFile)
    If errBackupLog <> 0 Then
        Wscript.Echo errBackupLog & strMSG
    Else
        objItem.ClearEventLog()
        WScript.echo "event log was backed up."
    End If
Next


Sub subCreateFileName
dim wmiQuery ' recycled variable. Same name outside.
Dim strDate ' only used in sub
Dim strName ' only used in sub

wmiQuery = "select domain from win32_computerSystem"
Set objWMIService = GetObject("winmgmts:\\" & strComputer & wmiNS)
Set colItems = objWMIService.execQuery(wmiQuery)

For Each objItem in colItems
 strName =  objItem.name
 strName = strName & "." & objItem.domain
Next

strDate = Replace (cstr(Date), "/", "_")
strLog = Replace (strLOG, "'", "_")
strFile = strName & strLog & strDate & ".evt"
End sub
```

Easing Windows Product Activation

A new class introduced in Windows XP is the *Win32_WindowsProductActivation* class. This class is very useful to help network administrators manage the deployment of Windows XP or Windows Server 2003. Windows XP and newer operating systems must be activated after installing them. Although this is not a problem for large organizations that have Select License agreements with Microsoft, because of the time and labor involved in completing the manual activation process, it can be a real problem for smaller customers who need to activate 10 or 15 copies of Windows XP.

If you need to activate Microsoft products on a number of computers, you can call the *Activate-Online* method or the *ActivateOffline* method. *ActivateOnline* is the easiest one to use, and it could be included as part of a setup script. The computer must be connected to the Internet to exchange the information with the Microsoft Clearinghouse license server. If you need to configure the Internet settings, you could use the *Win32_ProxyClass*, which has the *SetProxy-Setting* method.

Managing Windows product activation is not just a small-business problem—enterprise customers often have rogue departments that set up their own servers using retail software. To detect this, network administrators could use the DisplayWPAStatus.vbs script to locate servers that are about to crash as a result of inactivated licenses.

DisplayWPAStatus.vbs

```
strComputer = "."
wmiNS = "\root\cimv2"
wmiQuery = "Select * from Win32_WindowsProductActivation"
Set objWMIService = GetObject("winmgmts:\\" & strComputer & wmiNS)
Set colItems = objWMIService.ExecQuery(wmiQuery)

For Each objItem in colItems
    Wscript.Echo "ActivationRequired: " & objItem.ActivationRequired
    Wscript.Echo "IsNotificationOn: " & objItem.IsNotificationOn
    Wscript.Echo "ProductID: " & objItem.ProductID
    Wscript.Echo "RemainingEvaluationPeriod: " & objItem.RemainingEvaluationPeriod
    Wscript.Echo "RemainingGracePeriod: " & objItem.RemainingGracePeriod
    Wscript.Echo "ServerName: " & objItem.ServerName
Next
```

Summary

In this chapter, we looked at the operating system classes. Many classes and groups of classes can have immediate impact on the productivity of network administrators and consultants working in the field. The operating system WMI classes enable you to perform monitoring, logging, reporting, and various configuration activities by using scripts.

Quiz Yourself

Q: **What is the primary consideration when you use WMI to create a service from an application that is not configured to run as a service?**

A: The primary consideration when you use WMI to create a service from an application not configured to run as a service, besides possible service issues or stability issues, is security.

Q: **What must you remember when you use the *Win32_Volume* class to work with disk drives through WMI?**

A: When you use *Win32_Volume* to work with disk drives, remember that the class exists only in Windows Server 2003.

Q: **If you use *Win32_Registry* to set a new maximum size for the registry and a script reports that the proposed size and the maximum size of the registry are different numbers, what could be one reason for the difference?**

A: If you use *Win32_Registry* to set a new maximum size for the registry and the proposed size and the maximum size values are different, the most likely reason for this difference is that you did not reboot the computer subsequent to making the changes.

On Your Own

Lab 22 Monitoring the Shutdown of Applications

In this lab, you will use the *Win32_ProcessStopTrace* operating system event class to monitor the shutdown of applications. You will have two processes running on your computer, and when one of the processes stops, you want to capture the name and process ID of the process. When the second process stops, you will once again capture this information.

1. Open the WmiTemplate.vbs script and save it as StudentLab22.vbs.

2. Modify the *wmiQuery* to select everything from the *Win32_ProcessStopTrace* class. The line looks like the following:

   ```
   wmiQuery = "SELECT * FROM Win32_ProcessStopTrace"
   ```

3. Modify the *Set colItems* line to perform an *ExecNotificationQuery*. The line looks like the following:

   ```
   Set colItems = objWMIService.ExecNotificationQuery(wmiQuery)
   ```

4. Delete the *For Each Next* section and all the enclosed *Wscript.Echo* commands that were in the original template.

5. Because the *ExecNotificationQuery* might take a little while to actually work, you need to use *Wscript.Echo* to print out an appropriate message to inform the user that the script is waiting for a particular event. I added a line like the following under the *Set colItems* line:

   ```
   WScript.Echo "Waiting for process to stop ..."
   ```

6. Now put the script into a loop as it waits for the event to transpire. To do this, use the *Do Loop* command. It will be blank right now. Place *Do* under the *Wscript.Echo* command you added in step 5, add in a couple of blank lines, and type *Loop* on a separate line. It looks something like this when you are done:

   ```
   DO
   Loop
   ```

7. Just below the *Do* command, invoke your subscription to the event. Do this by using the *NextEvent* command. Assign what comes back from using *NextEvent* to the variable *objItem*. The completed line looks like the following:

   ```
   Set objItem = colItems.NextEvent
   ```

8. If an event occurs, you want to print out the *ProcessName* and the *ProcessID*. Do this by using *Wscript.Echo*. The completed *Do Loop* section now looks like the following:

   ```
   Do
        Set objItem = colItems.NextEvent
            Wscript.Echo "StoppedProcess Name: " & objItem.ProcessName
            Wscript.Echo "Process ID: " & objItem.ProcessId
       Loop
   ```

9. Save and run the script. You should see the message, "Waiting for process to stop..." in the output.

10. Run the LaunchMultipleProcesses.vbs script (in the Lab22 folder on the accompanying CD). This script starts Notepad and Calculator. Wait for a few seconds.

11. Open Task Manager, and find the Notepad.exe process and the Calc.exe process. Write down the process ID of the two processes you just started.

12. Kill Notepad. You should see a message that lists the process ID and the name of the process (*Notepad*) that you just killed.

13. Kill Calculator. You should see a message that lists the process ID and the name of the process (*Calc*) that you just killed.

14. If all goes smoothly, you have completed the lab. If you encounter errors, you must do the optional troubleshooting lab (just kidding). Compare your script to the Lab22Solution.vbs script in the Lab22 folder.

Lab 23 Performing a Controlled Shutdown of Apps

In this lab, you will expand upon the script you developed in Lab 22. Instead of simply reporting the process ID (PID) of an application that is no longer running (really lame, I will admit), this script will shut down an additional application. The idea of this lab is that in situations in which you have an application with multiple dependent processes, you can control the shutdown of the entire application by killing off the dependent processes in the correct order. For this lab, you will use Notepad and Calculator.

1. Open either your solution from Lab 22 or the Lab23Starter.vbs script. Whichever script you choose to use, make sure you save it as StudentLab23.vbs.

2. Create a subroutine called *SubKillProcess*. To do this, use the *Sub* and *End Sub* commands. It looks like the following:

```
Sub subKillProcess
End Sub
```

3. Under the *Sub SubKillProcess* line, declare three variables: *wmiQuery1*, *objItem1*, and *colItems1*.

4. You need to define *wmiQuery1*. Make it equal to selecting the *Name* property from the *Win32_Process* class. But do this only if the name is equal to Calc.exe. The query looks like the following:

```
wmiQuery1 = "select name from win32_Process where name='calc.exe'"
```

5. Use the variable *colItems1* to hold what comes back from executing the *wmiQuery1*. This line of code looks like the following:

```
Set colItems1 = objWMIService.execQuery(wmiQuery1)
```

6. To walk through the items in *colItems1*, use a *For Each Next* loop. Inside this loop, call the *Terminate* method of the *Win32_Process* class. The completed loop looks like the following:

```
For Each objItem1 in colItems1
   objItem1.terminate
Next
```

7. Save the script.

8. In the *Do* loop, just under the *Wscript.Echo "Process ID"* line, call the *SubKillProcess* subroutine. You do this simply by typing in the name of the subroutine: **SubKillProcess**.

9. Save and run your script.

10. Run the LaunchMultipleProcesses.vbs script. Wait a few seconds. The LaunchMultipleProcesses.vbs script will start Notepad and Calculator for you.

11. Now kill Notepad. You should see a confirmation message print the name *Notepad* and the process ID associated with Notepad. You should also see Calculator go away and see the printout for its process name and process ID as well.

This completes Lab 23.

Chapter 12

Using the Performance Counter Classes

In Chapter 11, we examined the operating system classes. We looked at several methods that enable us to make some useful configuration changes on our systems. In this chapter, we look at the performance counter classes. Network administrators love to use System Monitor; it gives them real-time insight into the performance of servers. System Monitor can quickly pinpoint trouble spots and offer insights for both hardware upgrades and system configuration changes. However much as administrators admit that they love using the tool, most lament that they do not have time to use it as much as they would like. Indeed, it seems that most administrators use System Monitor only when they are having problems. As an alternative, the Windows Management Instrumentation (WMI) performance counter classes enable harried administrators to retrieve real-time performance information proactively. In fact, when you incorporate a few well-crafted scripts, you can create a pretty sophisticated monitoring application.

Before You Begin

To work through this chapter, you should be familiar with the following concepts:
- The basics of network administration
- The basics of performance monitoring
- The basics of performing WMI queries

After you complete this chapter, you will be familiar with the following concepts:
- The difference between raw and cooked counters
- How to write WMI scripts that use performance counter classes
- How to refresh information retrieved from a performance counter class

 Note All the scripts used in this chapter are located on the CD that accompanies this book in the \Scripts\Chapter12 folder.

Using Formatted Performance Counter Classes

The performance counter WMI classes enable you to access performance information from within a script. By using this information, you can assess the health of your server. This information can also serve to feed into the decision portion of your script, enabling you to take either corrective or preventive action based on the actual statistical performance of the computer. The formatted performance counter classes are also called *cooked* performance counter classes and are listed in Appendix F, Table F-1. The big advantage of using the formatted performance counters is that many of the calculations are already made for you.

Understanding Performance Counter Classes

Two performance counter providers reside on computers running Microsoft Windows Server 2003: the cooked counter provider, and the performance counter provider. The cooked provider supplies WMI classes that calculate formatted data based on various sampling intervals that are used to supply the raw data to the class. The formatted data is then supplied to the class. This data should be the same data as is displayed in the System Monitor utility because the same formulas are used in the computations.

The classes are generated in the WMI repository when the system starts up by reading the performance libraries in the registry. The AutoDiscovery/AutoPurge (ADAP) process is responsible for adding classes to the repository. This process transfers performance counter objects into WMI performance classes in the WMI repository. The properties of these classes are used to represent the counters you would see in System Monitor. The ADAP process compares the list of counter objects found in the performance libraries to the list of counter classes in WMI. If an object is not represented in WMI, it is added. The process works in reverse as well: if a performance library has been uninstalled, the ADAP process will remove all the WMI performance classes derived from the registered performance libraries.

Obtaining Current Bandwidth

In Figure 12-1, you can see System Monitor reporting the current bandwidth of two network adapters. These values were selected from the Network Interface performance object. On my computer, I chose current bandwidth from all instances and obtained the results shown in Figure 12-1.

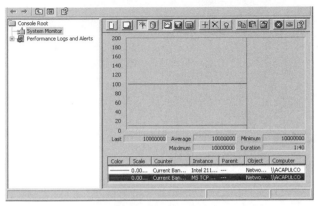

Figure 12-1   Checking the current bandwidth of a network interface using System Monitor

The two values reported in System Monitor correspond exactly to the output from the CurrentBandwidth.vbs script. In the script, I select a single property—*CurrentBandwidth*—from the *Win32_PerfFormattedData_Tcpip_NetworkInterface* class. I build up a variable, and then print the results. This gives me a real-time representation of the current bandwidth of the network interface—exactly the same information retrieved from System Monitor because of the ADAP process and the fact that the information comes from the same location.

CurrentBandwidth.vbs

```
strComputer = "."
wmiNS = "\root\cimv2"
wmiQuery = "Select CurrentBandwidth from _ Win32_PerfFormattedData_Tcpip_NetworkInterface"
Set objWMIService = GetObject("winmgmts:\\" & strComputer & wmiNS)
Set colItems = objWMIService.ExecQuery(wmiQuery)

For Each objItem in colItems
strMSG = strMSG & vbcrlf & "Name:  " & objItem.Name & vbcrlf & _
   vbtab & "CurrentBandwidth: " & objItem.CurrentBandwidth
Next
WScript.Echo strMSG
```

Quick Check

Q: What are the two kinds of performance counter classes available in WMI?

A: The two kinds of performance counter classes available in WMI are cooked and raw counters.

Q: What is the difference between a cooked counter class and a raw counter class?

A: The difference between a cooked counter class and a raw counter class is that a cooked counter class generally performs calculations for you, whereas the raw counter class does not. For instance, a cooked counter class can calculate the percentage of processor utilization by taking several measurements of the processor utilization, and then averaging them for you.

Refreshing the Data

When you perform a query into the performance-monitor counters, you might find illuminating results, but you cannot trend the data. If you loop through the counters without refreshing the data, you simply repeat the presentation of the information over and over again—certainly not a very useful operation. However, if you can go back to WMI and reload the data, you will have updated data to present to your script.

For example, if I want the capability of refreshing the WMI data available to my script, I must create a refresher object. The refresher object is called *SWbemRefresher*, and basically it is a container into which you can put data that needs to be refreshed. You can add multiple items to a refresher object. Individual items added to the refresher object are represented by an instance of *SWbemRefreshableItem*. Because this is the case, you can treat the entire object as a collection and can iterate through it if you choose. The refresher object will obtain updated data when you call the *Refresh* method. The tricky part of adding an item to the refresher is that you must specify two parameters: the connection that was made into WMI and the query that you want to use. This refresher object will take charge of refreshing the WMI query; additionally, the refresher object will execute the query for you.

Using the Refresher Object

In the Refresh_PerfOS_Objects.vbs script, you use a refresher object to update the information reported from the class. The first step is to create the refresher object. To do this, use the *Set* command to capture the object that comes back from using the *CreateObject* command to create the *SWbemRefresher* object. This line of code looks like the following:

```
Set objRefresher = CreateObject("WbemScripting.SWbemRefresher")
```

Once you have created the refresher object, you must add a query to the object that will be refreshed. You use the *AddEnum* method to tie the query and the WMI connection together using the refresher object. In the Refresh_PerfOS_Objects.vbs script, the line that adds the query and the WMI connection to the refresher object looks like the following:

```
Set objRefreshItem = objRefresher.AddEnum(objWMIService,wmiQuery)
```

After you use the *AddEnum* method, the last thing you must do is to use the *Refresh* method. You therefore call *objRefresher.Refresh* and pull back the information from WMI.

> **Tip**   At first glance, this might seem strange because you are refreshing data you have not yet received. But the key to understanding this concept is to realize that it is actually the refresher that makes the query in the first place. You need to refresh the data to obtain the data the first time. Failure to use the refresher to obtain the data prior to querying for the data is actually the biggest mistake that people make when first using the refresher.

Refresh_PerfOS_Objects.vbs

```
strComputer = "."
wmiNS = "\root\cimv2"
wmiQuery = "Win32_PerfFormattedData_PerfOS_Objects"
Set objWMIService = GetObject("winmgmts:\\" & strComputer & wmiNS)
Set objRefresher = CreateObject("WbemScripting.SWbemRefresher")
Set objRefreshItem = objRefresher.AddEnum(objWMIService,wmiQuery)
objRefresher.Refresh

For i = 1 To 4
For Each objItem in objRefreshItem.ObjectSet
objRefresher.refresh
 wscript.echo "Events: " & objItem.Events
 wscript.echo "Mutexes: " & objItem.Mutexes
 wscript.echo "Processes: " & objItem.Processes
 wscript.echo "Sections: " & objItem.Sections
 wscript.echo "Semaphores: " & objItem.Semaphores
 wscript.echo "Threads: " & objItem.Threads & vbcrlf
WScript.sleep 2000
next
Next
```

Refreshing a Single Counter

If you are interested in the performance characteristic of a single item, it does not make sense to retrieve everything that is running on the computer and walk through all the data when you need only monitor a single object. The procedure to monitor a single object is similar to one used in the Refresh_PerfOS_Objects.vbs script. You need to create a refresher object, add items to the refresher, and then use the *Refresh* method to obtain the data. This is where the similarities end. Working with a single counter entails identifying a single instance in the WMI query.

In the PercentProcessorUtilization.vbs script, I query only total processor utilization. The *Name* property is the key value for the *Win32_PerfFormattedData_PerfOS_Processor* class. Once I define the WMI query, I create a refresher object and use the *Add* method to add both the WMI connection and the WMI query to the refresher object. To query a single instance, I use the *Add* method instead of the *AddEnum* method because *AddEnum* is used to add a collection of objects to the refresher object. I then use the *Refresh* method to refresh the data in the refresher object. I loop through the data four times, refreshing the data each time.

PercentProcessorUtilization.vbs

```
strComputer = "."
wmiNS = "\root\cimv2"
wmiQuery = "Win32_PerfFormattedData_PerfOS_Processor.name='_Total'"
Set objWMIService = GetObject("winmgmts:\\" & strComputer & wmiNS)
Set objRefresher = CreateObject("WbemScripting.SWbemRefresher")
Set objItem = objRefresher.Add(objWMIService,wmiQuery).object
objRefresher.Refresh

For i = 1 To 4
```

```
objRefresher.refresh
Wscript.echo "InterruptsPersec:"  & objItem.InterruptsPersec
Wscript.echo "Name:"  & objItem.Name
Wscript.echo "PercentIdleTime:"  & objItem.PercentIdleTime
Wscript.echo "PercentInterruptTime:"  & objItem.PercentInterruptTime
Wscript.echo "PercentPrivilegedTime:"  & objItem.PercentPrivilegedTime
Wscript.echo "PercentProcessorTime:"  & objItem.PercentProcessorTime
Wscript.echo "PercentUserTime:"  & objItem.PercentUserTime & vbcrlf
WScript.sleep 3000
Next
```

Finding How Long Your System Has Been Up

One of the more intriguing formatted performance counter classes is the *Win32_PerfFormatted-Data_PerfOS_System* class. This class can retrieve a number of extremely valuable performance counters. It maps to the *System* object in System Monitor. As shown in Figure 12-2, the *System* object in the Performance console can provide very useful information about the computer system. You will use just one of these counters, the System Up Time counter.

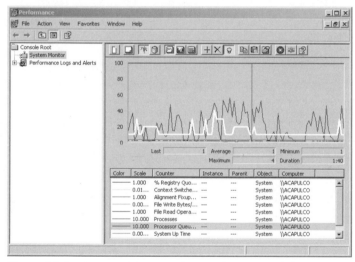

Figure 12-2   System object monitoring the status of the operating system

In the SystemUptime.vbs script, the *Win32_PerfFormattedData_PerfOS_System* class does not have a key value. I use the *Get* method to connect to the single instance of the operating system, which I specify as @. I then retrieve the *SystemUpTime* property, which is reported in seconds. I use two functions to format the output into a more palatable form. The first function reports the number of hours, and the second reports the number of days the system has been up. I do not need to use the refresher object in the SystemUptime.vbs script because I am interested in only a one-time number. There is no point in refreshing the data.

SystemUptime.vbs
```
strComputer = "."
wmiNS = "\root\cimv2"
```

```
wmiQuery = "Win32_PerfFormattedData_PerfOS_System=@"
Set objWMIService = GetObject("winmgmts:\\" & strComputer & wmiNS)
Set objItem = objWMIService.get(wmiQuery)
    numSeconds= objItem.SystemUpTime ' it is in seconds since last start
    WScript.echo "the system has been up " & convertHours(numSeconds) & " hours"
    WScript.echo "that translates to " & convertDays(numSeconds) & " days"
'### functions below ###
Function convertHours(numSeconds)
convertHours= int(numseconds/3600)  ' number of seconds in an hour
End Function

function convertDays(numseconds)
convertDays = Int(numSeconds/86400) ' number of seconds in a day
End Function
```

Examining Process Threads

At times, you need to examine the threads of a process. Some applications spin up many threads. For example, the system process in Microsoft Windows XP spins up more than 100 threads. Sometimes you will want to monitor these threads from a performance standpoint or from a troubleshooting perspective. To do so, you might use the MonitorProcessThreads.vbs script.

In the MonitorProcessThreads.vbs script, I define the WMI query, which is simply the name of the formatted data class. Next, I include a variable called *strProcess* that holds the name of the process that I want to monitor. In this script, I use the WinWord process, but you can change this value to any process you have running on your computer at the time. I make the connection into WMI by using the moniker and assign the returned *SWbemService* object to the variable *objWMIService*. I then create a refresher object and assign it to the variable *objRefresher*. Next, I add both the WMI connection and the WMI query to the refresher object by using the *AddEnum* method of the *SWbemRefresher* object. I do this instead of using the *Add* method because, although I am interested in only a single process, that process might have multiple threads associated with it. I would need to know the exact thread number to connect to only a specific thread. By performing the query as I do, I am actually retrieving all the processes and all the threads on the computer, but I use the *Instr* function to filter out the information to display only the process in which I am interested.

MonitorProcessThreads.vbs

```
strComputer = "."
wmiNS = "\root\cimv2"
wmiQuery = "Win32_PerfFormattedData_PerfProc_Thread"
strProcess = "winword"
Set objWMIService = GetObject("winmgmts:\\" & strComputer & wmiNS)
Set objRefresher = CreateObject("wbemScripting.SWbemRefresher")
Set objRefreshItem = objRefresher.AddEnum(objWMIService,wmiQuery)
objRefresher.Refresh

For i = 1 To 4
For Each objItem in objRefreshItem.ObjectSet
objRefresher.refresh
```

```
If InStr (1,objItem.name,strProcess,1) then
Wscript.echo "Caption:"  & objItem.Caption
Wscript.echo "ContextSwitchesPersec:"  & objItem.ContextSwitchesPersec
Wscript.echo "Description:"  & objItem.Description
Wscript.echo "ElapsedTime:"  & objItem.ElapsedTime
Wscript.echo "IDProcess:"  & objItem.IDProcess
Wscript.echo "IDThread:"  & objItem.IDThread
Wscript.echo "Name:"  & objItem.Name
Wscript.echo "PercentPrivilegedTime:"  & objItem.PercentPrivilegedTime
Wscript.echo "PercentProcessorTime:"  & objItem.PercentProcessorTime
Wscript.echo "PercentUserTime:"  & objItem.PercentUserTime
Wscript.echo "PriorityBase:"  & objItem.PriorityBase
Wscript.echo "PriorityCurrent:"  & objItem.PriorityCurrent
Wscript.echo "StartAddress:"  & objItem.StartAddress
Wscript.echo "ThreadState:"  & objItem.ThreadState
Wscript.echo "ThreadWaitReason:"  & objItem.ThreadWaitReason
WScript.sleep 2000
End if
next
Next
```

Measuring Memory Utilization

You can use the Win32_PerfFormattedData_PerfOS_Memory class to retrieve cooked perfor-mance counter data that reports memory utilization on your computer. In the Memory-Stats.vbs script, I examine four critical performance counters to determine the memory performance of the computer. The first counter is self-explanatory—AvailableMBytes. This counter reports available memory (both physical and virtual) in megabytes. What is nice about this property is that the number returned is easy to understand.

The next property I examine is the CommitLimit property, which determines how much mem-ory can be committed on the computer before you have to expand the page file to obtain addi-tional memory for the operating system. This is a critical performance counter because expanding the page file results in significant disk input/output (I/O) and processor utilization.

The CommittedBytes property indicates how much memory on the system is already commit-ted to various running applications. All this memory might not actually be in use, but it is reserved for specific applications and is therefore not available for other uses.

The PageFaultsPerSec property reports the average number of page faults during the polling period. It is important to monitor page faults because of the CPU expense involved in moving information to and from the page file. Paging also incurs a performance penalty when you read or write to the disk drive because typically the drives are the slowest parts of a computer. You want to avoid paging as much as possible. The only way you can track and understand this vital performance metric is to monitor it on a regular basis.

The MemoryStats.vbs script uses a refresher object that is created by using the CreateObject command. Once the refresher object is created, I add the WMI service connection and the WMI query to the refresher object by using the AddEnum method. I then execute the query by calling the *Refresh* method of the refresher object. This command populates the data into the refresher for the initial data retrieval. I then loop four times at 2-second intervals, each time refreshing the data retrieved.

MemoryStats.vbs

```
strComputer = "."
wmiNS = "\root\cimv2"
wmiQuery = "Win32_PerfFormattedData_PerfOS_Memory"
Set objWMIService = GetObject("winmgmts:\\" & strComputer & wmiNS)
Set objRefresher = CreateObject("WbemScripting.SWbemRefresher")
Set objRefreshItem = objRefresher.AddEnum(objWMIService,wmiQuery)
objRefresher.Refresh

For i = 1 To 4
For Each objItem in objRefreshItem.ObjectSet
objRefresher.refresh
 wscript.echo "AvailableMBytes: " & objItem.AvailableMBytes
 wscript.echo "CommitLimit: " & formatNumber(objItem.CommitLimit,,-1)
 wscript.echo "CommittedBytes: " & formatNumber(objItem.CommittedBytes,,-1)
 wscript.echo "PageFaultsPerSec: " & objItem.PageFaultsPerSec
 WScript.echo " "
WScript.sleep 2000
next
Next
```

Using Raw Performance Counter Classes

The raw performance counter classes are documented in Appendix F, Table F-2. By using the raw performance counter classes, you can make your own calculations in returning data to your scripts. You have more control over the data and can obtain the actual instantaneous performance counter data.

Monitoring Processor Utilization

In the PercentProcessorRaw.vbs script, I use the raw *Win32_PerfRawData_PerfOS_Processor* class and obtain total processor utilization. When I get the *PercentProcessorTime* property, I also get a time stamp. These values are written to variables *N1* and *D1*. After I have obtained the *PercentProcessorTime* property and the corresponding time stamp on the first pass (*TimeStamp_Sys100NS*), I save the values to the *N1* and *D1* variables. I then pause the execution of the script for a couple of seconds by using the *Wscript.Sleep* command. I perform the same WMI query a second time. This time I hold the results in a different variable—the *objItem2* variable. This enables me to work with the second set of properties. I once again obtain the value of *PercentProcessorTime* and the accompanying time stamp, which is stored in the *TimeStamp_Sys100NS* property.

I use two new variables to hold the *PercentProcessorTime* and the time stamp. *N2* holds the value of the *PercentProcessorTime*, and *D2* holds the time stamp. I subtract the value of *N1* from *N2*, which yields the difference in processor time from the first and second WMI queries. I divide the result by the difference in the two time stamps, subtract everything from 1, and multiple by 100, which yields the resultant processor utilization.

The *PercentProcessorTime* variable could contain a rather nasty number. I use the *Round* function to trim the number to two decimal places. Once the number is rounded, I use *Wscript.Echo* to print the results.

PercentProcessorRaw.vbs

```
strComputer = "."
wmiNS = "\root\cimv2"
wmiQuery = "Win32_PerfRawData_PerfOS_Processor.Name='_Total'"
Set objWMIService = GetObject("winmgmts:\\" & strComputer & wmiNS)
WScript.echo "Percent processor utilization"
For i = 1 to 8
Set objItem1 = objWMIService.get(wmiQuery)
    N1 = objItem1.PercentProcessorTime
    D1 = objItem1.TimeStamp_Sys100NS
WScript.Sleep 2000
Set objItem2 = objWMIService.get(wmiQuery)
    N2 = objItem2.PercentProcessorTime
    D2 = objItem2.TimeStamp_Sys100NS
PercentProcessorTime = (1 - ((N2 - N1)/(D2-D1)))*100
    WScript.Echo Round(PercentProcessorTime,2)
Next
```

Working with the Logical Disk

You can use the raw performance counters to retrieve information related to the performance of logical disks. Logical disks are different from physical disks; several logical disks can be defined on a single physical disk, and they represent an abstract arrangement on the physical drive. You often are concerned with the performance of a logical disk rather than the performance of a physical drive.

In the PercentLogicalDiskRAW.vbs script, I define the *wmiQuery* to equal the *Win32_PerfRawData_PerfDisk_LogicalDisk* class. I also specify the particular instance of the logical disk I want to monitor. I am interested in all the instances, so I connect to the counters representing all the logical drives.

Once I have defined the query, I make the connection into WMI. I use the WMI moniker for its ease of use and then assign the WMI service object returned to the variable *objWMIService*. I use a *For Next* loop and make eight passes. On each pass, I execute a WMI query retrieving both a performance counter and a time stamp. The time stamp is contained in the *TimeStamp_Sys100NS* property, which is the same property name used in the PercentProcessorRaw.vbs script. The classes used in both scripts are derived from the *Win32_Perf* class, and the *TimeStamp_Sys100NS* property is inherited from that class.

PercentLogicalDiskRAW.vbs

```
strComputer = "."
wmiNS = "\root\cimv2"
```

```
wmiQuery = "Win32_PerfRawData_PerfDisk_LogicalDisk.name='_total'"
Set objWMIService = GetObject("winmgmts:\\" & strComputer & wmiNS)
WScript.echo "Disk Utilization"
For i = 1 to 8
Set objItem1 = objWMIService.get(wmiQuery)
   N1 = objItem1.PercentDiskTime
   D1 = objItem1.TimeStamp_Sys100NS
WScript.Sleep 2000
Set objItem2 = objWMIService.get(wmiQuery)
   N2 = objItem2.PercentDiskTime
   D2 = objItem2.TimeStamp_Sys100NS
PercentUtilization = (1 - ((N2 - N1)/(D2-D1)))*100
   WScript.Echo Round(PercentUtilization,2)
Next
```

Summary

In this chapter, we looked at using the WMI performance counter classes. We examined the difference between raw and formatted (or cooked) performance counters and discussed when to use one type of counter rather than the other. We examined in detail the various categories of both cooked and raw counters. We discussed the use of the refresher object and when to use it, and we also looked at a script that did not need to use the refresher.

Quiz Yourself

Q: What is the refresher object and what is it used for?

A: The refresher object is the *SWbemRefresher* object. It is used to execute queries and is capable of refreshing the data after the query has been executed.

Q: Why do you need to use the refresher object?

A: You use the refresher object for certain performance counter classes that sample data over time. Typically, these classes are cooked counter classes that report data such as the percentage of processor utilization. To obtain the result, several measurements over a period of time are required to calculate the average utilization of the object, and for each measurement the data must be refreshed by using the refresher object.

Q: What is the primary consideration when using raw performance counter objects as opposed to using cooked performance counter objects?

A: When you use raw performance counter objects, you must sample the data twice and then perform your own calculation to obtain average values.

On Your Own

Lab 24 Working with Formatted Performance Classes

In this lab, you will work with the formatted performance counter classes to develop a script that is used to monitor real-time data on a server. During the course of this lab, you will develop a refresher template you can use whenever you need to refresh data in a script.

1.   Open the WmiTemplate.vbs script, and save it as RefresherTemplate.vbs. This will be a template script you can use in the future when you need to refresh data.

2.   In your newly named RefresherTemplate.vbs, turn off the *On Error Resume Next* line by remarking it out.

3.   Delete the *Dim* statement for the variable *colItems*.

4.   You need three variables to work with the refresher. Place them under the other variables that are declared under the line *Dim objItem*. Name the variables *objRefresher*, *objRefreshItem*, and *i*. The code to do this looks like the following:

```
Dim objRefresher, objRefreshItem, i
```

5.   Under the line that makes the connection into WMI by using the *GetObject* command, add a line that will create the *SWbemRefresher* object. Assign the refresher object that comes back to the *objRefresher* variable. The line that does this looks like the following:

```
Set objRefresher = CreateObject("WbemScripting.SWbemRefresher")
```

6.   Find the line that performs the *ExecQuery* method and populates the *colItems* variable with the result of the query. Once you find it, delete the line. You will not use *ExecQuery*. Instead, you will use a refresher. The line you must delete looks like the following:

```
Set colItems = objWMIService.ExecQuery(wmiQuery)
```

7.   In the location where you just deleted the *Set colItems* line, insert a line that adds the *wmiQuery* and the *objWMIService* to the refresher object. Use the *AddEnum* method from the refresher object to do this, and use the *objRefreshItem* variable to hold the collection of refreshable items:

```
Set objRefreshItem = objRefresher.AddEnum(objWMIService,wmiQuery)
```

8.   Now it is time to use the *Refresh* method from the refresher object to perform the initial data refresh. This is a very simple command that looks like the following:

```
objRefresher.Refresh
```

9.   Use a *For Next* loop to make four passes around the *For Each Next* loop. Use the i variable to count the iterations. The *For i = 1 to 4* line goes above the *For Each* statement, and the *Next* goes at the bottom of the script.

10.   At this point, the *For Each* statement should read as follows: *For Each objItem in colItems*. You deleted *colItems* earlier, so change this to iterate through the refresher-supplied data.

Keep the *For Each objItem* part of the command, but change the *colItems* to something else. When you use the *AddEnum* method to add items to the refresher, you add a collection—or an *objectSet*. To retrieve the items in the *objectSet* use *For Each* and a variable to hold an individual instance in the object set, and then refer to the actual collection of refreshable items. The code that does this looks like the following:

```
For Each objItem in objRefreshItem.ObjectSet
```

11. Go ahead and refresh the data in the refresher. You will again use the *Refresh* method:

```
objRefresher.refresh
```

12. After the last *Wscript.Echo* command, add a *Sleep* command to pause the execution of the script to enable the data to change possibly between iterations. Use a *Wscript.Echo 2000* command to pause execution for 2 seconds.

13. Save your work, but do not attempt to run the script because it will fail miserably.

14. Using the RefresherTemplate.vbs script you just created. Save the file as StudentLab24.vbs.

15. Modify the *wmiQuery* line so that it targets the *Win32_PerfFormattedData_PerfNet_Server* class. This is a simple value assignment to the *wmiQuery* variable that looks like the following:

```
wmiQuery = "Win32_PerfFormattedData_PerfNet_Server"
```

16. The only task left is to find the properties you wish to report. I picked out a few from the Platform software development kit (SDK) that looked interesting. Put the property on the other side of the *objItem*, and you can use the same name for the title. My completed *Wscript.Echo* section looks like the following:

```
wscript.echo "errorsLogon: " & objItem.errorsLogon
wscript.echo "logonTotal: " & objItem.logonTotal
wscript.echo "filesOpen: " & objItem.filesOpen
wscript.echo "ServerSessions: " & objItem.ServerSessions
wscript.echo "sessionsLoggedOff: " & objItem.sessionsLoggedOff
wscript.echo "sessionsTimedOut: " & objItem.sessionsTimedOut
```

17. Save and run the script. It should run perfectly. You can use the RefresherTemplate.vbs script to report on any property you wish to monitor on a refreshable basis. The only two items that must be changed are the name of the class and the property you wish to report.

Lab 25 Using Unformatted Performance Counters

In this lab, you will develop a script that uses the unformatted performance provider. The script you will write will be used to monitor the disk utilization on your computer. You will be using the *Win32_PerfRawData_PerfDisk_PhysicalDisk* class and taking several measurements over time to make the calculations.

1. Open the WmiTemplate.vbs script, and save it as StudentLab25.vbs.

2. To work with the raw performance counters, you need to perform two queries, track the time stamp, and make your own calculation. Declare two variables to use to walk through the WMI results: *objItem1* and *objItem2*. The code to do this looks like the following:

```
dim objItem1, objItem2
```

3. Declare a counter variable to use with the *For Next* loop, as well as some variables to hold the data that is read and the time stamp value. Use *i*, *n1*, *n2*, *d1*, and *d2*. The line that declares these variables looks like the following:

```
Dim i, n1, n2, d1, d2
```

4. You also need to declare a variable that will hold the result of the calculation. I used a variable called *PercentUtilization*. Declare this variable as shown here:

```
Dim PercentUtilization
```

5. Modify the *wmiQuery* line so that it points to the *Win32_PerfRawData_Perf-Disk_PhysicalDisk* class. Instead of performing a *Select ** query, connect to a specific instance of the *Win32_PerfRawData_PerfDisk_PhysicalDisk* class. Specify the name of the instance to which you wish to connect. You are connecting to the instance that represents a total of all the drives on the system. The *wmiQuery* line looks like the following:

```
wmiQuery = "Win32_PerfRawData_PerfDisk_PhysicalDisk.name='_total'"
```

6. Delete the *Set collItems = objWMIService.ExecQuery* line. You are not going to perform an *ExecQuery* in this script.

7. In place of the *Set collItems* line, add a *Wscript.Echo* line that will serve as the header for your output. I used a very basic line, as shown here:

```
WScript.echo "Disk Utilization"
```

8. Delete the *For Each objItem* in *CollItems* and all the *Wscript.Echo* lines that were in the template script. This actually comprises everything below the *Wscript.Echo* line you just added.

9. Add a *For i = 1 to 8* line and close it out with a *Next* at the bottom of your script. It looks like the following:

```
For i = 1 to 8
Next
```

10. You want to perform the first of two WMI queries. Under the *For i = 1 to 8* line, use the *objItem1* variable to hold the result of using *Get* to retrieve *wmiQuery*. It looks like the following:

```
Set objItem1 = objWMIService.get(wmiQuery)
```

11. Once you have executed the query, retrieve the *PercentDiskTime* property. Use the *N1* variable to hold the results. It looks like the following:

```
N1 = objItem1.PercentDiskTime
```

12. In addition to obtaining the *PercentDiskTime* property, you must also retrieve a time stamp to use in your calculations. The time stamp property to use is the *TimeStamp_Sys-100NS*. It will be associated with *objItem1*, and you will hold the value in the *D1* variable. The completed line of code looks like the following:

```
D1 = objItem1.TimeStamp_Sys100NS
```

13. You have just obtained your first raw performance counters, so pause the script for a couple of seconds to allow the values to change possibly. Use the *Wscript.Sleep* command to do this. It looks like the following:

```
WScript.Sleep 2000
```

14. Execute the second WMI query. It will be exactly the same query as the one you used earlier. Use the *objItem2* variable to hold the results. You are interested in obtaining the numbers and the time stamp so you can use them in your calculations. The line of code looks like the following:

```
Set objItem2 = objWMIService.get(wmiQuery)
```

15. Retrieve the *PercentDiskTime* property and the *TimeStamp_Sys100NS* property. Assign them to *N2* and *D2*, respectively. You can copy the *N1* and *D1* lines from earlier in the script, or you can type in code that looks like the following:

```
N2 = objItem2.PercentDiskTime
   D2 = objItem2.TimeStamp_Sys100NS
```

16. You need to figure out the percentage of disk time from the four numbers. To do this use the following line of code:

```
PercentUtilization = (1 - ((N2 - N1)/(D2-D1)))*100
```

17. Print out the value of *PercentUtilization* that you calculated in the previous line of code. You can use the *Round* function to obtain a cleaner number. The line of code that does this is as follows:

```
WScript.Echo Round(PercentUtilization,2)
```

18. Save and run the script. It should run just fine. If it does not, compare your script with the Lab25Solution.vbs script in the Chapter12\Lab25 folder on the accompanying CD.

Part V
Security and Troubleshooting

Chapter 13
Understanding WMI Security

In Chapter 12, we talked about the performance monitor classes. We discussed how we can use them to obtain real-time data that can either form the basis of a reporting script or a monitoring script. In this chapter, we examine WMI security. Everyone wants to talk about security—and for good reason. It does not make sense to have something that enables administrators to make changes to every workstation on the network if hackers can use the same tools to make changes to every workstation on the network! There is a balancing act between security and functionality. Some of the recent security changes made by Microsoft Corporation to both server and workstation operating systems require new behaviors on the part of network administrators. In this chapter, we look at the security we have built into Windows Management Instrumentation (WMI), and then we examine some of the special considerations for working in different environments.

Before You Begin

To work through this chapter, you should be familiar with the following concepts:

- The basics of WMI scripting

- The basics of WMI namespace organization

- The basics of the Microsoft Windows security model

After you complete this chapter, you will be familiar with the following concepts:

- The basics of using namespace security

- The basics of security descriptors

- The basics of access masks

- The basics of working with share-level permissions

> **Note** All the scripts used in this chapter are located on the CD that accompanies this book in the \Scripts\Chapter13 folder.

Using WMI Namespace Security

One of the fundamental changes network administrators undertake is to modify the security access on the different WMI namespaces. This can at times have unintended results. The problem is that each WMI client is responsible for handling security, and without a clear understanding of the required access, changes can break applications that use WMI. WMI maintains a list of users or groups that have access to a particular namespace. This list can be modified either by using the WMI Control tool or by using a script. Each WMI provider can require customized security settings such as encryption or other specific settings.

Understanding the Defaults

Before you can modify the WMI namespace security, you first must understand the defaults so you can assess whether they are sufficient to meet your needs. The default namespace permissions have been modified in Microsoft Windows XP and in Windows Server 2003. Each namespace in WMI is secured with a namespace security descriptor. This *security descriptor* is a byte array—it is not formatted in Security Descriptor Definition Language (SDDL) and therefore cannot be modified or manipulated by using the *Win32_SecurityDescriptor* class. You cannot manipulate the byte array directly. If you examine it closely, you might find a security identifier (SID) hidden in there. You will also find an indicator of the access rights granted, but you cannot edit this byte array because the structure of the array is not documented, and there are no tools available to edit it. The default namespace security makes the administrator owner and grants all rights—including remotely accessing WMI on another computer. By default, remote access to WMI requires Administrator rights on the computer.

A normal user has the ability to read static data in the WMI namespace—including WMI class definitions. The normal user can also execute methods and read and write to objects supplied by WMI providers. If a user attempts to execute a method, WMI will impersonate the user to see whether that user has the permission to execute the method. WMI does this by checking the access control list (ACL).

Administrators can do only three things that a normal user cannot do: edit static data in the namespace, connect to remote computers, and change namespace security permissions. That is it. Keep in mind, however, that a normal user is authenticated on the network—a normal user is not an anonymous user. If these security settings do not meet your needs, you might want to modify the security on the WMI namespaces, which we discuss in the next section.

Modifying Security on WMI Namespaces

At some time you might need to modify the security on a particular WMI namespace to change it from the defaults. Essentially, you can do this in two ways: programmatically by using a WMI script or by using the WMI Control Properties console. In this section, we examine both of these procedures.

You secure the WMI namespace by adjusting the namespace security descriptor. The security descriptor determines who is able to access the namespace, whether that user can write to the namespace, and whether the user is able to execute any operations in the namespace. If you need to change the security descriptor, you can use the methods from the *__SystemSecurity* class. If the *RequiresEncryption* qualifier is set on a namespace, the WMI client application or script will be required to use an authentication level that supports encrypted remote procedure calls. When this is done, both the incoming and the outgoing calls are encrypted.

Working with Namespace Security Descriptors

Because each namespace has its own security descriptor, you can work with the permissions that are described by WMI. The default WMI namespace security makes the local administrator the owner and provides the local Administrators group Full Control. If you connect to a remote computer, you need to use an account that has local administrator rights by default. You can also grant account permissions for each namespace in the WMI repository. If you connect to a remote computer, you must use administrator credentials or connect with a user account that has privileges to the namespace on the target computer. If you attempt to make a guest connection, even if the Guest account has privileges on the namespace, the connection will fail because Distributed Component Object Model (DCOM) denies access to nonauthenticated users.

This illustrates the two facets of WMI security. The first element of security in WMI is the namespace security that controls a user's access to a namespace and the rights and privileges the user has once inside the namespace. The other element of WMI security is DCOM, which is used to control remote access to the methods of WMI. These two components of security work together. Setting security for WMI involves working with both namespace security and DCOM security. In Windows Server 2003, changes were made to DCOM that prevent anonymous connections to WMI. This means you cannot use the Guest account to make a connection, even if the Guest account is enabled and has namespace security permissions. DCOM security on WMI does not permit nonauthenticated access.

Examining Inherited Security Settings

In WMI, namespace security is inherited. Subordinate namespaces inherit an ACL and security settings from a parent namespace, and an inheritance flag is set for each namespace. This makes it possible for you to set security at both the parent namespace and at the child namespace. If you do not want a namespace to inherit security settings, you can disable the inheritance flag by clicking the Advanced button in the graphical user interface (GUI) of the WMI Control tool (in the Security tab of the WMI Control tool, click Security, and select Advanced). As shown in Figure 13-1, setting WMI namespace security is similar to setting Microsoft Windows NT file system (NTFS) security permissions.

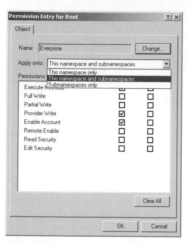

Figure 13-1   Setting namespace security using the WMI Control tool

If you disable inheritance of security permissions, you must set the security access control entries (ACEs) specifically. When you define the security settings in the ACL that control security for the namespace, pay close attention to the order of each entry because you can use a Deny access or an Allow access entry and change the security for an entire group. Once the entire group of entries is parsed, a given user's security privileges are calculated and the user is granted the appropriate level of access to the namespace.

Remember that just like with NTFS permissions, a Deny ACE overrides all other granted permissions. If a user is a member of two groups, one that has been granted Full Control and the other that has been denied access, the user will not have access. The Administrators group is the exception: administrators always have Full Control of the WMI namespace and cannot be denied access. This is a security measure that keeps a program (or malware) from locking out the admin. Also, this scheme protects intrepid admins from locking themselves out.

> **Administrators Always Have Full Control**   You cannot apply a Deny ACE against a user that is a member of the local Administrators group. Actually, it *is* physically possible to apply a Deny ACE to a member of the Administrators group, but the ACE will be ignored. Whether because of membership in the Domain Administrators group or the local Administrators group, members of the Administrators group have Full Control of all WMI namespaces on the computer. This is another good reason not to allow normal users to have Administrator rights on the local machine. It also points to the need for administrators to have a second user account that is not a member of the Administrators group to use for normal day-to-day use. Network administrators should never read e-mail, surf the Web, or perform other such activities while logged on to the machine with Administrator rights. Most of the users at Microsoft no longer run with admin rights on their local machines; instead, they use the RunAs command to obtain administrative permissions when such permissions are needed for an advanced task.

Using the WMI Control Tool to Set Security

Assuming you need to make one or two changes on one or two machines, the easiest way to modify the WMI namespace security settings is to use the WMI Control Properties console. Before you start changing the security settings for WMI on your computer, perform a backup of the Web-Based Enterprise Management (WBEM) repository. How to back up the repository is covered in Chapters 1 and 14. The backup does include security permissions. If you really mess up the security settings and you have made a recent WBEM repository backup, it is a simple matter to recover. If, however, you do not have a backup of the repository, you will have to delete and rebuild the WMI database.

By using the WMI Control Properties console to set security permissions (in the Security tab of the WMI Control tool, click Security, and select Advanced) as shown in Figure 13-2, you cannot directly block inheritance. You can remove an entry and then add it back in with the appropriate permissions, but you do not have the option to block the inheritance of a setting. You can clearly see this behavior in Figure 13-2: the option to block is unavailable.

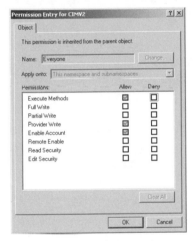

Figure 13-2   Setting security permissions when inheritance cannot be directly blocked

Scripting WMI Namespace Security

If you have more than one or two computers, or you need to make several complicated changes, the best method to set namespace security is to use a script to make the changes for you. Indeed, if you were to mess up, it would be much easier to undo the effects of the script because you have a record of the exact configuration settings applied. On the other hand, there is generally no such record if you were to go on a "clicking frenzy."

Using the __*SystemSecurity* Class

There is only one instance of the __*SystemSecurity* class running on your machine at any time—it is therefore a singleton class. Even though there is only one instance of the class, you can find the __*SystemSecurity* class in every namespace that is defined in WMI, and this makes it very easy to work with. The first thing you need to do when working with namespace security is find out which access rights are actually defined for the user. In the GetAccessRights.vbs script, I use the *GetCallerAccessRights* method to retrieve the rights of the user who launched the script. If you were connecting remotely and using the *ConnectServer* method to specify alternative credentials, the rights returned would be those of the person specified. Additionally, if you use *RunAs* to run the script, the rights returned would be those of the person specified in *RunAs*. This is an easy way to test security access rights for various users. All users, by default, have the ability to call the *GetCallerAccessRights* method.

When you use the *GetCallerAccessRights* method of the __*SystemSecurity* class in the Get-AccessRights.vbs script, you must specify an output variable to hold the rights bitmap that is returned. If you do not specify an output variable, the call will not fail, but it will, in fact, return an error status of 0, meaning the call succeeded—which is technically true because it worked, but it just did not do anything.

If you change the value of *wmiNS* to a different namespace, the access rights that have been defined for the calling user in that namespace will be returned.

GetAccessRights.vbs

```
strComputer = "."
wmiNS = "\root\cimv2"
wmiQuery = "__SystemSecurity=@"
Set objWMIService = GetObject("winmgmts:\\" & strComputer & wmiNS)
Set objItem = objWMIService.get(wmiQuery)

  Wscript.Echo objItem.GetCallerAccessRights(strSD)
  Wscript.Echo strSD
```

To obtain all the access rights for all the WMI namespaces, you can do a recursive query. To do a recursive script, pass a parameter to the subroutine. You can call a subroutine by using the name of the sub—the word *Call* is optional: you can use *Call* to make it a bit more obvious that you are going into the subroutine, but it is not required. Once into the subroutine, you loop through each namespace and use a function to obtain the security descriptor on the namespace. The function you call is *FunAccess*, and you pass the namespace path that is contained in the variable *strNameSpace*. You need to preface the namespace name with a backslash (\) to use the *GetCallerAccessRights* method of the __*SystemSecurity* class.

Note that in the GetAccessRights.vbs script, I used *Wscript.Echo* to "capture the return code" from using the method. The *GetCallerAccessRights* method requires you to capture the return code. You cannot simply call the method without a provision for the return code. The return code is a number—0 means no errors, any other number means you have a problem. I use

ErrRTN to capture the return code in the GetAccessRightsInAllNamespaces.vbs script; however, as it currently stands, I am doing nothing with the return code. To get the security descriptor from the *GetCallerAccessRights* method, I have to use a variable to hold the number—*strSD* in this script. I assign *strSD* to the function name, *FunAccess* in this case, and I have the security descriptor.

Translating the Access Security Descriptor

The access security descriptor number values are added together and are reported as a single number. Once you have obtained the security descriptor for the WMI namespace, you must translate it. To do this, use a function (contained in the Utilities folder on the accompanying CD) that is called *FunNSSec*. The *FunNSSec* function matches each of the number codes contained in the security descriptor by ANDing the numerical values with the security descriptor—if a match is found, it echoes out the permissions granted by the value.

GetAccessRightsInAllNamespaces.vbs

```
strComputer = "."

Call EnumNameSpaces("root")

WScript.Echo("all done " & Now)

'#### functions and Subs below #####

Sub EnumNameSpaces(strNameSpace)
  secSTR= funAccess("\" & strNameSpace)
    WScript.Echo ("\" & strNameSpace)
    WScript.Echo myTab & secSTR & myTab & funNSSEC(secSTR)
  Set objSWbemServices = _
    GetObject("winmgmts:\\" & strComputer & "\" & strNameSpace)
  Set colNameSpaces = objSWbemServices.InstancesOf("__NAMESPACE")
    For Each objNameSpace In colNameSpaces
     Call EnumNameSpaces(strNameSpace & "\" & objNameSpace.Name)
    Next
End Sub

Function funAccess(wmiNS) 'retrieves security descriptor from NS
dim wmiQuery
dim objWMIService
dim strSD
dim objItem
Dim errRTN
wmiQuery = "__SystemSecurity=@"
Set objWMIService = GetObject("winmgmts:\\" & strComputer & wmiNS)
Set objItem = objWMIService.get(wmiQuery)
  errRTN=objItem.GetCallerAccessRights(strSD)
  funAccess= strSD
End Function

Function funNSSEC (inMASK) 'Deciphers the security descriptor
Dim strPerm
If inMask AND 1 Then strPerm = strPerm & "WBEM_ENABLE, "
```

```
If inMask AND 2 Then strPerm = strPerm & "WBEM_METHOD_EXECUTE, "
If inMask AND 4 Then strPerm = strPerm & "WBEM_FULL_WRITE_REP, "
If inMask AND 8 Then strPerm = strPerm & "WBEM_PARTIAL_WRITE_REP, "
If inMask AND 16 Then strPerm = strPerm & "WBEM_WRITE_PROVIDER, "
If inMask AND 32 Then strPerm = strPerm & "WBEM_REMOTE_ACCESS, "
If inMask AND 131072 Then strPerm = strPerm & "READ_CONTROL, "
If inMask AND 262144 Then strPerm = strPerm & "WRITE_DAC, "
funNSSEC = strPerm
End function
```

Quick Check

Q: For what are WMI namespace security masks used?

A: WMI namespace security masks are used to control user access into a WMI namespace.

Q: How can you determine whether a person running a script has access rights to a certain namespace?

A: To determine whether a person running a script has access rights to a certain namespace, you can connect to the namespace and use the *GetCallerAccessRights* method from the *__SystemSecurity* class.

Working with the Namespace Security Descriptor

As mentioned earlier, the namespace security is a byte array, and no tools enable you to translate it, manipulate it, or do anything to it other than read and set the security descriptor. If you want to set namespace security on a WMI namespace, the best way to do so programmatically is to set the security on a namespace using the WMI Control Properties console, and then retrieve the namespace security descriptor as illustrated in the GetSecurityDescriptor-OfNS.vbs script.

The GetSecurityDescriptorOfNS.vbs script uses the *Get* method in a similar capacity as to how it is used in other scripts that use the *__SystemSecurity* class. Once you have a connection into WMI, and you have the *__SystemSecurity* class, use the *GetSD* method. Capture the return code with the *errRTN* variable, and go into a subroutine to check for errors. If no error is returned, use a function to format the security descriptor into a semireadable format. Because the namespace security descriptor is an array, you use the Microsoft Visual Basic Scripting Edition (VBScript) *Join* function to convert it into an array using a comma as the delimiter.

GetSecurityDescriptorOfNS.vbs

```
strComputer = "."
wmiNS = "\root\wmi"
wmiQuery = "__SystemSecurity=@"
Set objWMIService = GetObject("winmgmts:\\" & strComputer & wmiNS)
Set objItem = objWMIService.Get(wmiQuery)

errRTN = objItem.GetSD(strSD)
```

```
SubCheckERR

  Wscript.Echo forMatSD(strSD)

Sub subCheckERR
If errRTN <> 0 Then
WScript.Echo "an error occurred. It was " & errRTN
WScript.Quit
End If
End sub

Function forMatSD(strSD)
forMatSD = "{" & join(strSD,",") & "}"
End Function
```

Working with Share Permissions

For many network administrators, creating a share is very easy. It is also easy to create a share by using a script. But what if you need to work with the security permissions on those shares? This is where you need to begin to work with security permissions with WMI. In the following Share.vbs script, I query for the existence of a specific share—a share simply called *a*. Once I find the share, I print out the share name, the path, and the *ShareMask* property. I then proceed to obtain the share access mask by using the *GetAccessMask* method.

When Is a Mask Not a Mask?   In Windows XP and Windows Server 2003, the *Access-Mask* property is deprecated but is still defined for backward compatibility. As a result, the *AccessMask* property always returns a null value. On systems running Windows XP and Windows Server 2003, do not use this property—instead, use the *GetAccessMask* method of the *Win32_Share* class.

If you were to look at the Managed Object Format (MOF) file for the *Win32_Share class*, you would see the *AccessMask* property listed as follows:

```
[read: ToSubClass, DEPRECATED: ToSubClass] uint32 AccessMask;
```

Even if a property is deprecated, at times it will still return data, but that is not the case here. The *AccessMask* property still works, however, for earlier versions of the Windows operating system.

Once an item is marked as deprecated, no further development work is going into it, and you should begin planning to move to something else or to find another manner to retrieve the information.

Use *Wbemtest* to Troubleshoot Scripts

If you ever have a problem getting a property or a method to work, and it is not throwing an error but rather is just not working, use Wbemtest.exe. You can launch Wbemtest.exe by clicking Start, Run, and typing **wbemtest.exe** in the Open box. Once it is running, click Connect to connect to a particular namespace. Generally, you will want to open a class.

Then, at this point, you have several options. Often, I open the MOF file by clicking Show MOF. As you can see in the graphic below, the MOF file can provide a good look inside a class and can let you know what the class expects from the script. This is where you will find information about special privileges that might be required, what type of data a property expects (string, array, integer), or even whether a property is deprecated.

Wbemtest can be an invaluable tool for troubleshooting scripts. If a script does not work, look at the MOF file. If the script is not returning data, look for instances. If you wonder whether a query is right, click the Query button. Wbemtest is a Swiss Army knife for scripters, and everyone should know how to use it—plus, it is always installed.

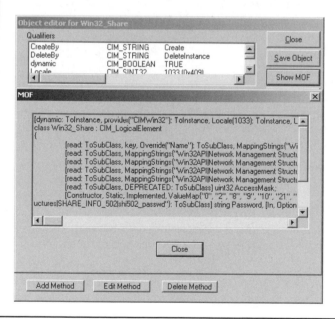

In the Share.vbs script, after I use the *GetAccessMask* method, I get back an access mask that describes the rights to the share held by the person running the script. To interpret the rights that are represented by the access mask, I use the *StrAccessMask* function. In the function, I use ANDing to look for the presence of the numerical values of the right in the access mask. If I find them, I add the name of the right represented by the integer to the *strPerm* string. When I am done with this analysis, the function returns the completed access string.

Share.vbs

```
strComputer = "."
wmiNS = "\root\cimv2"
wmiQuery = "Select * from win32_share where name = 'a'"
Set objWMIService = GetObject("winmgmts:\\" & strComputer & wmiNS)
Set colItems = objWMIService.ExecQuery(wmiQuery)

For Each objItem in colItems
    Wscript.Echo "Share Name: " & objItem.name
    Wscript.Echo "Share Path: " & objItem.path
    Wscript.Echo "Share Mask Property: " & objItem.accessMask 'NULL
wscript.echo "Share Mask method:" &strAccessMask(objItem.getAccessMask)
'WScript.Echo(strMask)
Next

Function strAccessMask(inMask)
Dim strPerm
    If inMask AND 1048576 Then strPerm = strPerm & "Synchronize, "
    If inMask AND 524288 Then strPerm = strPerm & "Write Owner, "
    If inMask AND 262144 Then strPerm = strPerm & "Write DAC, "
    If inMask AND 131072 Then strPerm = strPerm & "Read Control, "
    If inMask AND 65536 Then strPerm = strPerm & "Delete, "
    If inMask AND 256 Then strPerm = strPerm & "File Write Attrib, "
    If inMask AND 128 Then strPerm = strPerm & "File Read Attrrib, "
    If inMask AND 64 Then strPerm = strPerm & "File Delete Child, "
    If inMask AND 32 Then strPerm = strPerm & "File Traverse, "
    If inMask AND 16 Then strPerm = strPerm & "File Write Ext Attr, "
    If inMask AND 8 Then strPerm = strPerm & "File Read Ext Attr, "
    If inMask AND 4 Then strPerm = strPerm & "File Add Sub, "
    If inMask AND 2 Then strPerm = strPerm & "File Add File, "
    If inMask AND 1 Then strPerm = strPerm & "File List Dir. "
strAccessMask = strPerm
End Function
```

Who Has Access to This Share?

At times you need to know who has access to a particular share. In the Share.vbs script, you can connect to a specific share and look at the access of a specific user who has rights on that share. In the PermissionsOnShare.vbs script, I use an *associators of* query and look at the relationship between the *Win32_LogicalShareSecuritySetting* class and the *Win32_Sid* class. I again connect to a specific share, but now the SID and the account name of all the users who have permissions defined on the share are returned.

In the *associators of* query in the PermissionsOnShare.vbs script, I specify the *ResultClass* is a *Win32_Sid*. In this way I can retrieve the SID and the *AccountName* property, which enables me from having to make additional queries and use extra WMI classes that would complicate the script and make it more difficult to troubleshoot and maintain.

PermissionsOnShare.vbs

```
strComputer = "."
wmiNS = "\root\cimv2"
strShare = "'a'" 'name of a Share on the system
wmiQuery = "associators of{win32_LogicalShareSecuritySetting="_
    & strShare & "}where resultClass = win32_sid"
Set objWMIService = GetObject("winmgmts:\\" & strComputer & wmiNS)
Set colItems = objWMIService.ExecQuery(wmiQuery)

For Each objItem in colItems
    Wscript.Echo "SID: " & objItem.sid
        WScript.Echo objItem.accountName
Next
```

Mapping Users and Rights

Next you need to look at the users and their associated rights to the share. The LogicalShare-AccessRights.vbs script answers the questions "What shares are defined on my server?" and "Who has access to them?" In this script, I use the *Win32_LogicalShareAccess* class. First, I make the connection into WMI by using the moniker and specifying the name of the computer and the namespace to which I wish to connect. Because the *Win32_LogicalShareAccess* resides in the *root\cimv2* namespace, that is the one you assign to the *wmiNS* variable.

The *ExecQuery* method returns a collection, and I use *For Each Next* to walk through the collection. The *MyFun* function uses the intrinsic *String* function from VBScript to repeat a character a specified number of times. I use the *Len* function from VBScript to determine the length of the line that contains the name of the security setting value and the string label. I feed that number to the *String* function while specifying the equal sign as the character to repeat. When I run the script, this provides an output listing that is easier to read. I use the *FunShare* function to translate the access mask into something a bit more readable, and I also retrieve the SID of the user who has access to the share. This script prints out the information on every share defined on the server. On a large file and print server, it could take a little while for this script to complete.

LogicalShareAccessRights.vbs

```
strComputer = "."
wmiNS = "\root\cimv2"
wmiQuery = "Select * from Win32_LogicalShareAccess"
Set objWMIService = GetObject("winmgmts:\\" & strComputer & wmiNS)
Set colItems = objWMIService.ExecQuery(wmiQuery)

For Each objItem in colItems
    Wscript.Echo myFun("SecuritySetting: " & objItem.SecuritySetting)
    Wscript.Echo "AccessMask: " & funShare(objItem.AccessMask)
```

```
    WScript.Echo "Trustee" &  objItem.Trustee
    Wscript.Echo "Type: " & objItem.Type
    Wscript.Echo "Inheritance : " & objItem.Inheritance
    Wscript.Echo "GuidObjectType: " & objItem.GuidObjectType & vbcrlf
Next

'##### Functions are below ###

Function funShare(inMask)
Dim strPerm
If inMask AND 0 Then strPerm = strPerm & "FILE_LIST_DIRECTORY, "
If inMask AND 1 Then strPerm = strPerm & "FILE_ADD_FILE, "
If inMask AND 2 Then strPerm = strPerm & "FILE_ADD_SUBDIRECTORY, "
If inMask AND 3 Then strPerm = strPerm & "FILE_READ_EA, "
If inMask AND 4 Then strPerm = strPerm & "FILE_WRITE_EA, "
If inMask AND 5 Then strPerm = strPerm & "FILE_TRAVERSE, "
If inMask AND 6 Then strPerm = strPerm & "FILE_DELETE_CHILD, "
If inMask AND 7 Then strPerm = strPerm & "FILE_WRITE_ATTRIBUTES, "
If inMask AND 8 Then strPerm = strPerm & "FILE_DELETE_CHILD, "
If inMask AND 16 Then strPerm = strPerm & "DELETE, "
If inMask AND 17 Then strPerm = strPerm & "READ_CONTROL, "
If inMask AND 18 Then strPerm = strPerm & "WRITE_DAC, "
If inMask AND 19 Then strPerm = strPerm & "WRITE_OWNER, "
If inMask AND 20 Then strPerm = strPerm & "SYNCHRONIZE, "
funShare = strPerm
End function

Function myFun(input)
Dim lstr
lstr = Len(input)
myFun = input & vbcrlf & string(lstr,"=")
End function
```

Quick Check

Q: If you want to match a user and a SID to each other, which WMI class can you use?

A: If you want to match a user and a SID to each other, the *Win32_Sid* class is the easiest to use.

Q: Name one tool that is easy to use to test WMI functionality.

A: Wbemtest.exe is a good tool to use to test WMI functionality.

Summary

In this chapter, we looked at the fundamentals of WMI security. We examined WMI namespace security and discussed methods for retrieving calling user access rights, getting the namespace security masks, and setting WMI security descriptors. These tasks were done by using the *__SystemSecurity* WMI class. Then we examined the use of security descriptors on shares and looked at several WMI classes.

Quiz Yourself

Q: What is an easy way to set namespace security on a WMI namespace?

A: An easy way to set namespace security on a WMI namespace is to use the *GetSD* method of the *__SystemSecurity* class to retrieve the security descriptor of a namespace that has the rights you want to duplicate. Then use the *SetSD* method of the *__SystemSecurity* class to write the security descriptor to the namespace you wish to secure.

Q: You are using the *Win32_Share* class to generate a listing of shares that are on a workstation that runs Windows XP. When you query the *AccessMask* property of the *Win32_Share* class, it does not return any information. What could be the problem?

A: When you query the *AccessMask* property of the *Win32_Share* class on a computer running Windows XP or later, it will not return any information because the property has been deprecated and is no longer supported.

Q: You are working with a security class in WMI, and the results are not coming back the way you expect. You look up the class in the documentation and on the Internet, but you do not find any information that can help you. What is one step you can take to see what the class expects or whether the property is even implemented in your operating system?

A: If you are working with a security class (or any other class, for that matter) and it does not seem to be working properly, use Wbemtest.exe to open the class and examine its properties and instances. Next, open the MOF file to see whether the property you are working with is implemented or deprecated.

On Your Own

Lab 26 Creating a WMI Namespace

In this lab, you will create a WMI namespace called *myNS1*. You will use the WMI Control Properties console to assign custom permissions to *myNS1*, and then you will use a script to retrieve and interpret those permissions.

1. Before you start creating namespaces and changing security descriptors, make sure you have a current backup of the WMI repository.

2. Open a blank Microsoft Management Console (MMC). Click Start, Run, and type **MMC** in the Open box.

3. Add the WMI Control Properties console by clicking File, Add/Remove Snap-in.

4. Click Add, select WMI Control, and click Add.

5. Click Local Computer, and then click Finish.

6. Click Close, and then click OK to finish adding the console.

7. Right-click WMI Control (Local), and click Properties.

8. Click the Backup/Restore tab, and click Back Up Now.

9. Create a folder off the root called wmiBackup.

10. Use your *DateTime* for the backup as the backup file name (it might look something like July23PM.rec).

11. Click Open, and the backup will start. (For reference, it takes only a few seconds to perform the backup on my laptop.)

12. Create a namespace called *myNS1* under the *root* namespace. To create the namespace, open and run the CreateWMINS.vbs script from the Chapter13\Lab26 folder on the accompanying CD.

13. To confirm the namespace was created, open and run the ListNameSpaces.vbs script from the Chapter13\Lab26 folder. You should see the *myNS1* namespace listed.

14. Click the Security tab, and navigate to the *myNS1* namespace.

15. Click the *myNS1* namespace, and then click Security.

16. Click the LOCAL SERVICE user, and deny all rights by clicking each check box in the Deny column

17. Do the same thing for the NETWORK SERVICE user. (Do not worry about this breaking anything because you just created this namespace and nothing is using it—plus, you have a backup.)

18. Now you will develop a script to retrieve the security descriptor from the *myNS1* namespace. Begin by opening the WmiTemplate.vbs script and saving it as StudentLab26.vbs.

19. Add two variables in the header section of the script. The first is *strSD*, which is an output variable and will hold the security descriptor from the *GetSD* method. The second variable is *errRTN*, which will hold the return code from calling the *GetSD* method. The code to do this looks like the following:

```
dim strSD 'outPut variable holds security descriptor from GetSD.
dim errRTN 'captures return code from the GetSD method.
```

20. Modify the value of *wmiNS* so it points to the new namespace. It will be *root\myNS1*. The code looks like the following:

```
wmiNS = "\root\myNS1"
```

21. Modify the *wmiQuery*. It will select the *__SystemSecurity* class as a singleton class, so use @ to specify the singleton. The code for this looks like the following:

```
wmiQuery = "__SystemSecurity=@"
```

22. Change *Set colItems* to *Set objItem*. Also, instead of using *ExecQuery*, use the *Get* method. The revised line looks like the following:

```
Set objItem = objWMIService.Get(wmiQuery)
```

23. Delete the entire *For Each Next* loop. The section looks like the following:

```
For Each objItem in colItems
    Wscript.Echo ":  " & objItem.
    Wscript.Echo ":  " & objItem.
    Wscript.Echo ":  " & objItem.
    Wscript.Echo ":  " & objItem.
    Wscript.Echo ":  " & objItem.
    Wscript.Echo ":  " & objItem.
Next
```

24. Call the *GetSD* method from the *__SystemSecurity* class. Also, capture the return code with the *errRTN* variable. This line looks like the following:

```
errRTN = objItem.GetSD(strSD)
```

25. Create a subroutine called *SubCheckERR*. Evaluate *errRTN*. If *errRTN* is not equal to 0, print out the value of *errRTN* and end the script. The code looks like the following:

```
Sub subCheckERR
If errRTN <> 0 Then
WScript.Echo "an error occurred. It was " & errRTN
WScript.Quit
End If
End sub
```

26. Under the *errRTN = objItem.GetSD(strSD)* line, enter the subroutine to evaluate the return code. To do this, simply call the subroutine: *SubCheckERR*.

27. Create a function to format the security descriptor for ease of use. Call the function *ForMatSD* and name your input *strSD*. You will need to prefix the security descriptor with an opening curly brace enclosed in quotation marks ("{") and then end it with a closing curly brace enclosed in quotation marks ("}"). Because the security descriptor is contained in an array, use the *Join* function to put it into a string and specify each separator as a comma. The completed function looks like the following:

```
Function forMatSD(strSD)
forMatSD = "{" & join(strSD,",") & "}"
End Function
```

28. Save and run the script. It will return something like the following (but on a single line):

```
{1,0,4,129,192,0,0,0,208,0,0,0,0,0,0,0,20,0,0,0,2,0,172,0,8,0,0,0,1,0,20,0,63,0,6,0,1,
1,0,0,0,0,0,5,20,0,0,0,1,0,20,0,63,0,6,0,1,1,0,0,0,0,0,5,19,0,0,0,0,18,24,0,63,0,6,0,1
,2,0,0,0,0,0,5,32,0,0,0,32,2,0,0,0,18,20,0,19,0,0,0,1,1,0,0,0,0,0,5,20,0,0,0,0,18,20,0
,19,0,0,0,1,1,0,0,0,0,0,5,19,0,0,0,0,18,20,0,19,0,0,0,1,1,0,0,0,0,0,1,0,0,0,0,0,18,20,
0,19,0,0,0,1,1,0,0,0,0,0,5,20,0,0,0,0,18,20,0,19,0,0,0,1,1,0,0,0,0,0,5,19,0,0,0,1,2,0,
0,0,0,0,5,32,0,0,0,32,2,0,0,1,2,0,0,0,0,0,5,32,0,0,0,32,2,0,0}
```

This completes the lab.

Lab 27 Setting WMI Namespace Permissions

In this lab, you will use the permissions you retrieve from the *myNS1* WMI namespace and apply those permissions to a new WMI namespace called *myNS2*. You will then use a script to delete both namespaces.

1. Open the CreateWMINS.vbs script from the Chapter13\Lab27 folder, and make sure it is set to create a namespace called *myNS2*. Run the script to create the namespace. Close the script when you are finished.

2. Run the ListNameSpace.vbs script to confirm that you now have a namespace called *myNS1* and a namespace called *myNS2*. Close the script when you are finished.

3. Open either your completed student script StudentLab26.vbs or the Lab27Starter.vbs script. Save the file as StudentLab27.vbs.

4. You need to add some variables to hold the new connection to the new namespace. The variables will be *objWMIService1*, *objItem1*, *wmiNS1*, and *errMSG*. The code looks like the following:

```
Dim objWMIService1
Dim objItem1
Dim wmiNS1
Dim errMSG
```

5. Copy the *Set objWMIService* line and paste it under the original. Change *objWMIService* to *objWMIService1* on the copied line. It looks like the following:

```
Set objWMIService1 = GetObject("winmgmts:\\" & strComputer & wmiNS1)
```

6. Copy the *Set objItem* line and paste it below the original. Change *objItem* to *objItem1* and *objWMIService* to *objWMIService1* in the copied line. It looks like the following:

```
Set objItem1 = objWMIService1.Get(wmiQuery)
```

7. Assign the string *"Get security descriptor"* to the *errMSG* variable. This value will be passed to the error checker to inform you whether the operation was successful. The code looks like the following:

```
errMSG = "Get security descriptor"
```

8. Because you are not interested in the text of the security descriptor, you can delete the *Wscript.Echo ForMatSD* line as well as the *ForMatSD* function from the bottom of the script.

9. Set the security descriptor on the *myNS2* namespace. To do this, use the *SetSD* method from the connection to the *myNS2* namespace. The line of code looks like the following:

```
errRTN =objItem1.SetSD(strSD)
```

10. Assign the message *"Set security descriptor"* to the *errMSG* variable. The code looks like the following:

```
errMSG = "Set security descriptor"
```

11. Call the *SubCheckERR* subroutine to see whether the method was successful.

12. Add an *Else* clause to the *SubCheckERR* subroutine. The *Else* clause will echo out *"no errors for: "* and the *errMSG*. Insert this after the *Wscript.Quit* command and before the *End If*. The code looks like the following:

```
Else
WScript.Echo "no errors for: " & errMSG
```

13. Save and run the script. You should see two messages that indicate the get security descriptor process succeeded and the set security descriptor process succeeded.

14. Open the WMI Control Properties console, and navigate to the *myNS2* namespace. You should see the same security settings as you have on *myNS1* namespace.

15. Now let's clean up. Open the DeleteNameSpace.vbs script. Look at the *wmiQuery* line. Run it once to delete the *myNS2* namespace.

16. Edit the *wmiQuery* line, change *wmiNS2* to *wmiNS1*, and run it a second time.

17. Run the ListNameSpaces.vbs to ensure that both the *myNS1* and the *myNS2* namespaces are indeed gone. Once the cleanup is complete, so is the lab.

Chapter 14

Troubleshooting WMI

In Chapter 13, we examined Windows Management Instrumentation (WMI) security. We looked at the concept of WMI namespace security and discussed two ways to modify security on the namespaces. In this chapter, we look at troubleshooting WMI. In the past, troubleshooting WMI was not as difficult, but with the widespread adoption of WMI by many critical network monitoring software packages, the WMI environment has become more complex.

Before You Begin

To work through this chapter, you should be familiar with the following concepts:
- The basics of working with WMI namespaces
- The basics of writing a WMI script, connecting to namespaces, and retrieving class information
- The basics of how to write a script using alternate credentials to make a connection

After you complete this chapter, you will be familiar with the following concepts:
- The services involved in making WMI work
- The dependencies that must be met for WMI to work
- The symptoms of a corrupt database
- The common methods of recovering from problems with WMI

 Note All the scripts used in this chapter are located on the CD that accompanies this book in the \Scripts\Chapter14 folder.

Identifying the Problem

WMI is one of those services that simply works. Most people never have to troubleshoot WMI; in fact, many network administrators do not even know that WMI exists or that their sophisticated monitoring and tracking application relies heavily on the services of WMI. For many, the only time that they even begin to learn about WMI is when a critical application suddenly quits. Unfortunately, this is the wrong time to begin to learn about WMI and, more important, how to troubleshoot WMI.

Spotting Common Sources of Errors

What are some of the more common types of WMI errors? In general, problems with WMI are in one of the following four categories:

- WMI database corruption
- Distributed Component Object Model (DCOM) security issues
- Provider security issues
- Firewall issues

Basically, that's it. The preceding comprise 90 percent of all the WMI support calls that Microsoft Product Support Services (PSS) support professionals receive. The other 10 percent are truly strange, esoteric, or downright exotic problems. In this chapter, we therefore focus on the four categories that cause 90 percent of the problems.

Testing the Local WMI Service

The first task when troubleshooting WMI is to test the local WMI service to see if it responds to requests. Check whether WMI is actually working or whether it is corrupt, hung, or in some other nonfunctioning state. In fact, many problems that at first appear to be WMI problems are not WMI problems at all. The application that is using WMI could have a problem, or the script you are trying to run could have a problem.

You can use two utilities to test WMI easily, reliably, and effectively: the WMI Control Properties console and the Windows Management Instrumentation Tester (Wbemtest.exe). Although these utilities do not determine specifically whether you have a problem with WMI, they do detect whether WMI is working. If the two tools do not work, you have a problem that bears further investigation.

Using the WMI Control Tool

The most basic check you can make to see whether WMI is working properly is to open the WMI Control Properties console and see if it will connect. If it will not connect to the local instance of WMI running on your computer, you have a symptom of a more serious problem with WMI. On the other hand, if it does connect, it does not mean that there is no problem, but that at least some things are working correctly. This is the easiest check to make and should be the first step in troubleshooting. If the WMI service does not have the appropriate configuration, the connection will fail.

If the connection with WMI succeeds, the WMI Control Properties console, shown in Figure 14-1, appears. In the General tab, you can see the operating system version build number, service pack version, and the WMI version. In Microsoft Windows XP and Windows Server 2003, the operating system build number and the WMI version number should match. In Microsoft Windows 2000, the WMI version number is 1085.0005. The other important piece of information in this tab is the WMI location, which should be *%SystemRoot%*\System32\WBEM. (In most cases, *%SystemRoot%* is reported as C:\WINDOWS, as shown in Figure 14-1.)

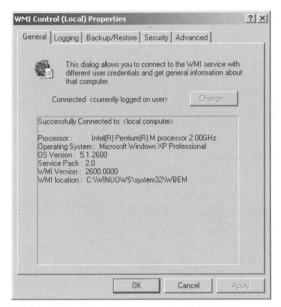

Figure 14-1   The General tab in the WMI Control Properties console displays troubleshooting information

Pay Attention to Dependencies

You can examine service dependencies as another way of obtaining an indicator of the health of the WMI service. This is very important in the troubleshooting process; I have seen cases in which administrators believed they had a WMI problem, uninstalled the WMI service or deleted the WMI database to rebuild it, and still the actions did not solve the "WMI problem." Although not definitive, the state of a dependent service can provide a clue as to the health of WMI.

If the WMI service is not running, several other services will not function either. The Security Center, SMS Agent Host, and Windows Firewall are some of the services that depend on WMI. These service dependencies can be found in the Services console, as shown in Figure 14-2. If WMI is not functioning, you should notice several errors in the Windows system event log indicating service failures.

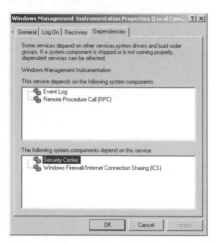

Figure 14-2   Listing of WMI service dependencies

Using Scriptomatic

Scriptomatic is a tool created by Microsoft that is useful in troubleshooting scenarios. Scriptomatic connects to any WMI namespace and lists all the classes in the namespace. When you choose a class, Scriptomatic generates a Microsoft Visual Basic Scripting Edition (VBScript) file listing all the properties of the class. You can then run the script from within Scriptomatic. If no properties are listed or if the script that is generated does not produce output when it is run, you might have a problem with WMI. You can read more about and download Scriptomatic from the following Web site: *http://www.microsoft.com/technet/scriptcenter/tools/wmimatic.mspx*.

Examining the Status of the WMI Service

If the WMI Control Properties console cannot make a local connection, check to see whether the WMI service is running. The following steps list the easy way to do this:

1.   Open a CMD prompt.

2.   Type **net start**.

3.   Near the bottom of the list, look for Windows Management Instrumentation.

If it appears in the list, it is started. If it does not appear, it is not running. This would be rather strange because the WMI service should restart itself if it stops or is stopped. The recovery setting for WMI is set to restart the service on the first and subsequent failures. The recovery interval is set to 1 minute. If the WMI service fails, it will attempt a restart of the service every minute.

Next, examine the service settings. To do this use the Services console. The following steps walk you through using this console:

- Click Start, and then click Run.

- In the Run dialog box, type **Services.msc** in the Open box, and then click OK.

- Scroll down the list until you find Windows Management Instrumentation. Double-click it.

- Click the Log On tab. Under Log On As, Local System Account should be selected. The Allow Service To Interact With Desktop option should not be selected.

- Click the Recovery tab. Under Select The Computer's Response If This Service Fails, for First Failure, Second Failure, and Subsequent Failures the Restart The Service option should be selected. The Reset Fail Count After option should read 1 Days, and the Restart Service After option should read 1 Minutes. This is illustrated in Figure 14-3.

Figure 14-3   Recovery settings of the WMI service

Using Wbemtest.exe

You can use the Windows Management Instrumentation Tester (Wbemtest.exe) to troubleshoot WMI. In addition to checking whether WMI is actually running and accepting connections (as the WMI Control Properties console does), Wbemtest can be used to test the functionality of almost every aspect of WMI, including security. When using Wbemtest, keep in mind that it cannot be used to specify alternate credentials for a local connection. To test alternate credentials, you must make a remote connection. In effect, Wbemtest is using the *SWbemLocator* method to supply alternate credentials, and *SWbemLocator* does not permit supplying alternate credentials for a local connection.

> ## Quick Check
>
> **Q: What is the easiest way to check whether WMI is really broken?**
>
> A: The easiest way to check whether WMI is really broken is to open the WMI Control Properties console. If it makes a connection to WMI, it indicates that WMI is not totally broken—but there might be other problems. On the other hand, if the WMI Control tool cannot connect, you have a problem with WMI.
>
> **Q: Why is Wbemtest unable to permit you to make a local connection into WMI using alternative credentials?**
>
> A. Wbemtest does not permit you to make a local connection into WMI using alternative credentials because WMI does not permit it.

Testing Remote WMI Service

WMI is already set up to run remotely. The procedures for testing the remote WMI service are essentially the same procedures that you use when working locally. In the initial stages of testing the ability of WMI to respond to remote requests, the tools and procedures are very similar.

Using the WMI Control Tool Remotely

The first tool you can use is the WMI Control tool. Make sure that you start the tool in the correct manner or else the remote function of the tool will not be available. The following steps illustrate how to use the WMI Control tool to make a remote connection:

1. Click Start, and then click Run.
2. In the Run dialog box, type **wmimgmt.msc** in the Open box, and then click OK.
3. Right-click WMI Control (Local).
4. Click Connect To Another Computer.
5. Click Another Computer, and then enter the name of the remote computer.
6. If needed, click Change to provide user credentials.
7. Click OK.
8. Right-click WMI Control (*remote system name*).
9. Click Properties.

If you cannot make a remote connection using the WMI Control tool, you must ensure that you have checked WMI locally on each computer. If you have checked both computers locally, the next steps are as follows:

1. Check connectivity.
2. Check firewall issues.
3. Check rights/permissions.
4. Check DCOM settings.

Testing the Scripting Interface

After you have checked for local and remote WMI functionality, you might need to test the scripting interface. To do this, check both the core WMI provider and the provider host interface. You can use a script to do this. In the RetrieveWMISettings.vbs script, I use the *Connect-Server* method from the *SWbemLocator* object because it is already set up to accept alternative connections on a remote computer, which enables a fuller range of tests. I connect to the *Win32_WMISetting* class. There is only one instance of the *Win32_WMISetting* class. I use the at symbol (@) to get the one instance of the *Win32_WMISetting* class that represents the WMI settings for the computer. After the query is executed, I use the *GetObjectText_* method, which retrieves all the properties in the class as well as the values assigned to those properties. The output text will be in Managed Object Format (MOF) format. I cannot specify any modifiers for this method. The input flag is optional. If you choose to specify the input flag, you must supply a zero because zero is the only value allowed for this flag. It will not change the way the method operates, so I omit it in the RetrieveWMISettings.vbs script.

RetrieveWMISettings.vbs

```
strComputer = "."
wmiNS = "\root\cimv2"
wmiQuery = "Win32_WMISetting=@"
strUsr =""'Blank for current security. Domain\Username
strPWD = ""'Blank for current security.
strLocl = "MS_409" 'U.S. English. Can leave blank for current language
strAuth = ""'if specify domain in strUsr, this must be blank
iFlag = "0" 'only two values allowed here: 0 (wait for connection), 128 (wait max two min)

Set objLocator = CreateObject("wbemScripting.SWbemLocator")
Set objWMIService = objLocator.ConnectServer(strComputer, _
    wmiNS, strUsr, strPWD, strLocl, strAuth, iFLag)
Set objItem = objWMIService.get(wmiQuery)

WScript.Echo objItem.GetObjectText_
```

If the RetrieveWMISettings.vbs script works, you have successfully tested the core WMI functionality. You have not, however, tested other WMI providers, only the WBEMCore provider. The RetrieveComputerSystem.vbs script uses the *Win32_ComputerSystem* class. *Win32_Computer-System* relies on the CIMWin32 provider, and a query to this class exercises an extremely important WMI provider. I specify the name of the computer in the variable *strComputer*, but because I want to use the *Get* method, I must specify a particular instance of *Win32_ComputerSystem*, which happens to be the local machine. When I use the WMI moniker to make a WMI connection, I do not supply the computer name in single quotes, but contain it in a variable called *str-Computer* enclosed in double quotes. When I supply a computer name for the key name property of *Win32_ComputerSystem* class, the computer name must be enclosed in single quotes. To use a single variable for both of these instances that have different requirements, I devised the simple *FunFix* function and included it at the bottom of the script. This function takes the string that is supplied to it, appends a single quote as both a prefix and a suffix, and assigns the resultant string to be equal to the function name. This enables dual use of the same variable name.

RetrieveComputerSystem.vbs

```
strComputer = "Mred1" 'name of the target computer system.
wmiNS = "\root\cimv2"
wmiQuery = "win32_ComputerSystem.name=" & funFix(strComputer)
Set objWMIService = GetObject("winmgmts:\\" & strComputer & wmiNS)
Set objItem = objWMIService.get(wmiQuery)

    Wscript.Echo myFun(wmiQuery) & objItem.getObjectText_

Function myFun(input)
Dim lstr
lstr = Len(input)
myFun = input & vbcrlf & string(lstr,"=")
End Function

Function funFix(strIN) 'computer name needs single '
funFix = "'" & strIN & "'"
End function
```

Obtaining Diagnostic Information

If the preceding checks do not point to an immediate solution, the next step is to obtain more information. To do this, you have several tools at your disposal. The primary source of troubleshooting information is WMI logging. By changing the logging level to verbose, you can generate a diagnostic trace of WMI events in several WMI logs.

Enabling Verbose WMI Logging

There are three logging levels for WMI: disabled, errors only, and verbose. These logging levels are recorded in the registry at the following location:

```
HKEY_LOCAL_MACHINE\SOFTWARE\Microsoft\WBEM\CIMOM\Logging
```

A value of 0 disables all logging, a value of 1 enables errors-only logging, and a value of 2 sets the logging level to verbose.

You can set the logging levels by using the WMI Control Properties console. As shown in Figure 14-4, the logging levels are displayed in the Logging tab—the same tab used to increase or decrease the logging level. After the WMI problem is solved, it is important that you reduce the logging level back to errors only, or the increased logging activity could cause performance problems for WMI and for all applications that rely on its services. To increase the logging level, follow these steps:

1. Click Start, and then click Run.

2. In the Run dialog box, type **wmimgmt.msc** in the Open box, and then click OK.

3. Right-click WMI Control (Local).

4. Click Properties.

5. Click the Logging tab.

6. Change the Logging Level to Verbose.

7. Increase the maximum log size (that is, set it to 256,000 or more).

8. Click OK, and then close the WMI console.

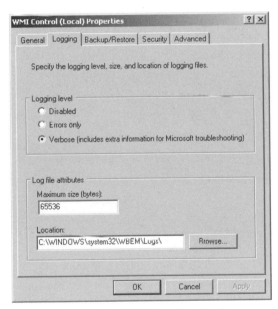

Figure 14-4   Setting WMI Logging levels

The increased logging level takes effect after the WMI service has been stopped and restarted; no reboot is required.

Examining the WMI Log Files

The WMI log files are stored in the *%SystemRoot%*\System32\WBEM\Logs directory by default. This location is configurable in the Logging tab, as shown in Figure 14-4. In addition, the WMI log file directory is recorded in the registry at the following location:

```
HKEY_LOCAL_MACHINE\SOFTWARE\Microsoft\WBEM\CIMOM\Logging Directory
```

If you open the logs directory, you will find a number of WMI logs. Perhaps one of the challenges in troubleshooting WMI is to select the correct log file in which to look for the information that is needed. Table 14-1 provides a quick listing of the most common WMI log files and the purpose of each file.

Table 14-1   WMI Log Files and Their Purposes

Log File	Purpose
Dsprovider.log	Trace information and error messages for the Directory Services provider
Framework.log	Trace information and error messages for the provider framework and the Win32 provider
Mofcomp.log	Compilation details from the MOF compiler, including mofcomp failures during setup
Ntevt.log	Trace messages from the Event Log provider
Setup.log	Reports on MOF files that failed to load during the setup process
Viewprovider.log	Trace information from the View provider
Wbemcore.log	Logging from the Wbemcore provider
Wbemess.log	Log entries related to events
Wbemprox.log	Trace information for the WMI proxy server; remote logons
Winmgmt.log	Trace information that is typically not used for diagnostics
Wmiadap.log	Error messages related to the AutoDiscovery/AutoPurge (ADAP) process
Wmiprov.log	Management data and events from WMI-enabled Windows Driver Model (WDM) drivers; hardware

Your computer system might not have all these log files. Some of the providers have their own procedure for configuring logging levels. For example, the View provider requires adding a registry key to the following location:

```
HKEY_LOCAL_MACHINE\SOFTWARE\Microsoft\WBEM\
PROVIDERS\Logging\ViewProvider\Level
```

Once the registry key is added, you use the same 0, 1, 2 values to configure no logging, error-only logging, or verbose logging, respectively. This works the same as setting the overall WMI logging level.

The key WMI log files that you will probably view the most are the following:

- Wbemcore.log
- Mofcomp.log
- Wbemprox.log

> **Use the Date**   When I am troubleshooting a WMI problem, once I bump up the diagnostic logging level, I then try to reproduce the problem. If I am successful in reproducing the problem, I note the time, open the WMI logging directory, and sort by time. Sometimes, if I am lucky, I will find a log file with a time stamp that is very nearly the time I noted when I was able to reproduce the error. Also, I like to use the VBScript *Now* function in my script that is generating the error because it will give me a time stamp I can refer back to when I am analyzing a diagnostic log file. If you follow this simple procedure, you can easily eliminate having to review more than half of the WMI log files in troubleshooting because they were not updated around the same time as when you reproduced the error.

Using the Err Tool

As you look through the WMI log files, you will quickly see that they are filled with strange numbers. The Err.exe tool is sometimes called the Microsoft Exchange Server Error Code Look-Up tool, but it is much more than that. It pulls error codes from header files installed on your computer. At home on my computer that runs Windows XP, Err.exe can supply information on nearly 20,000 error messages that come from more than 170 different sources—and I don't even have Exchange Server installed at home! You can download the Err.exe tool for free from the Microsoft Download Center (*http://www.microsoft.com/downloads*). If you do a search for "Exchange Server Error Code," it is easy to find. You use the Err.exe tool in Lab 28 when you troubleshoot some WMI script problems. The Err.exe tool is a single executable and does not need to be installed, which means it can easily be copied to any machine. Once the downloaded file has been extracted, you copy it to an easily accessed location on your machine. To use the Err.exe tool type **err** (if it is in your path, or change to the directory containing the Err.exe tool) and supply an error number. An example of this is shown here:

```
c:\Utils>err 0x80041003
```

The tool will then return every match it has for the error number, which can be only one item or might be many, depending on the number. You should always look for a source that is related to what you are troubleshooting. For example, in the following output, two sources generate error 0x80041003. But as you are troubleshooting a WMI problem, you choose the meaning access denied because it is generated from Wbemcli.h. You choose this meaning from the Err.exe output because *Wbemcli* looks similar to *Wbem client*—which sounds like an application that is using WMI.

```
# for hex 0x80041003 / decimal -2147217405 :
  REC_E_TOODIFFERENT                                    reconcil.h
  WBEM_E_ACCESS_DENIED                                  wbemcli.h
# 2 matches found for "0x80041003"
```

Using Mofcomp.exe

Mofcomp.exe is a tool that is used to compile MOF files. You use Mofcomp.exe in Lab 29. Basically, you will need to use Mofcomp.exe at two times. If you have a MOF file you need in WMI, you must run Mofcomp.exe to add the MOF file to the repository. You would use Mofcomp.exe in these situations to add additional functionality to WMI. Some applications do not register themselves with WMI for autorecovery, and if you ever delete the repository, you must recompile those MOF files back into WMI after rebuilding the repository. In either case, the syntax is the same. If you look at the number of switches listed for Mofcomp.exe, it looks like a rather complicated tool:

```
Microsoft (R) 32-bit MOF Compiler Version 5.1.2600.2180
Copyright (c) Microsoft Corp. 1997-2001. All rights reserved.

usage: mofcomp [-check] [-N:<Path>]
               [-class:updateonly|-class:createonly]
               [-instance:updateonly|-instance:createonly]
               [-B:<filename>] [-P:<Password>] [-U:<UserName>]
               [-A:<Authority>] [-WMI] [-AUTORECOVER]
               [-MOF:<path>] [-MFL:<path>] [-AMENDMENT:<Locale>]
               [-ER:<ResourceName>] [-L:<ResourceLocale>]
               <MOF filename>

    -check                     Syntax check only
    -N:<path>                  Load into this namespace by default
    -class:updateonly          Do not create new classes
    -class:safeupdate          Update unless conflicts exist
    -class:forceupdate         Update resolving conflicts if possible
    -class:createonly          Do not change existing classes
    -instance:updateonly       Do not create new instances
    -instance:createonly       Do not change existing instances
    -U:<UserName>              User Name
    -P:<Password>              Login password
    -A:<Authority>             Example: NTLMDOMAIN:Domain
    -B:<destination filename>  Creates a binary MOF file, does not add to DB
    -WMI                       Do Windows Driver Model (WDM) checks, requires -B switch
    -AUTORECOVER               Adds MOF to list of files compiled during DB recovery
    -Amendment:<LOCALE>        splits MOF into language neutral and specific versions
                               where locale is of the form "MS_4??"
    -MOF:<path>                name of the language neutral output
    -MFL:<path>                name of the language specific output
    -ER:<ResourceName>         extracts binary mof from named resource
    -L:<ResourceLocale>        optional specific locale number when using -ER switch

    Example c:>mofcomp -N:root\default yourmof.mof
```

Most of the time, you will not need any of these switches. In its most basic form, the MOF file tells WMI where to compile the class, namespace, or instance of an event provider. Using Mofcomp.exe in this fashion requires only that you type **mofcomp mymof.mof** with no switches. Of course, *Mymof.mof* must be the name of the MOF file you are trying to compile.

The next most common Mofcomp command is one in which you must specify the namespace into which the MOF file will be compiled. This is as follows:

```
C:\mofcomp -N:root\myNameSpace myMofFile.mof
```

Using WMIchk

WMIchk.exe is a tool that was developed by Microsoft Premier Support Services to aid administrators in quickly gathering all the information they need to perform initial troubleshooting of WMI configuration problems. The amount of information supplied by this tool can save you hours of information gathering. It is included in the WMIcheck folder on the CD accompanying this book. To use the WMIchk.exe tool you, open a CMD prompt and type the following command:

```
C:\>wmichk >wmiChk.txt
```

Open the WmiChk.txt file in Notepad. Some of the items reported by this program are listed here:

- WMI settings—Registry settings for WMI, including default namespace, logging levels, and log file sizes

- Operating system version and service pack level

- Software installed on the computer

- Services and processes running on the computer

- A listing of namespaces, providers, and event filters defined on the computer

General WMI Troubleshooting Steps

If you determine that there is in fact a problem with WMI, you must consider several steps:

- **DCOM security**   WMI uses DCOM. Changes in DCOM security settings might prevent WMI from working properly.

- **Service settings**   The Windows Management Instrumentation service must be running for WMI to work. If this service is disabled, WMI will not work. The Windows Management Instrumentation service must log on with local system privileges. If this account is changed, WMI will not have the permissions needed to operate properly.

- **Module registration**   The basic WMI service is very robust. Because of the flexible nature of WMI, many software vendors use it to provide management of everything from applications to hardware monitoring. Often, special modules are required to be registered. You can use the WMI Check tool (WMIchk.exe) to report on the state of these modules. If the application is not working and the modules are not registered, you might need to reinstall the application; at a minimum, the modules must be registered.

- **Rebuilding the WBEM repository**   Rebuilding the WMI repository should be the last step—not the first step—in troubleshooting WMI. It is easy to do. You stop the WMI service, delete the database, and restart the database. Make sure you have a backup of the WMI database prior to deleting the database. But if this does not fix the problem, what do you do? If rebuilding does not solve the problem and you have custom settings, you can always perform a restoration.

Summary

In this chapter, we looked at troubleshooting WMI-related issues on both local computers and remote computers. We examined several tools that can help in diagnostic attempts. We discussed the most fundamental tool to use in troubleshooting WMI issues, the WMI Control tool. We discussed using the Windows Management Instrumentation Tester tool and several scripts to exercise WMI functionality.

Quiz Yourself

Q: What are two tools you can use to see whether WMI is accepting connections?

A: The two tools you can use to see whether WMI is accepting connections are the WMI Control tool and Wbemtest.exe.

Q: If you want to produce a list of WMI classes in a namespace, choose a class, and see a sample WMI script produced that you can run to test WMI, what tool would you use?

A: If you need to produce a list of WMI classes in a namespace, choose a class, and see a sample WMI script produced that you can run to test WMI, you would use Scriptomatic.

Q: If you want to test user credentials for a WMI connection on a remote computer, which tool can you use?

A: If you need to test user credentials for a WMI connection on a remote computer, you can use Wbemtest.exe.

Q: If you receive a strange error number in the event log and you need to look up the meaning quickly and easily, which tool can you use?

A: If you receive a strange error number in the event log and you need to look up the meaning quickly and easily, you can use Err.exe to translate the error number into something a bit more meaningful.

Q: If you need to compile a MOF file into the repository, which tool can you use?

A: If you need to compile a MOF file into the repository, you can use Mofcomp.exe.

On Your Own

Lab 28 Working with Logging

In this lab, you will use WMI logging capabilities to assist you in troubleshooting a scripting problem. To do this, you will increase the logging level to verbose and run two scripts that have a few problems in them. You will conclude the lab by running a good script and comparing the information that is logged from this script with the results from running the bad scripts.

1. First you must increase the WMI logging level. Click Start, and then click Run.

2. In the Open dialog box, type **wmimgmt.msc**, and then click OK.

3. Right-click WMI Control (Local).

4. Click Properties.

5. Click the Logging tab.

6. Change Logging Level to Verbose.

7. Increase the maximum log size (that is, set it to 256,000 or more).

8. Click OK, and close the WMI console.

9. Open the WMI logging directory in Windows Explorer. The directory is listed here:

   `C:\WINDOWS\system32\wbem\Logs`

10. Sort the file view by date; you can do this by clicking the Date Modified tab at the top of the Date column. Ensure that the most recent dates are listed at the top.

11. Open the BadScript1.vbs script and run it. (Don't worry, it will not break anything.) Do not close the script output window. You will need the time stamp that is returned from the *Now* function.

12. Make a note of the exact date and time when the script completed.

13. Go to the WMI log file directory and press F5 to refresh the view of the file dates. Examine the file dates closely. Do you see any that match (or are very close) to the time stamp produced by running BadScript1.vbs? You should see at least three files with time stamps very near the time indicated by running the BadScript1.vbs. The three files should be WinMgmt.log, Wbemprox.log, and WbemCore.log.

14. If you do not see any recent files with recent Date Modified time stamps, you might need to refresh the folder view by pressing F5 again. If you still do not see any log files with an appropriate Date Modified time stamp, go back and double-check to ensure the verbose WMI logging level is set properly. If you are using an operating system earlier than Windows XP, you will need to restart the WMI service for the logging level change to take effect. Windows XP and Windows Server 2003 dynamically apply the changes.

15. Once you have found the log files, open WinMgmt.log by using Notepad and scroll to the bottom of the file. Look for the time stamp that matches (or at least is within a few seconds of the time produced by BadScript1.vbs). You will see some errors that look similar to the following:

```
(Sat Jul 30 06:41:16 2005.36668000) : Got a provider can unload event
(Sat Jul 30 06:41:46 2005.36698000) : Got a TIMEOUT work item
(Sat Jul 30 06:41:46 2005.36698000) : Got a FinalCoreShutdown work item
(Sat Jul 30 06:41:59 2005.36710921) : CForwardFactory::CreateInstance
(Sat Jul 30 06:42:01 2005.36713000) : Got a provider can unload event
```

16. Open the Wbemprox.log file using Notepad and scroll to the bottom of the file. Again look for a close time stamp. You will see some errors that look similar to the following:

```
(Sat Jul 30 06:41:59 2005.36710921) : Using the principal -RPCSS/
Acapulco.NWTraders.MSFT-
(Sat Jul 30 06:41:59 2005.36710921) : ConnectViaDCOM, CoCreateInstanceEx resulted in h
r = 0x0
(Sat Jul 30 06:41:59 2005.36710921) : NTLMLogin resulted in hr = 0x8004100e
```

17. Once you find the *NTLMLogin resulted in* line, note that it says the *hr = 0x8004100e*. This is the result code that is returned from trying to connect to WMI. If you look up the error 0x8004100e using Err.exe, you might be able to find more information.

18. Open a command prompt window, and change to the directory in which you have Err.exe installed. Type the following command:

```
Err 0x8004100e
```

19. Examine the output from Err.exe. The output looks like the following:

```
C:\Utils>err 0x8004100e
# for hex 0x8004100e / decimal -2147217394 :
  WBEM_E_INVALID_NAMESPACE                                    wbemcli.h
# 1 matches found for "0x8004100e"
```

20. From the output you can see that part of the problem is related to an invalid namespace.

21. Open the WbemCore.log file and find the time stamp close to when you ran the BadScript1.vbs. You will find an entry that looks similar to the one listed here:

```
Sat Jul 30 06:41:59 2005.36710921) : CALL ConnectionLogin::NTLMLogin
    wszNetworkResource = \\.\root\cimv1
    pPreferredLocale = (null)
    lFlags = 0x0
(Sat Jul 30 06:41:59 2005.36710921) : DCOM connection from NWtraders\LondonAdmin at au
thentiction level Privacy, AuthnSvc = 10, AuthzSvc = 0, Capabilities = 0
(Sat Jul 30 06:42:01 2005.36713000) : + DllCanUnloadNow()
(Sat Jul 30 06:42:01 2005.36713000) : - DllCanUnloadNow() S_FALSE
(Sat Jul 30 06:42:01 2005.36713000) : + DllCanUnloadNow()
(Sat Jul 30 06:42:01 2005.36713000) : - DllCanUnloadNow() S_FALSE
```

22. By examining the output, can you determine the problem with the script? Can you see the reason for the failed login reported in the Wbemprox.log file? Do you see why the error that was reported was invalid namespace? WMI is unable to authenticate a user against a WMI namespace that does not exist.

23. Run the BadScript2.vbs script. Retain the time stamp from the script.

24. Open the WinMgmt.log file, and locate the time that is closest to the time stamp retrieved from running BadScript2.vbs. The error messages should appear near the bottom of the script. Compare the results from BadScript1.vbs in the WinMgmt.log file with the results from BadScript2.vbs. What is the difference between the two results? The BadScript2.vbs script should not record any errors in the WinMgmt.log file. The entry from BadScript2.vbs should look like the following:

```
(Sat Jul 30 07:39:35 2005.40167562) : CForwardFactory::CreateInstance
```

25. Open Wbemprox.log and locate the entries closest to the time stamp retrieved from BadScript2.vbs. The entries should be near the bottom of the file. Do you find any errors listed in the Wbemprox.log file? No.

26. Compare the results in Wbemprox.log from BadScript2.vbs to the results generated by BadScript1.vbs. Are there any differences? Yes. The following line was generated by BadScript1.vbs but was not generated by BadScript2.vbs:

```
(Sat Jul 30 06:41:59 2005.36710921) : NTLMLogin resulted in hr = 0x8004100e
```

27. What does the absence of an error here mean? It indicates that the NTLMLogin operation succeeded. The connection to *root\cimv2* was successful.

28. Open the WbemCore.log file, and find the time stamp from the BadScript2.vbs run. It should be near the bottom. Compare the results from running BadScript2.vbs to the results from running BadScript1.vbs in the log file. Notice there are far more entries in the log file. You should find entries that look similar to the following:

```
(Sat Jul 30 07:39:35 2005.40167562) : CALL ConnectionLogin::NTLMLogin
    wszNetworkResource = \\.\root\cimv2
    pPreferredLocale = (null)
    lFlags = 0x0
(Sat Jul 30 07:39:35 2005.40167562) : DCOM connection from NWTRADERS\LondonAdmin at au
thenticion level Privacy, AuthnSvc = 10, AuthzSvc = 0, Capabilities = 0
(Sat Jul 30 07:39:35 2005.40167562) : CALL CWbemNamespace::ExecQuery
    BSTR QueryFormat = WQL
    BSTR Query = Select * from win32_Processer
    IEnumWbemClassObject **pEnum = 0x28FD0C8
(Sat Jul 30 07:39:35 2005.40167562) : CALL CWbemNamespace::ExecQueryAsync
    BSTR QueryFormat = WQL
    BSTR Query = Select * from win32_Processer
    IWbemObjectSink* pHandler = 0x0
(Sat Jul 30 07:39:35 2005.40167562) : STARTING a main queue thread 548 for a total of
1
(Sat Jul 30 07:39:35 2005.40167578) : CALL CWbemNamespace::ExecQuery
    BSTR QueryFormat = Wql
```

```
      BSTR Query = Select * from __ClassProviderRegistration
      IEnumWbemClassObject **pEnum = 0xF7F9C0
(Sat Jul 30 07:39:35 2005.40167578) : CALL CWbemNamespace::ExecQueryAsync
      BSTR QueryFormat = Wql
      BSTR Query = Select * from __ClassProviderRegistration
      IWbemObjectSink* pHandler = 0x0
(Sat Jul 30 07:39:35 2005.40167578) : STARTING a main queue thread 2032 for a total of
  2
(Sat Jul 30 07:39:47 2005.40179578) : STOPPING a main queue thread 548 for a total of
  1
(Sat Jul 30 07:39:47 2005.40179578) : STOPPING a main queue thread 2032 for a total of
  0
```

29. In examining the log file, were you able to parse a WMI Query Language (WQL) query? Yes. This is indicated by the following line in the log file:

```
(Sat Jul 30 07:39:35 2005.40167562) : CALL CWbemNamespace::ExecQuery
      BSTR QueryFormat = WQL
      BSTR Query = Select * from win32_Processer
      IEnumWbemClassObject **pEnum = 0x28FD0C8
```

30. Did BadScript1.vbs succeed in parsing a WQL query? No. There is no entry similar to the preceding one listed in WbemCore.log around the time the BadScript1.vbs script ran.

31. After the query is parsed, it now tries to find the class that is referenced in the query. Locate the entries that try to identify the class provider. It looks like the following:

```
(Sat Jul 30 07:39:35 2005.40167578) : CALL CWbemNamespace::ExecQuery
      BSTR QueryFormat = Wql
      BSTR Query = Select * from __ClassProviderRegistration
      IEnumWbemClassObject **pEnum = 0xF7F9C0
```

32. Examine the WbemCore.log file. Did the query for the class provider succeed? No. There is no indication in the log file that the query succeeded. The next entry in the log indicates the main thread queue stops, as shown here:

```
(Sat Jul 30 07:39:47 2005.40179578) : STOPPING a main queue thread 548 for a total of
  1
```

33. To compare your results from bad scripts with the results of a good script, run the GoodScript1.vbs script. Pay attention to the script complete time stamp.

34. Open WinMgmt.log, and find the time stamp from running GoodScript1.vbs. Compare your results from running GoodScript1.vbs with the results from running BadScript2.vbs. They are similar.

35. Open Wbemprox.log, find the time stamp from running GoodScript1.vbs. Compare with the results from running BadScript2.vbs. They are similar. This indicates that both BadScript2.vbs and GoodScirpt2.vbs were able to make a connection into WMI and have the query parsed.

36. Open WbemCore.log and compare the results from running BadScript2.vbs and the results from running GoodScript1.vbs. What do you notice? There are far more entries from GoodScript1.vbs. Why is this the case? The good script ran to completion.

37. Can you identify the name of the provider that supplies *Win32_Processor*? Yes. It is CIMWin32.

This concludes the lab.

Lab 29 Compiling MOF Files

In this lab, you will use Mofcomp.exe to compile MOF files into the WBEM repository. You will first create a new namespace using Mofcomp, and then you will delete that namespace. Next you will create an instance of the active script consumer, and then you will delete the instance of the active script consumer you created.

1. Copy the four MOF files in the Chapter14\Lab 29 folder to a directory you can easily access from a command prompt window.

2. Open a command prompt window.

3. In the command prompt window, use Mofcomp.exe to compile Createnamespace.mof, which will create a new namespace called *MyNamespace* in WMI off the *root* namespace. The syntax of the command looks something like the following:

```
D:\>mofcomp createnamespace.mof
```

4. The output from this command looks like the following:

```
Microsoft (R) 32-bit MOF Compiler Version 5.1.2600.2180
Copyright (c) Microsoft Corp. 1997-2001. All rights reserved.
Parsing MOF file: createnamespace.mof
MOF file has been successfully parsed
Storing data in the repository...
Done!
```

5. Run the ListWMINameSpace.vbs script to confirm the namespace was created.

6. Now delete the namespace. In the command prompt window, use Mofcomp.exe to compile the Deletenamespace.mof. The command looks like the following:

```
D:\>mofcomp deletenamespace.mof
```

7. The output from the command looks like the following:

```
Microsoft (R) 32-bit MOF Compiler Version 5.1.2600.2180
Copyright (c) Microsoft Corp. 1997-2001. All rights reserved.
Parsing MOF file: deletenamespace.mof
MOF file has been successfully parsed
Storing data in the repository...
Done!
```

8. Next create a new instance of the active script event consumer. You have a MOF file that will write to an event log when Calc.exe is closed out. It requires a reboot to take effect.

9. In the command prompt window, use Mofcomp.exe to compile the Asec.mof MOF file. This MOF file takes about a minute to compile, so do not get alarmed when it does not compile as quickly as the two previous examples. The command to do this looks like the following:

   ```
   D:\>mofcomp asec.mof
   ```

10. When it is completed compiling, the output looks like the following:

    ```
    Microsoft (R) 32-bit MOF Compiler Version 5.1.2600.2180
    Copyright (c) Microsoft Corp. 1997-2001. All rights reserved.
    Parsing MOF file: asec.mof
    MOF file has been successfully parsed
    Storing data in the repository...
    Done!
    ```

11. Reboot your computer and launch Calc.exe. Use it for a minute or so, and perform come calculations with it. Exit Calculator.

12. Navigate to your C drive, and you should see a text file called Asec.log. Delete the log file. If you do not see a log file there within 5 to 10 seconds, check the Windows Application event log for errors.

13. The last thing you need to do is to delete the instance of the active script event consumer. To do this, compile the DeleteAsec.mof file using Mofcomp. The command to do this looks like the following:

    ```
    D:\>mofcomp deleteasec.mof
    ```

14. If the delete is successful, you will see an output similar to the following:

    ```
    Microsoft (R) 32-bit MOF Compiler Version 5.1.2600.2180
    Copyright (c) Microsoft Corp. 1997-2001. All rights reserved.
    Parsing MOF file: deleteasec.mof
    MOF file has been successfully parsed
    Storing data in the repository...
    Done!
    ```

This concludes the lab.

Part VI
Appendixes

Appendix A
Scripting API Methods and Properties

This appendix provides documentation for the scripting application programming interface (API) methods and properties. These are discussed in detail in Chapter 4.

Table A-1 *SWbemServices* **Methods**

Method	Meaning
AssociatorsOf	Returns a collection of objects (classes or instances) that are associated with a specified object
AssociatorsOfAsync	Asynchronously returns a collection of objects (classes or instances) that are associated with a specified object
Delete	Deletes an instance or class
DeleteAsync	Asynchronously deletes an instance or class
ExecMethod	Executes an object method
ExecMethodAsync	Asynchronously executes a method
ExecNotificationQuery	Executes a query to receive events
ExecNotificationQueryAsync	Asynchronously executes a query to receive events
ExecQuery	Executes a query to retrieve a collection of objects (classes or instances)
ExecQueryAsync	Asynchronously executes a query to retrieve a collection of objects (classes or instances)
Get	Retrieves a class or instance
GetAsync	Asynchronously retrieves a class or instance
InstancesOf	Returns a collection of instances of a specified class
InstancesOfAsync	Asynchronously returns a collection of instances of a specified class
ReferencesTo	Returns a collection of objects (classes or instances) that refer to a single object
ReferencesToAsync	Asynchronously returns a collection of objects (classes or instances) that refer to a single object

Table A-1   *SWbemServices* Methods

Method	Meaning
SubclassesOf	Returns a collection of subclasses of a specified class
SubclassesOfAsync	Asynchronously returns a collection of subclasses of a specified class

Table A-2   *SWbemObjectSet Iflags* and Meanings

Flag	Value	Meaning
wbemFlagForwardOnly	0x20	Returns a forward-only enumerator. Forward-only enumerators are faster and use less memory. They do not allow calls to *SWbem-Object.Clone_.*
wbemFlagBidirectional	0x0	Retains pointers to objects of the enumeration until the client releases the enumerator.
wbemFlagReturnImmediately	0x10	The call returns immediately.
wbemFlagReturnWhenComplete	0x0	Blocks until the query is complete.
wbemQueryFlagPrototype	0x2	Stops the query from executing and returns an object that looks like a typical result.
wbemFlagUseAmendedQualifiers	0x20000	Returns class amendment data with the base class definition.

Table A-3   Properties of *SWbemObjectPath*

Property	Description
Authority	String that defines the *Authority* component of the object path.
Class	Name of the class that is part of the object path.
DisplayName	String that contains the path in a form that can be used as a moniker display name.
IsClass	Boolean value that indicates whether this path represents a class.
IsSingleton	Boolean value that indicates whether this path represents a singleton instance.
Keys	An *SWbemNamedValueSet* object that contains the key value bindings.
Locale	String containing the locale for this object path.
Namespace	Name of the namespace that is part of the object path.
ParentNamespace	Name of the parent of the namespace that is part of the object path.
Path	Contains the absolute path. This is the default property of this object.
Relpath	Contains the relative path.
*Security_*	Used to read or change the security settings.
Server	Name of the server.

Table A-4   Methods of the *SWbemNamedValueSet* Object

Method	Description
Add	Adds an *SWbemNamedValue* object to the collection.
Clone	Makes a copy of this *SWbemNamedValueSet* collection.
DeleteAll	Removes all items from the collection, making the *SWbemNamedValueSet* object empty.
Item	Retrieves an *SWbemNamedValue* object from the collection. This is the default method of the object.
Remove	Removes an *SWbemNamedValue* object from the collection.

Table A-5   *SWbemProperty* Properties

Property	Description
CIMType	Type of this property.
IsArray	Boolean value that indicates whether this property has an array type.
IsLocal	Boolean value that indicates whether this is a local property.
Name	Name of this property.
Origin	Contains the originating class of this property.
*Qualifiers_*	An *SWbemQualifierSet* object, which is the collection of qualifiers for this property.
Value	Actual value of this property. This is the default automation property of this object.

Table A-6   *WbemCimTypeEnum* Constants

Constant	Decimal Value	Description
wbemCimtypeSint16	2	Signed 16-bit integer
wbemCimtypeSint32	3	Signed 32-bit integer
wbemCimtypeReal32	4	32-bit real number
wbemCimtypeReal64	5	64-bit real number
wbemCimtypeString	8	String
wbemCimtypeBoolean	11	Boolean value
wbemCimtypeObject	13	Common Information Model (CIM) object
wbemCimtypeSint8	16	Signed 8-bit integer
wbemCimtypeUint8	17	Unsigned 8-bit integer
wbemCimtypeUint16	18	Unsigned 16-bit integer
wbemCimtypeUint32	19	Unsigned 32-bit integer
wbemCimtypeSint64	20	Signed 64-bit integer
wbemCimtypeUint64	21	Unsigned 64-bit integer
wbemCimtypeDatetime	101	Date/time value
wbemCimtypeReference	102	Reference to a CIM object.
wbemCimtypeChar16	103	16-bit character

Table A-7   *SWbemQualifierSet* Methods

Method	Description
Add	Adds an *SWbemQualifier* object to the *SWbemQualifierSet* collection.
Item	Retrieves an *SWbemQualifier* object from the collection. This is the default method of this object.
Remove	Removes an *SWbemQualifier* object from the collection.

Table A-8   *SWbemQualifier* Properties

Property	Description
IsAmended	Boolean value that indicates whether this qualifier has been localized using a merge operation.
IsLocal	Boolean value that indicates whether this is a local qualifier.
IsOverridable	Boolean value that indicates whether this qualifier can be overridden when propagated.
Name	Name of this qualifier.
PropagatesToInstance	Boolean value that indicates whether this qualifier can be propagated to an instance.
PropagatesToSubclass	Boolean value that indicates whether this qualifier can be propagated to a subclass.
Value	Actual value of this qualifier. This is the default property of this object.

Table A-9   Methods of the *SWbemRefresher* Object

Method	Description
Add	Adds a new refreshable object to the refresher object
AddEnum	Adds a new enumerator to the refresher
DeleteAll	Removes all items from the refresher
Item	Returns a specified item from the collection in the refresher
Refresh	Refreshes all items in the refresher
Remove	Removes object or object set with a specified index from the refresher

Table A-10   Properties of the *SWbemRefreshableItem* Object

Properties	Description
Index	Index of the item in the refresher object
IsSet	Indicates whether the item is a single object or an object set
Object	The *SWbemObject* that represents the item
ObjectSet	The *SWbemObjectSet* that represents the item
Refresher	The *SWbemRefresher* object in which this item resides

Appendix B
WMI Security Constants

This appendix provides documentation for the security constants that are defined in WMI. These constants are used throughout the book but are discussed in detail in Chapter 7.

Constant	Value	Meaning
wbemPrivilegeCreateToken	1	Required to create a primary token.
wbemPrivilegePrimaryToken	2	Required to assign the primary token of a process.
wbemPrivilegeLockMemory	3	Required to lock physical pages in memory.
wbemPrivilegeIncreaseQuota	4	Required to increase the quota assigned to a process.
wbemPrivilegeMachineAccount	5	Required to create a machine account.
wbemPrivilegeTcb	6	Identifies its holder as part of the trusted computer base. Some trusted protected subsystems are granted this privilege.
wbemPrivilegeSecurity	7	Required to perform a number of security-related functions such as controlling and viewing audit messages. This privilege identifies its holder as a security operator.
wbemPrivilegeTakeOwnership	8	Required to take ownership of an object without being granted discretionary access. This privilege allows the owner value to be set only to those values that the holder might legitimately assign as the owner of an object.
wbemPrivilegeLoadDriver	9	Required to load or unload a device driver.
wbemPrivilegeSystemProfile	10	Required to gather profiling information for the entire system.
wbemPrivilegeSystemtime	11	Required to modify the system time.
wbemPrivilegeProfileSingleProcess	12	Required to gather profiling information for a single process.
wbemPrivilegeIncreaseBasePriority	13	Required to increase the base priority of a process.
wbemPrivilegeCreatePagefile	14	Required to create a paging file.

Constant	Value	Meaning
wbemPrivilegeCreatePermanent	15	Required to create a permanent object.
wbemPrivilegeBackup	16	Required to perform backup operations.
wbemPrivilegeRestore	17	Required to perform restore operations. This privilege enables you to set any valid user or group security identifier (SID) as the owner of an object.
wbemPrivilegeShutdown	18	Required to shut down a local system.
wbemPrivilegeDebug	19	Required to debug a process.
wbemPrivilegeAudit	20	Required to generate audit log entries.
wbemPrivilegeSystemEnvironment	21	Required to modify the nonvolatile RAM of systems that use this type of memory to store configuration information.
wbemPrivilegeChangeNotify	22	Required to receive notifications of changes to files or directories. This privilege also causes the system to skip all traversal access checks. It is enabled by default for all users.
wbemPrivilegeRemoteShutdown	23	Required to shut down a system using a network request.
wbemPrivilegeUndock	24	Required to remove computer from docking station.
wbemPrivilegeSyncAgent	25	Required to synchronize directory service data.
wbemPrivilegeEnableDelegation	26	Required to enable computer and user accounts to be trusted for delegation.
wbemPrivilegeManageVolume	27	Required to perform volume maintenance tasks.

Appendix C
WMI Security Privileges and Operations

This appendix provides documentation on the use of privileged operations in WMI. This information is supplemental to Chapter 7.

Class Name	Privilege	Purpose
Win32_NTLogEvent	SeSecurityPrivilege	For security event log
Win32_NTEventlogFile	SeSecurityPrivilege, SeBackup-Privilege	*ClearEventlog*
	SeSecurityPrivilege, SeBackup-Privilege	*BackupEventlog*
Win32_PageFile	SeCreatePagefileNamePrivilege	*Create an instance*
Win32_ComputerSystem	SeSystemEnvironmentPrivilege	*SystemStartupDelay*
	SeSystemEnvironmentPrivilege	*SystemStartupOptions*
	SeSystemEnvironmentPrivilege	*SystemStartupSetting*
Win32_OperatingSystem	SeShutdownPrivilege	*Reboot*
	SeShutdownPrivilege	*Shutdown*
	SeShutdownPrivilege	*Win32ShutDown*
	SeSystemTimePrivilege	*SetDateTime*
Win32_Process	SeDebugPrivilege	*MinimumWorkingSetSize*
	SeDebugPrivilege	*MaximumWorkingSetSize*
	SeDebugPrivilege	*ExecutablePath*
	SeDebugPrivilege	*Terminate*
	SeAssignPrimaryTokenPrivilege, SeIncreaseQuotaPrivilege	*Create*
Win32_ProcessStartup Process-StartupInformation	SeDebugPrivilege	Create an instance
Win32_TCPIPPrinterPort	SeLoadDriverPrivilege	Create an instance

Class Name	Privilege	Purpose
Win32_SecuritySetting	SeSecurityPrivilege, SeRestore-Privilege	*GetSecurityDescriptor*
	SeSecurityPrivilege, SeRestore-Privilege	*SetSecurityDescriptor*
Win32_LogicalFileSecuritySetting	SeSecurityPrivilege, SeRestore-Privilege	Create an instance
Win32_LogicalShareSecuritySetting	SeSecurityPrivilege, SeRestore-Privilege	Create an instance
Win32_PageFileSetting	SeCreatePagefilePrivilege	*Name*
CIM_ProcessExecutable	SeDebugPrivilege	*ProcessCount*
Win32_NTLogEventLog	SeSecurityPrivilege	Query security log
Win32_NTLogEventUser	SeSecurityPrivilege	Query security log
Win32_NTLogEventComputer	SeSecurityPrivilege	Query security log
Win32_Trustee	SeSecurityPrivilege, SeRestore-Privilege	*SIDString*
	SeSecurityPrivilege, SeRestore-Privilege	*SID*
	SeSecurityPrivilege, SeRestore-Privilege	*Name*
	SeSecurityPrivilege, SeRestore-Privilege	*SidLength*
Win32_ACE	SeSecurityPrivilege, SeRestore-Privilege	*Domain*
	SeSecurityPrivilege, SeRestore-Privilege	*AccessMask*
	SeSecurityPrivilege, SeRestore-Privilege	*AceFlags*
	SeSecurityPrivilege, SeRestore-Privilege	*AceType*
	SeSecurityPrivilege, SeRestore-Privilege	*GuidInheritedObjectType*
	SeSecurityPrivilege, SeRestore-Privilege	*GuidObjectType*
Win32_SecurityDescriptor	SeSecurityPrivilege, SeRestore-Privilege	Create an instance
Win32_Trustee Owner	SeSecurityPrivilege, SeRestore-Privilege	Create an instance

Appendix D

Computer System Hardware Classes

This appendix provides documentation on the computer system hardware classes. These classes are discussed in detail in Chapter 10.

Table D-1   Cooling Device Classes

Class	Properties	Methods	Description
Win32_Fan	22	3	Represents the properties of a fan device
Win32_HeatPipe	20	2	Represents the properties of a heat pipe cooling device
Win32_Refrigeration	20	2	Represents the properties of a refrigeration device
Win32_TemperatureProbe	35	2	Represents the properties of a temperature sensor (electronic thermometer)

Table D-2   Input Device Classes

Class	Properties	Methods	Description
Win32_Keyboard	23	2	Represents a keyboard
Win32_PointingDevice	33	2	Represents an input device used to point to and select regions on the display

Table D-3   Mass Storage Classes

Class	Properties	Methods	Description
Win32_AutoChkSetting	4	0	Represents the settings for the auto-check operation of a disk
Win32_CDROMDrive	48	2	Represents a CD-ROM drive
Win32_DiskDrive	49	2	Represents a physical disk drive
Win32_FloppyDrive	30	2	Manages the capabilities of a floppy disk drive

Table D-3   Mass Storage Classes

Class	Properties	Methods	Description
Win32_PhysicalMedia	23	0	Represents any type of documentation or storage medium
Win32_TapeDrive	40	2	Represents a tape drive

Table D-4   Motherboard, Controller, and Port Classes

Class	Properties	Methods	Description
Win32_1394Controller	23	2	Represents the capabilities and management of a 1394 controller
Win32_1394ControllerDevice	7	0	Relates the high-speed serial bus (IEEE 1394 Firewire) controller and the *CIM_Logical-Device* instance connected to it
Win32_AssociatedProcessorMemory	3	0	Relates a processor and its cache memory
Win32_AllocatedResource	2	0	Relates a logical device to a system resource
Win32_BaseBoard	29	1	Represents a baseboard (also known as a motherboard or system board)
Win32_BIOS	27	0	Represents the attributes of the computer system's basic input/output system (BIOS)
Win32_Bus	21	2	Represents a physical bus
Win32_CacheMemory	53	2	Represents cache memory (internal and external)
Win32_ControllerHasHub	7	0	Represents the hubs downstream from the universal serial bus (USB) controller
Win32_DeviceBus	2	0	Relates a system bus and a logical device using the bus
Win32_DeviceMemoryAddress	11	0	Represents a device memory address
Win32_DeviceSettings	2	0	Relates a logical device and a setting that can be applied to it
Win32_DMAChannel	19	0	Represents a direct memory access (DMA) channel
Win32_FloppyController	23	2	Represents the capabilities and management capacity of a floppy disk drive controller

Table D-4 Motherboard, Controller, and Port Classes

Class	Properties	Methods	Description
Win32_IDEController	23	2	Represents the capabilities of an Integrated Drive Electronics (IDE) controller device
Win32_IDEControllerDevice	7	0	Association class that relates an IDE controller and the logical device
Win32_InfraredDevice	23	2	Represents the capabilities and management of an infrared device
Win32_IRQResource	15	0	Represents an interrupt request (IRQ) line number
Win32_MemoryArray	39	2	Represents the properties of the computer system memory array and mapped addresses
Win32_MemoryArrayLocation	2	0	Relates a logical memory array and the physical memory array upon which it exists
Win32_MemoryDevice	39	2	Represents the properties of a computer system's memory device along with its associated mapped addresses
Win32_MemoryDeviceArray	2	0	Relates a memory device and the memory array in which it resides
Win32_MemoryDeviceLocation	2	0	Association class that relates a memory device and the physical memory on which it exists
Win32_MotherboardDevice	22	2	Represents a device that contains the central components of the computer system
Win32_OnBoardDevice	20	0	Represents common adapter devices built into the motherboard (system board)
Win32_ParallelPort	26	2	Represents the properties of a parallel port
Win32_PCMCIAController	23	2	Manages the capabilities of a Personal Computer Memory Card International Association (PCMCIA) controller device

Table D-4 Motherboard, Controller, and Port Classes

Class	Properties	Methods	Description
Win32_PhysicalMemory	30	0	Represents a physical memory device located on a computer as available to the operating system
Win32_PhysicalMemoryArray	27	1	Represents details about the computer system's physical memory
Win32_PhysicalMemoryLocation	3	0	Relates an array of physical memory to the physical memory locations
Win32_PNPAllocatedResource	2	0	Represents an association between logical devices and system resources
Win32_PNPDevice	2	0	Relates a device (known to Configuration Manager as a PNPEntity) and the function it performs
Win32_PNPEntity	22	2	Represents the properties of a Plug and Play device
Win32_PortConnector	20	0	Represents physical connection ports, such as DD-25 pin male, Centronics, and PS/2
Win32_PortResource	11	0	Represents an input/output (I/O) port
Win32_Processor	44	2	Represents a device capable of interpreting a sequence of machine instructions
Win32_SCSIController	31	2	Represents a Small Computer System Interface (SCSI) controller
Win32_SCSIControllerDevice	7	0	Relates a SCSI controller and the logical device (disk drive) connected to it
Win32_SerialPort	47	2	Represents a serial port
Win32_SerialPortConfiguration	29	0	Represents the settings for data transmission on a serial port
Win32_SerialPortSetting	2	0	Relates a serial port and its configuration settings
Win32_SMBIOSMemory	38	2	Represents the capabilities and management of memory-related logical devices

Table D-4 Motherboard, Controller, and Port Classes

Class	Properties	Methods	Description
Win32_SoundDevice	23	2	Represents the properties of a sound device
Win32_SystemBIOS	2	0	Relates a computer system (including data such as start-up properties, time zones, boot configurations, or administrative passwords) and a system BIOS (services, languages, system management properties)
Win32_SystemDriverPNPEntity	2	0	Relates a Plug and Play device and the driver that supports the Plug and Play device
Win32_SystemEnclosure	37	1	Represents the properties associated with a physical system enclosure
Win32_SystemMemoryResource	10	0	Represents a system memory resource
Win32_SystemSlot	31	0	Represents physical connection points (including ports, motherboard slots, and peripherals) and proprietary connections points
Win32_USBController	23	2	Manages the capabilities of a universal serial bus (USB) controller
Win32_USBControllerDevice	7	0	Relates a USB controller and the CIM_LogicalDevice instances connected to it
Win32_USBHub	28	3	Represents the management characteristics of a USB hub

Table D-5 Network Device Classes

Class	Properties	Methods	Description
Win32_NetworkAdapter	36	2	Represents a network adapter
Win32_NetworkAdapterConfiguration	60	41	Represents the attributes and behaviors of a network adapter
Win32_NetworkAdapterSetting	2	0	Relates a network adapter and its configuration settings

Table D-6   Power Classes

Class	Properties	Methods	Description
Win32_AssociatedBattery	2	0	Relates a logical device and the battery it is using
Win32_Battery	33	2	Represents a battery connected to the computer system
Win32_CurrentProbe	35	2	Represents the properties of a current monitoring sensor (ammeter)
Win32_PortableBattery	36	2	Represents the properties of a portable battery, such as one used for a notebook computer
Win32_PowerManagementEvent	4	0	Represents power management events resulting from power state changes
Win32_UninterruptiblePowerSupply	43	2	Represents the capabilities and management capacity of an uninterruptible power supply (UPS)
Win32_VoltageProbe	35	2	Represents the properties of a voltage sensor (electronic voltmeter)

Table D-7   Printing Classes

Class	Properties	Methods	Description
Win32_DriverForDevice	2	0	Relates a printer to a printer driver
Win32_Printer	86	9	Represents a printer device
Win32_PrinterConfiguration	33	0	Defines the configuration for a printer device
Win32_PrinterController	7	0	Relates a printer and the local device to which the printer is connected
Win32_PrinterDriver	22	3	Represents the drivers for a *Win32_Printer* instance
Win32_PrinterDriverDll	2	0	Relates a local printer and its driver file (not the driver itself)
Win32_PrinterSetting	2	0	Relates a printer and its configuration settings

Table D-7   Printing Classes

Class	Properties	Methods	Description
Win32_PrintJob	24	2	Represents a print job generated by a Microsoft Windows application
Win32_TCPIPPrinterPort	17	0	Represents a Transmission Control Protocol/Internet Protocol (TCP/IP) service access point

Table D-8   Telephony Classes

Class	Properties	Methods	Description
Win32_POTSModem	79	2	Represents the services and characteristics of a Plain Old Telephone Service (POTS) modem
Win32_POTSModemToSerialPort	7	0	Relates a modem and the serial port the modem uses

Table D-9   Video and Monitor Classes

Class	Properties	Methods	Description
Win32_DesktopMonitor	28	2	Represents the type of monitor or display device attached to the computer system.
Win32_DisplayConfiguration	15	0	Represents configuration information for the display device. This class is obsolete. In place of this class, use the properties in the *Win32_VideoController*, *Win32_DesktopMonitor*, and *CIM_VideoControllerResolution* classes.
Win32_DisplayController-Configuration	14	0	Represents the video adapter configuration information. This class is obsolete. In place of this class, use the properties in the *Win32_VideoController*, *Win32_DesktopMonitor*, and *CIM_VideoController-Resolution* classes.
Win32_VideoConfiguration	30	0	This class has been eliminated from Microsoft Windows XP and later operating systems; attempts to use it generate a fatal error. In place of this class, use the properties in the *Win32_VideoController*, *Win32_DesktopMonitor*, and *CIM_VideoControllerResolution* classes.

Table D-9   Video and Monitor Classes

Class	Properties	Methods	Description
Win32_VideoController	59	2	Represents the capabilities and management capacity of the video controller.
Win32_VideoSettings	2	0	Relates a video controller and video settings that can be applied to it.

Appendix E
Operating System Classes

This appendix provides documentation on the operating system classes. These classes are discussed in detail in Chapter 11.

Table E-1   COM Classes

Class	Properties	Methods	Description
Win32_ClassicCOM-ApplicationClasses	2	0	Association class. Relates a Distributed Component Object Model (DCOM) application and a Component Object Model (COM) component grouped under it
Win32_ClassicCOMClass	6	0	Instance class. Represents the properties of a COM component
Win32_ClassicCOMClass-Settings	2	0	Association class. Relates a COM class and the settings used to configure instances of the COM class
Win32_ClientApplication-Setting	2	0	Association class. Relates an executable and a DCOM application that contains the DCOM configuration options for the executable file
Win32_COMApplication	5	0	Instance class. Represents a COM application
Win32_COMApplication-Classes	2	0	Association class. Relates a COM component and the COM application where it resides
Win32_COMApplication-Settings	2	0	Association class. Relates a DCOM application and its configuration settings
Win32_COMClass	5	0	Instance class. Represents the properties of a COM component
Win32_ComClassAuto-Emulator	2	0	Association class. Relates a COM class and another COM class that it automatically emulates
Win32_ComClassEmulator	2	0	Association class. Relates two versions of a COM class

Table E-1   COM Classes

Class	Properties	Methods	Description
Win32_ComponentCategory	6	0	Instance class. Represents a component category
Win32_COMSetting	3	0	Instance class. Represents the settings associated with a COM component or COM application
Win32_DCOMApplication	6	0	Instance class. Represents the properties of a DCOM application
Win32_DCOMApplication-AccessAllowedSetting	2	0	Association class. Relates the Win32_DCOMApplication instance and the user security identifiers (SIDs) that can access it
Win32_DCOMApplication-LaunchAllowedSetting	2	0	Association class. Relates the Win32_DCOMApplication instance and the user SIDs that can launch it
Win32_DCOMApplication-Setting	12	0	Instance class. Represents the settings of a DCOM application
Win32_Implemented-Category	2	0	Association class. Relates a component category and the COM class using its interfaces

Table E-2   Desktop Classes

Class	Properties	Methods	Description
Win32_Desktop	21	0	Instance class. Represents the common characteristics of a user's desktop
Win32_Environment	8	0	Instance class. Represents an environment or system environment
Win32_TimeZone	24	0	Instance class. Represents the time zone information
Win32_UserDesktop	2	0	Association class. Relates a user account and desktop settings that are specific to it

Table E-3   Driver Classes

Class	Properties	Methods	Description
Win32_DriverVXD	21	0	Instance class. Represents a virtual device driver
Win32_SystemDriver	22	10	Instance class. Represents the system driver for a base service

Table E-4 File System Classes

Class	Properties	Methods	Description
Win32_CIMLogicalDeviceCIM-DataFile	4	0	Association class. Relates logical devices and data files, indicating the driver files used by the device
Win32_Directory	31	14	Represents a directory entry
Win32_DirectorySpecification	13	1	Instance class. Represents the directory layout for the product
Win32_DiskDriveToDiskPartition	2	0	Association class. Relates a disk drive and a partition existing on it
Win32_DiskPartition	34	2	Instance class. Represents the capabilities and management capacity of a partitioned area of a physical disk
Win32_DiskQuota	6	0	Association class. Tracks disk space usage for NTFS file system volumes
Win32_LogicalDisk	40	5	Represents a data source that resolves to an actual local storage device
Win32_LogicalDiskRootDirectory	2	0	Association class. Relates a logical disk and its directory structure
Win32_LogicalDiskToPartition	4	0	Association class. Relates a logical disk drive and the disk partition on which it resides
Win32_MappedLogicalDisk	38	2	Represents network storage devices that are mapped as logical disks on the computer system
Win32_OperatingSystem-AutochkSetting	2	0	Association class. Represents the association between a CIM_ManagedSystemElement instance and the settings defined for it
Win32_QuotaSetting	9	0	Instance class. Contains setting information for disk quotas on a volume
Win32_ShortcutFile	34	14	Instance class. Represents files that are shortcuts to other files, directories, and commands
Win32_SubDirectory	2	0	Association class. Relates a directory (folder) and one of its subdirectories (subfolders)

Table E-4 File System Classes

Class	Properties	Methods	Description
Win32_SystemPartitions	2	0	Association class. Relates a computer system and a disk partition on that system
Win32_Volume	2	0	Instance class. Represents an area of storage on a hard disk
Win32_VolumeQuota	2	0	Association class. Relates a volume to the per-volume quota settings
Win32_VolumeQuotaSetting	2	0	Association class. Relates disk quota settings with a specific disk volume
Win32_VolumeUserQuota	2	0	Association class. Relates per-user quotas to quota-enabled volumes

Table E-5 Job Object Classes

Class	Properties	Methods	Description
Win32_CollectionStatistics	2	0	Association class. Relates a managed system element collection and the class representing statistical information about the collection
Win32_LUID	2	0	Instance class. Represents a locally unique identifier (LUID)
Win32_LUIDandAttributes	2	0	Instance class. Represents a LUID and its attributes
Win32_NamedJobObject	4	0	Instance class. Represents a kernel object that is used to group processes for the sake of controlling the life and resources of the processes within the job object
Win32_NamedJobObjectActgInfo	19	0	Instance class. Represents the input/output (I/O) accounting information for a job object
Win32_NamedJobObjectLimit	2	0	Instance class. Represents an association between a job object and the job object limit settings
Win32_NamedJobObjectLimitSetting	14	0	Instance class. Represents the limit settings for a job object
Win32_NamedJobObjectProcess	2	0	Instance class. Relates a job object and the process contained in the job object

Table E-5   Job Object Classes

Class	Properties	Methods	Description
Win32_NamedJobObjectSecLimit	2	0	Instance class. Relates a job object and the job object security limit settings
Win32_NamedJobObjectSecLimit-Setting	7	0	Instance class. Represents the security limit settings for a job object
Win32_NamedJobObjectStatistics	2	0	Instance class. Represents an association between a job object and the job object I/O accounting information class
Win32_SIDandAttributes	2	0	Instance class. Represents a security identifier (SID) and its attributes
Win32_TokenGroups	2	0	Event class. Represents information about the group SIDs in an access token
Win32_TokenPrivileges	2	0	Event class. Represents information about a set of privileges for an access token

Table E-6   Memory and Page File Classes

Class	Properties	Methods	Description
Win32_LogicalMemoryConfiguration	8	0	Instance class. This class is obsolete and has been replaced by the *Win32_OperatingSystem* class.
Win32_PageFile	36	14	Instance class. Represents the file used for handling virtual memory file swapping
Win32_PageFileElementSetting	2	0	Association class. Relates the initial settings of a page file and the state of those settings during normal use.
Win32_PageFileSetting	6	0	Instance class. Represents the settings of a page file.
Win32_PageFileUsage	9	0	Instance class. Represents the file used for handling virtual memory file swapping.
Win32_SystemLogicalMemory-Configuration	2	0	Association class. This class is obsolete because the properties existing in the *Win32_Logical-MemoryConfiguration* class are now a part of the *Win32_OperatingSystem* class.

Table E-7   Media and Audio Class

Class	Properties	Methods	Description
Win32_CodecFile	34	14	Instance class. Represents the audio or video codec installed on the computer system

Table E-8   Networking Classes

Class	Properties	Methods	Description
Win32_ActiveRoute	2	0	Association class. Relates the current Internet Protocol 4 (IP4) route to the persisted IP route table
Win32_IP4PersistedRouteTable	9	0	Instance class. Represents persisted IP routes
Win32_IP4RouteTable	18	0	Instance class. Represents information that governs the routing of network data packets
Win32_IP4RouteTableEvent	2	0	Event class. Represents IP route change events
Win32_NetworkClient	6	0	Instance class. Represents a network client
Win32_NetworkConnection	17	0	Instance class. Represents an active network connection
Win32_NetworkProtocol	23	0	Instance class. Represents a protocol and its network characteristics
Win32_NTDomain	27	0	Instance class. Represents a Microsoft Windows NT domain
Win32_PingStatus	24	0	Instance class. Represents the values returned by the standard ping command
Win32_ProtocolBinding	3	0	Association class. Relates a system level driver, network protocol, and network adapter

Table E-9   Operating System Event Classes

Class	Properties	Methods	Description
Win32_ComputerShutdownEvent	4	0	Represents computer shutdown events
Win32_ComputerSystemEvent	3	0	Represents events related to a computer system
Win32_DeviceChangeEvent	3	0	Represents device change events resulting from the addition, removal, or modification of devices on the computer system
Win32_ModuleLoadTrace	6	0	Indicates that a process has loaded a new module

Table E-9   Operating System Event Classes

Class	Properties	Methods	Description
Win32_ModuleTrace	2	0	Base event for module events
Win32_ProcessStartTrace	8	0	Indicates that a new process has started
Win32_ProcessStopTrace	8	0	Indicates that a process has terminated
Win32_ProcessTrace	8	0	Base event for process events
Win32_SystemConfiguration-ChangeEvent	3	0	Indicates that the device list on the system has been refreshed (a device has been added or removed, or the configuration changed)
Win32_SystemTrace	2	0	Base class for all system trace events, including module, process, and thread traces
Win32_ThreadStartTrace	11	0	Indicates a new thread has started
Win32_ThreadStopTrace	4	0	Indicates that a thread has stopped
Win32_ThreadTrace	4	0	Base event class for thread events
Win32_VolumeChangeEvent	4	0	Represents a network-mapped drive event resulting from the addition of a network drive letter or mounted drive

Table E-10   Operating System Settings Classes

Class	Properties	Methods	Description
Win32_BootConfiguration	9	0	Instance class. Represents the boot configuration
Win32_ComputerSystem	54	4	Instance class. Represents a computer system
Win32_ComputerSystemProcessor	2	0	Association class. Relates a computer system and a processor running on that system
Win32_ComputerSystemProduct	8	0	Instance class. Represents a product
Win32_DependentService	3	0	Association class. Relates two interdependent base services
Win32_LoadOrderGroup	7	0	Instance class. Represents a group of system services that define execution dependencies

Table E-10   Operating System Settings Classes

Class	Properties	Methods	Description
Win32_LoadOrderGroupService-Dependencies	2	0	Instance class. Represents an association between a base service and a load order group that the service depends on to start running
Win32_LoadOrderGroupService-Members	2	0	Association class. Relates a load order group and a base service
Win32_OperatingSystem	61	4	Instance class. Represents an installed operating system
Win32_OperatingSystemQFE	2	0	Association class. Relates an operating system and product updates applied as represented in Win32_QuickFixEngineering
Win32_OSRecoveryConfiguration	15	0	Instance class. Represents the types of information that will be gathered from memory when the operating system fails
Win32_QuickFixEngineering	11	0	Instance class. Represents system-wide Quick Fix Engineering (QFE) or updates that have been applied to the current operating system
Win32_StartupCommand	7	0	Instance class. Represents a command that runs automatically when a user logs on to the computer system
Win32_SystemBootConfiguration	2	0	Association class. Relates a computer system and its boot configuration
Win32_SystemDesktop	2	0	Association class. Relates a computer system and its desktop configuration
Win32_SystemDevices	2	0	Association class. Relates a computer system and a logical device installed on that system
Win32_SystemLoadOrderGroups	2	0	Association class. Relates a computer system and a load order group

Table E-10   Operating System Settings Classes

Class	Properties	Methods	Description
Win32_SystemNetworkConnections	2	0	Association class. Relates a network connection and the computer system on which it resides
Win32_SystemOperatingSystem	3	0	Association class. Relates a computer system and its operating system
Win32_SystemProcesses	2	0	Association class. Relates a computer system and a process running on that system
Win32_SystemProgramGroups	2	0	Association class. Relates a computer system and a logical program group
Win32_SystemResources	2	0	Association class. Relates a system resource and the computer system on which it resides
Win32_SystemServices	2	0	Association class. Relates a computer system and a service program that exists on the system
Win32_SystemSetting	2	0	Association class. Relates a computer system and a general setting on that system
Win32_SystemSystemDriver	2	0	Association class. Relates a computer system and a system driver running on that computer system
Win32_SystemTimeZone	2	0	Association class. Relates a computer system and a time zone
Win32_SystemUsers	2	0	Association class. Relates a computer system and a user account on that system

Table E-11   Processes Classes

Class	Properties	Methods	Description
Win32_Process	45	6	Instance class. Represents a sequence of events on a computer system
Win32_ProcessStartup	14	0	Instance class. Represents the startup configuration of a Microsoft Windows process
Win32_Thread	22	0	Instance class. Represents a thread of execution

Table E-12   Registry Class

Class	Properties	Methods	Description
Win32_Registry	8	0	Instance class. Represents the system registry

Table E-13   Scheduler Job Classes

Class	Properties	Methods	Description
Win32_LocalTime	10	0	Instance class. Represents an instance in time as component seconds, minutes, day of the week, and so on
Win32_ScheduledJob	19	2	Instance class. Represents a job scheduled using the Windows NT schedule service (AT command)

Table E-14   Security Classes

Class	Properties	Methods	Description
Win32_AccountSID	2	0	Association class. Relates a security account instance with a security descriptor instance
Win32_ACE	6	0	Instance class. Represents an access control entry (ACE)
Win32_LogicalFileAccess	7	0	Association class. Relates the security settings of a file/directory and one member of its discretionary access control list (DACL)
Win32_LogicalFileAuditing	7	0	Association class. Relates the security settings of a file/directory and one member of its system access control list (SACL)
Win32_LogicalFileGroup	2	0	Association class. Relates the security settings of a file/directory and its group
Win32_LogicalFileOwner	2	0	Association class. Relates the security settings of a file/directory and its owner
Win32_LogicalFileSecuritySetting	6	2	Instance class. Represents security settings for a logical file
Win32_LogicalShareAccess	7	0	Association class. Relates the security settings of a share and one member of its DACL
Win32_LogicalShareAuditing	7	0	Association class. Relates the security settings of a share and one member of its SACL
Win32_LogicalShareSecurity-Setting	5	2	Instance class. Represents security settings for a logical file

Table E-14   Security Classes

Class	Properties	Methods	Description
Win32_PrivilegesStatus	7	0	Instance class. Represents information about privileges required to complete an operation
Win32_SecurityDescriptor	5	0	Instance class. Represents a structural representation of a SECURITY_DESCRIPTOR
Win32_SecuritySetting	4	2	Instance class. Represents security settings for a managed element
Win32_SecuritySettingAccess	7	0	Instance class. Represents the rights granted and denied to a trustee for a given object
Win32_SecuritySettingAuditing	7	0	Instance class. Represents the auditing for a given trustee on a given object
Win32_SecuritySettingGroup	2	0	Association class. Relates the security of an object and its group
Win32_SecuritySettingOfLogical-File	2	0	Instance class. Represents security settings of a file or directory object
Win32_SecuritySettingOfLogical-Share	2	0	Instance class. Represents security settings of a share object
Win32_SecuritySettingOfObject	2	0	Association class. Relates an object to its security settings
Win32_SecuritySettingOwner	2	0	Association class. Relates the security settings of an object and its owner
Win32_SID	5	0	Instance class. Represents an arbitrary SID
Win32_Trustee	5	0	Instance class. Represents a trustee

Table E-15   Service Classes

Class	Properties	Methods	Description
Win32_BaseService	22	10	Instance class. Represents executable objects that are installed in a registry database maintained by the Service Control Manager
Win32_Service	25	10	Instance class. Represents a service

Table E-16   Share Classes

Class	Properties	Methods	Description
Win32_ConnectionShare	2	0	Association class. Relates a shared resource on the computer and the connection made to the shared resource
Win32_DFSNode	25	10	Association class. Represents a root or junction node of a domain-based or stand-alone distributed file system (DFS)
Win32_DFSNodeTarget	25	10	Association class. Represents the relationship of a DFS node to one of its targets
Win32_DFSTarget	25	10	Association class. Represents the target of a DFS node
Win32_PrinterShare	2	0	Association class. Relates a local printer and the share that represents it as it is viewed over a network
Win32_ServerConnection	12	0	Instance class. Represents the connections made from a remote computer to a shared resource on the local computer
Win32_ServerSession	13	0	Instance class. Represents the sessions that are established with the local computer by users on a remote computer
Win32_SessionConnection	2	0	Association class. Represents an association between a session established with the local server by a user on a remote machine and the connections that depend on the session
Win32_SessionProcess	2	0	Association class. Represents an association between a logon session and the processes associated with that session
Win32_Share	10	4	Instance class. Represents a shared resource
Win32_ShareToDirectory	2	0	Association class. Relates a shared resource on the computer system and the directory to which it is mapped

Table E-17   Start Menu Classes

Class	Properties	Methods	Description
Win32_LogicalProgramGroup	7	0	Instance class. Represents a program group.
Win32_LogicalProgramGroup-Directory	2	0	Association class. Relates logical program groups (groupings on the Start menu) and the file directories in which they are stored.

Table E-17 **Start Menu Classes**

Class	Properties	Methods	Description
Win32_LogicalProgramGroup-Item	5	0	Instance class. Represents an element contained by a *Win32_ProgramGroup* instance that is not itself another *Win32_ProgramGroup* instance.
Win32_LogicalProgramGroup-ItemDataFile	2	0	Association class. Relates the program group items of the Start menu and the files in which they are stored.
Win32_ProgramGroup	6	0	Instance class. Deprecated. Represents a program group. Use the *Win32_LogicalProgramGroup* class instead.
Win32_ProgramGroupContents	2	0	Association class. Relates a program group order and an individual program group or item contained in it.
Win32_ProgramGroupOrItem	5	0	Instance class. Represents a logical grouping of programs on the Programs menu on the Start menu.

Table E-18 **Storage Classes**

Class	Properties	Methods	Description
Win32_ShadowBy	5	0	Association class. Represents the association between a shadow copy and the provider that creates the shadow copy
Win32_ShadowContext	5	0	Association class. Specifies how a shadow copy is to be created, queried, or deleted
Win32_ShadowCopy	5	0	Instance class. Represents a duplicate copy of the original volume at a previous time
Win32_ShadowDiffVolumeSupport	5	0	Association class. Represents an association between a shadow copy provider and a storage volume
Win32_ShadowFor	5	0	Association class. Represents an association between a shadow copy and the volume for which the shadow copy is created
Win32_ShadowOn	5	0	Association class. Represents an association between a shadow copy and where the differential data is written

Table E-18   Storage Classes

Class	Properties	Methods	Description
Win32_ShadowProvider	5	0	Association class. Represents a component that creates and represents volume shadow copies
Win32_ShadowStorage	5	0	Association class. Represents an association between a shadow copy and where the differential data is written
Win32_ShadowVolumeSupport	5	0	Association class. Represents an association between a shadow copy provider with a supported volume
Win32_Volume	42	9	Instance class. Represents an area of storage on a hard disk
Win32_VolumeUserQuota	6	0	Association class. Represents a volume to the per-volume quota settings

Table E-19   User Classes

Class	Properties	Methods	Description
Win32_Account	9	0	Instance class. Represents information about user accounts and group accounts
Win32_Group	9	1	Instance class. Represents data about a group account
Win32_GroupInDomain	2	0	Association class. Identifies the group accounts associated with a Windows NT domain
Win32_GroupUser	2	0	Association class. Relates a group and an account that is a member of that group
Win32_LogonSession	9	0	Instance class. Describes the logon session or sessions associated with a user logged on to Windows NT, Microsoft Windows 2000, or Microsoft Windows Server 2003
Win32_LogonSessionMappedDisk	2	0	Association class. Represents the mapped logical disks associated with the session
Win32_NetworkLoginProfile	32	0	Instance class. Represents the network logon information of a specific user
Win32_SystemAccount	9	0	Instance class. Represents a system account

Table E-19   User Classes

Class	Properties	Methods	Description
Win32_UserAccount	16	1	Instance class. Represents information about a user account
Win32_UserInDomain	2	0	Association class. Relates a user account and a Windows NT domain

Table E-20   Event Log Classes

Class	Properties	Methods	Description
Win32_NTEventlogFile	39	16	Instance class. Represents data stored in a Windows NT/Windows 2000 log file
Win32_NTLogEvent	16	0	Instance class. Represents Windows NT/Windows 2000 events
Win32_NTLogEventComputer	2	0	Association class. Relates instances of Win32_NTLogEvent and Win32_ComputerSystem
Win32_NTLogEventLog	2	0	Association class. Relates instances of Win32_NTLogEvent and Win32_NTEventLogFile classes
Win32_NTLogEventUser	2	0	Association class. Relates instances of Win32_NTLogEvent and Win32_UserAccount

Table E-21   Windows Product Activation Classes

Class	Properties	Methods	Description
Win32_ComputerSystemWindowsProductActivationSetting	2	0	Association class. Relates instances of Win32_ComputerSystem and Win32_WindowsProductActivation
Win32_Proxy	6	1	Instance class. Contains properties and methods to query and configure an Internet connection related to Windows Product Activation (WPA)
Win32_WindowsProductActivation	9	5	Instance class. Contains properties and methods related to WPA

Appendix F
Performance Monitor Classes

This appendix provides documentation on the performance monitor classes. These classes are discussed in detail in Chapter 12.

Table F-1   Formatted Data Classes

Class	Properties	Methods	Description
Win32_PerfFormattedData	9	0	Abstract base class for the formatted data classes
Win32_PerfFormattedData_ ASP_ActiveServerPages	9	0	Represents performance counters for the Active Server Pages (ASP) device on the computer system
Win32_PerfFormattedData_ ContentFilter_IndexingServiceFilter	12	0	Represents performance information about an Indexing service filter
Win32_PerfFormattedData_ ContentIndex_IndexingService	20	0	Represents performance data about the state of the Indexing service
Win32_PerfFormattedData_Inet-Info_InternetInformationServices-Global	20	0	Represents counters that monitor Microsoft Internet Information Services (IIS) (the Web service and the FTP service) as a whole
Win32_PerfFormattedData_ ISAPISearch_HttpIndexingService	17	0	Represents performance data from the Hypertext Transfer Protocol (HTTP) Indexing service
Win32_PerfFormattedData_ MSDTC_DistributedTransaction-Coordinator	22	0	Represents Microsoft Distributed Transaction Coordinator (DTC) performance counters
Win32_PerfFormattedData_ NTFSDRV_SMTPNTFSStoreDriver	22	0	Represents global counters for the Microsoft Exchange NTFS Store driver
Win32_PerfFormattedData_ PerfDisk_LogicalDisk	32	0	Represents counters that monitor logical partitions of a hard or fixed disk drive
Win32_PerfFormattedData_ PerfDisk_PhysicalDisk	30	0	Represents counters that monitor hard or fixed disk drives on a computer

Table F-1   Formatted Data Classes

Class	Properties	Methods	Description
Win32_PerfFormattedData_Perf-Net_Browser	29	0	Represents counters that measure the rates of announcements, enumerations, and other browser transmissions
Win32_PerfFormattedData_Perf-Net_Redirector	46	0	Represents counters that monitor network connections originating at the local computer
Win32_PerfFormattedData_Perf-Net_Server	35	0	Represents counters that monitor communications using the Windows Internet Naming Service (WINS) Server service
Win32_PerfFormattedData_Perf-Net_ServerWorkQueues	26	0	Represents counters that monitor the length of the queues and objects in the queues
Win32_PerfFormattedData_Perf-OS_Cache	26	0	Represents counters that monitor the file system cache, an area of physical memory that stores recently used data as long as possible to permit access to the data without having to read from the disk
Win32_PerfFormattedData_Perf-OS_Memory	26	0	Represents counters that describe the behavior of physical and virtual memory on the computer
Win32_PerfFormattedData_Perf-OS_Objects	26	0	Represents calculated counts of the objects contained by the operating system such as events, mutexes, processes, sections, semaphores, and threads
Win32_PerfFormattedData_Perf-OS_PagingFile	26	0	Represents counters that monitor the paging file(s) on the computer
Win32_PerfFormattedData_Perf-OS_Processor	26	0	Represents counters that measure aspects of processor activity
Win32_PerfFormattedData_Perf-OS_System	26	0	Represents counters that apply to more than one instance of a component processor on the computer
Win32_PerfFormattedData_Perf-Proc_FullImage_Costly	17	0	Represents counters that monitor the virtual address usage of images executed by processes on the computer
Win32_PerfFormattedData_Perf-Proc_Image_Costly	17	0	Represents counters that monitor the virtual address usage of images executed by processes on the computer

Table F-1   Formatted Data Classes

Class	Properties	Methods	Description
Win32_PerfFormattedData_Perf-Proc_JobObject	22	0	Represents the accounting and processor usage data collected by each active named job object
Win32_PerfFormattedData_Perf-Proc_JobObjectDetails	36	0	Represents detailed performance information about the active processes that make up a job object
Win32_PerfFormattedData_Perf-Proc_Process	36	0	Represents counters that monitor running application program and system processes
Win32_PerfFormattedData_Perf-Proc_ProcessAddressSpace_Costly	46	0	Represent counters that monitor memory allocation and use for a selected process
Win32_PerfFormattedData_Perf-Proc_Thread	21	0	Represents counters that measure aspects of thread behavior
Win32_PerfFormattedData_Perf-Proc_ThreadDetails_Costly	10	0	Represents counters that measure aspects of thread behavior that are difficult or time-consuming to collect
Win32_PerfFormattedData_PSched_PSchedFlow	10	0	Represents flow statistics from the packet scheduler
Win32_PerfFormattedData_PSched_PSchedPipe	10	0	Represents pipe statistics from the packet scheduler
Win32_PerfFormattedData_RemoteAccess_RASPort	10	0	Represents counters that monitor individual Remote Access Service (RAS) ports of the RAS device on the computer
Win32_PerfFormattedData_RemoteAccess_RASTotal	10	0	Represents counters that combine values for all ports of the RAS device on the computer
Win32_PerfFormattedData_RSVP_ACSRSVPInterfaces	10	0	Represents the number of local network interfaces visible to and used by the Resource Reservation Setup Protocol (RSVP) service
Win32_PerfFormattedData_RSVP_ACSRSVPService	10	0	Represents RSVP or ACS service performance counters
Win32_PerfFormattedData_SMTPSVC_SMTPServer	10	0	Represents counters specific to the Simple Mail Transfer Protocol (SMTP) server
Win32_PerfFormattedData_Spooler_PrintQueue	22	0	Represents performance statistics about a print queue
Win32_PerfFormattedData_TapiSrv_Telephony	18	0	Represents the telephony system

Table F-1   Formatted Data Classes

Class	Properties	Methods	Description
Win32_PerfFormattedData_Tcpip_ ICMP	18	0	Represents counters that measure the rates at which messages are sent and received by using Internet Control Message Protocol (ICMP) protocols
Win32_PerfFormattedData_Tcpip_ IP	18	0	Represents counters that measure the rates at which IP datagrams are sent and received by using Internet Protocol (IP)
Win32_PerfFormattedData_Tcpip_ NBTConnection	18	0	Represents counters that measure the rates at which bytes are sent and received over the NetBIOS over TCP/IP (NBT) connection between the local computer and a remote computer
Win32_PerfFormattedData_Tcpip_ NetworkInterface	18	0	Represents counters that measure the rates at which bytes and packets are sent and received over a TCP/IP network connection
Win32_PerfFormattedData_Tcpip_ TCP	18	0	Represents counters that measure the rates at which TCP segments are sent and received by using the Transmission Control Protocol (TCP)
Win32_PerfFormattedData_Tcpip_ UDP	18	0	Represents counters that measure the rates at which UDP datagrams are sent and received by using the User Datagram Protocol (UDP)
Win32_PerfFormattedData_ TermService_TerminalServices	12	0	Represents Terminal Services summary information
Win32_PerfFormattedData_Term-Service_TerminalServicesSession	84	0	Represents Terminal Services per-session resource monitoring
Win32_PerfFormattedData_ W3SVC_WebService	84	0	Represents counters specific to the World Wide Web Publishing service

Table F-2   Raw Performance Monitor Classes

Class	Properties	Methods	Description
Win32_PerfRawData	9	0	Abstract base class for all concrete raw performance counter classes
Win32_PerfRawData_ASP_ ActiveServerPages	9	0	Represents the Active Server Pages device on the computer system
Win32_PerfRawData_Content-Filter_IndexingServiceFilter	12	0	Represents performance information about an Indexing service filter

Table F-2   **Raw Performance Monitor Classes**

Class	Properties	Methods	Description
Win32_PerfRawData_Content-Index_IndexingService	20	0	Represents performance data about the state of the Indexing service
Win32_PerfRawData_InetInfo_InternetInformationServices-Global	20	0	Represents counters that monitor IIS (the Web service and the FTP service) as a whole
Win32_PerfRawData_ISAPI-Search_HttpIndexingService	19	0	Represents performance data from the HTTP Indexing service
Win32_PerfRawData_MSDTC_DistributedTransactionCoordinator	22	0	Represents Microsoft Distributed Transaction Coordinator performance counters
Win32_PerfRawData_NTFS-DRV_SMTPNTFSStoreDriver	22	0	Represents global counters for the Microsoft Exchange NTFS Store driver
Win32_PerfRawData_PerfDisk_LogicalDisk	43	0	Represents counters that monitor logical partitions of a hard or fixed disk drive
Win32_PerfRawData_PerfDisk_PhysicalDisk	40	0	Represents counters that monitor hard or fixed disk drives on a computer
Win32_PerfRawData_PerfNet_Browser	29	0	Represents counters that measure the rates of announcements, enumerations, and other browser transmissions
Win32_PerfRawData_PerfNet_Redirector	46	0	Represents counters that monitor network connections originating at the local computer
Win32_PerfRawData_PerfNet_Server	35	0	Represents counters that monitor communications using the WINS Server service
Win32_PerfRawData_PerfNet_ServerWorkQueues	26	0	Represents counters that monitor the length of the queues and objects in the queues
Win32_PerfRawData_PerfOS_Cache	26	0	Represents counters that monitor the file system cache
Win32_PerfRawData_PerfOS_Memory	26	0	Represents counters that describe the behavior of physical and virtual memory on the computer
Win32_PerfRawData_PerfOS_Objects	26	0	Represents calculated counts of the objects contained by the operating system such as events, mutexes, processes, sections, semaphores, and threads

Table F-2   Raw Performance Monitor Classes

Class	Properties	Methods	Description
Win32_PerfRawData_PerfOS_ PagingFile	26	0	Represents counters that monitor the paging file(s) on the computer
Win32_PerfRawData_PerfOS_ Processor	26	0	Represents counters that measure aspects of processor activity
Win32_PerfRawData_PerfOS_ System	26	0	Represents counters that apply to more than one instance of a component processor on the computer
Win32_PerfRawData_PerfProc_ FullImage_Costly	17	0	Represents counters that monitor the virtual address usage of images executed by processes on the computer
Win32_PerfRawData_PerfProc_ Image_Costly	17	0	Represents counters that monitor the virtual address usage of images executed by processes on the computer
Win32_PerfRawData_PerfProc_ JobObject	22	0	Represents the accounting and processor usage data collected by each active, named job object
Win32_PerfRawData_PerfProc_ JobObjectDetails	36	0	Represents detailed performance information about the active processes that make up a job object
Win32_PerfRawData_PerfProc_ Process	36	0	Represents counters that monitor running application program and system processes
Win32_PerfRawData_PerfProc_ ProcessAddressSpace_Costly	46	0	Represent counters that monitor memory allocation and use for a selected process
Win32_PerfRawData_PerfProc_ Thread	21	0	Represents counters that measure aspects of thread behavior
Win32_PerfRawData_PerfProc_ ThreadDetails_Costly	10	0	Represents counters that measure aspects of thread behavior that are difficult or time-consuming to collect
Win32_PerfRawData_PSched_ PSchedFlow	10	0	Represents flow statistics from the packet scheduler
Win32_PerfRawData_PSched_ PSchedPipe	10	0	Represents pipe statistics from the packet scheduler
Win32_PerfRawData_Remote-Access_RASPort	10	0	Represents counters that monitor individual RAS ports of the RAS device on the computer
Win32_PerfRawData_Remote-Access_RASTotal	10	0	Represents counters that combine values for all ports of the RAS device on the computer

Table F-2   Raw Performance Monitor Classes

Class	Properties	Methods	Description
Win32_PerfRawData_RSVP_ ACSRSVPInterfaces	10	0	Represents the number of local network interfaces visible to and used by the RSVP service
Win32_PerfRawData_RSVP_ ACSRSVPService	10	0	Represents RSVP or ACS service performance counters
Win32_PerfRawData_ SMTPSVC_SMTPServer	10	0	Represents the counters specific to the SMTP server
Win32_PerfRawData_Spooler_ PrintQueue	22	0	Represents performance statistics about a print queue
Win32_PerfRawData_TapiSrv_ Telephony	18	0	Represents the telephony system
Win32_PerfRawData_Tcpip_ ICMP	18	0	Represents counters that measure the rates at which messages are sent and received by using ICMP protocols
Win32_PerfRawData_Tcpip_IP	18	0	Represents counters that measure the rates at which IP datagrams are sent and received by using IP protocols
Win32_PerfRawData_Tcpip_ NBTConnection	18	0	Represents counters that measure the rates at which bytes are sent and received over the NBT connection between the local computer and a remote computer
Win32_PerfRawData_Tcpip_ NetworkInterface	18	0	Represents counters that measure the rates at which bytes and packets are sent and received over a TCP/IP network connection
Win32_PerfRawData_Tcpip_ TCP	18	0	Represents counters that measure the rates at which TCP segments are sent and received by using TCP
Win32_PerfRawData_Tcpip_ UDP	18	0	Represents counters that measure the rates at which UDP datagrams are sent and received by using UDP
Win32_PerfRawData_Term-Service_TerminalServices	12	0	Represents Terminal Services summary information
Win32_PerfRawData_Term-Service_TerminalServices-Session	84	0	Represents Terminal Services per-session resource monitoring
Win32_PerfRawData_W3SVC_ WebService	84	0	Represents counters specific to the World Wide Web Publishing service

Index

Symbols

& (ampersand), line continuation, 61
, (commas), separating properties, 61
= (equal sign), comparison operators, 64
\>= (greater than or equal to sign), comparison operators, 64
\> (greater than sign), comparison operators, 64
\<= (less than or equal to sign), comparison operators, 64
\< (less than sign), comparison operators, 64
\\ (not equal), comparison operators, 64
!= (not equal to sign), comparison operators, 64
_ (underscores), line continuation, 61

A

abstract base classes, 158
abstract classes, 168–170
access rights, system security, 162
actions, 6
ActivateOnline method, 249
ActiveScriptEventConsumer class
    event consumers, 111–112
    properties, 112
AdapterMicrosoft.vbs, 67
Add method, privileges, 143
AddAsString method, privileges, 144
AddPrinterPort.vbs, 148
Add/Remove Snap-In command (File menu), 10
Add/Remove Snap-In dialog box, 10
Administrative tools, download Web site, 110
ampersand (&), line continuation, 61
Anonymous impersonation levels, 57
APIs (application programming interfaces), 19, 83
appendixes, v
application programming interfaces (APIs), 19, 83
applications
    activation, 249
    controlled shutdown, 252–253
    provider managed, 20
    shutdown, 250–252
    startup, process classes, 233
    Win32 WMI classes, 174–175
    WMI infrastructure, 21–22
ASPScriptDefaultNamespace property, 181
associations, 83
Associators method, SWbemObject, 73, 94
associators of command, queries, 83–85

ASSOCIATORS OF method, schema query, 71
AssociatorsAsync method, SWbemObject, 73
AssociatorsOf method, SWbemServices, 94
AssociatorsOfLogonSession.vbs, 85
AssociatorsOfNetAdapterRequiredQualifier.vbs, 87
AssociatorsOfNetAdapterResultClass.vbs, 87
AssociatorsOfW32SystemDriver.vbs, 128
audience, ii–iii
audiovisual classes, operating systems, 229
Authority parameter, ConnectServer method, 127
Authority property, SWbemObjectPath, 74
AutoChkSetting class, 195
AutoDiscovery process, 99–100
automatic recovery, providers, 42
    Autorecover MOF key manual edit, 44
    installation, 42–44
    Mofcomp.exe utility, 45
    #pragma autorecover tag add to MOF file, 44
Autorecover MOF keys
    manual edit, 44
    provider autorecovery, 42
Availability property
    CIM_pointingDevice class, 17
    CIM_UserDevice class, 18
    WIN32_PointingDevice class, 18

B

BackupAppLog.vbs, 143
BackupEventLog method, 247
BackupEventLogCreateFileName.vbs, 248
BackUpLastTime property, 183
backups, event logs, 247–248
bandwidth, performance-counter classes, 256–257
base classes, 158
BaseBoard class, 164
BaseService class, 240
batteries
    portable, 205–207
    power classes, 204–205
Battery class, 205

About the Author

Ed Wilson is a senior consultant on the Microsoft Corporation ProActive Consulting team. He has worked with some of the world's largest Microsoft customers, helping them leverage the power of Microsoft Windows Management Instrumentation (WMI) scripting to manage their enterprise server farms. He is a Microsoft Certified Trainer and has taught numerous networking and administration classes. He has delivered his Microsoft Visual Basic Scripting Edition (VBScript) workshop to hundreds of premier customers, as well as to Microsoft employees. Ed has written or contributed to nine books and holds nearly two dozen industry certifications, including the Microsoft Certified System Engineer (MCSE) and the Certified Information System Security Professional (CISSP) certifications. Ed is the author of the extremely popular *Microsoft Windows Scripting Self-Paced Learning Guide*.

What do you think of this book?
We want to hear from you!

Do you have a few minutes to participate in a brief online survey? Microsoft is interested in hearing your feedback about this publication so that we can continually improve our books and learning resources for you.

To participate in our survey, please visit:
www.microsoft.com/learning/booksurvey

And enter this book's ISBN, 0-7356-2231-0. As a thank-you to survey participants in the United States and Canada, each month we'll randomly select five respondents to win one of five $100 gift certificates from a leading online merchant.* At the conclusion of the survey, you can enter the drawing by providing your e-mail address, which will be used for prize notification *only*.

Thanks in advance for your input. Your opinion counts!

Sincerely,

Microsoft Learning

Learn More. Go Further.

To see special offers on Microsoft Learning products for developers, IT professionals, and home and office users, visit: *www.microsoft.com/learning/booksurvey*.